Some time ago, because of school homework or something, I asked my grandfather what it was like when he was young.

"The no-good son of the business owner at the place where I was an apprentice was not a nice person" and "I played baseball in Manchuria. I was the ace pitcher and the clean-up batter" were things he said. The stories felt fresh to me because they were obviously from a specific time period.

Recently, there seems to be an increase in the number of older people who are writing and self-publishing their personal memoirs. Whether they publish them or not is a separate matter, but I think it's a great thing for the younger generation (because it gives them a chance to know their history). So, in accordance with that idea, a story of the past begins here.

—HIROSHI SHIIBASHI, 2009

**HIROSHI SHIIBASHI** debuted in BUSINESS JUMP magazine with *Aratama*. NURA: RISE OF THE YOKAI CLAN is his breakout hit. He was an assistant to manga artist Hirohiko Araki, the creator of *Jojo's Bizarre Adventure*. *Steel Ball Run* by Araki is one of his favorite manga.

# NURA: RISE OF THE YOKAI CLAN
## VOLUME 7
### SHONEN JUMP Manga Edition

**Story and Art by HIROSHI SHIIBASHI**

Translation — Yumi Okamoto
Adaptation — Mark Giambruno
Touch-up Art and Lettering — Annaliese Christman
Graphics and Cover Design — Fawn Lau
Editor — Joel Enos

NURARIHYON NO MAGO © 2008 by Hiroshi Shiibashi. All rights reserved. First published in Japan in 2008 by SHUEISHA Inc., Tokyo. English translation rights arranged by SHUEISHA Inc.

The rights of the author(s) of the work(s) in this publication to be so identified have been asserted in accordance with the Copyright, Designs and Patents Act 1988. A CIP catalogue record for this book is available from the British Library.

Printed in the U.S.A.

Published by VIZ Media, LLC
P.O. Box 77010
San Francisco, CA 94107

10 9 8 7 6 5 4 3 2 1
First printing, February 2012

www.viz.com   www.shonenjump.com

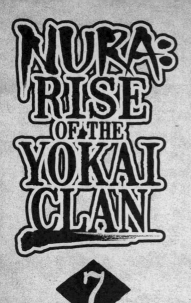

# NURA: RISE OF THE YOKAI CLAN

## 7

## THE THREE KEIKAIN SIBLINGS

STORY AND ART BY
**HIROSHI SHIIBASHI**

# CHARACTERS

## NURARIHYON

Rikuo's grandfather and the Lord of Pandemonium. He intends to pass leadership of the Nura clan—leaders of the yokai world—to Rikuo.

## RIKUO NURA

Though he appears to be a human boy, he's actually the grandson of Nurarihyon, a yokai. His grandfather's blood makes him one-quarter yokai, and he transforms into a yokai at times.

## KIYOTSUGU

Rikuo's classmate. He has adored yokai ever since Rikuo saved him in his yokai form, leading him to form The Kiyojuji Paranormal Patrol.

## KANA IENAGA

Rikuo's classmate and a childhood friend. Even though she hates scary things, she's a member of the Kiyojuji Paranormal Patrol for some reason.

## YUKI-ONNA

A yokai of the Nura clan who is in charge of looking after Rikuo. She disguises herself as a human and attends the same school as Rikuo to protect him from danger. When in human form, she goes by the name Tsurara Oikawa.

## YURA KEIKAIN

Rikuo's classmate and a descendant of the Keikain family of onmyoji. She transferred into Ukiyoe Middle School to do field training in yokai exorcism. She has the power to control her shikigami and uses them to destroy yokai.

## KUROTABO

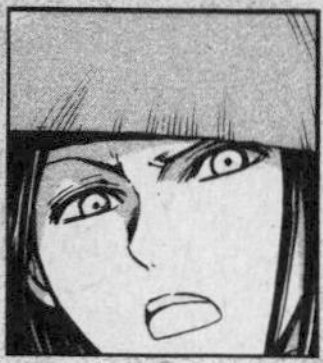

A Nura clan yokai, also known as the Father of Destruction, and one of the clan's best warriors. He hides numerous weapons under his priest's robe.

## AOTABO

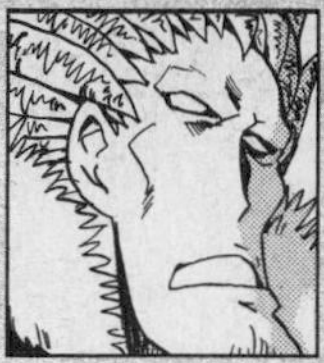

A Nura clan yokai who is in charge of looking after Rikuo. He attends school to protect Rikuo, along with Yuki-Onna. His alias as a human is Kurata.

## MAMIRU KEIKAIN

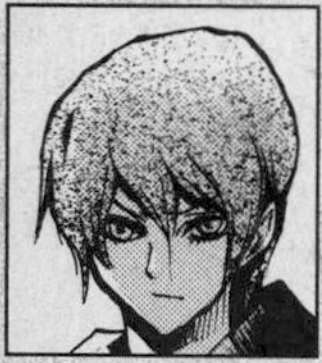

Onmyoji of the Keikain family. Appears to be quite skilled, but the details are uncertain. Came to Ukiyoe Town to look for Yura.

## RYUJI KEIKAIN

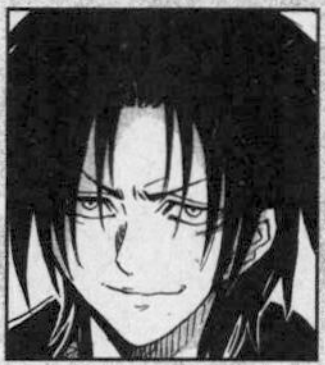

Onmyoji of the Keikain family. Appears to be Yura's brother, but the details are uncertain. Came to Ukiyoe Town to look for Yura.

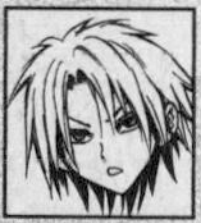

KUBINASHI

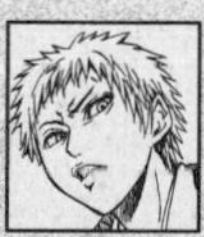

ZEN

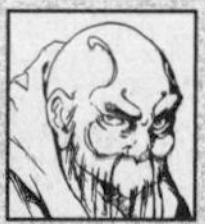

MOKUGYO-DARUMA

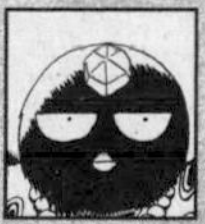

KARASU-TENGU

# STORY SO FAR

Rikuo Nura appears to be just your average seventh-grader at Ukiyoe Middle School. But he's actually the grandson of the yokai overlord Nurarihyon and has just been promoted to become the Underboss of the Nura clan, the Tokyo region's powerful yokai syndicate! For now, he lives his days as a human boy, but eventually, he is expected to take his grandfather's place as the leader of the clan.

The Nura clan is locked in battle with The Shikoku clan. The leader of the Shikoku, Tamazuki, slaughters his own allies to increase his yokai aura using the legendary sword, the Devil's Hammer, which captures the power of the yokai it kills. Using a new power called Kyokasuigetsu, Rikuo defeats Tamazuki. Rikuo's new powers and natural charms are winning him allies inside the Nura clan and drawing the attention of rivals as well. However, the brothers of Rikuo's friend Yura have shown up in Ukiyoe Town, and they may not be looking to make friends.

# TABLE OF CONTENTS

## NURA: RISE OF THE YOKAI CLAN

# Act 52: Warriors Black and Blue

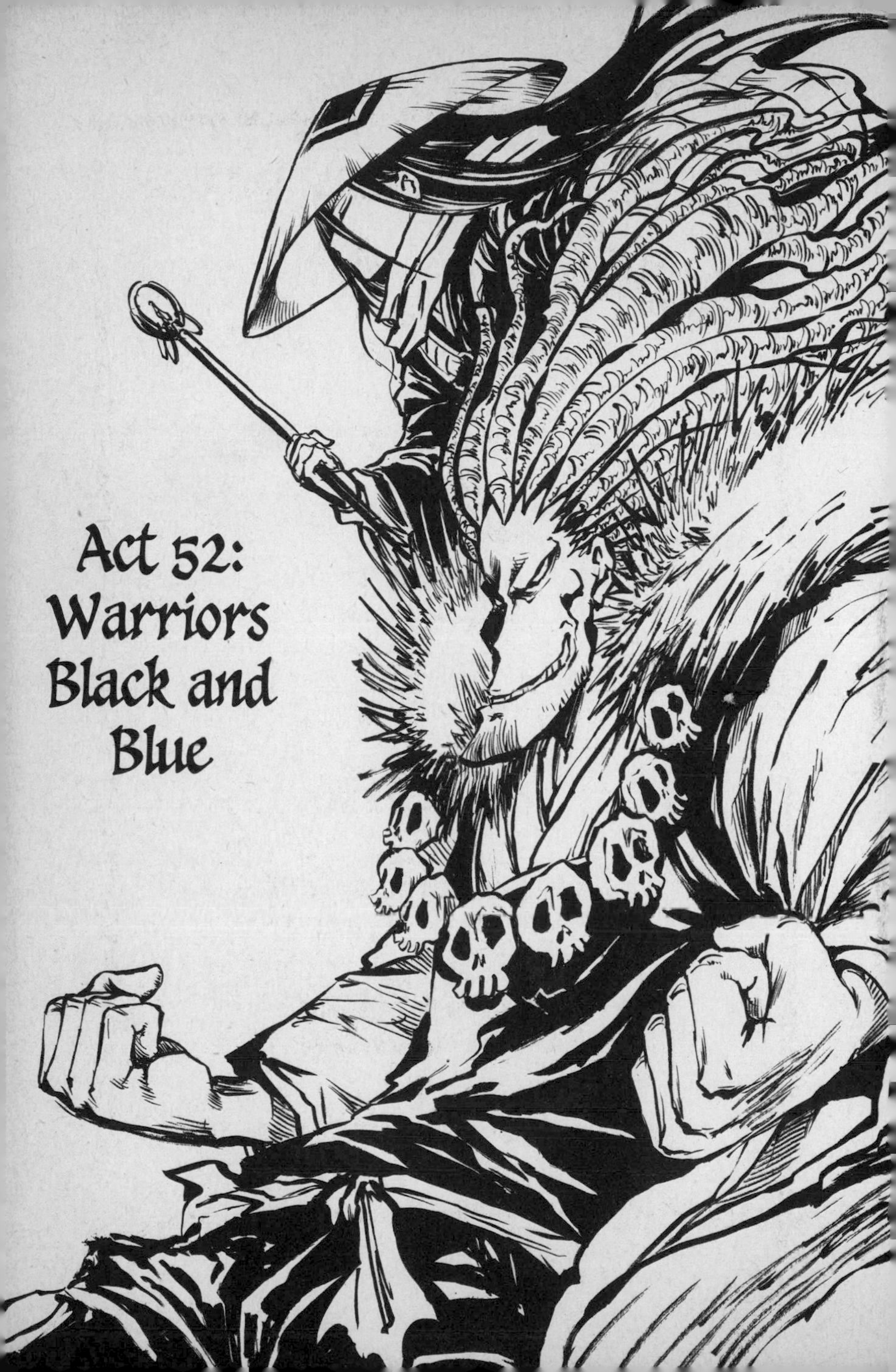

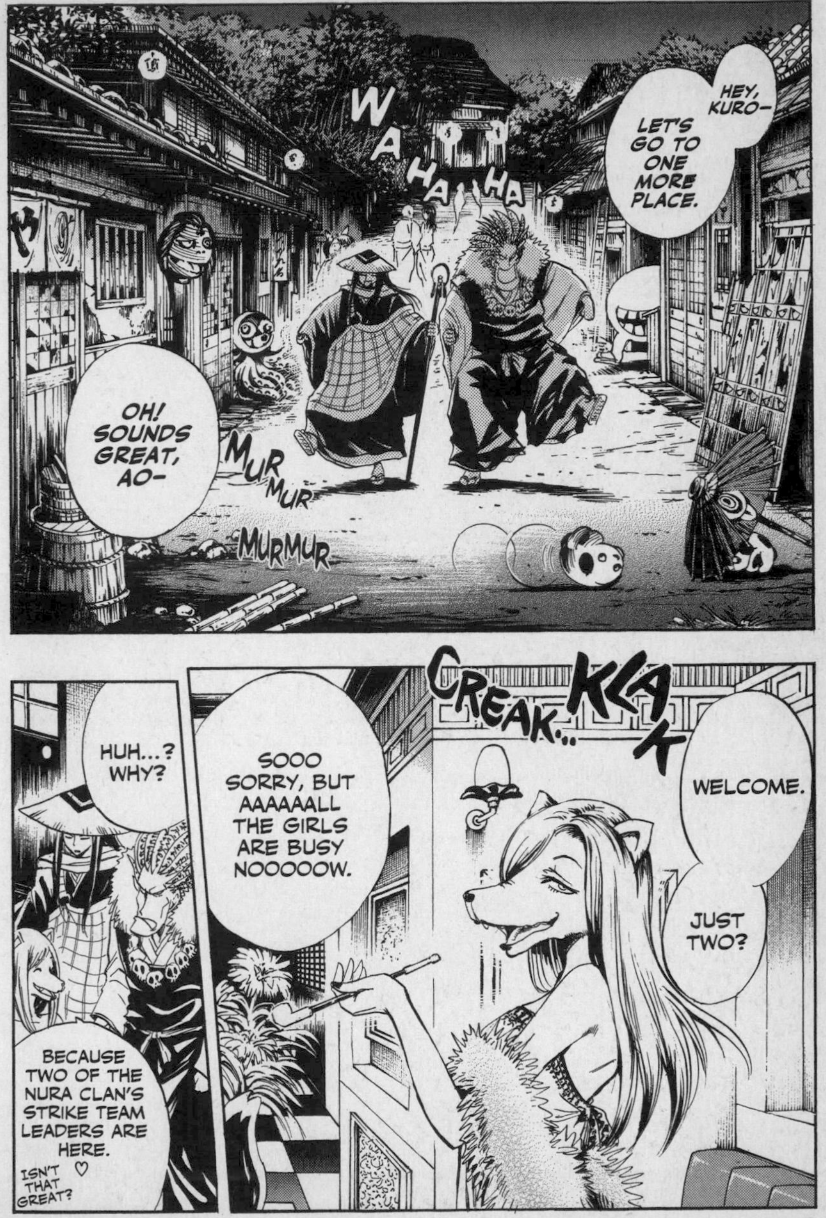
HEY, KURO— LET'S GO TO ONE MORE PLACE.
WAHAHA
OH! SOUNDS GREAT, AO—
MURMUR
MURMUR
CREAK... KLAK
WELCOME.
JUST TWO?
SOOO SORRY, BUT AAAAAALL THE GIRLS ARE BUSY NOOOOOW.
HUH...? WHY?
BECAUSE TWO OF THE NURA CLAN'S STRIKE TEAM LEADERS ARE HERE.
ISN'T THAT GREAT? ♡

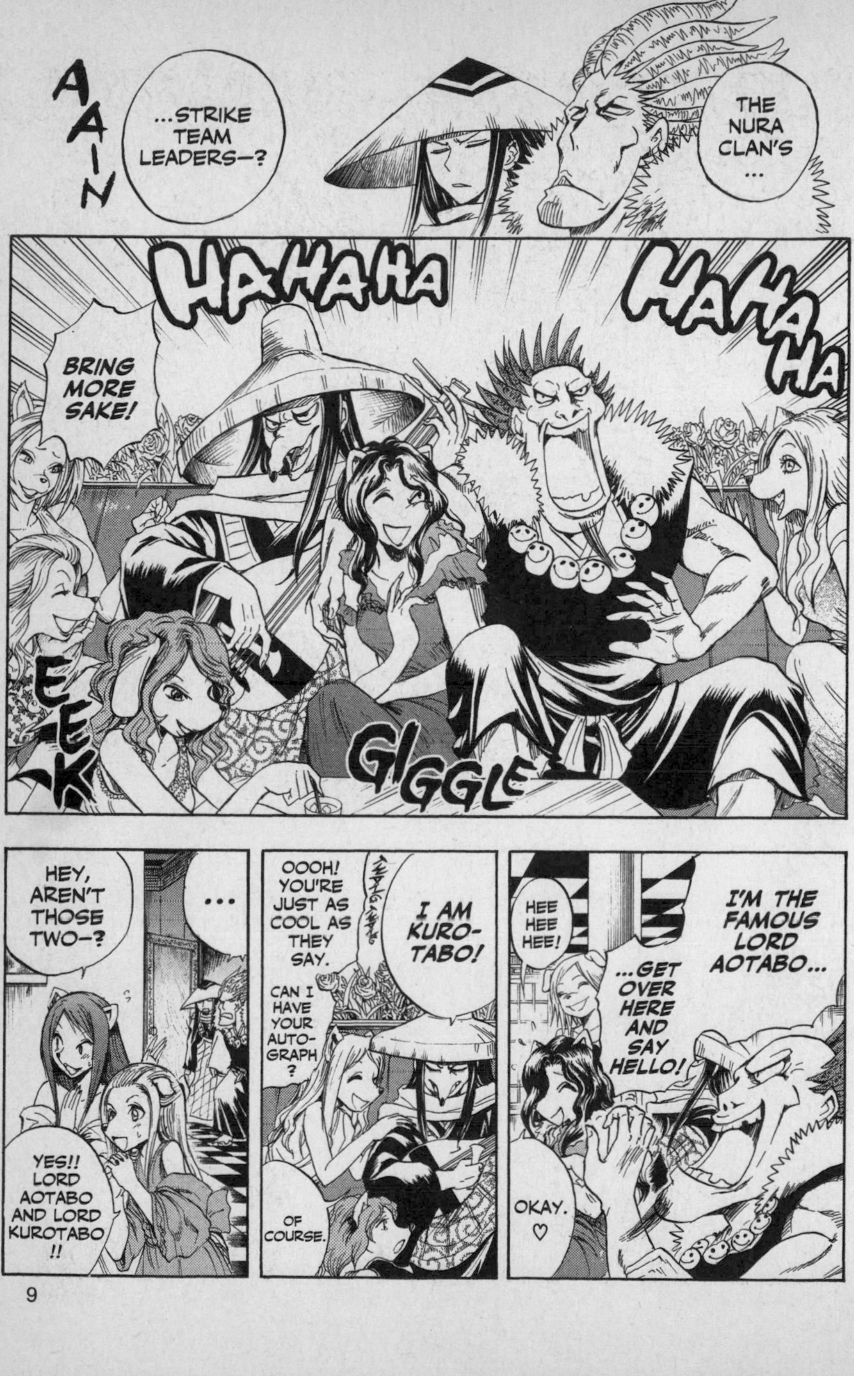
THE NURA CLAN'S ...
...STRIKE TEAM LEADERS—?
AAIN
HAHAHA
HAHAHA
BRING MORE SAKE!
GIGGLE
EEEK
I'M THE FAMOUS LORD AOTABO...
...GET OVER HERE AND SAY HELLO!
HEE HEE HEE!
OKAY. ♡
I AM KURO-TABO!
OOOH! YOU'RE JUST AS COOL AS THEY SAY.
CAN I HAVE YOUR AUTO-GRAPH?
OF COURSE.
...
HEY, AREN'T THOSE TWO—?
YES!! LORD AOTABO AND LORD KUROTABO!!

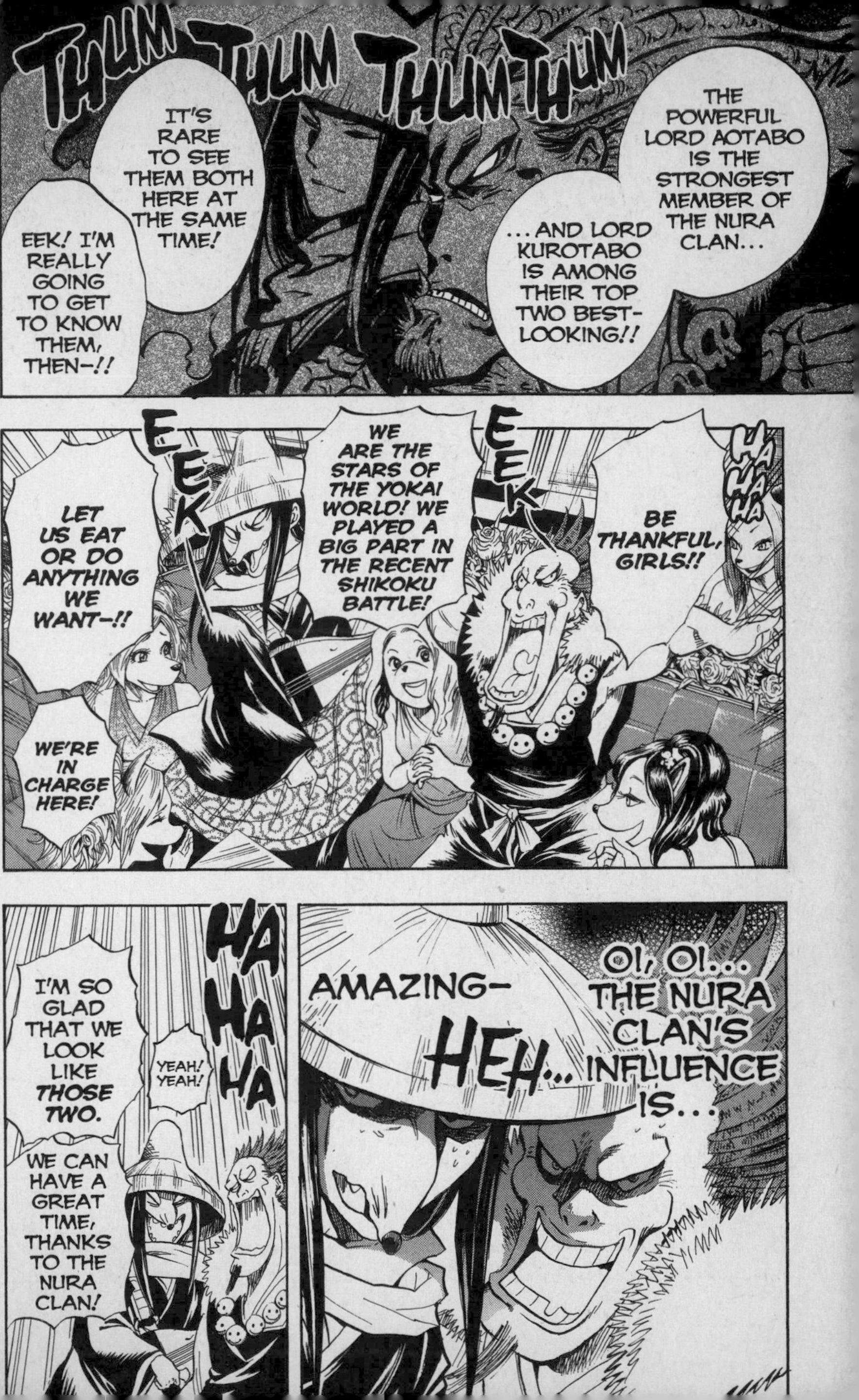

THUM THUM THUM THUM
THE POWERFUL LORD AOTABO IS THE STRONGEST MEMBER OF THE NURA CLAN...
...AND LORD KUROTABO IS AMONG THEIR TOP TWO BEST-LOOKING!!
IT'S RARE TO SEE THEM BOTH HERE AT THE SAME TIME!
EEK! I'M REALLY GOING TO GET TO KNOW THEM, THEN-!!
HA HA HA HA
BE THANKFUL, GIRLS!!
EEK
WE ARE THE STARS OF THE YOKAI WORLD! WE PLAYED A BIG PART IN THE RECENT SHIKOKU BATTLE!
EEK
LET US EAT OR DO ANYTHING WE WANT-!!
WE'RE IN CHARGE HERE!
OI, OI... THE NURA CLAN'S INFLUENCE IS...
HEH...
AMAZING-
HA HA HA HA
YEAH! YEAH!
I'M SO GLAD THAT WE LOOK LIKE THOSE TWO.
WE CAN HAVE A GREAT TIME, THANKS TO THE NURA CLAN!

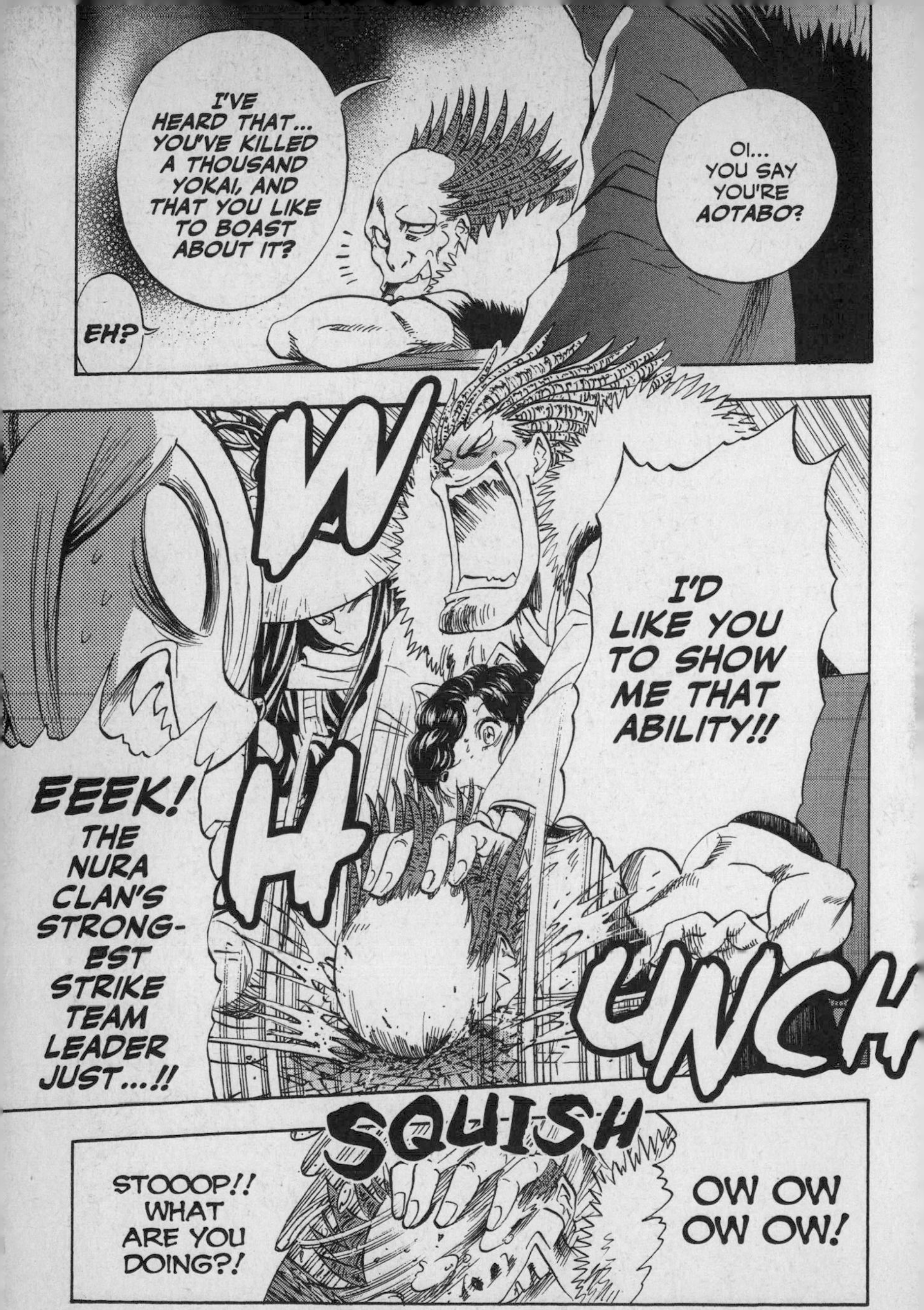
OI... YOU SAY YOU'RE AOTABO?
I'VE HEARD THAT... YOU'VE KILLED A THOUSAND YOKAI, AND THAT YOU LIKE TO BOAST ABOUT IT?
EH?
I'D LIKE YOU TO SHOW ME THAT ABILITY!!
WHUNCH
EEEK! THE NURA CLAN'S STRONG-EST STRIKE TEAM LEADER JUST...!!
SQUISH
OW OW OW OW!
STOOOP!! WHAT ARE YOU DOING?!

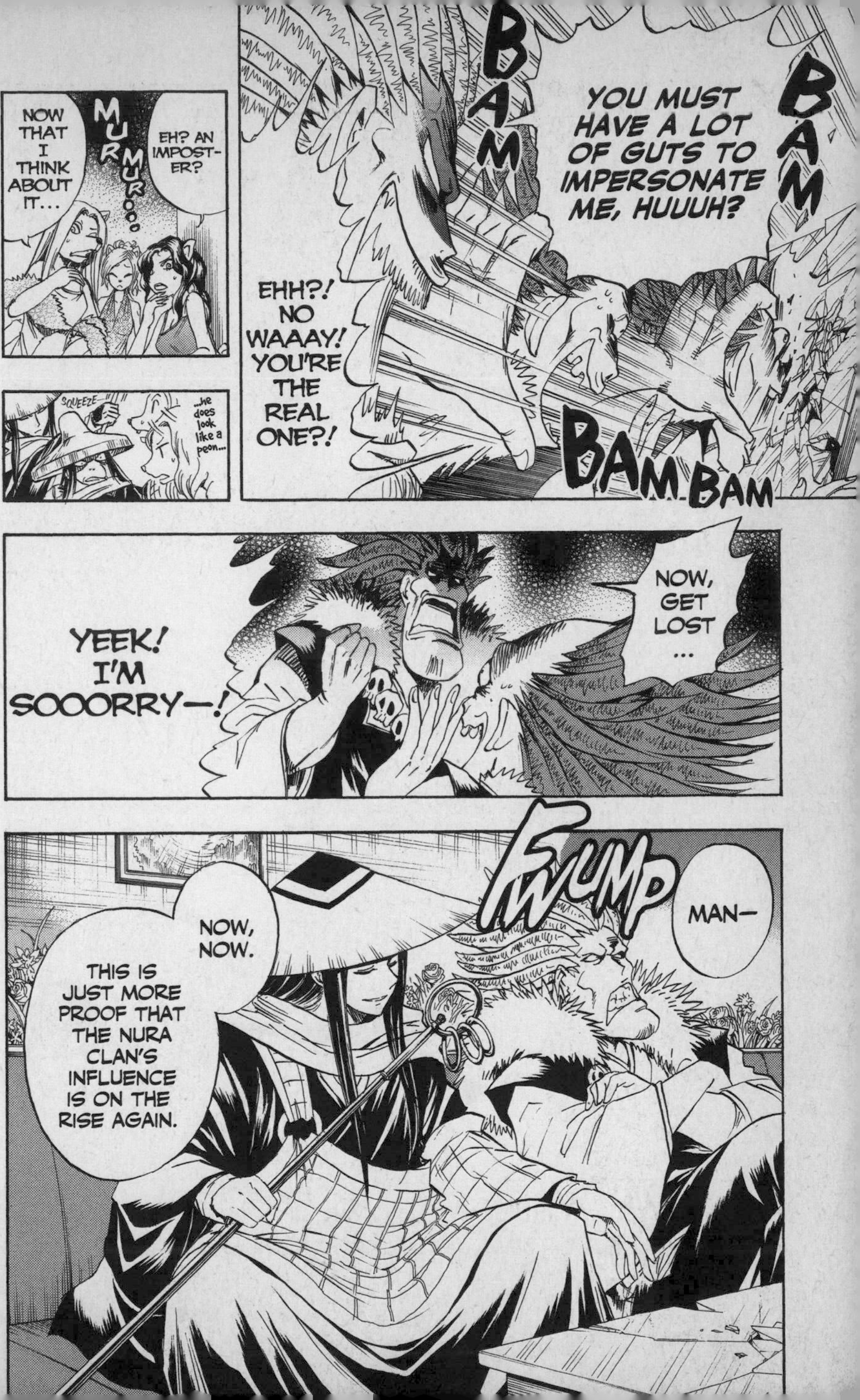

BAM
BAM
YOU MUST HAVE A LOT OF GUTS TO IMPERSONATE ME, HUUUH?
EHH?! NO WAAAY! YOU'RE THE REAL ONE?!
BAM BAM
EH? AN IMPOSTER?
MURMUR
NOW THAT I THINK ABOUT IT...
...he does look like a peon...
SQUEEZE
NOW, GET LOST...
YEEK! I'M SOOORRY—!
MAN—
FWUMP
NOW, NOW.
THIS IS JUST MORE PROOF THAT THE NURA CLAN'S INFLUENCE IS ON THE RISE AGAIN.

READ THIS WAY

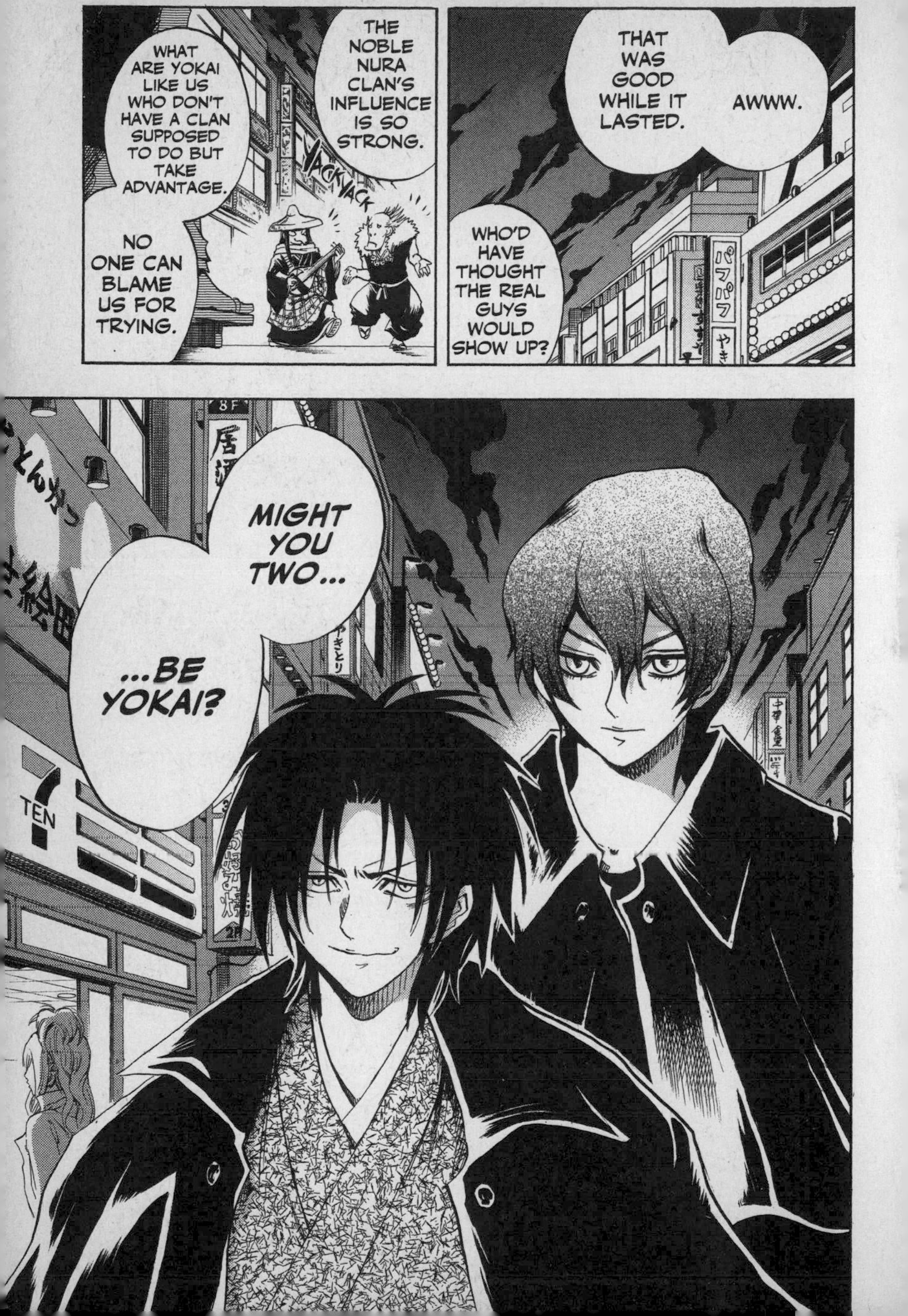
AWWW.
THAT WAS GOOD WHILE IT LASTED.
WHO'D HAVE THOUGHT THE REAL GUYS WOULD SHOW UP?
パフパフ
THE NOBLE NURA CLAN'S INFLUENCE IS SO STRONG.
WHAT ARE YOKAI LIKE US WHO DON'T HAVE A CLAN SUPPOSED TO DO BUT TAKE ADVANTAGE.
YACK YACK
NO ONE CAN BLAME US FOR TRYING.
MIGHT YOU TWO...
...BE YOKAI?
やきとり
TEN

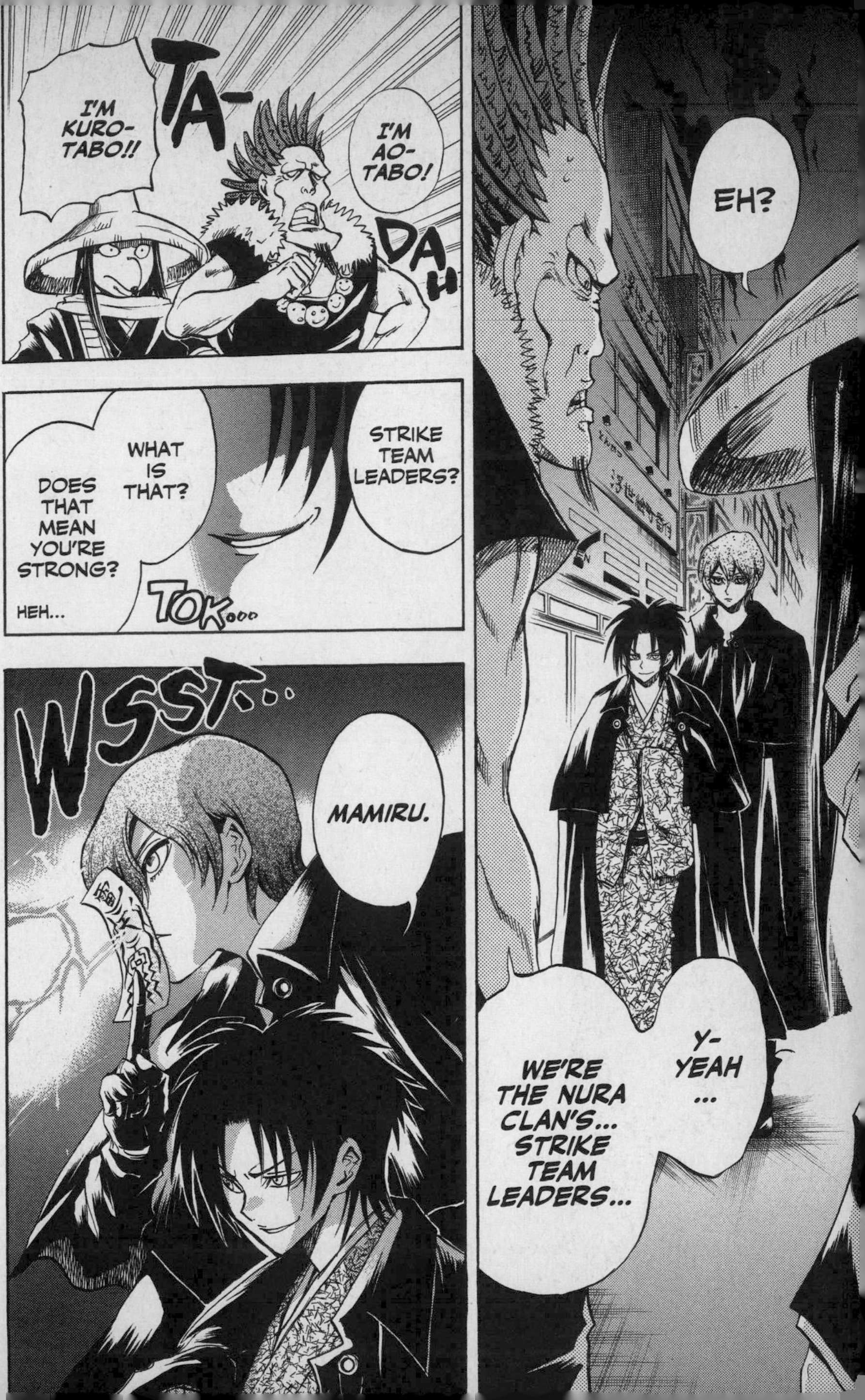
EH?
Y-YEAH...
WE'RE THE NURA CLAN'S... STRIKE TEAM LEADERS...
I'M AO-TABO!
TA-
I'M KURO-TABO!!
DAH
STRIKE TEAM LEADERS?
WHAT IS THAT?
DOES THAT MEAN YOU'RE STRONG?
TOK...
HEH...
WSST...
MAMIRU.

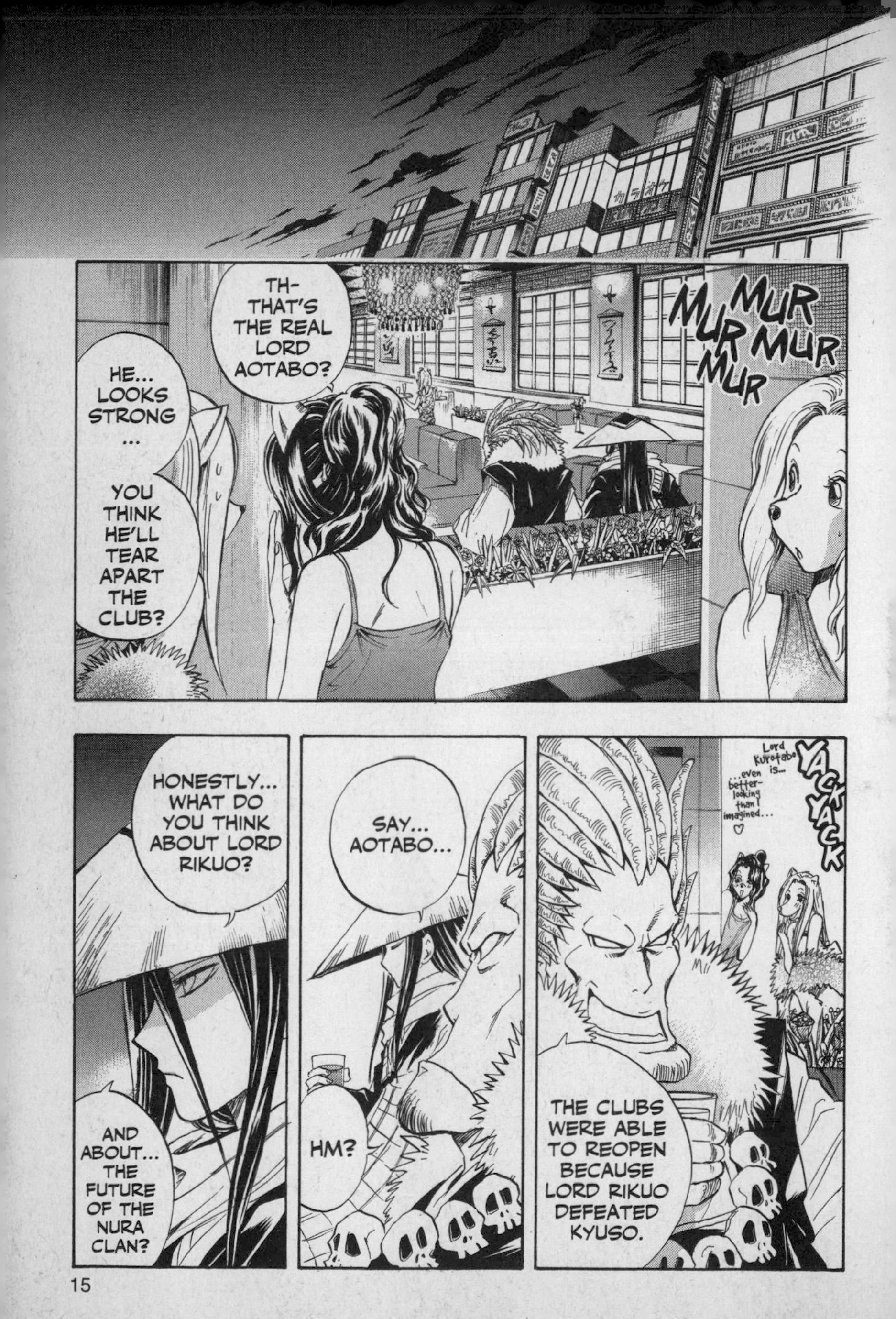
MUR MUR MUR MUR
TH- THAT'S THE REAL LORD AOTABO?
HE... LOOKS STRONG...
YOU THINK HE'LL TEAR APART THE CLUB?
YACK YACK
Lord Kurotabo is... ...even better-looking than I imagined... ♡
THE CLUBS WERE ABLE TO REOPEN BECAUSE LORD RIKUO DEFEATED KYUSO.
SAY... AOTABO...
HM?
HONESTLY... WHAT DO YOU THINK ABOUT LORD RIKUO?
AND ABOUT... THE FUTURE OF THE NURA CLAN?

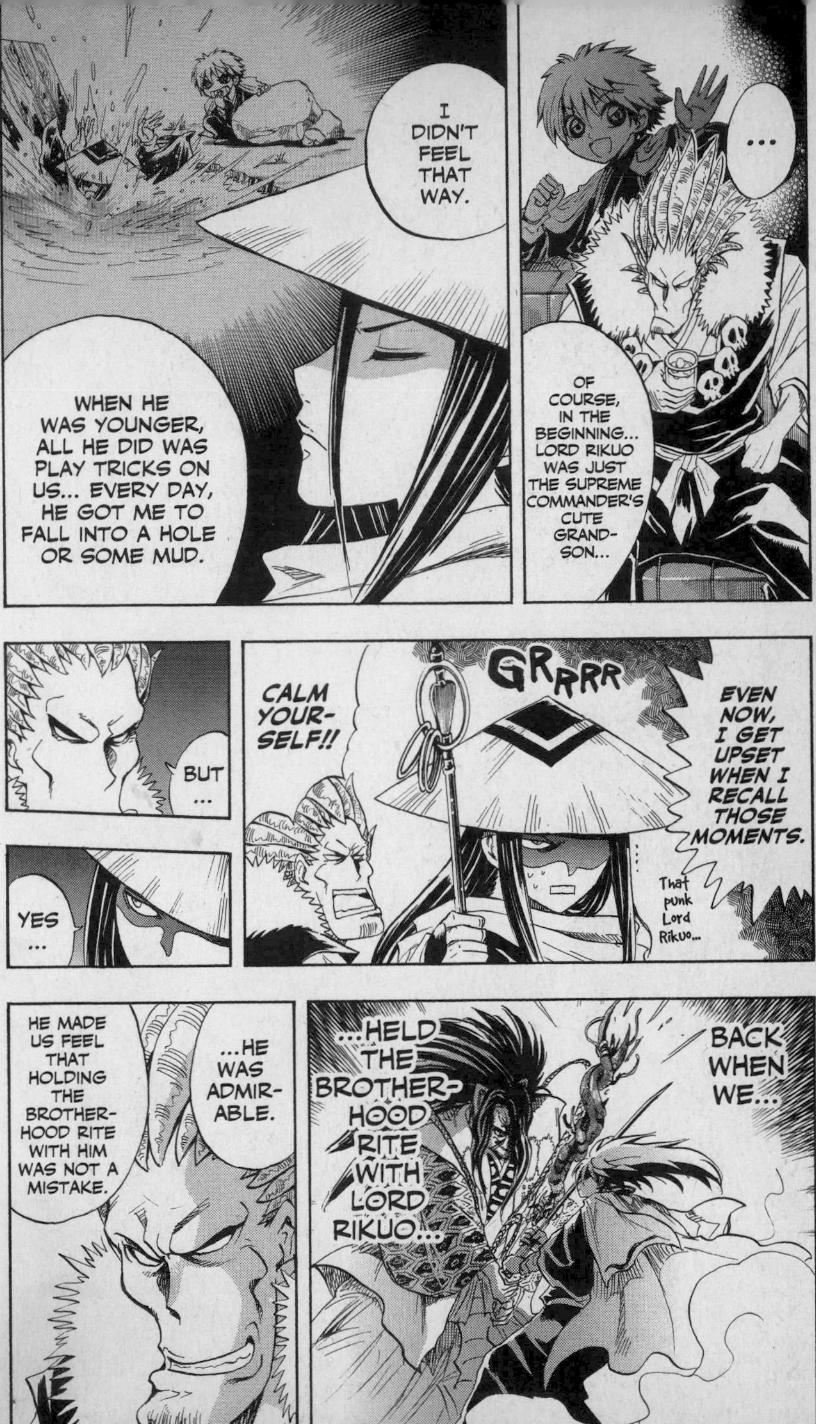
...
OF COURSE, IN THE BEGINNING... LORD RIKUO WAS JUST THE SUPREME COMMANDER'S CUTE GRANDSON...
I DIDN'T FEEL THAT WAY.
WHEN HE WAS YOUNGER, ALL HE DID WAS PLAY TRICKS ON US... EVERY DAY, HE GOT ME TO FALL INTO A HOLE OR SOME MUD.
EVEN NOW, I GET UPSET WHEN I RECALL THOSE MOMENTS.
GRRRR
That punk Lord Rikuo...
CALM YOURSELF!!
BUT...
YES...
BACK WHEN WE...
...HELD THE BROTHERHOOD RITE WITH LORD RIKUO...
...HE WAS ADMIRABLE.
HE MADE US FEEL THAT HOLDING THE BROTHERHOOD RITE WITH HIM WAS NOT A MISTAKE.

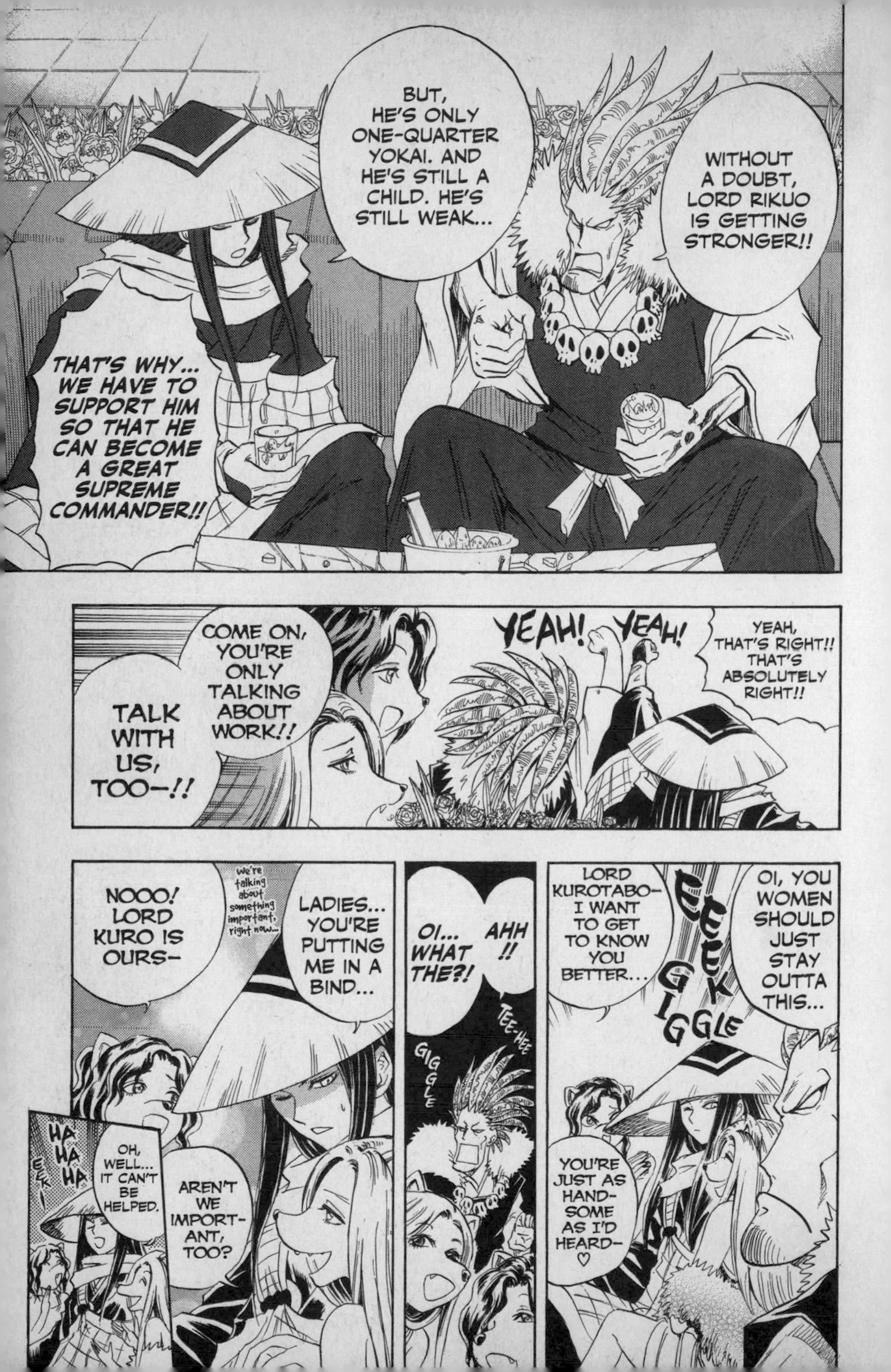
WITHOUT A DOUBT, LORD RIKUO IS GETTING STRONGER!!
BUT, HE'S ONLY ONE-QUARTER YOKAI. AND HE'S STILL A CHILD. HE'S STILL WEAK...
THAT'S WHY... WE HAVE TO SUPPORT HIM SO THAT HE CAN BECOME A GREAT SUPREME COMMANDER!!
YEAH, THAT'S RIGHT!! THAT'S ABSOLUTELY RIGHT!!
YEAH! YEAH!
COME ON, YOU'RE ONLY TALKING ABOUT WORK!!
TALK WITH US, TOO-!!
OI, YOU WOMEN SHOULD JUST STAY OUTTA THIS...
EEEK
GIGGLE
LORD KUROTABO- I WANT TO GET TO KNOW YOU BETTER...
YOU'RE JUST AS HAND-SOME AS I'D HEARD-♡
AHH!!
OI... WHAT THE?!
TEE-HEE
GIGGLE
LADIES... YOU'RE PUTTING ME IN A BIND...
we're talking about something important, right now...
NOOO! LORD KURO IS OURS-
AREN'T WE IMPORTANT, TOO?
OH, WELL... IT CAN'T BE HELPED.
HA HA HA
EEK!

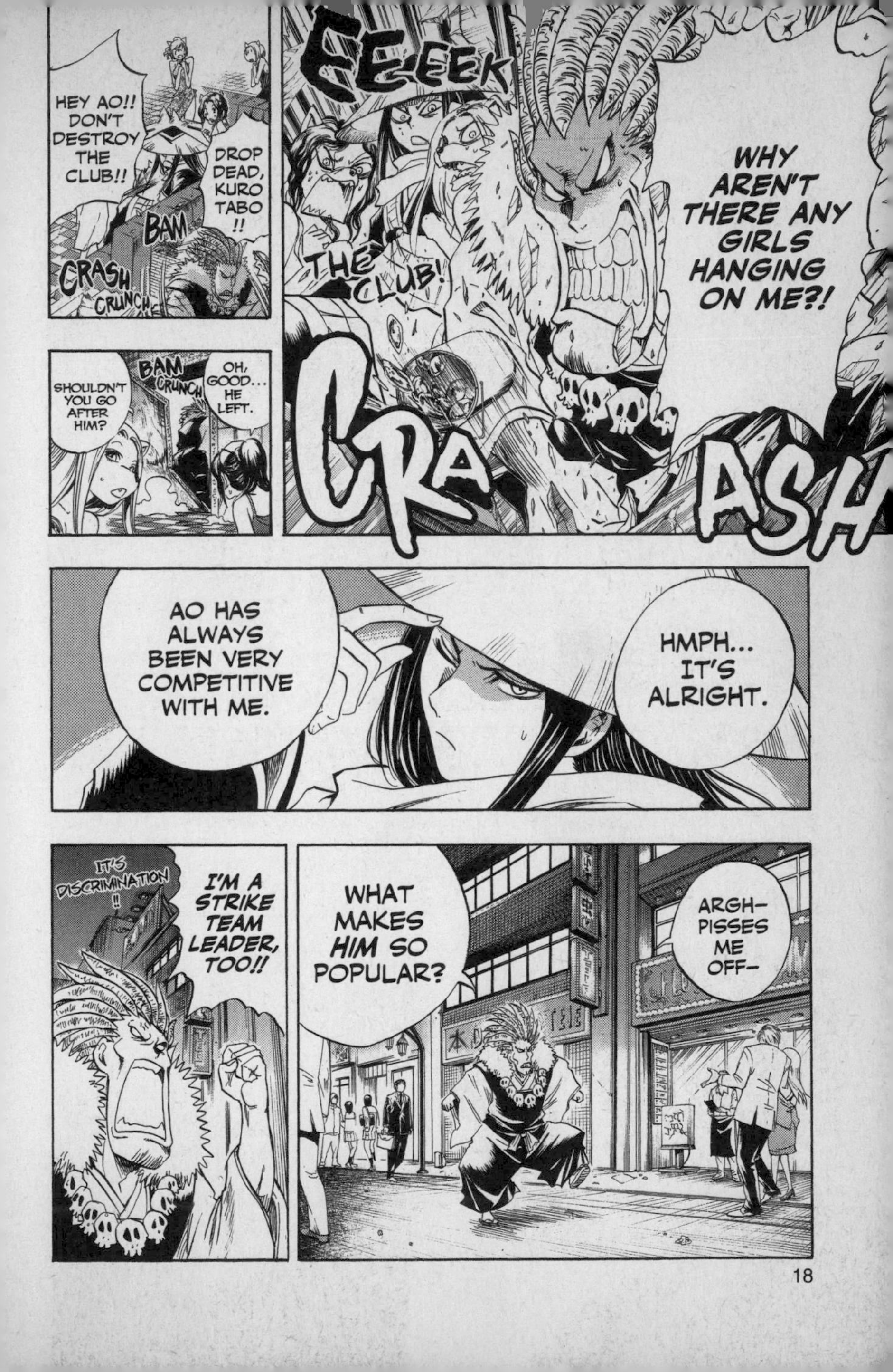
WHY AREN'T THERE ANY GIRLS HANGING ON ME?!
EE-EEK
THE CLUB!
CRA ASH
DROP DEAD, KURO TABO!!
HEY AO!! DON'T DESTROY THE CLUB!!
BAM
CRASH
CRUNCH
OH, GOOD... HE LEFT.
BAM CRUNCH
SHOULDN'T YOU GO AFTER HIM?
HMPH... IT'S ALRIGHT.
AO HAS ALWAYS BEEN VERY COMPETITIVE WITH ME.
ARGH- PISSES ME OFF-
WHAT MAKES *HIM* SO POPULAR?
I'M A STRIKE TEAM LEADER, TOO!!
IT'S DISCRIMINATION!!

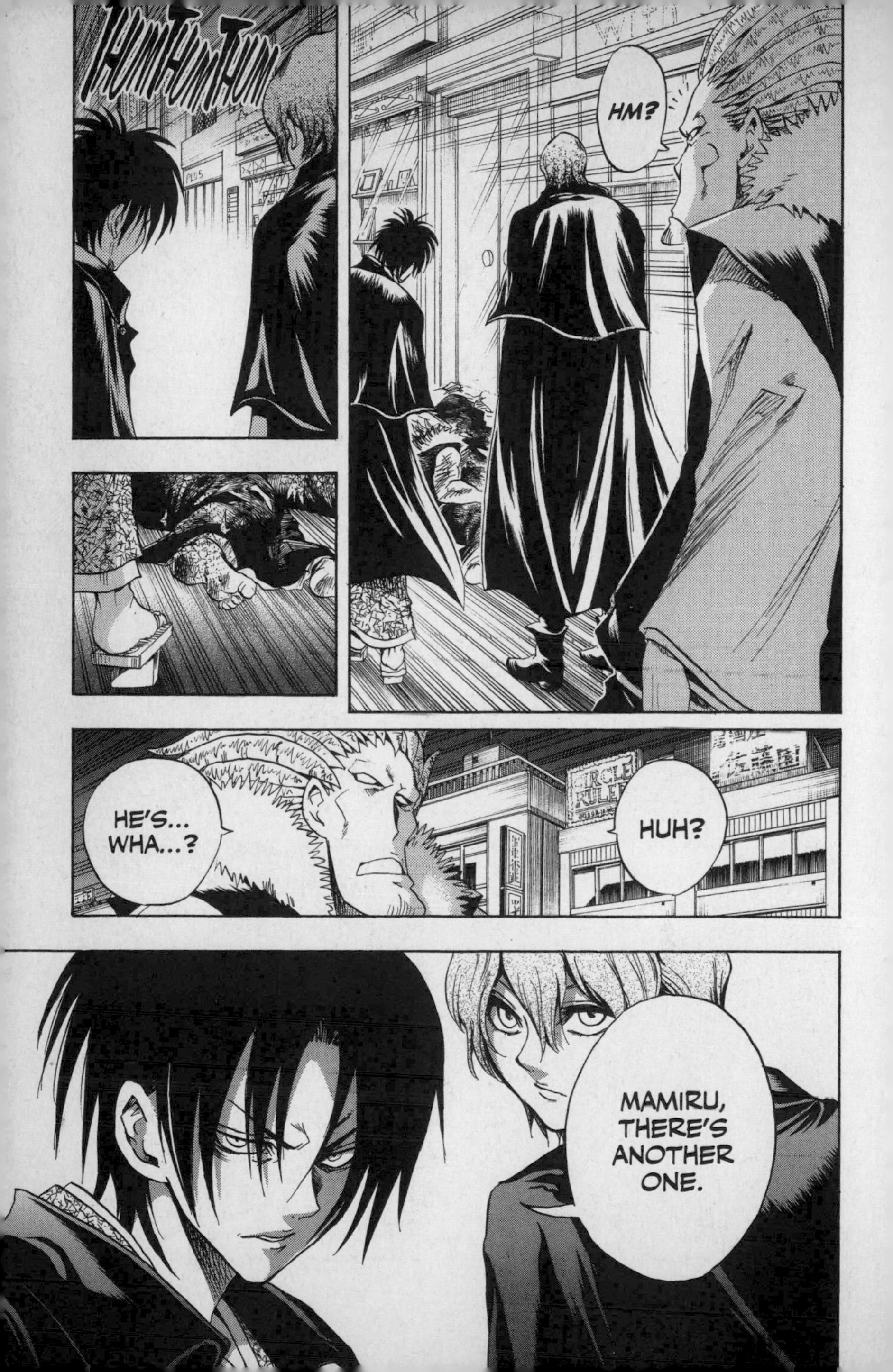
HM?
HUH?
HE'S... WHA...?
MAMIRU, THERE'S ANOTHER ONE.

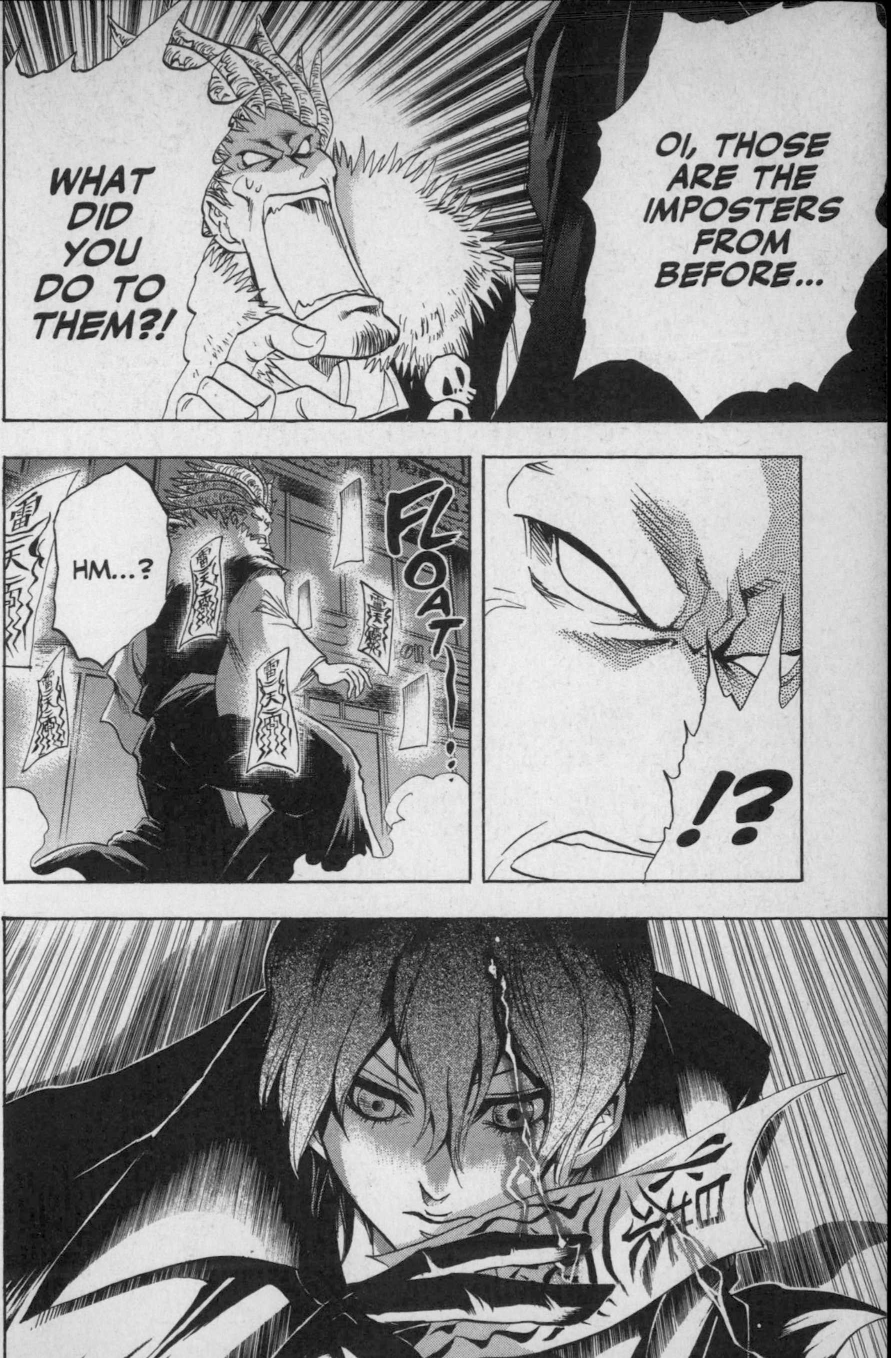
OI, THOSE ARE THE IMPOSTERS FROM BEFORE...
WHAT DID YOU DO TO THEM?!
!?
FLOAT!!
HM...?

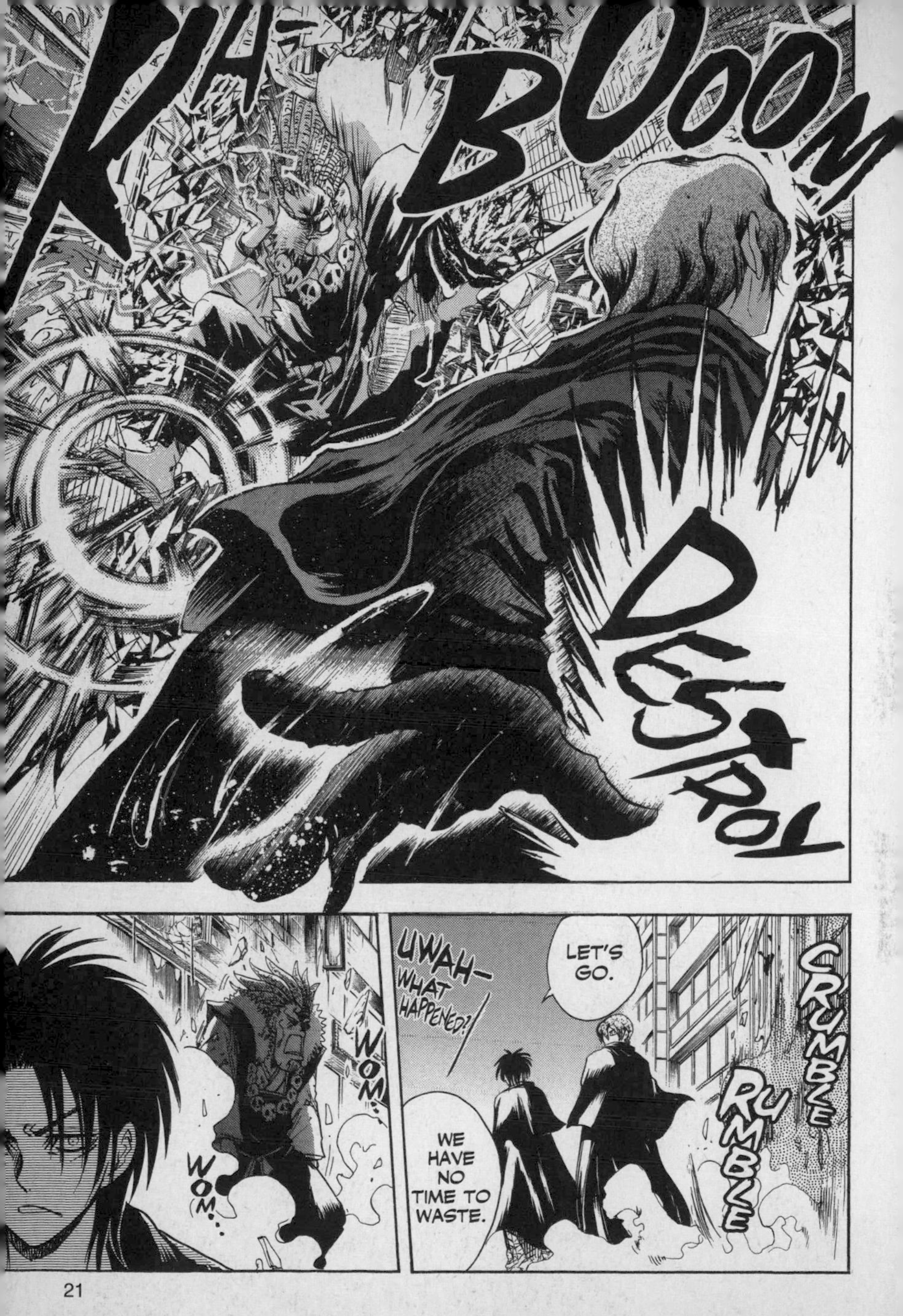
KA-BOOM
DESTROY
CRUMBLE
LET'S GO.
UWAH- WHAT HAPPENED?!
RUMBLE
WE HAVE NO TIME TO WASTE.
WOM...
WOM...

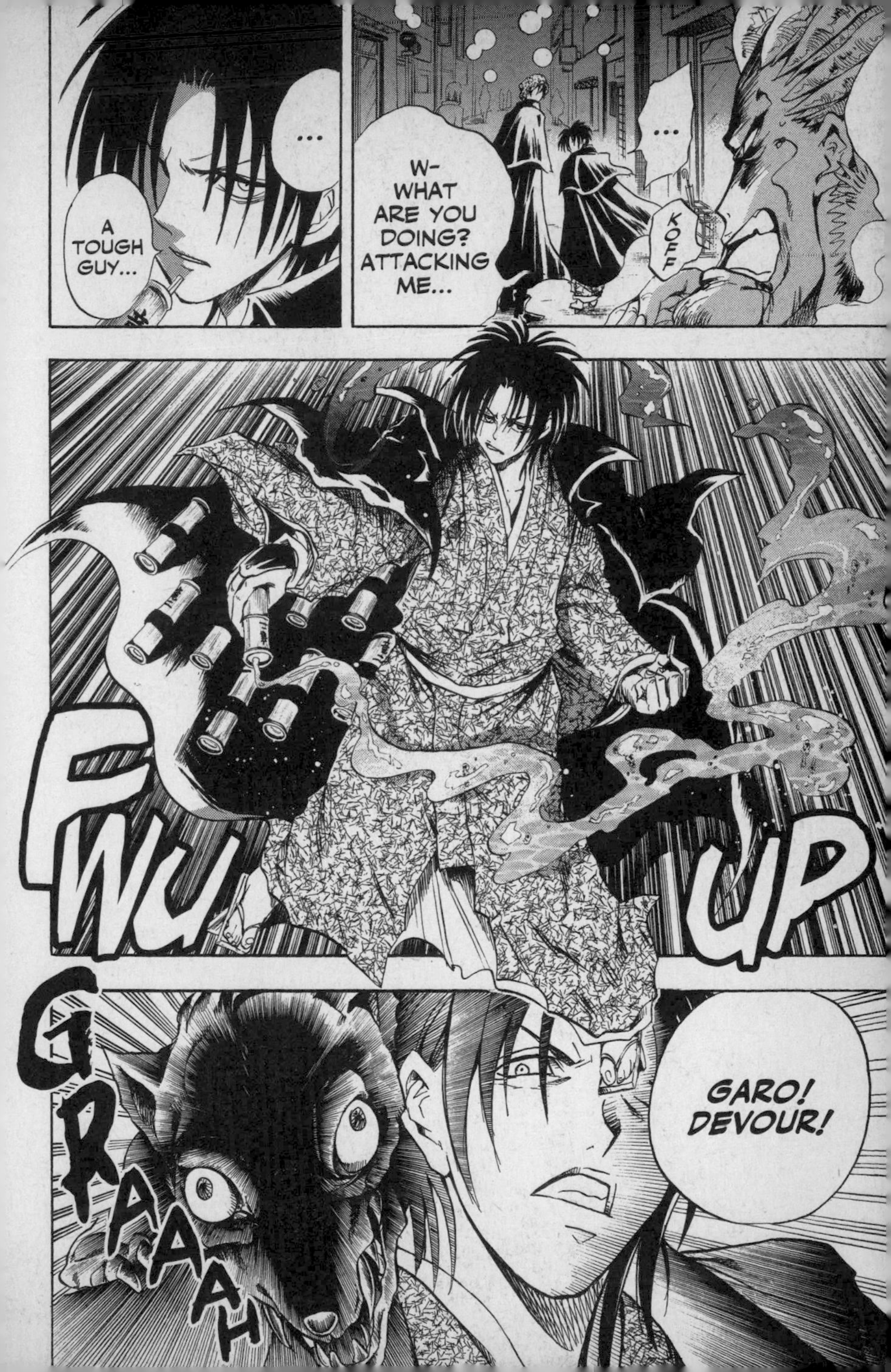
...
KOFF
W- WHAT ARE YOU DOING? ATTACKING ME...
...
A TOUGH GUY...
FWU UP
GARO! DEVOUR!
GRAAAH

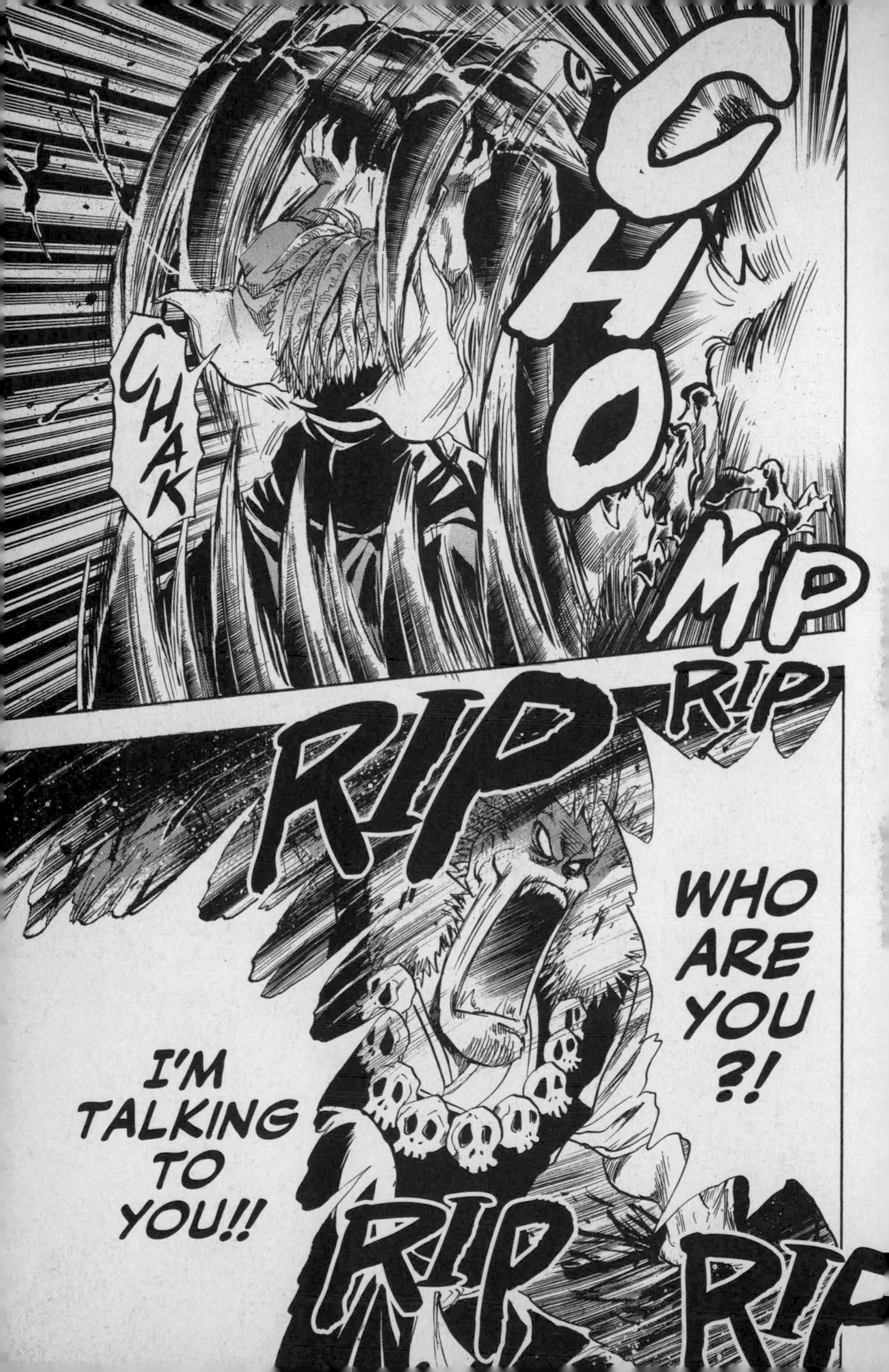
CHOMP
CHAK
RIP
RIP
WHO ARE YOU?!
I'M TALKING TO YOU!!
RIP
RIP

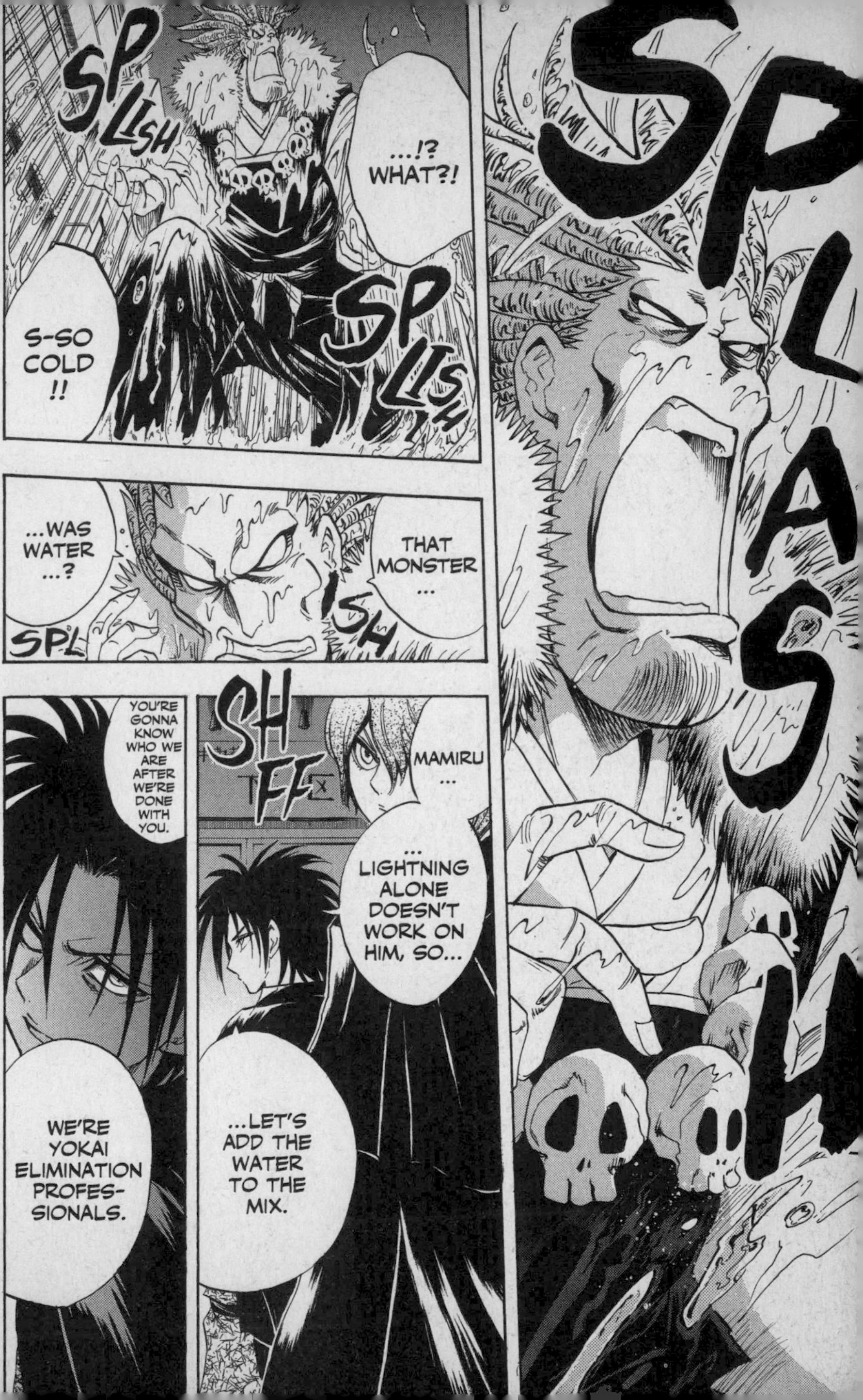
SPLASH
...!? WHAT?!
SPLISH
S-SO COLD !!
SPLISH
THAT MONSTER ...
...WAS WATER ...?
ISH
SPL
SHFF
MAMIRU ...
... LIGHTNING ALONE DOESN'T WORK ON HIM, SO...
...LET'S ADD THE WATER TO THE MIX.
YOU'RE GONNA KNOW WHO WE ARE AFTER WE'RE DONE WITH YOU.
WE'RE YOKAI ELIMINATION PROFES-SIONALS.

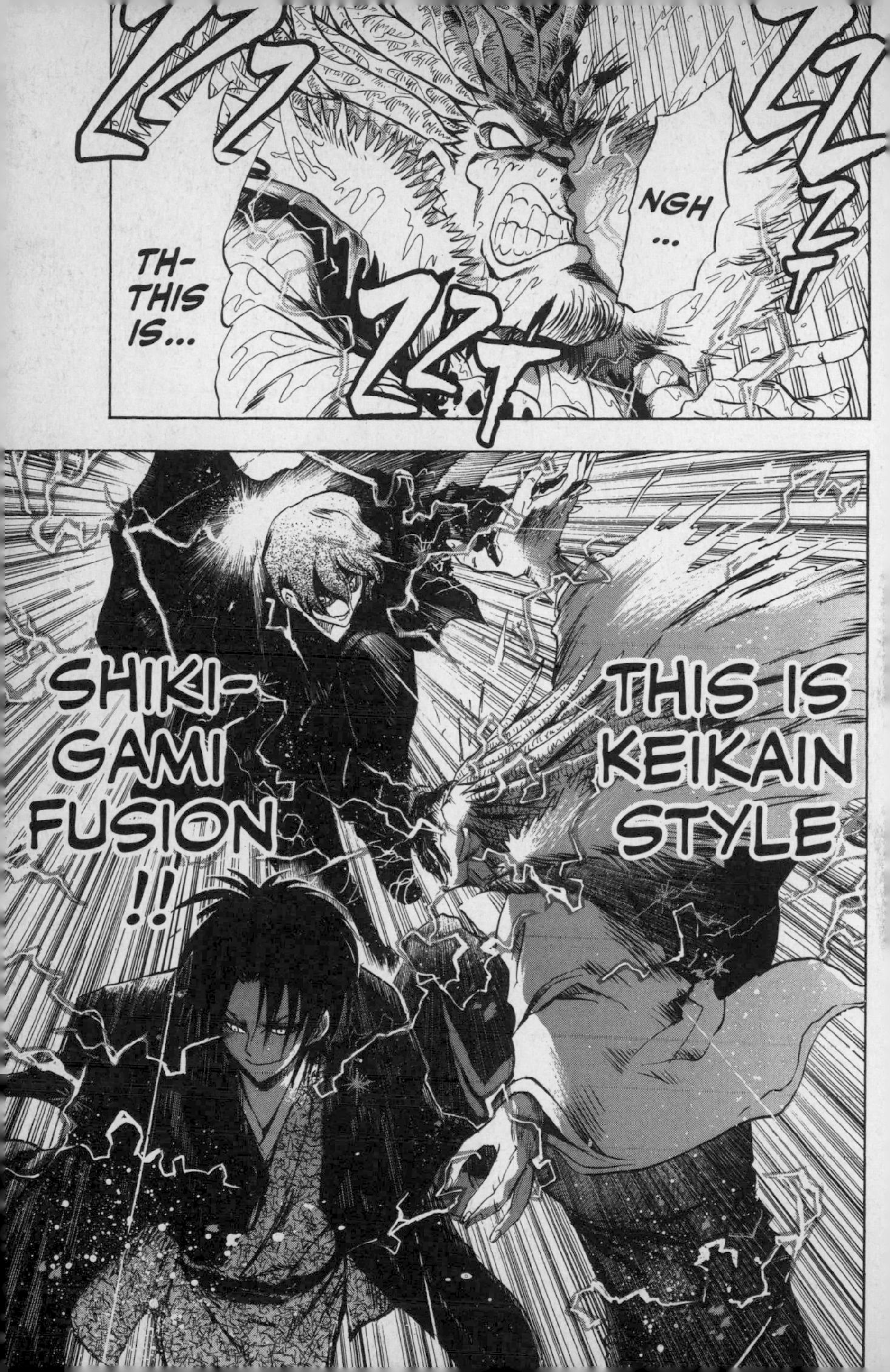
NGH...
TH-THIS IS...
THIS IS KEIKAIN STYLE
SHIKIGAMI FUSION!!

NURA: RISE OF THE YOKAI CLAN

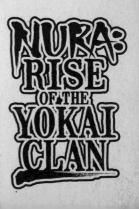

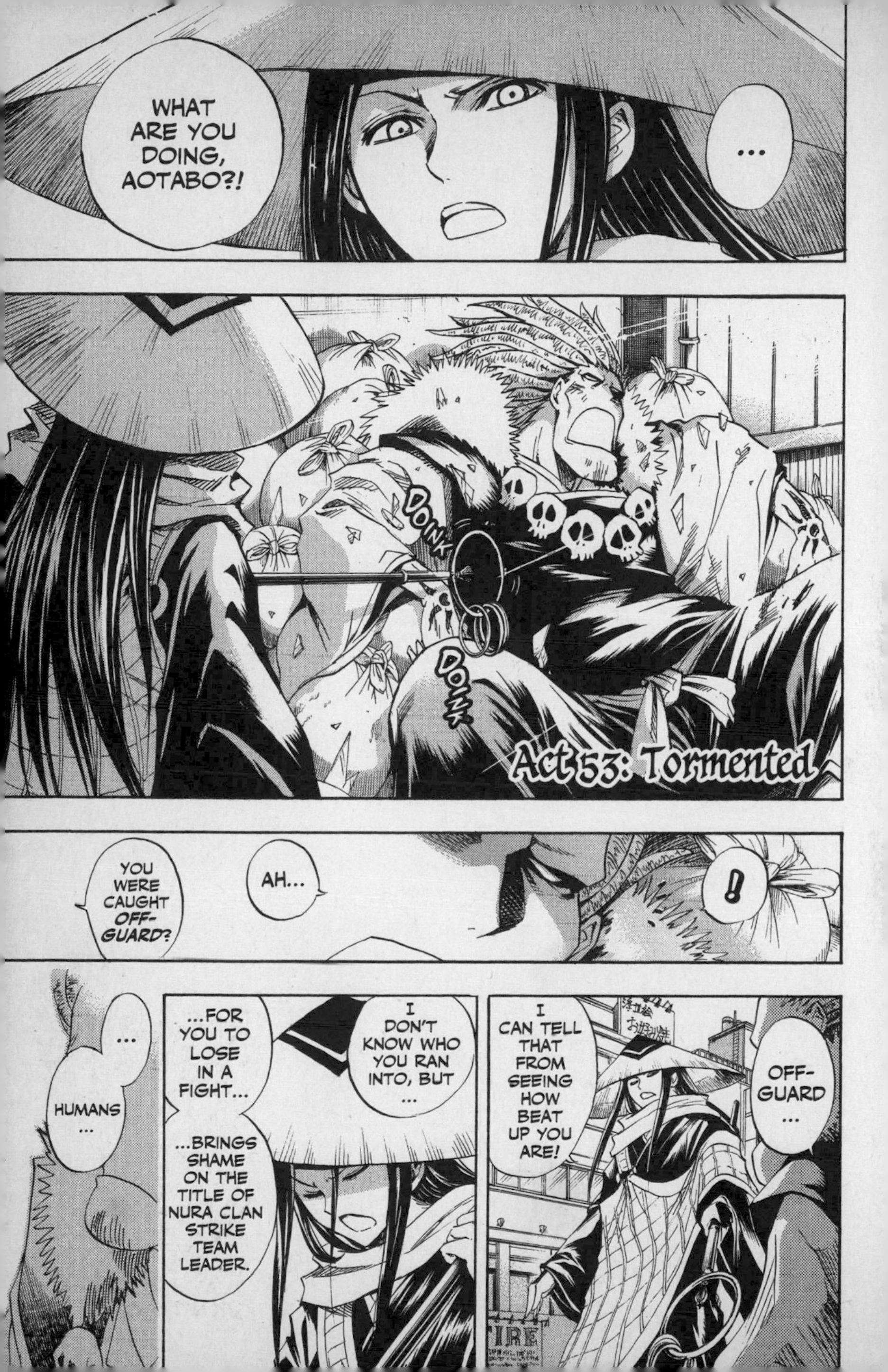
...
WHAT ARE YOU DOING, AOTABO?!
DOINK
DOINK
Act 53: Tormented
!
AH...
YOU WERE CAUGHT OFF-GUARD?
OFF-GUARD ...
I CAN TELL THAT FROM SEEING HOW BEAT UP YOU ARE!
I DON'T KNOW WHO YOU RAN INTO, BUT ...
...FOR YOU TO LOSE IN A FIGHT...
...BRINGS SHAME ON THE TITLE OF NURA CLAN STRIKE TEAM LEADER.
...
HUMANS ...

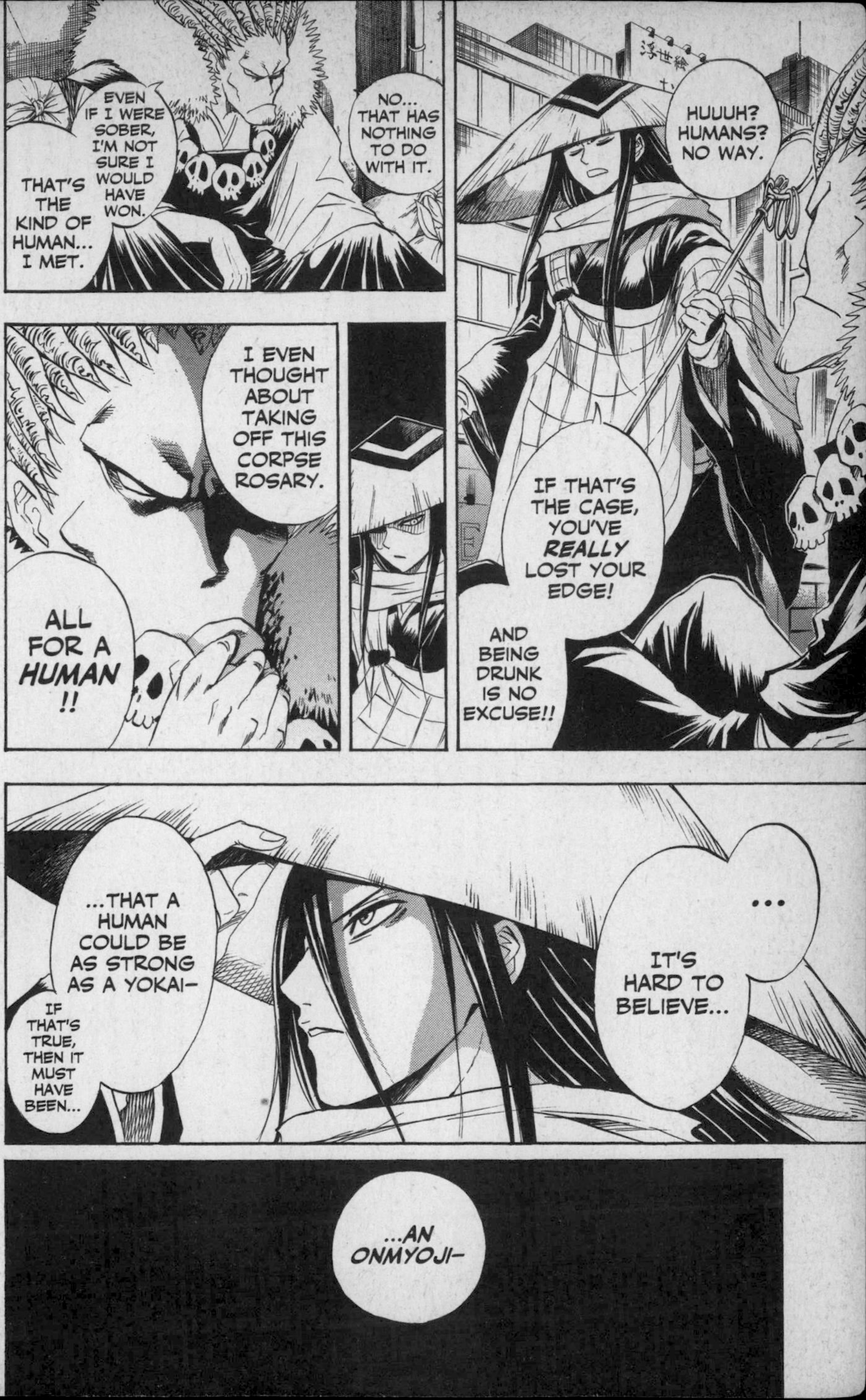
HUUUH? HUMANS? NO WAY.
IF THAT'S THE CASE, YOU'VE *REALLY* LOST YOUR EDGE!
AND BEING DRUNK IS NO EXCUSE!!
NO... THAT HAS NOTHING TO DO WITH IT.
EVEN IF I WERE SOBER, I'M NOT SURE I WOULD HAVE WON.
THAT'S THE KIND OF HUMAN... I MET.
I EVEN THOUGHT ABOUT TAKING OFF THIS CORPSE ROSARY.
ALL FOR A *HUMAN* !!
...
IT'S HARD TO BELIEVE...
...THAT A HUMAN COULD BE AS STRONG AS A YOKAI–
IF THAT'S TRUE, THEN IT MUST HAVE BEEN...
*...AN ONMYOJI–*

# Act 53: Tormented

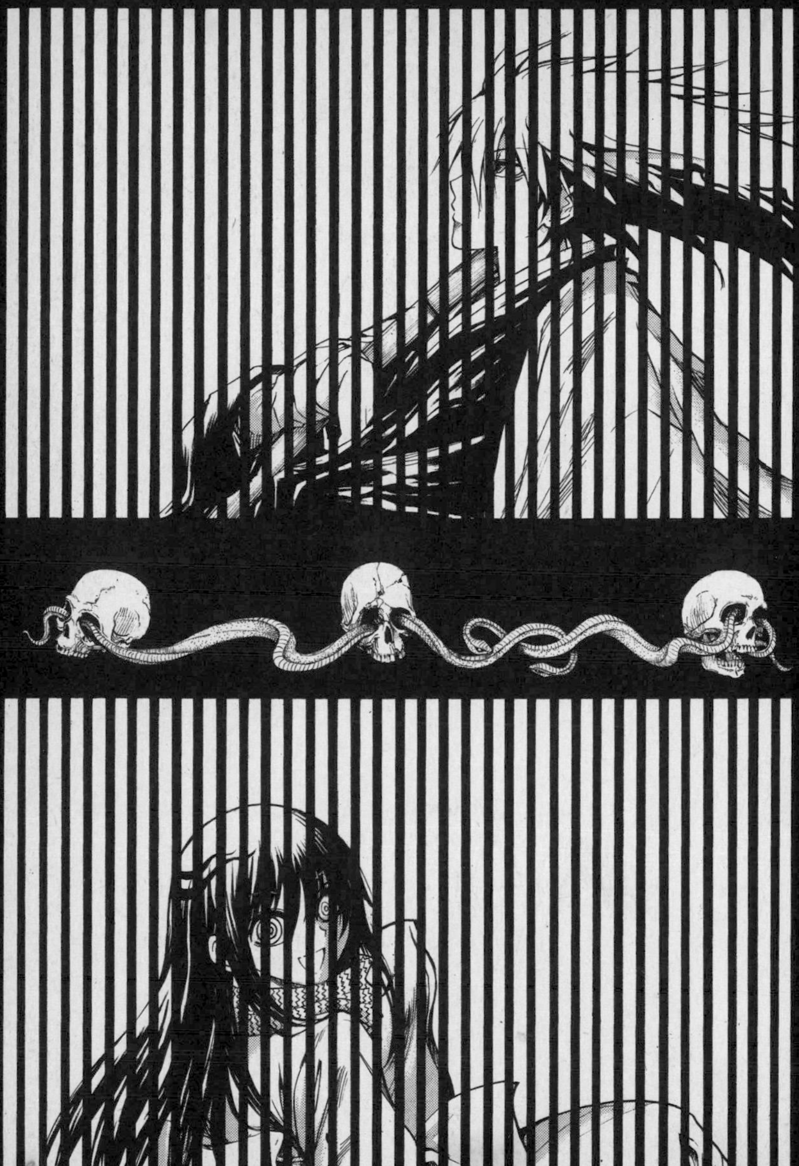

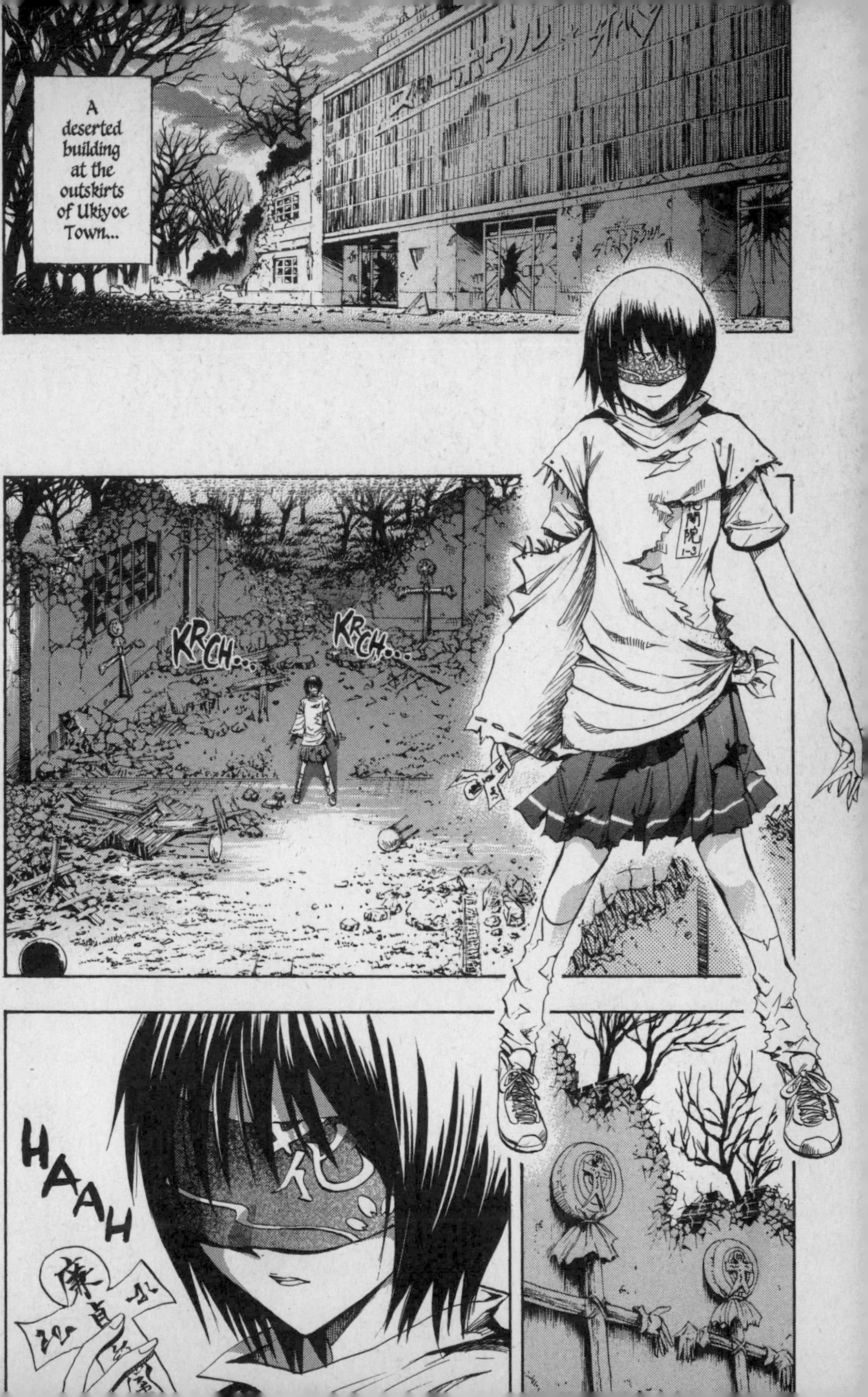
A deserted building at the outskirts of Ukiyoe Town...
KRCH...
KRCH...
HAAAH

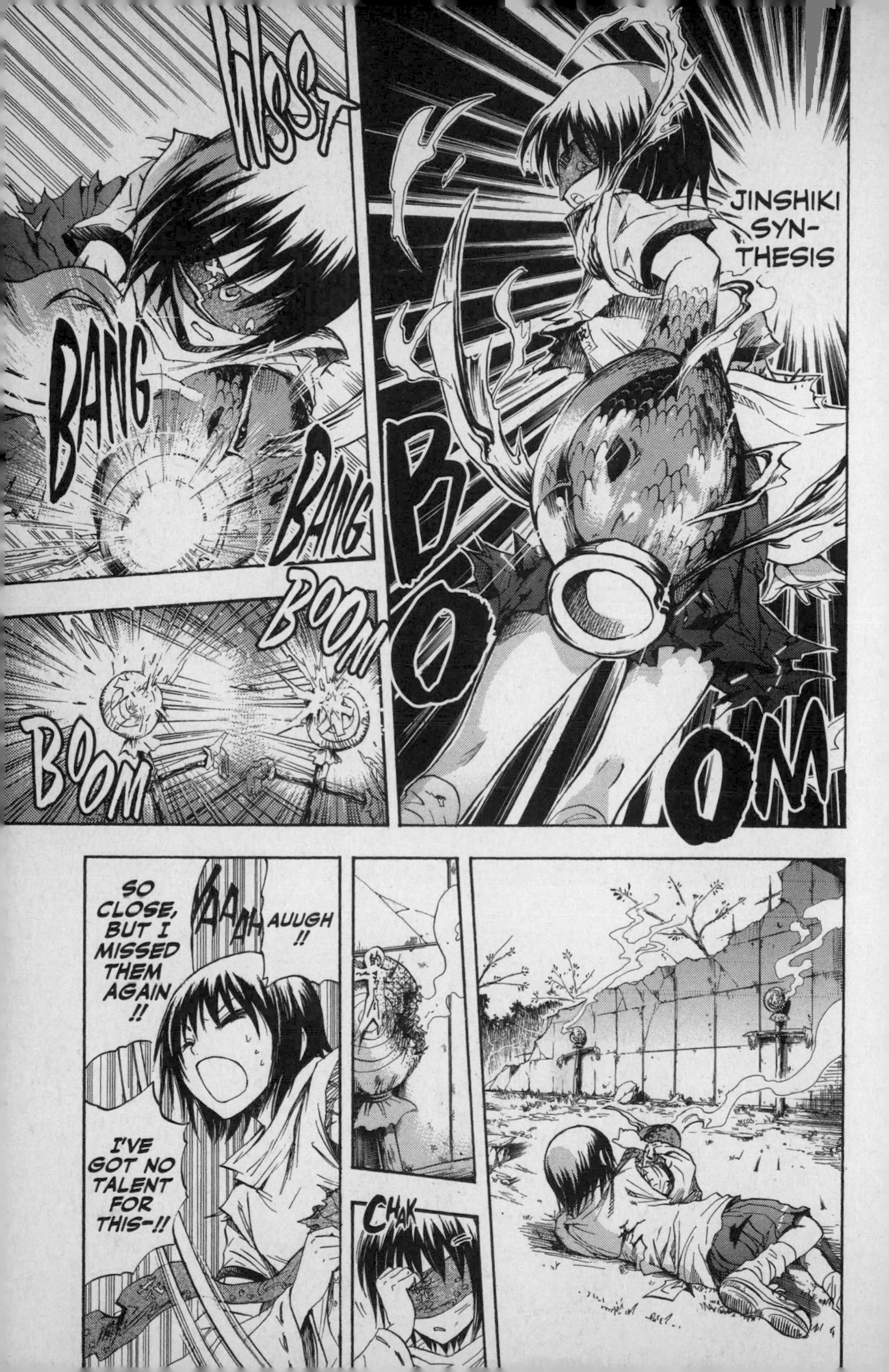
JINSHIKI SYN-THESIS
BOOM
WHSST
BANG
BANG
BOOM
BOOM
CHAK
AUUGH !!
YAAAH
SO CLOSE, BUT I MISSED THEM AGAIN !!
I'VE GOT NO TALENT FOR THIS-!!

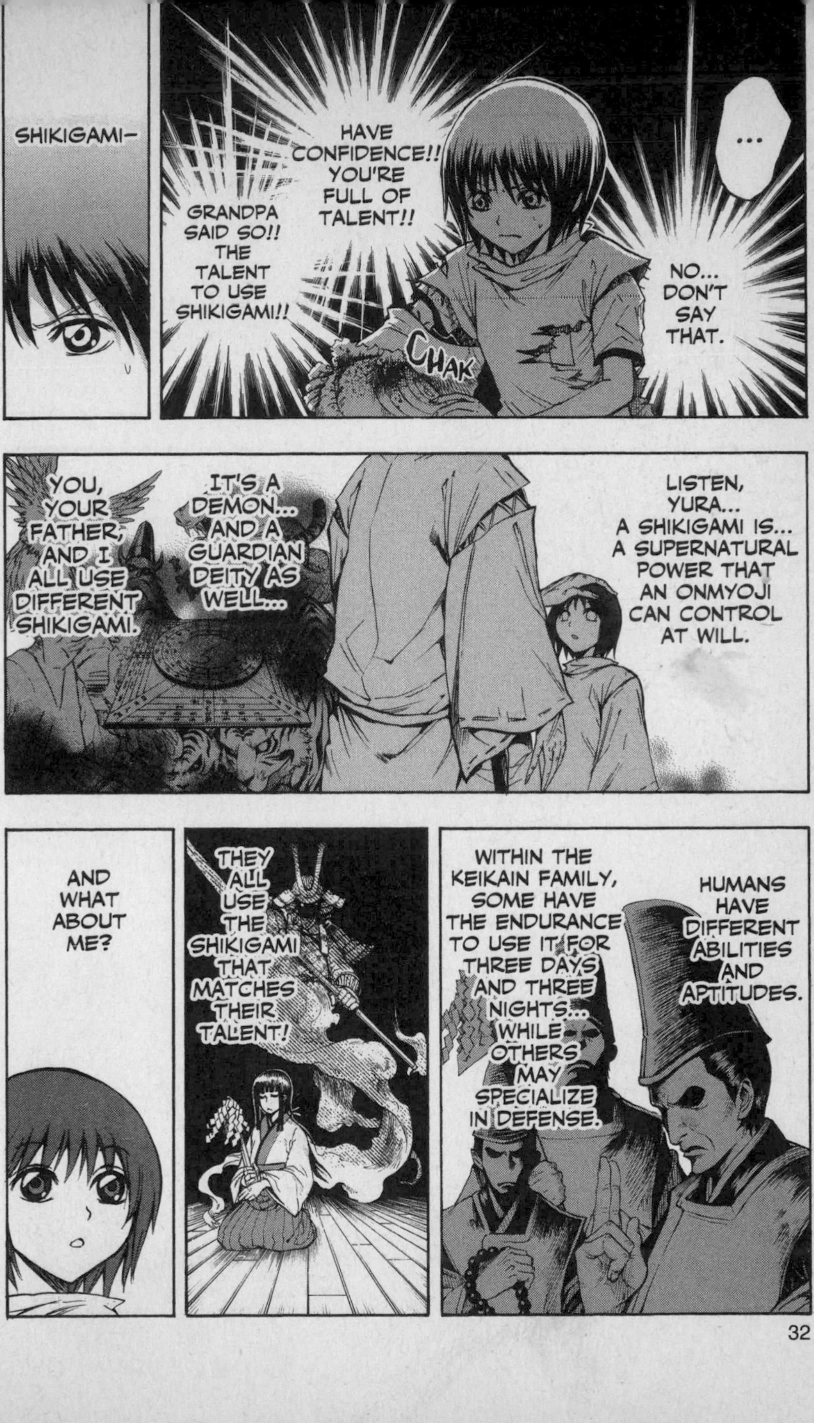
...
NO... DON'T SAY THAT.
HAVE CONFIDENCE!! YOU'RE FULL OF TALENT!!
GRANDPA SAID SO!! THE TALENT TO USE SHIKIGAMI!!
CHAK
SHIKIGAMI–
LISTEN, YURA... A SHIKIGAMI IS... A SUPERNATURAL POWER THAT AN ONMYOJI CAN CONTROL AT WILL.
IT'S A DEMON... AND A GUARDIAN DEITY AS WELL...
YOU, YOUR FATHER, AND I ALL USE DIFFERENT SHIKIGAMI.
HUMANS HAVE DIFFERENT ABILITIES AND APTITUDES.
WITHIN THE KEIKAIN FAMILY, SOME HAVE THE ENDURANCE TO USE IT FOR THREE DAYS AND THREE NIGHTS... WHILE OTHERS MAY SPECIALIZE IN DEFENSE.
THEY ALL USE THE SHIKIGAMI THAT MATCHES THEIR TALENT!
AND WHAT ABOUT ME?

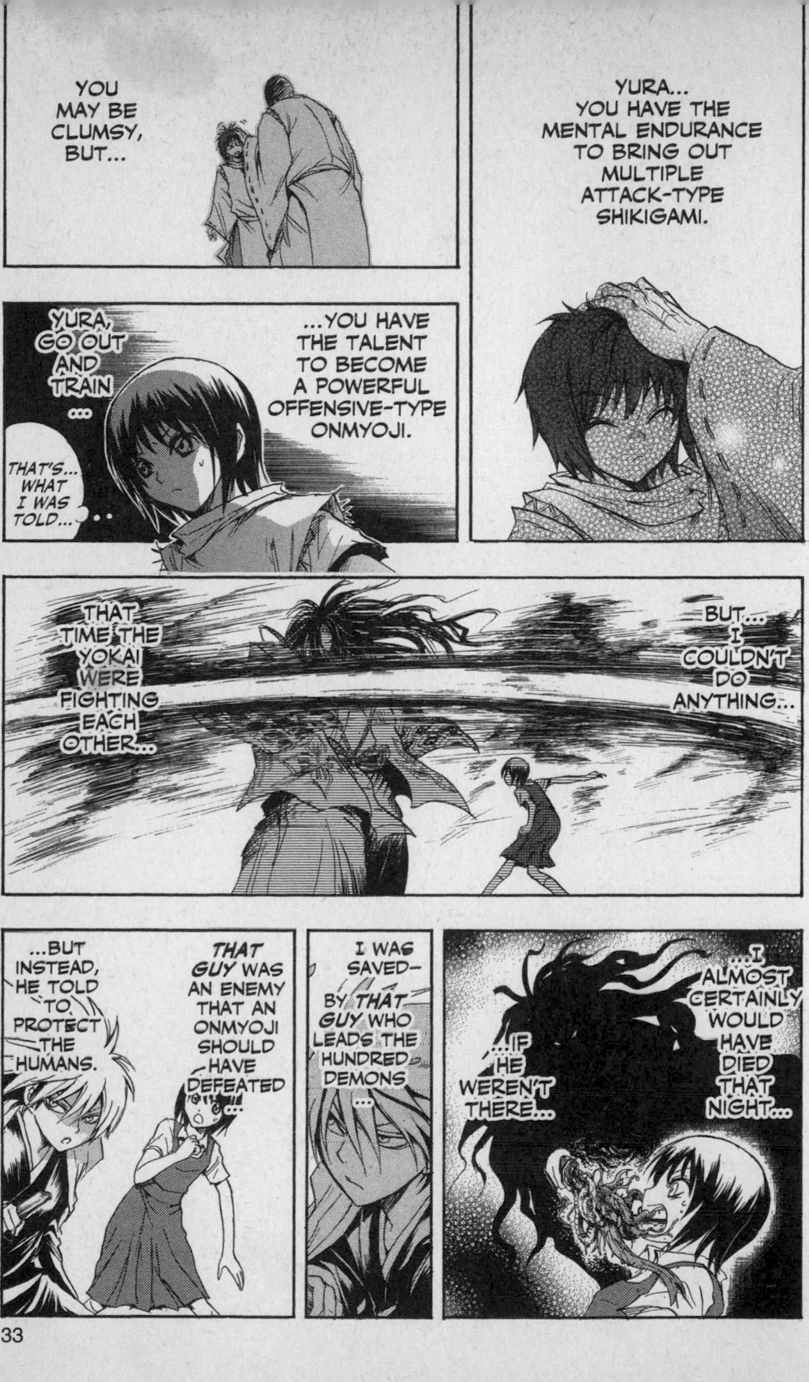
YURA... YOU HAVE THE MENTAL ENDURANCE TO BRING OUT MULTIPLE ATTACK-TYPE SHIKIGAMI.
YOU MAY BE CLUMSY, BUT...
...YOU HAVE THE TALENT TO BECOME A POWERFUL OFFENSIVE-TYPE ONMYOJI.
YURA, GO OUT AND TRAIN...
THAT'S... WHAT I WAS TOLD...
BUT... I COULDN'T DO ANYTHING...
THAT TIME THE YOKAI WERE FIGHTING EACH OTHER...
...I ALMOST CERTAINLY WOULD HAVE DIED THAT NIGHT...
...IF HE WEREN'T THERE...
I WAS SAVED— BY *THAT GUY* WHO LEADS THE HUNDRED DEMONS...
*THAT GUY* WAS AN ENEMY THAT AN ONMYOJI SHOULD HAVE DEFEATED...
...BUT INSTEAD, HE TOLD TO PROTECT THE HUMANS.

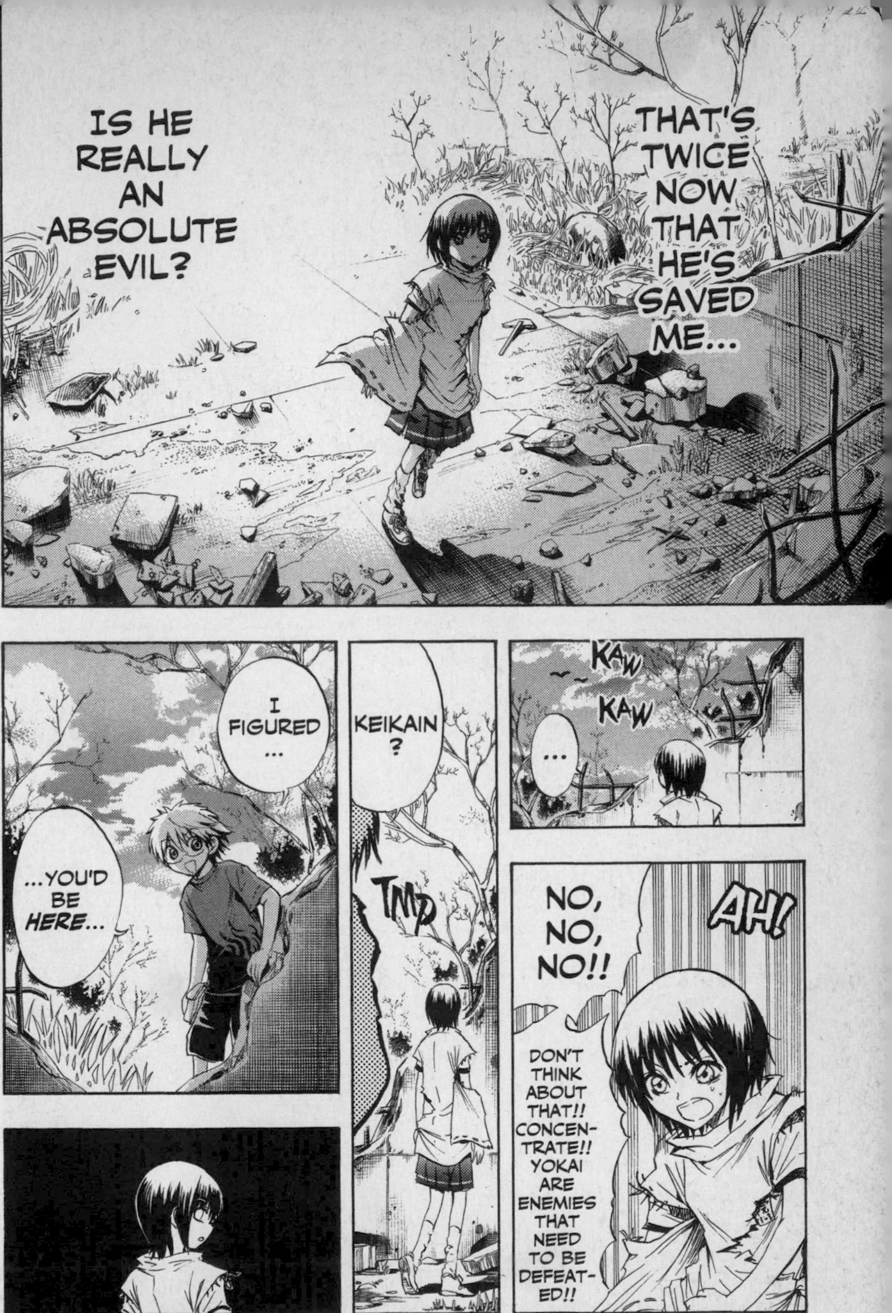
THAT'S TWICE NOW THAT HE'S SAVED ME...
IS HE REALLY AN ABSOLUTE EVIL?
KAW
KAW
...
AH!
NO, NO, NO!!
DON'T THINK ABOUT THAT!! CONCENTRATE!! YOKAI ARE ENEMIES THAT NEED TO BE DEFEATED!!
KEIKAIN?
TMP
I FIGURED...
...YOU'D BE *HERE*...

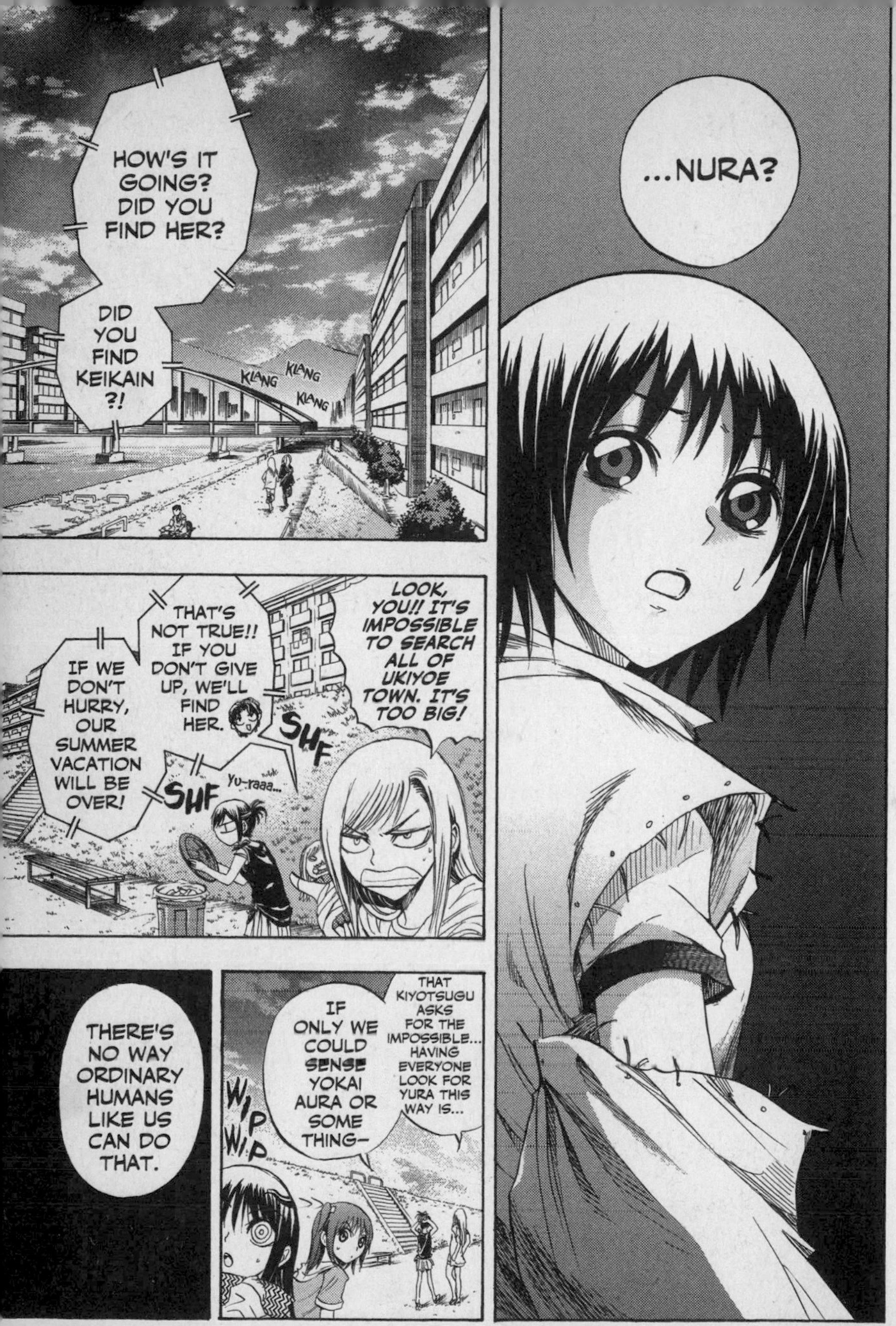
...NURA?
HOW'S IT GOING? DID YOU FIND HER?
DID YOU FIND KEIKAIN ?!
KLANG
KLANG
KLANG
LOOK, YOU!! IT'S IMPOSSIBLE TO SEARCH ALL OF UKIYOE TOWN. IT'S TOO BIG!
SHF
THAT'S NOT TRUE!! IF YOU DON'T GIVE UP, WE'LL FIND HER.
IF WE DON'T HURRY, OUR SUMMER VACATION WILL BE OVER!
SHF
Yu-raaa...
THAT KIYOTSUGU ASKS FOR THE IMPOSSIBLE... HAVING EVERYONE LOOK FOR YURA THIS WAY IS...
IF ONLY WE COULD SENSE YOKAI AURA OR SOME THING—
WIP WIP
THERE'S NO WAY ORDINARY HUMANS LIKE US CAN DO THAT.

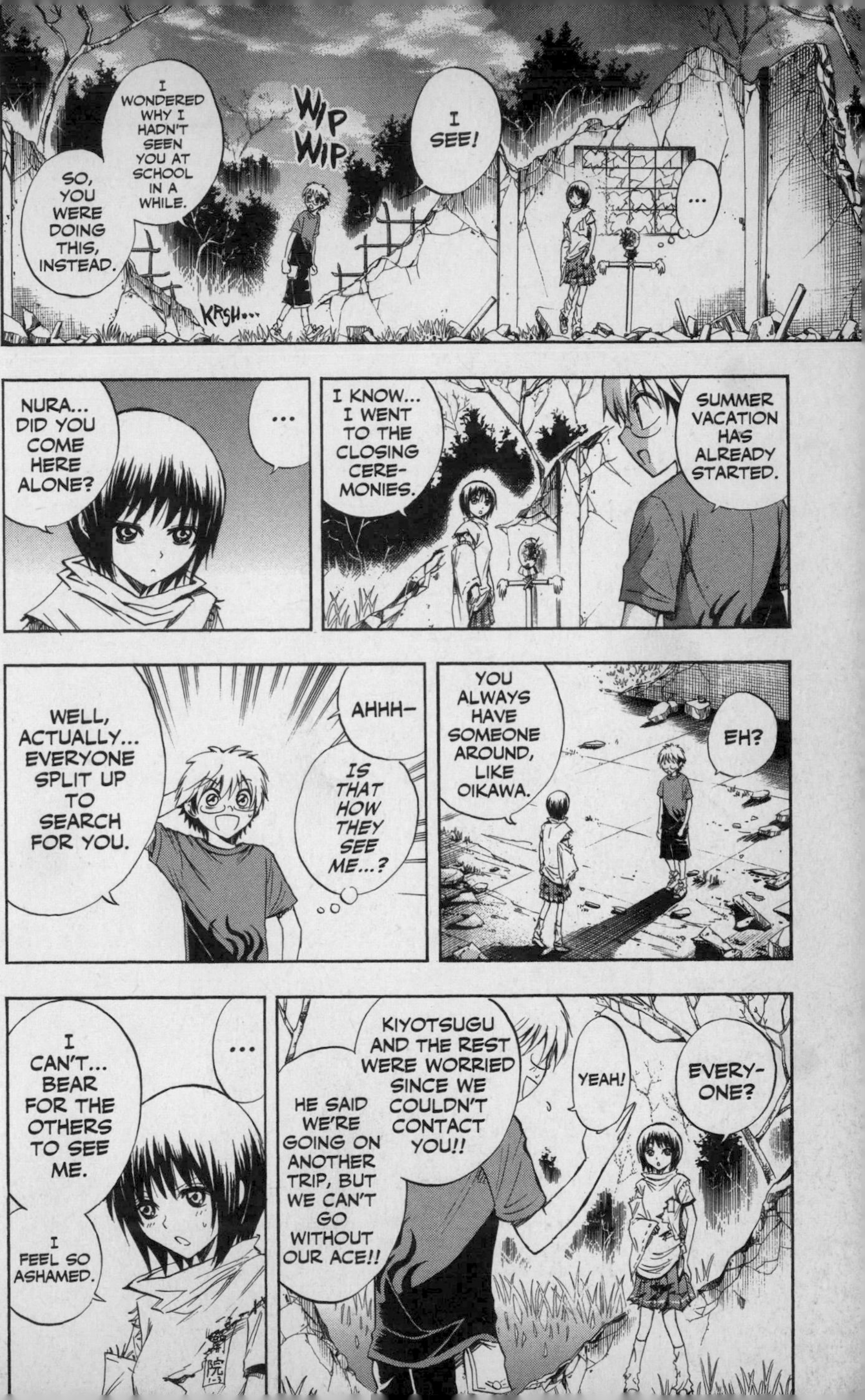
...
I SEE!
WIP WIP
I WONDERED WHY I HADN'T SEEN YOU AT SCHOOL IN A WHILE.
SO, YOU WERE DOING THIS, INSTEAD.
KRSH...
SUMMER VACATION HAS ALREADY STARTED.
I KNOW... I WENT TO THE CLOSING CERE-MONIES.
...
NURA... DID YOU COME HERE ALONE?
EH?
YOU ALWAYS HAVE SOMEONE AROUND, LIKE OIKAWA.
AHHH—
IS THAT HOW THEY SEE ME...?
WELL, ACTUALLY... EVERYONE SPLIT UP TO SEARCH FOR YOU.
EVERY-ONE?
YEAH!
KIYOTSUGU AND THE REST WERE WORRIED SINCE WE COULDN'T CONTACT YOU!!
HE SAID WE'RE GOING ON ANOTHER TRIP, BUT WE CAN'T GO WITHOUT OUR ACE!!
...
I CAN'T... BEAR FOR THE OTHERS TO SEE ME.
I FEEL SO ASHAMED.

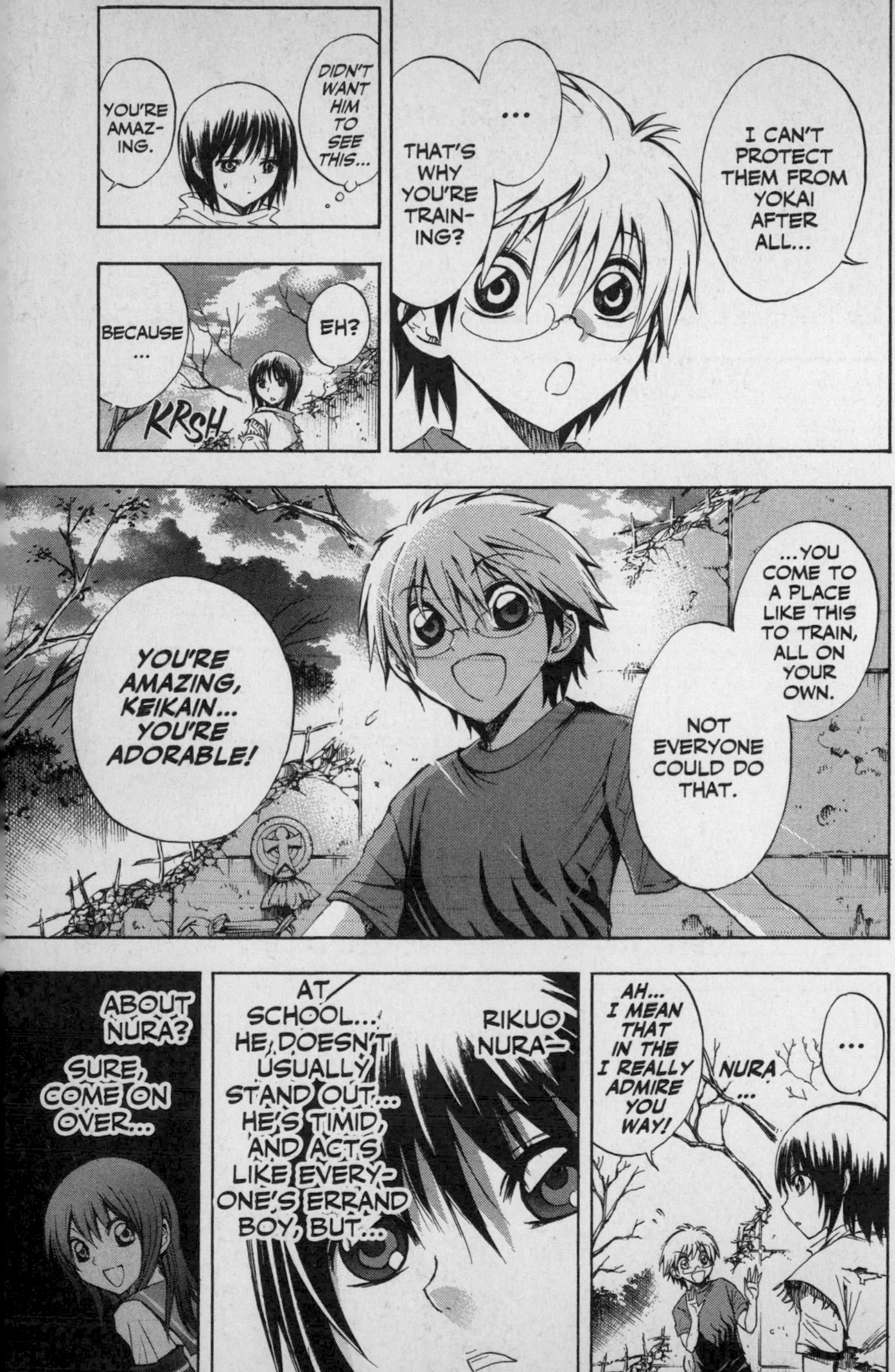
I CAN'T PROTECT THEM FROM YOKAI AFTER ALL...
...
THAT'S WHY YOU'RE TRAINING?
DIDN'T WANT HIM TO SEE THIS...
YOU'RE AMAZING.
EH?
BECAUSE ...
KRSH
...YOU COME TO A PLACE LIKE THIS TO TRAIN, ALL ON YOUR OWN.
NOT EVERYONE COULD DO THAT.
YOU'RE AMAZING, KEIKAIN... YOU'RE ADORABLE!
...
NURA ...
AH... I MEAN THAT IN THE I REALLY ADMIRE YOU WAY!
RIKUO NURA—
AT SCHOOL... HE DOESN'T USUALLY STAND OUT... HE'S TIMID, AND ACTS LIKE EVERY-ONE'S ERRAND BOY, BUT...
ABOUT NURA?
SURE, COME ON OVER...

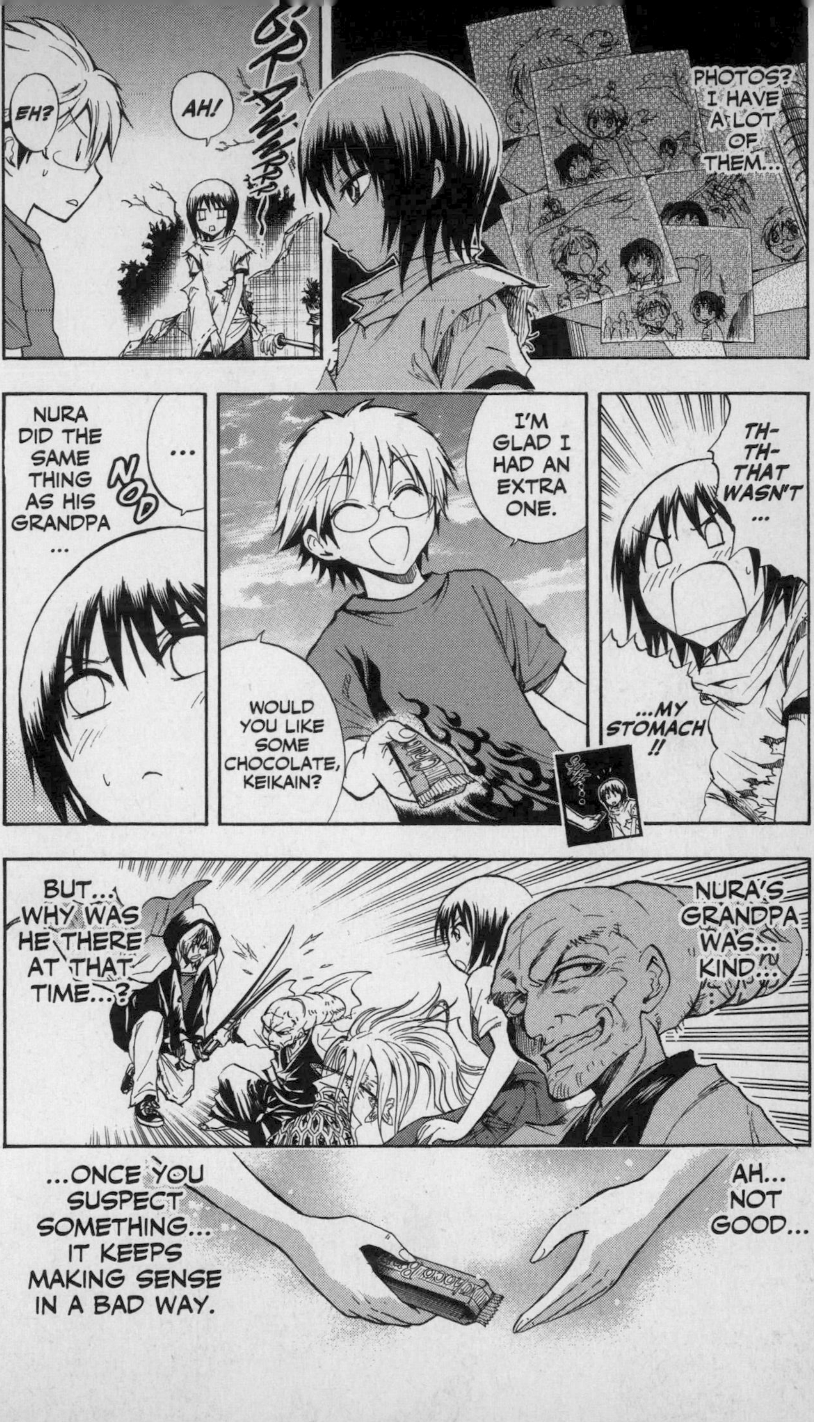
PHOTOS? I HAVE A LOT OF THEM...
AH!
EH?
TH-TH-THAT WASN'T ...
...MY STOMACH !!
I'M GLAD I HAD AN EXTRA ONE.
WOULD YOU LIKE SOME CHOCOLATE, KEIKAIN?
...
NOD
NURA DID THE SAME THING AS HIS GRANDPA ...
NURA'S GRANDPA WAS... KIND...
BUT... WHY WAS HE THERE AT THAT TIME...?
AH... NOT GOOD...
...ONCE YOU SUSPECT SOMETHING... IT KEEPS MAKING SENSE IN A BAD WAY.

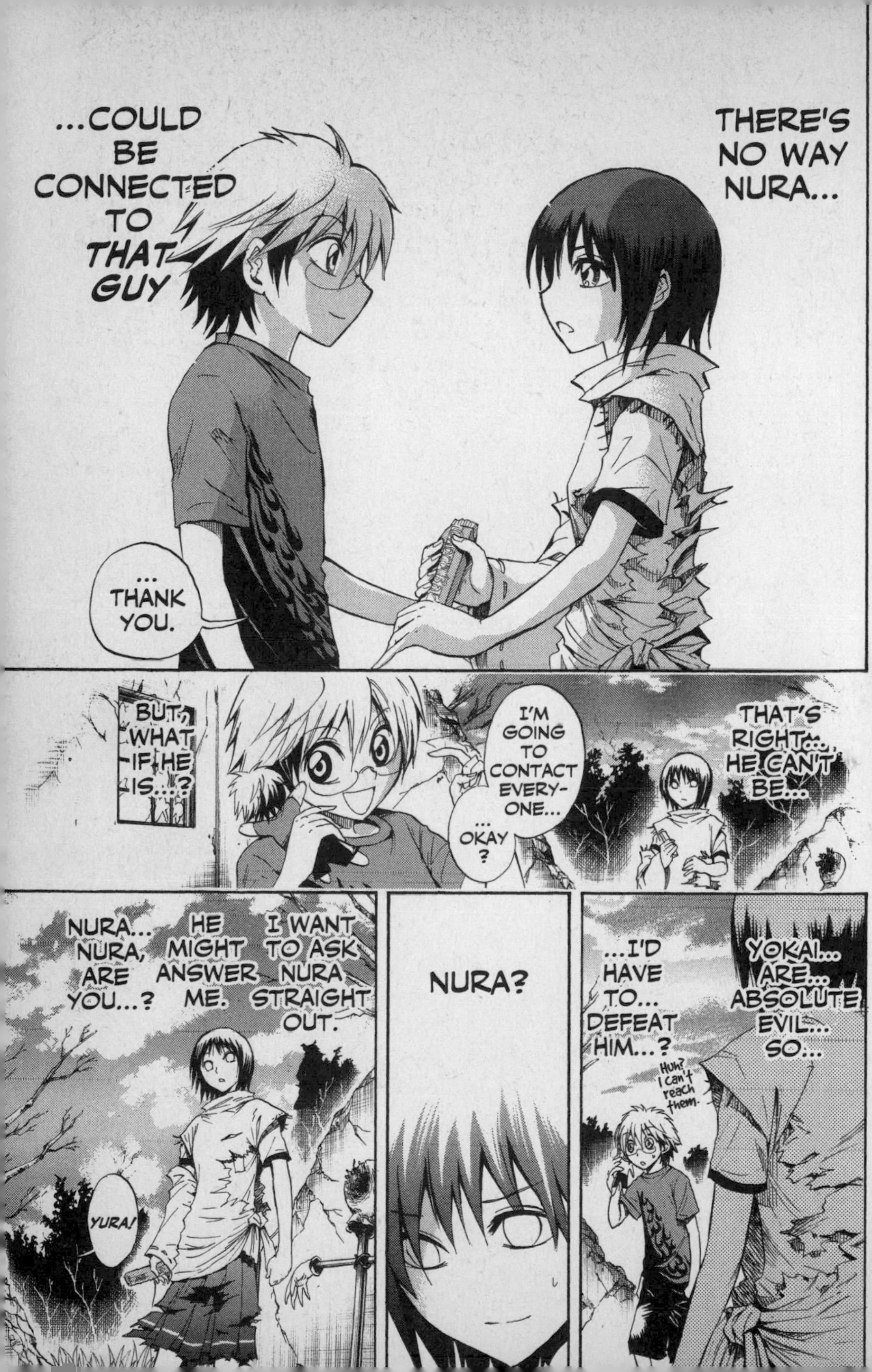
THERE'S NO WAY NURA...
...COULD BE CONNECTED TO THAT GUY
... THANK YOU.
THAT'S RIGHT..., HE CAN'T BE...
I'M GOING TO CONTACT EVERY-ONE...
... OKAY?
BUT, WHAT IF HE IS...?
YOKAI... ARE... ABSOLUTE EVIL... SO...
...I'D HAVE TO... DEFEAT HIM...?
Huh? I can't reach them.
NURA?
I WANT TO ASK NURA STRAIGHT OUT.
HE MIGHT ANSWER ME.
NURA... NURA, ARE YOU...?
YURA!

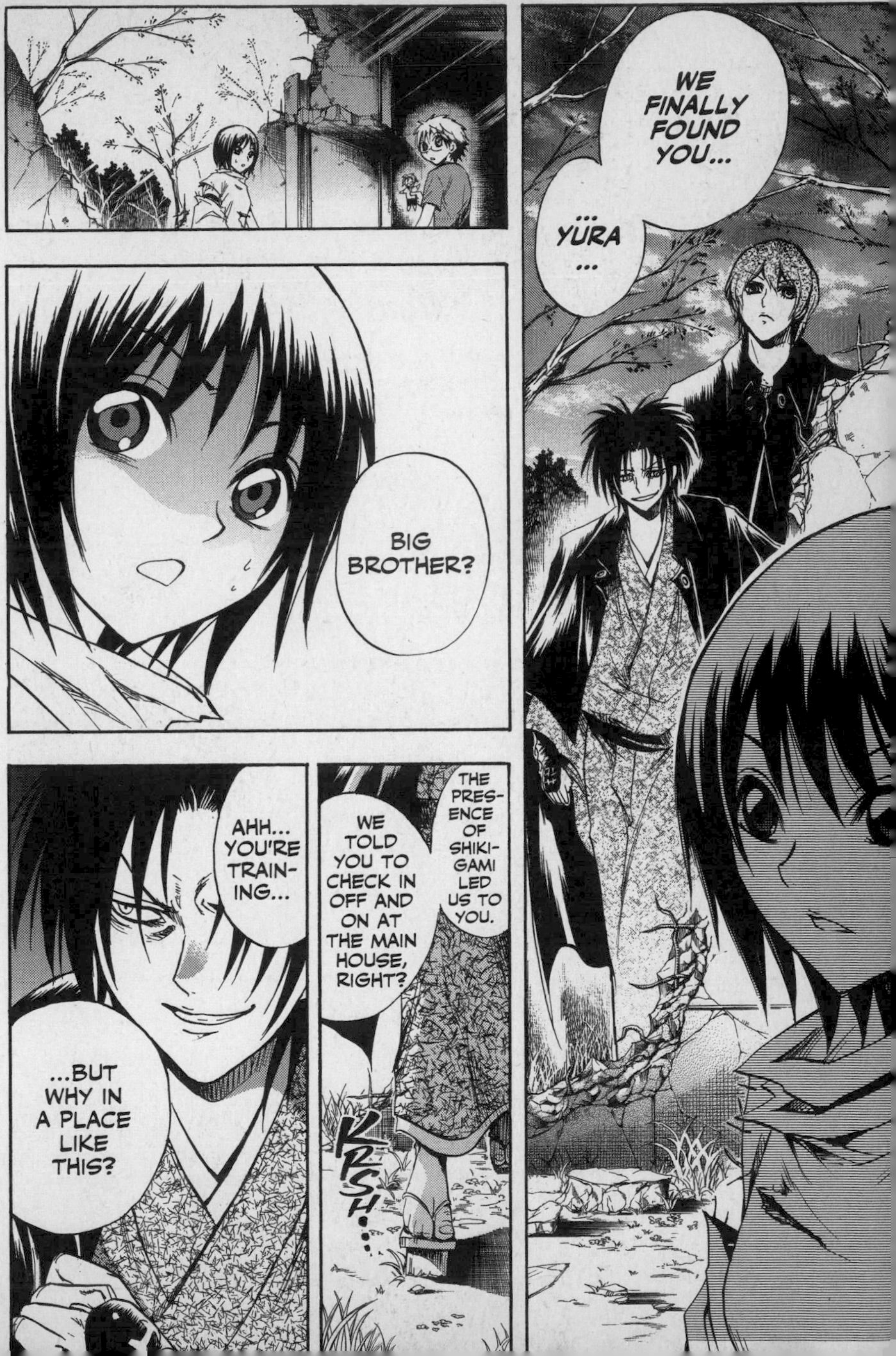
WE FINALLY FOUND YOU...
...YÜRA...
BIG BROTHER?
THE PRESENCE OF SHIKIGAMI LED US TO YOU.
WE TOLD YOU TO CHECK IN OFF AND ON AT THE MAIN HOUSE, RIGHT?
KRSH...
AHH... YOU'RE TRAINING...
...BUT WHY IN A PLACE LIKE THIS?

READ THIS WAY

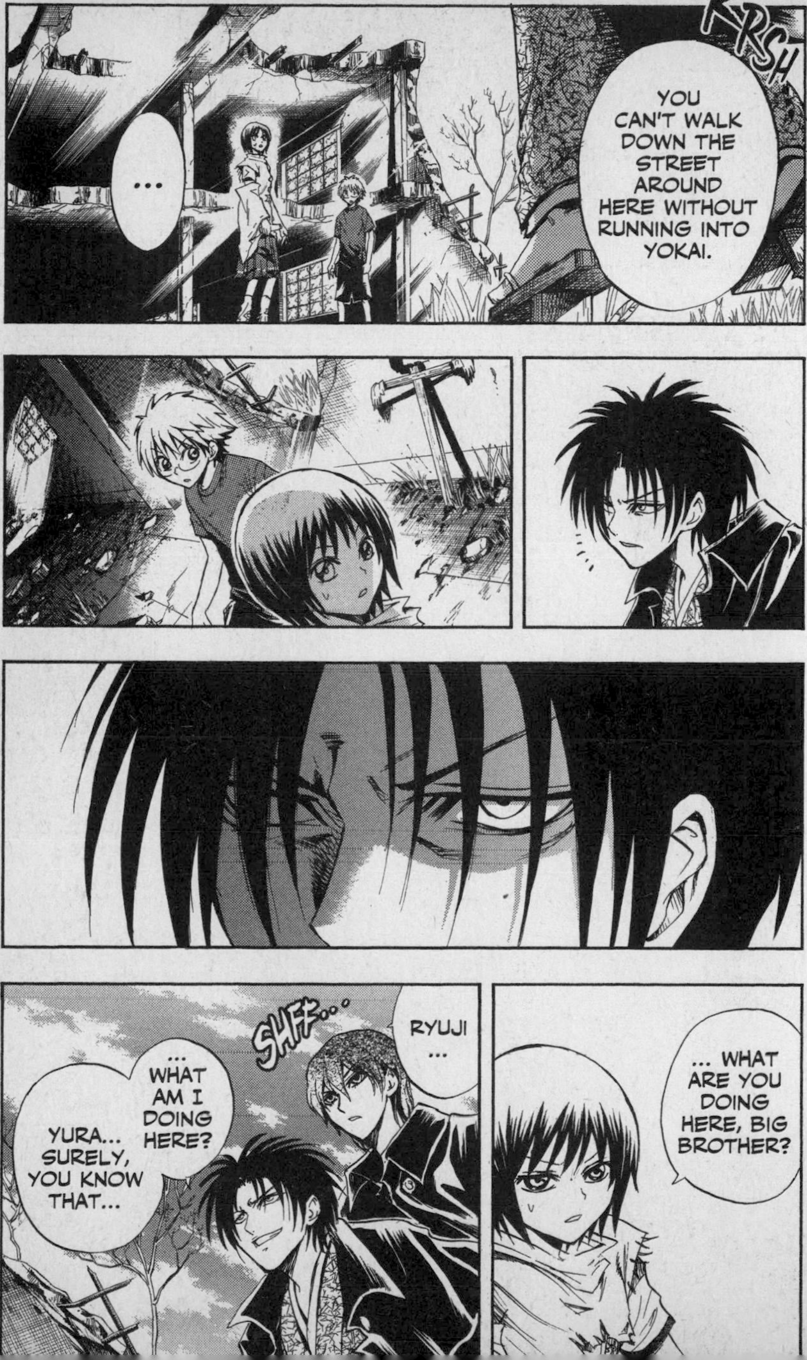
KRSH
YOU CAN'T WALK DOWN THE STREET AROUND HERE WITHOUT RUNNING INTO YOKAI.
...
... WHAT ARE YOU DOING HERE, BIG BROTHER?
RYUJI ...
SHFF...
... WHAT AM I DOING HERE?
YURA... SURELY, YOU KNOW THAT...

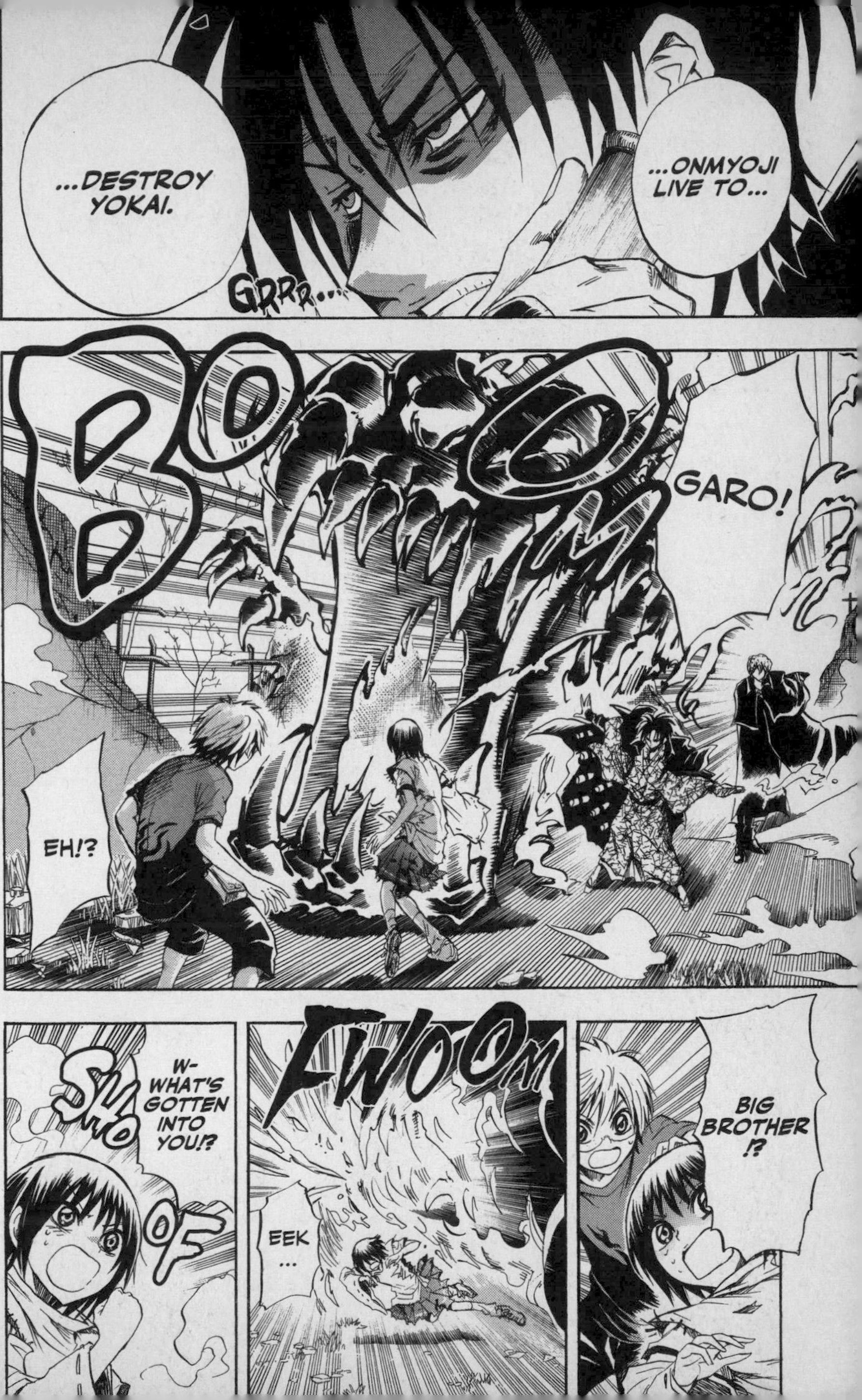
...ONMYOJI LIVE TO...
...DESTROY YOKAI.
GRRR...
GARO!
EH!?
BIG BROTHER!?
FWOOM
EEK...
W-WHAT'S GOTTEN INTO YOU!?

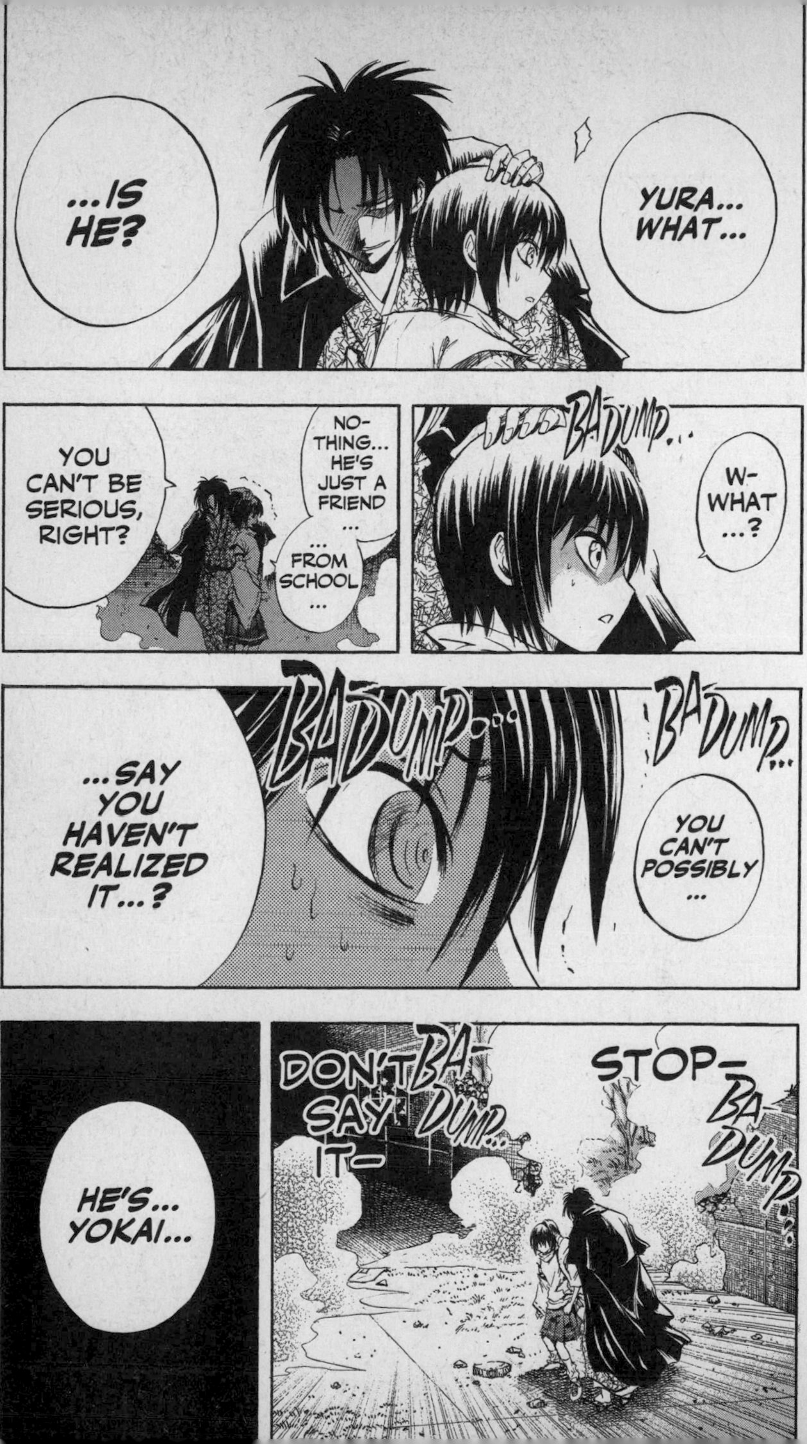
YURA... WHAT...
...IS HE?
BA-DUMP...
W-WHAT...?
NO-THING... HE'S JUST A FRIEND...
...FROM SCHOOL...
YOU CAN'T BE SERIOUS, RIGHT?
BA-DUMP...
YOU CAN'T POSSIBLY...
BA-DUMP...
...SAY YOU HAVEN'T REALIZED IT...?
BA-DUMP...
STOP—
BA-DUMP...
DON'T SAY IT—
HE'S... YOKAI...

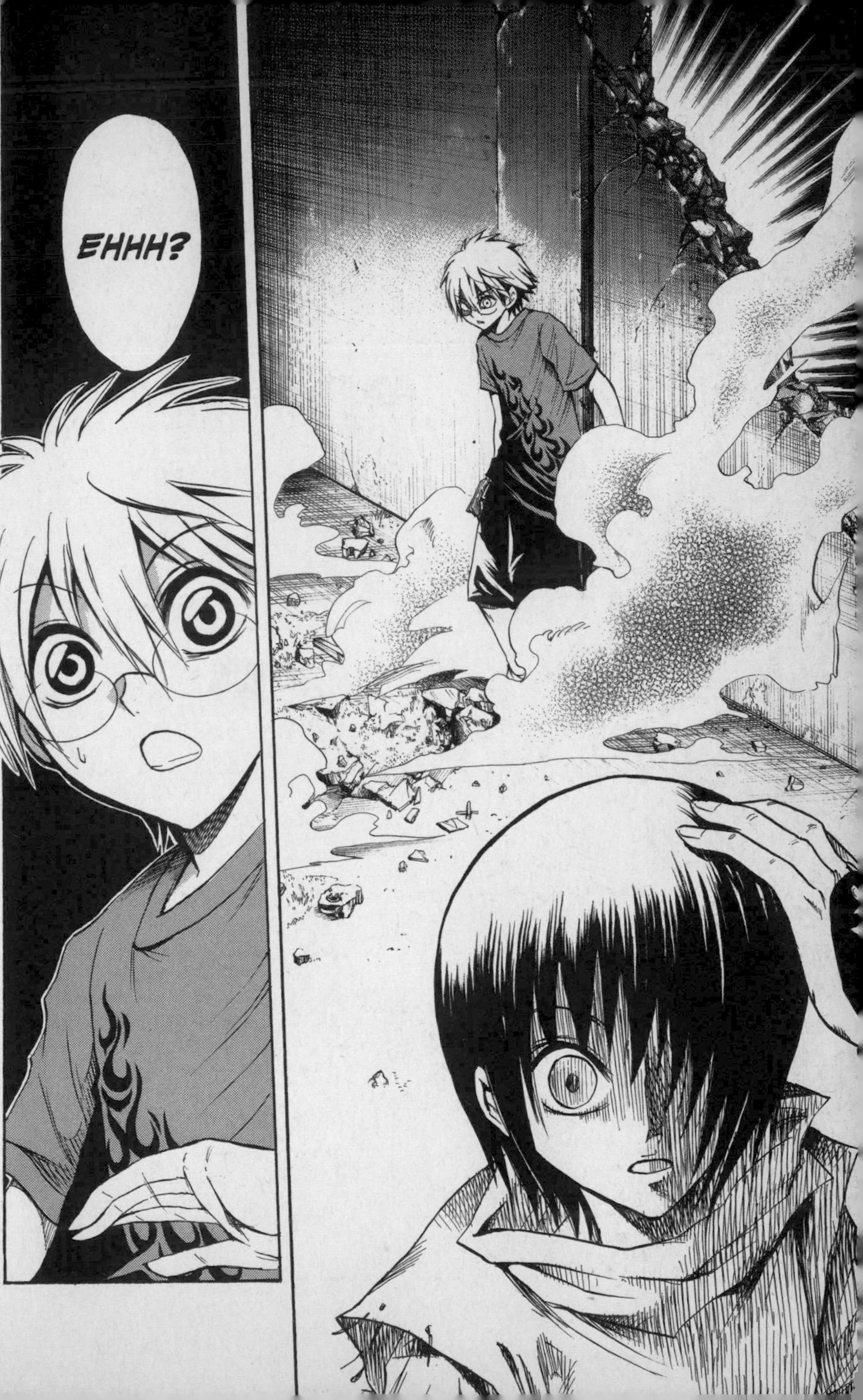
EHHH?

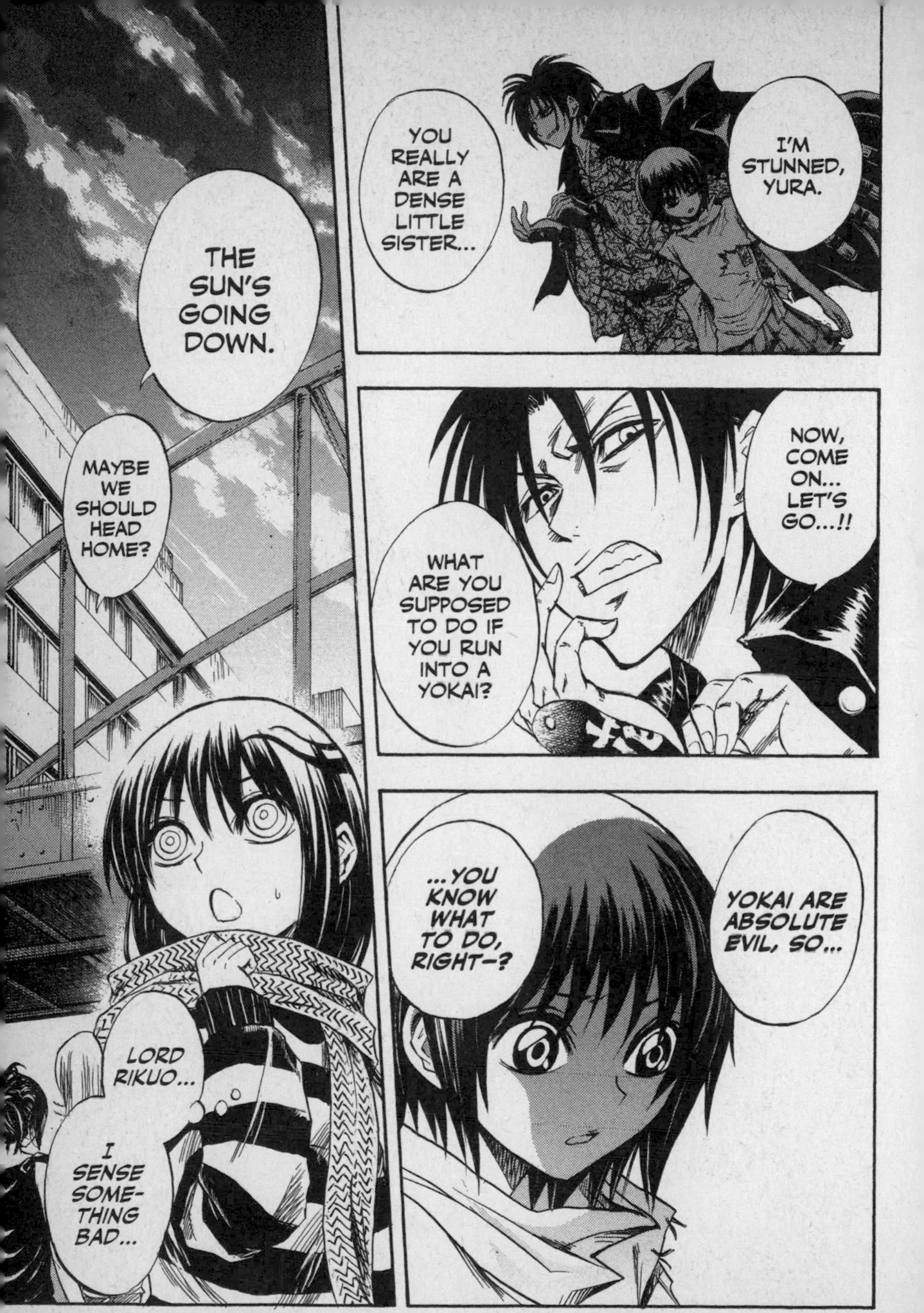
I'M STUNNED, YURA.
YOU REALLY ARE A DENSE LITTLE SISTER...
NOW, COME ON... LET'S GO...!!
WHAT ARE YOU SUPPOSED TO DO IF YOU RUN INTO A YOKAI?
YOKAI ARE ABSOLUTE EVIL, SO...
...YOU KNOW WHAT TO DO, RIGHT-?
THE SUN'S GOING DOWN.
MAYBE WE SHOULD HEAD HOME?
LORD RIKUO...
I SENSE SOMETHING BAD...

NURA: RISE OF THE YOKAI CLAN

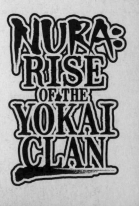

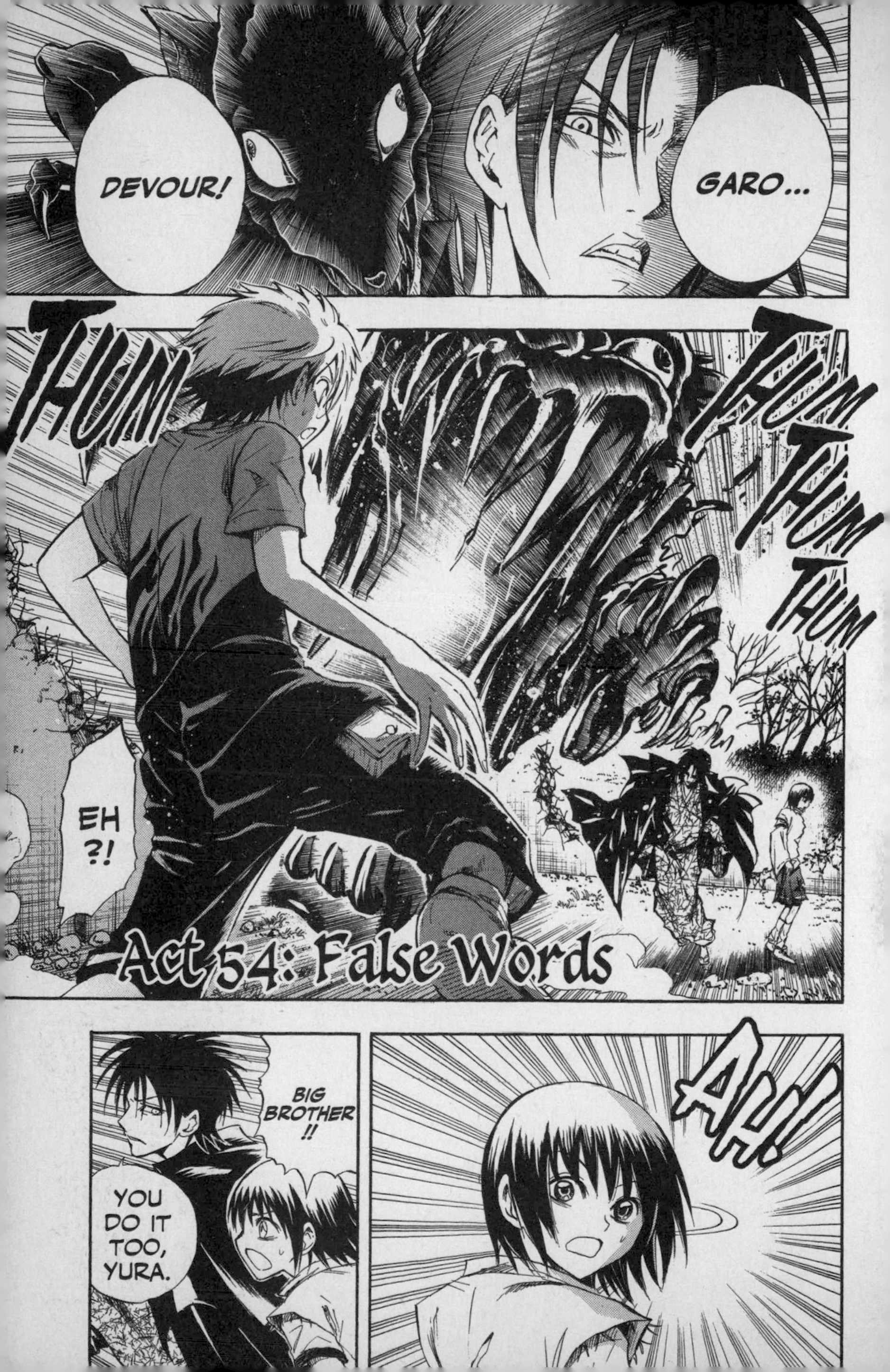
GARO...
DEVOUR!
THUM THUM THUM THUM
THUM
EH ?!
Act 54: False Words
AH!
BIG BROTHER !!
YOU DO IT TOO, YURA.

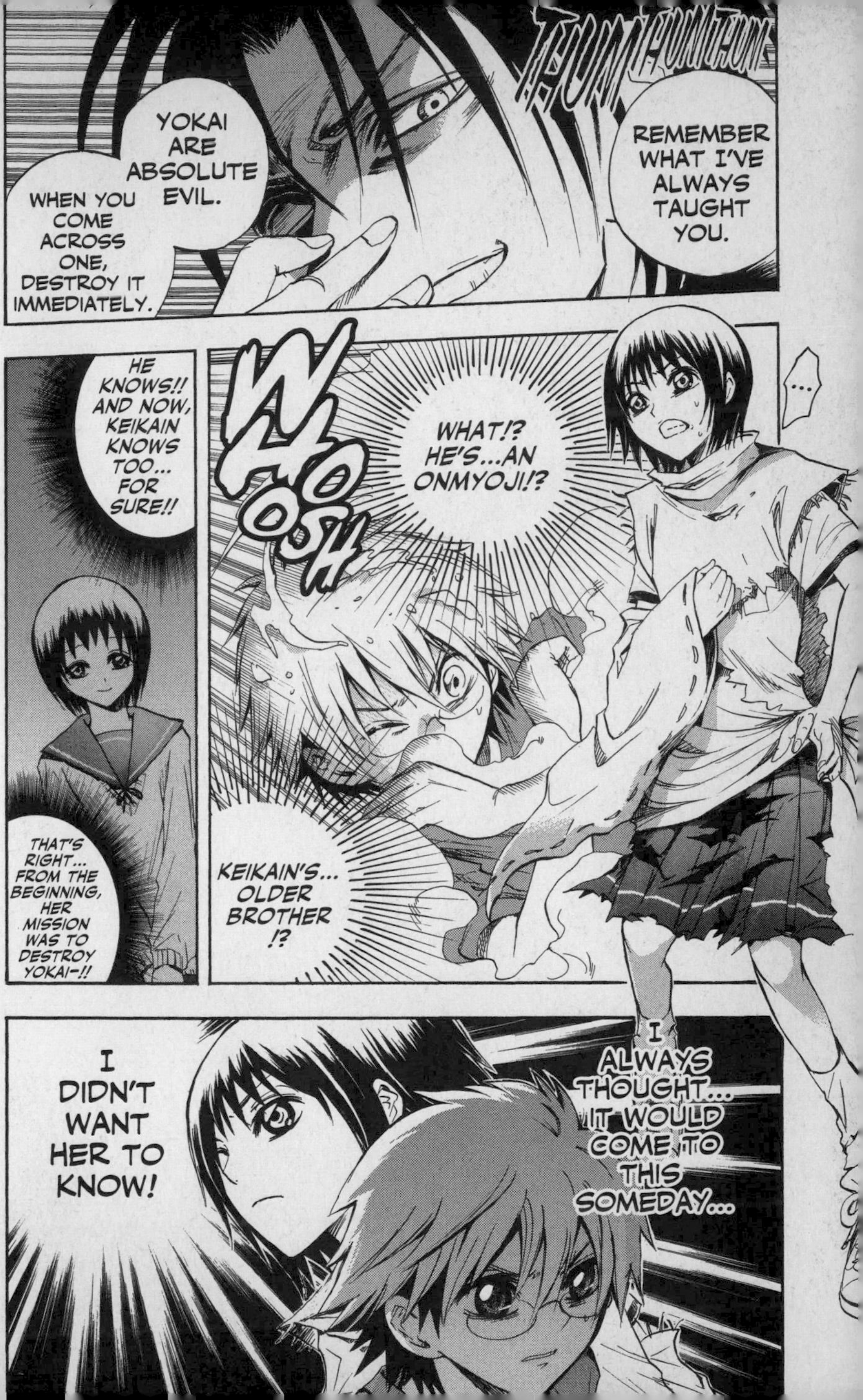
REMEMBER WHAT I'VE ALWAYS TAUGHT YOU.
YOKAI ARE ABSOLUTE EVIL.
WHEN YOU COME ACROSS ONE, DESTROY IT IMMEDIATELY.
...
WHOOSH
WHAT!? HE'S...AN ONMYOJI!?
KEIKAIN'S... OLDER BROTHER !?
HE KNOWS!! AND NOW, KEIKAIN KNOWS TOO... FOR SURE!!
THAT'S RIGHT... FROM THE BEGINNING, HER MISSION WAS TO DESTROY YOKAI-!!
I ALWAYS THOUGHT... IT WOULD COME TO THIS SOMEDAY...
I DIDN'T WANT HER TO KNOW!

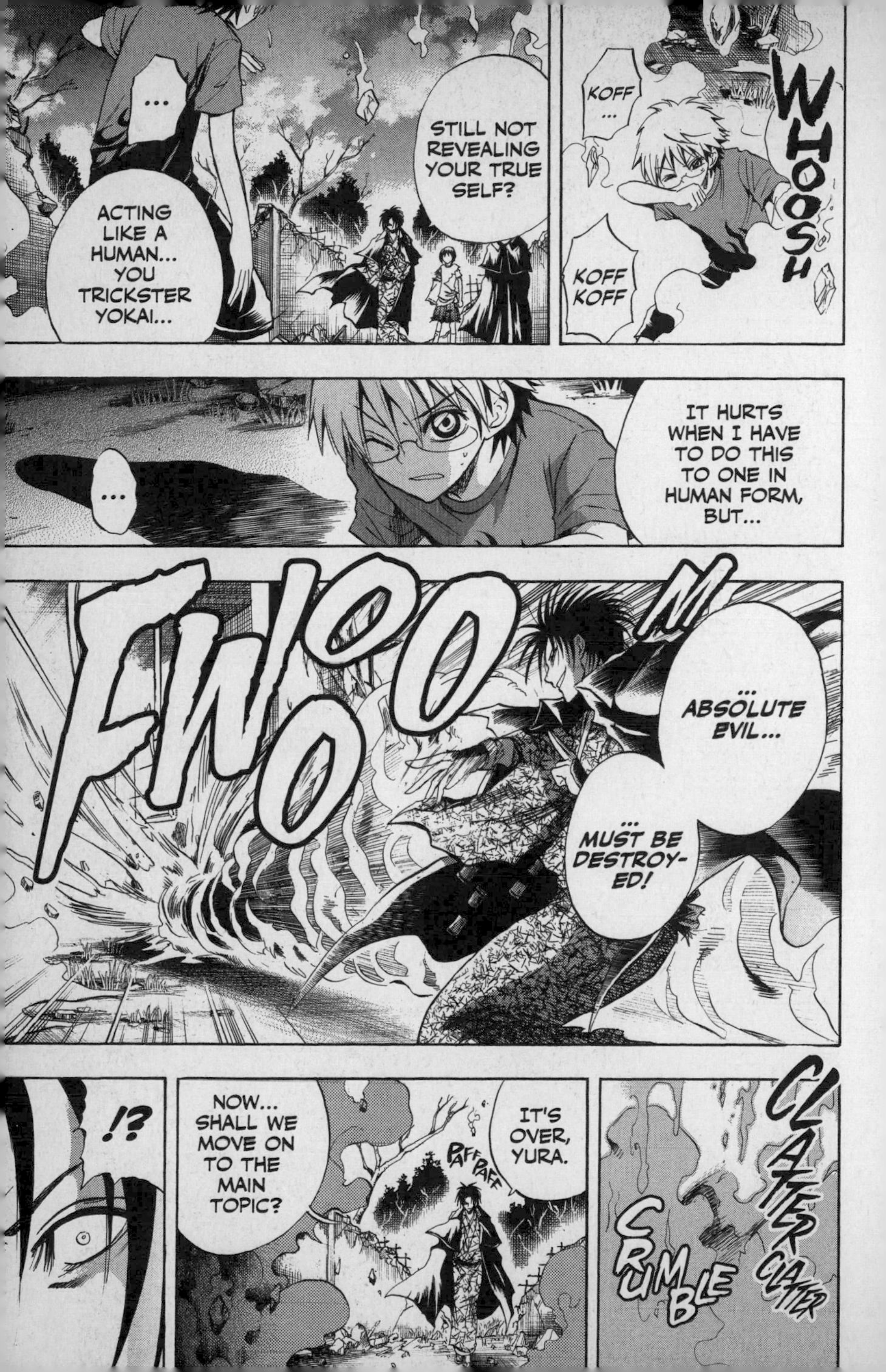
WHOOSH
KOFF ...
KOFF KOFF
STILL NOT REVEALING YOUR TRUE SELF?
...
ACTING LIKE A HUMAN... YOU TRICKSTER YOKAI...
IT HURTS WHEN I HAVE TO DO THIS TO ONE IN HUMAN FORM, BUT...
...
FWOOOM
... ABSOLUTE EVIL...
... MUST BE DESTROY-ED!
CLATTER CLATTER
CRUMBLE
IT'S OVER, YURA.
PAFF PAFF
NOW... SHALL WE MOVE ON TO THE MAIN TOPIC?
!?

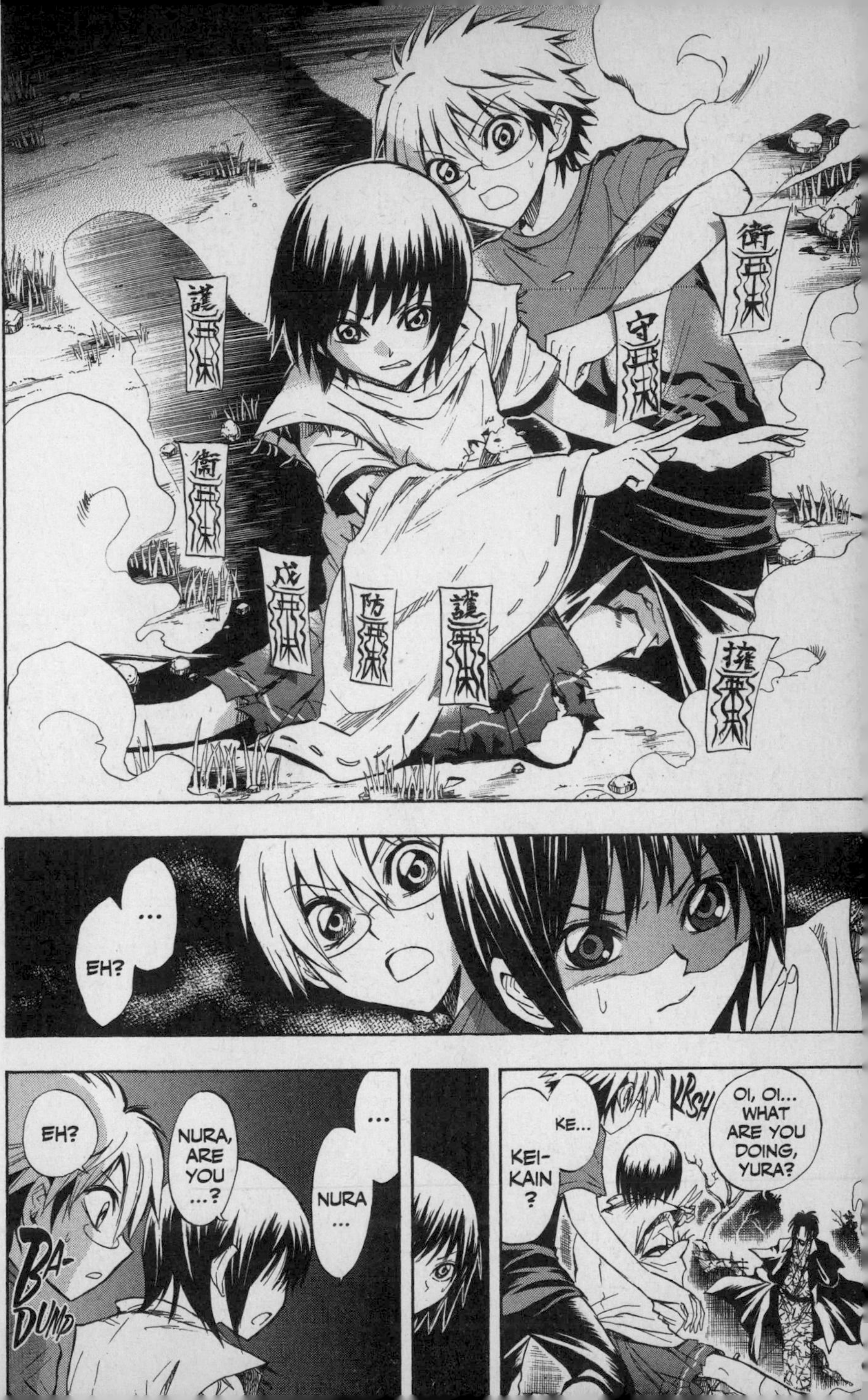
衛
守
護
衛
護
防
...
EH?
KRSH
OI, OI... WHAT ARE YOU DOING, YURA?
KE... KEI-KAIN?
...
NURA ...
NURA, ARE YOU ...?
EH?
BA-DUMP

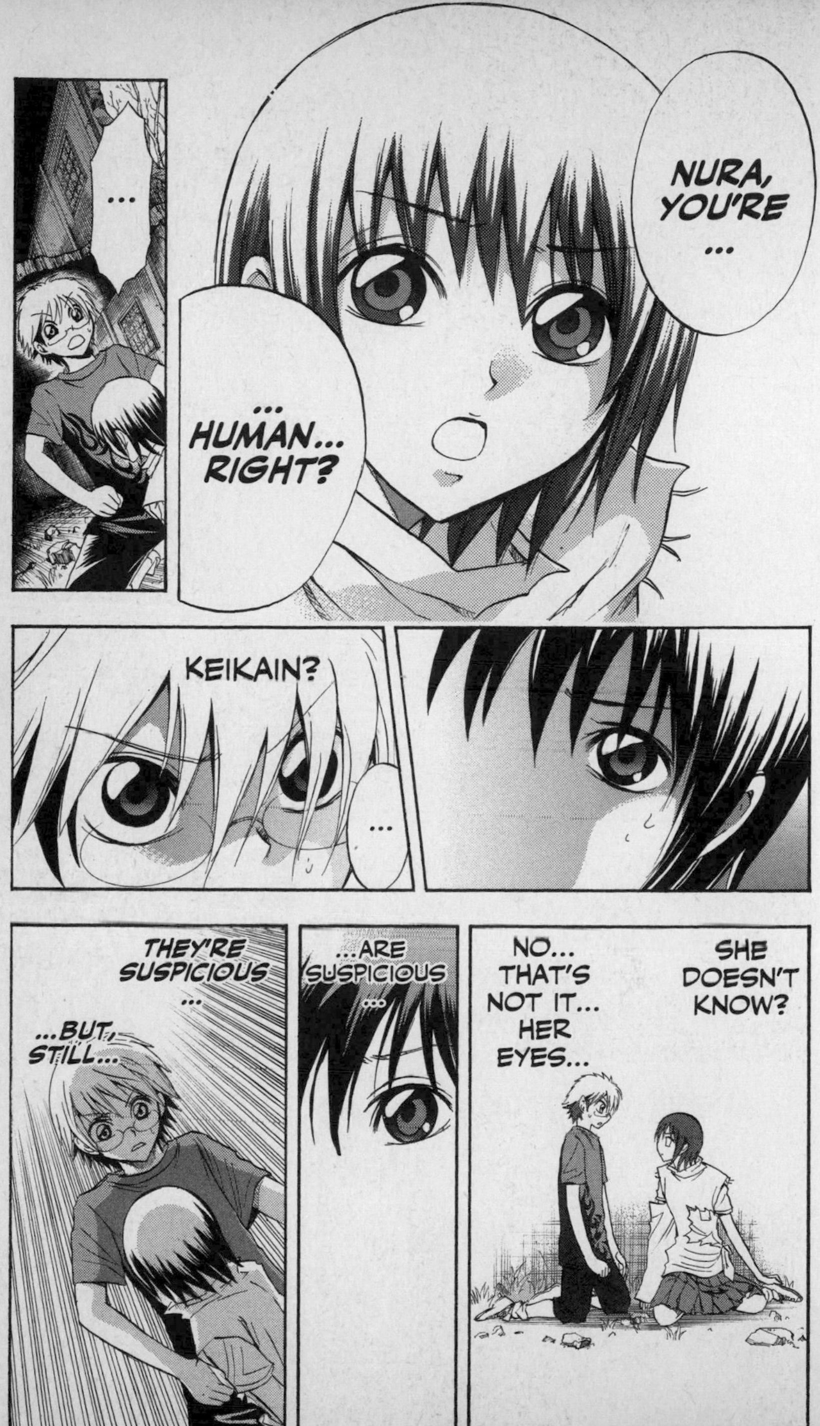
NURA, YOU'RE ...
... HUMAN... RIGHT?
...
KEIKAIN?
...
SHE DOESN'T KNOW?
NO... THAT'S NOT IT... HER EYES...
...ARE SUSPICIOUS ...
THEY'RE SUSPICIOUS ...
...BUT, STILL...

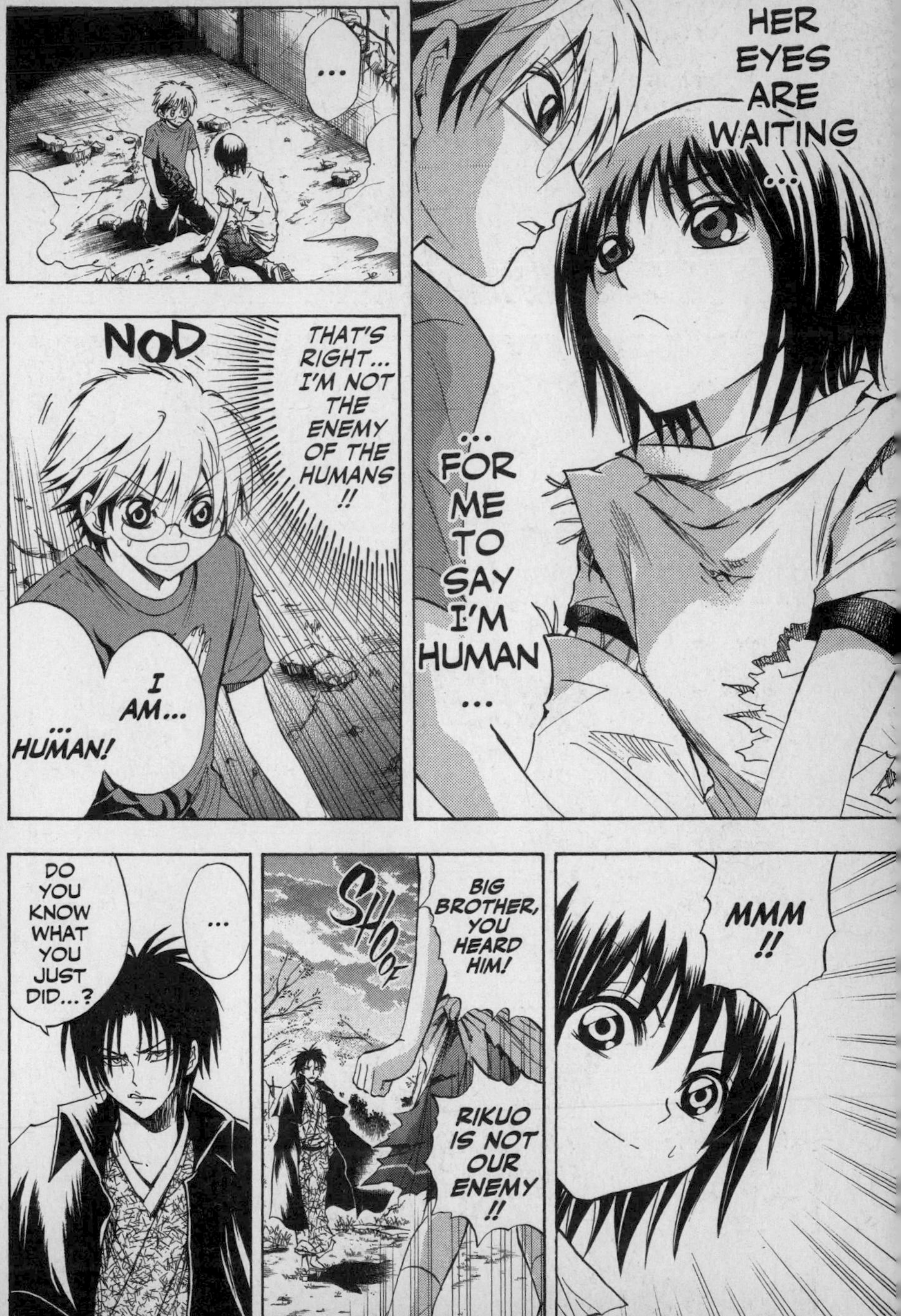
HER EYES ARE WAITING...
...FOR ME TO SAY I'M HUMAN...
...
THAT'S RIGHT... I'M NOT THE ENEMY OF THE HUMANS!!
NOD
I AM... ...HUMAN!
MMM!!
BIG BROTHER, YOU HEARD HIM!
SHOOF
RIKUO IS NOT OUR ENEMY!!
...
DO YOU KNOW WHAT YOU JUST DID...?

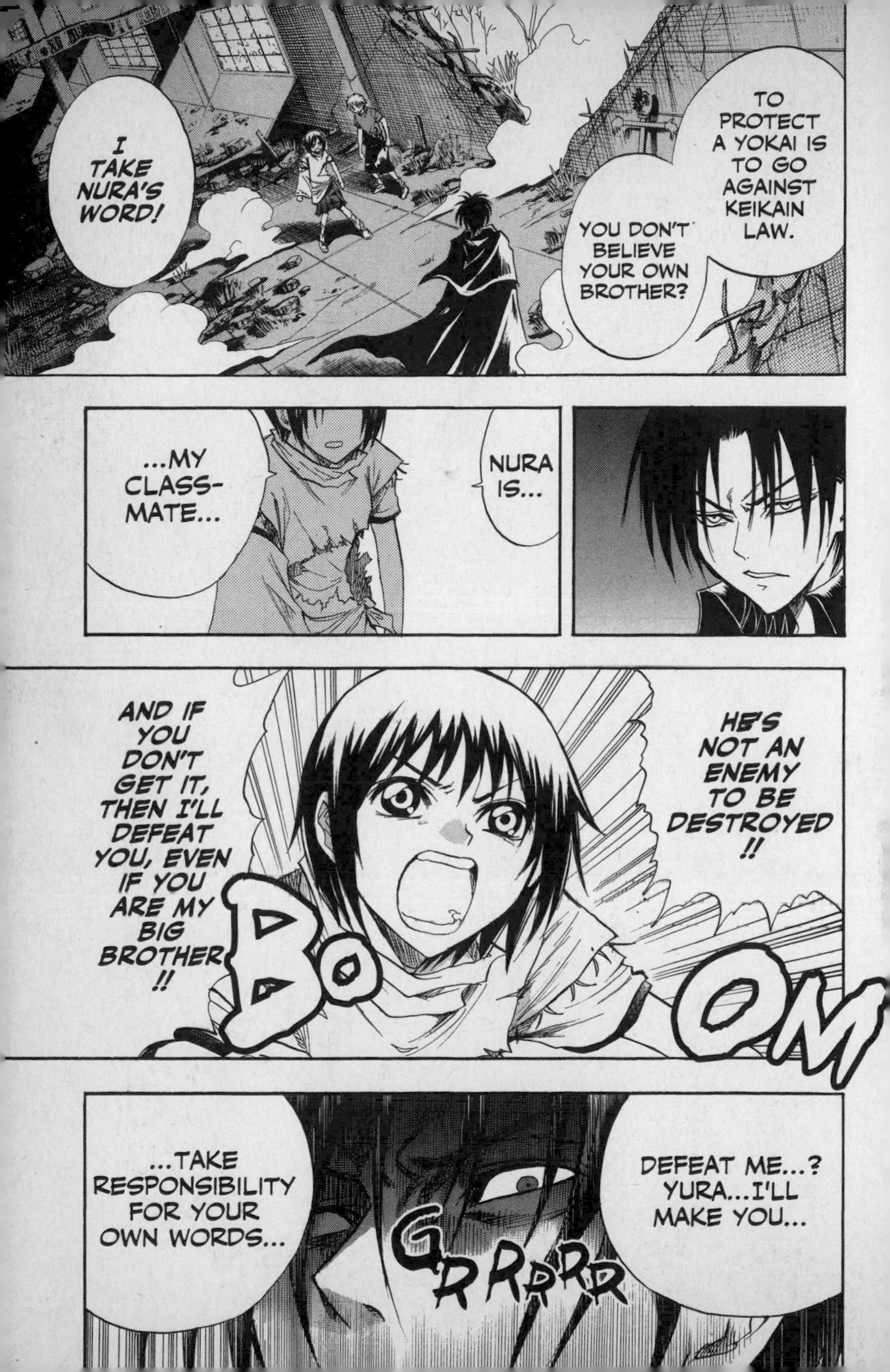
TO PROTECT A YOKAI IS TO GO AGAINST KEIKAIN LAW.
YOU DON'T BELIEVE YOUR OWN BROTHER?
I TAKE NURA'S WORD!
NURA IS...
...MY CLASSMATE...
HE'S NOT AN ENEMY TO BE DESTROYED!!
AND IF YOU DON'T GET IT, THEN I'LL DEFEAT YOU, EVEN IF YOU ARE MY BIG BROTHER!!
BOOM
DEFEAT ME...? YURA...I'LL MAKE YOU...
...TAKE RESPONSIBILITY FOR YOUR OWN WORDS...
GRRRRR

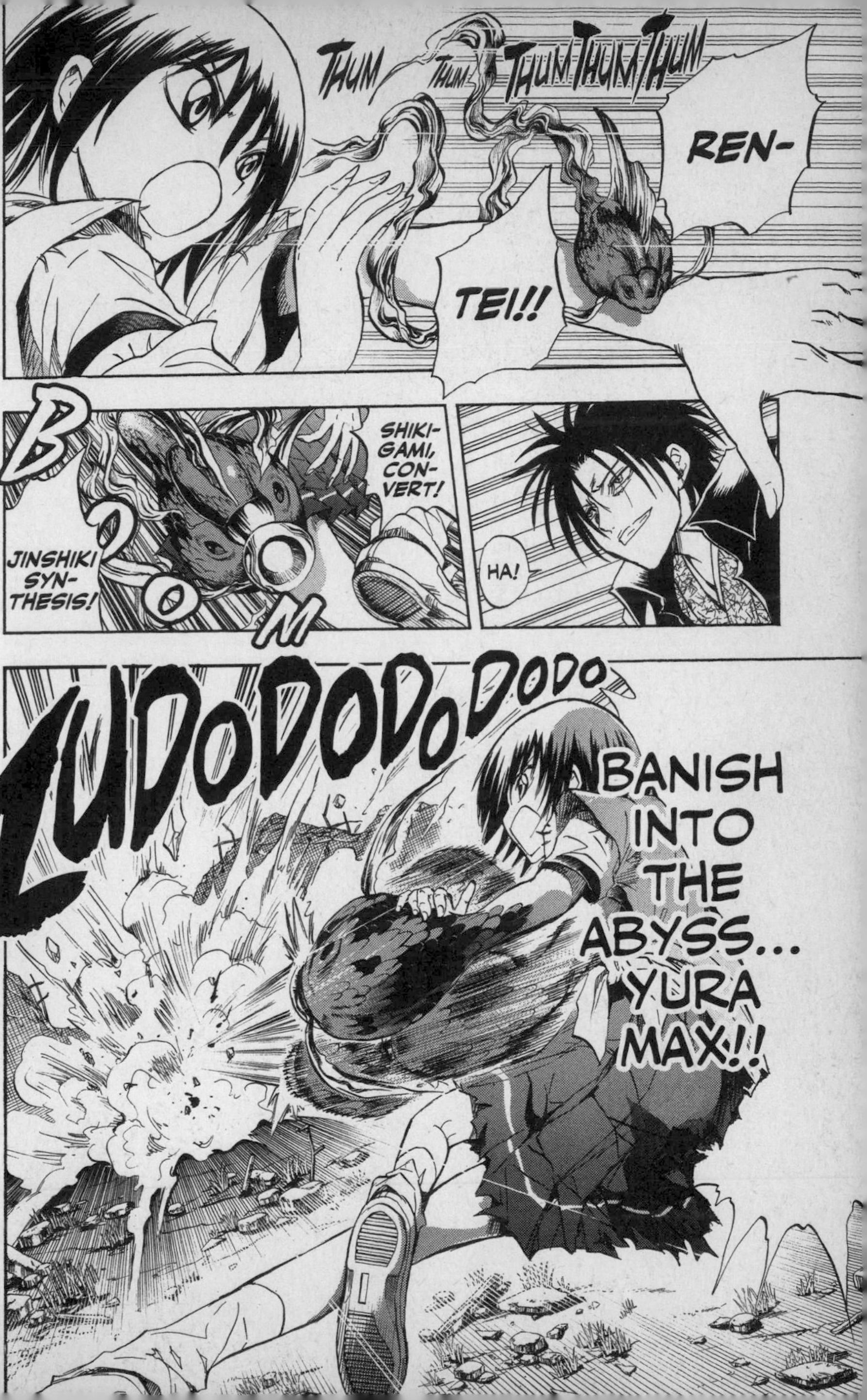
THUM THUM THUM THUM THUM
REN-
TEI!!
HA!
SHIKI-GAMI, CONVERT!
JINSHIKI SYN-THESIS!
BOOM
ZUDODODODODO
BANISH INTO THE ABYSS... YURA MAX!!

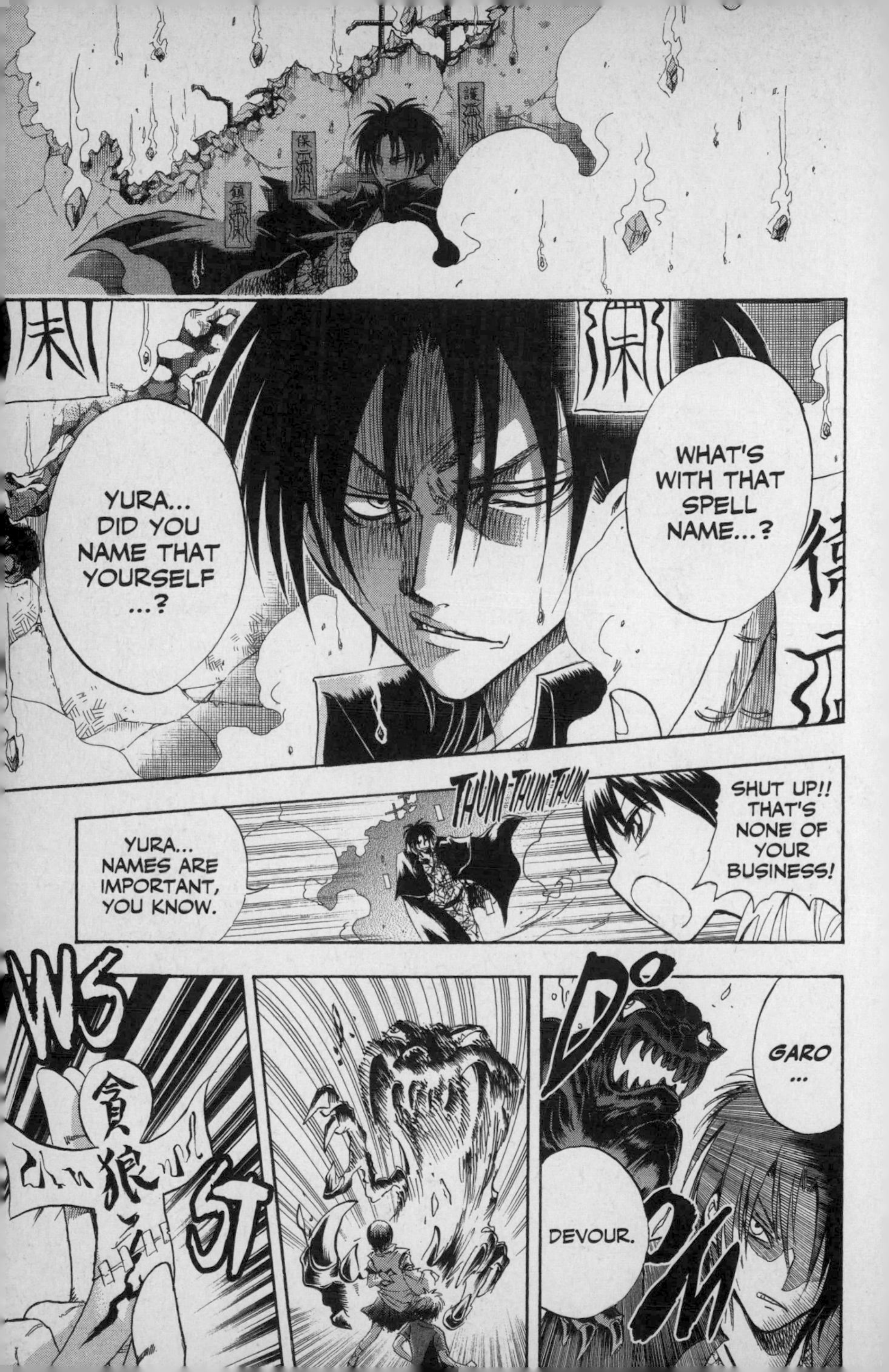
WHAT'S WITH THAT SPELL NAME...?
YURA... DID YOU NAME THAT YOURSELF...?
SHUT UP!! THAT'S NONE OF YOUR BUSINESS!
THUM-THUM-THUM
YURA... NAMES ARE IMPORTANT, YOU KNOW.
GARO...
DEVOUR.
貪狼

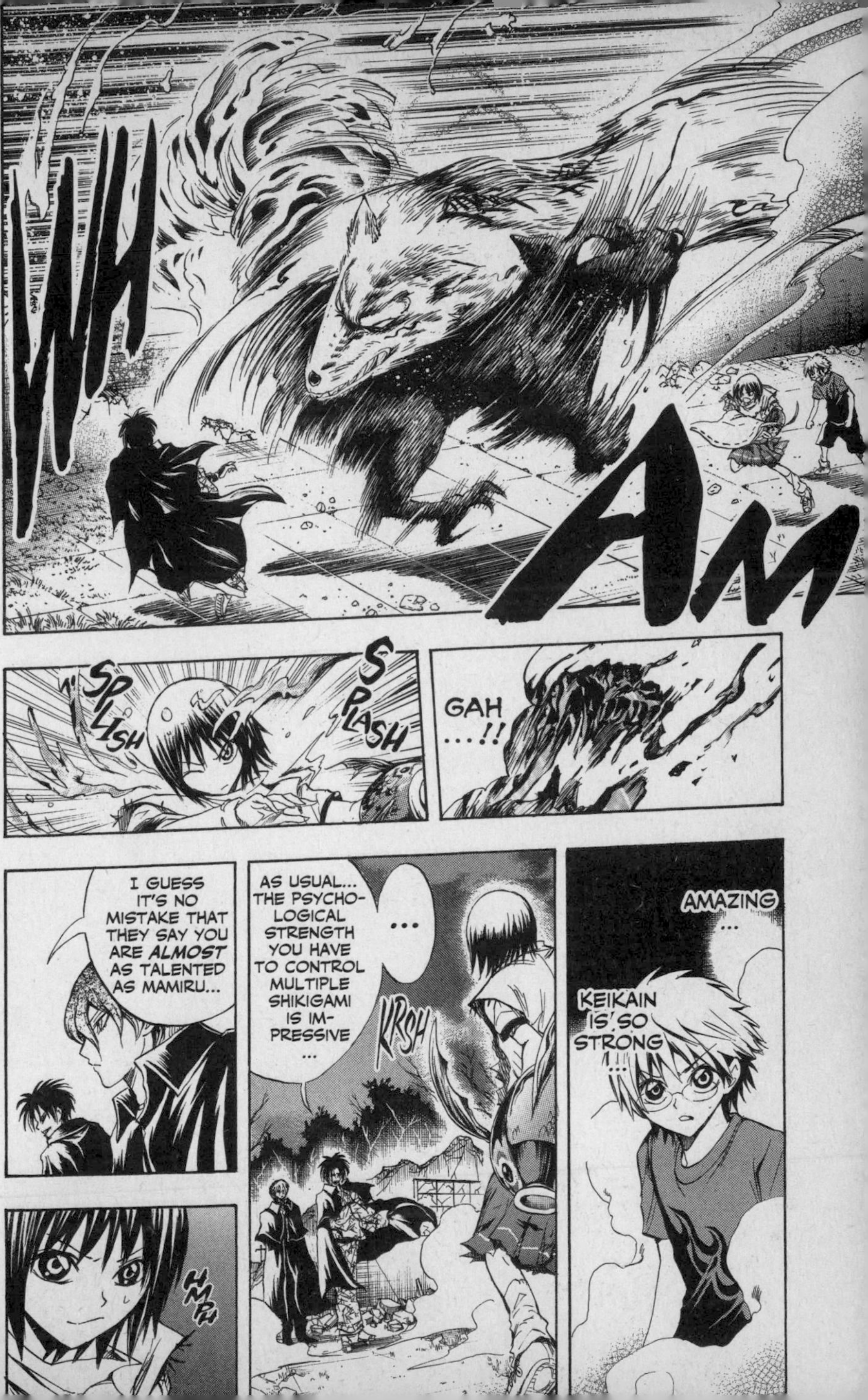
WH
AM
GAH ...!!
S PLASH
SPLISH
AMAZING ...
KEIKAIN IS SO STRONG ...
...
AS USUAL... THE PSYCHOLOGICAL STRENGTH YOU HAVE TO CONTROL MULTIPLE SHIKIGAMI IS IMPRESSIVE ...
KRSH
I GUESS IT'S NO MISTAKE THAT THEY SAY YOU ARE *ALMOST* AS TALENTED AS MAMIRU...
HMPH

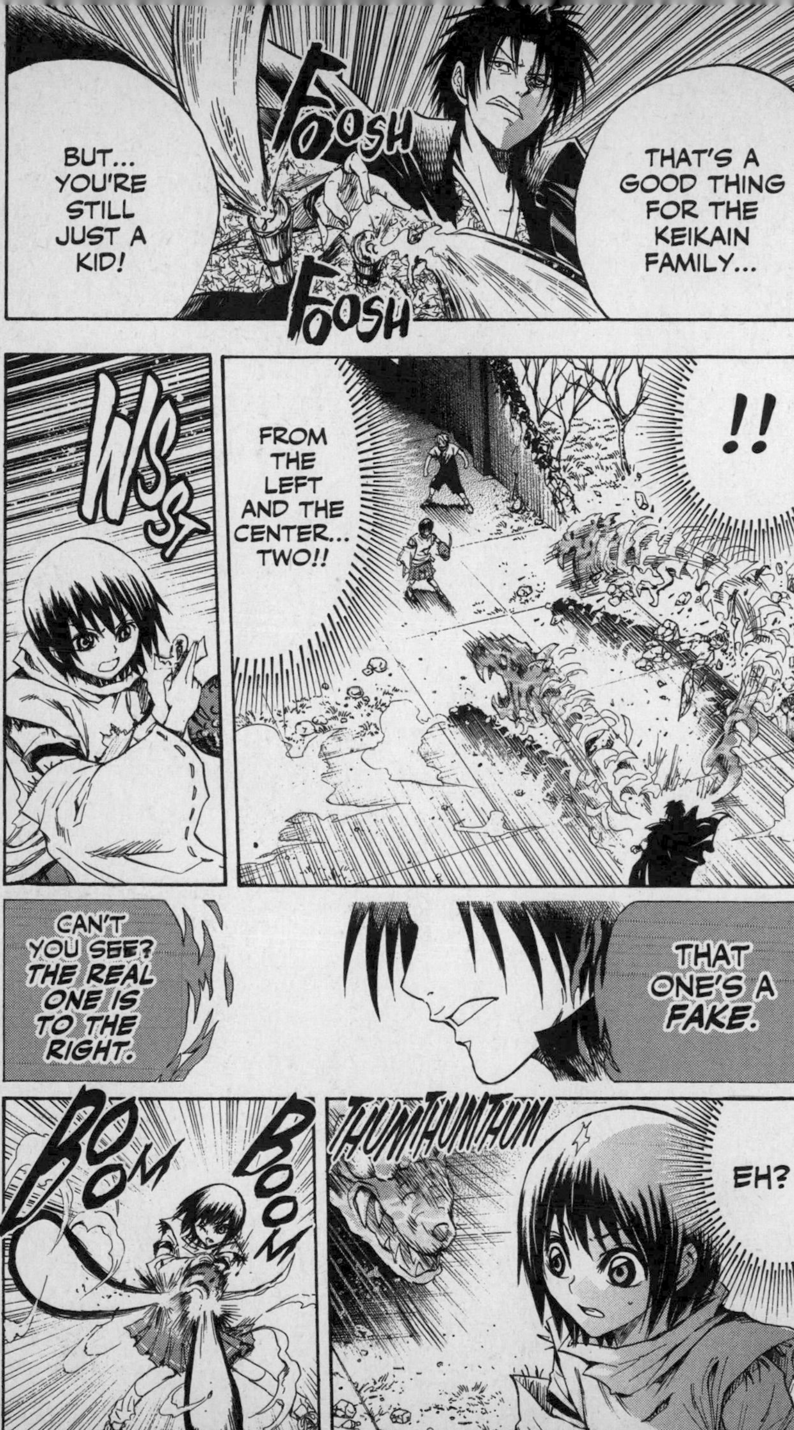
THAT'S A GOOD THING FOR THE KEIKAIN FAMILY...
FOOSH
BUT... YOU'RE STILL JUST A KID!
FOOSH
!!
FROM THE LEFT AND THE CENTER... TWO!!
THAT ONE'S A FAKE.
CAN'T YOU SEE? THE REAL ONE IS TO THE RIGHT.
THUMTHUMTHUM
EH?
BOOM
BOOM

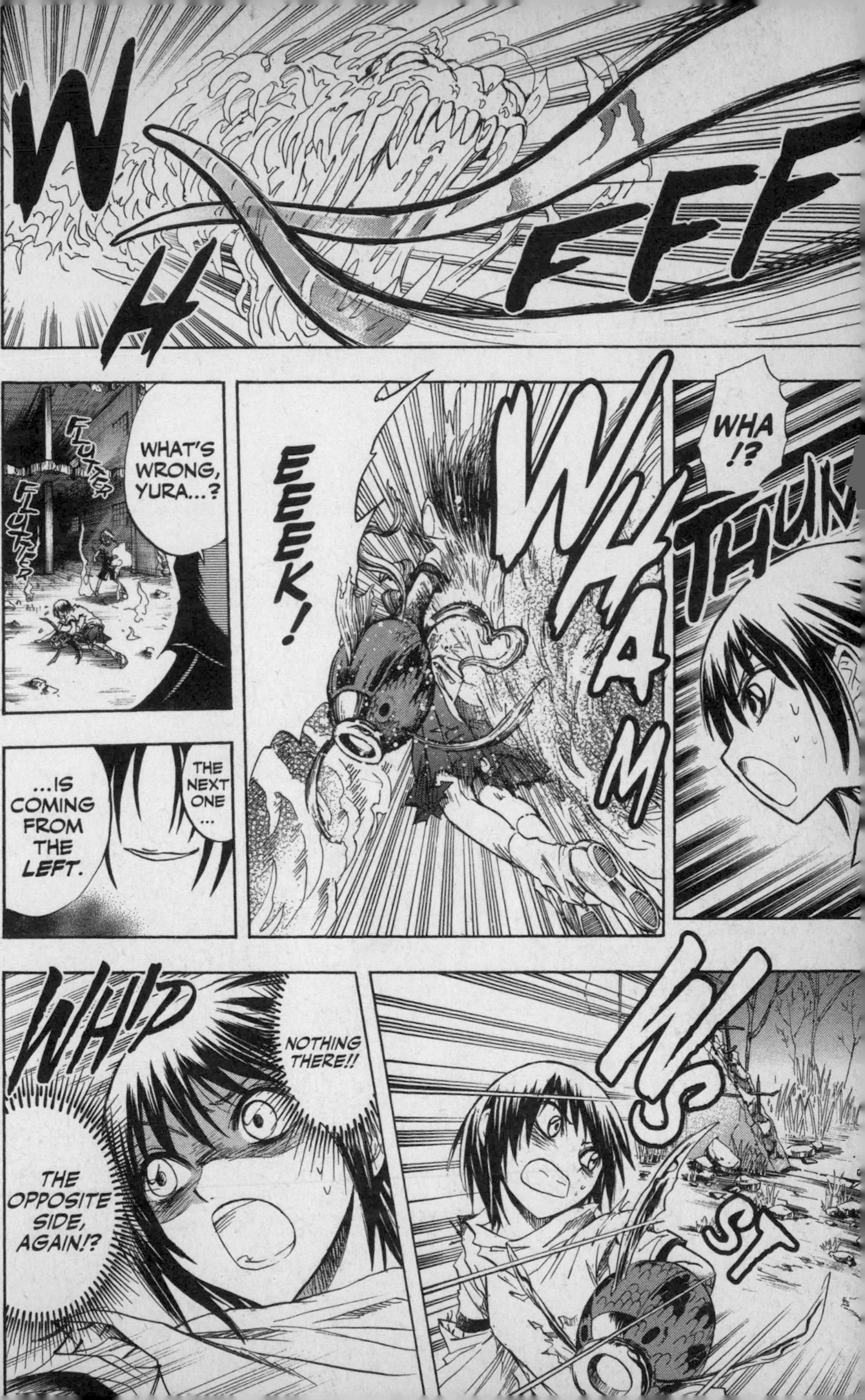
WHFFF
WHA!?
THUN
WHAM
EEEEK!
WHAT'S WRONG, YURA...?
FLUTTER
FLUTTER
THE NEXT ONE...
...IS COMING FROM THE LEFT.
WHIP
NOTHING THERE!!
THE OPPOSITE SIDE, AGAIN!?

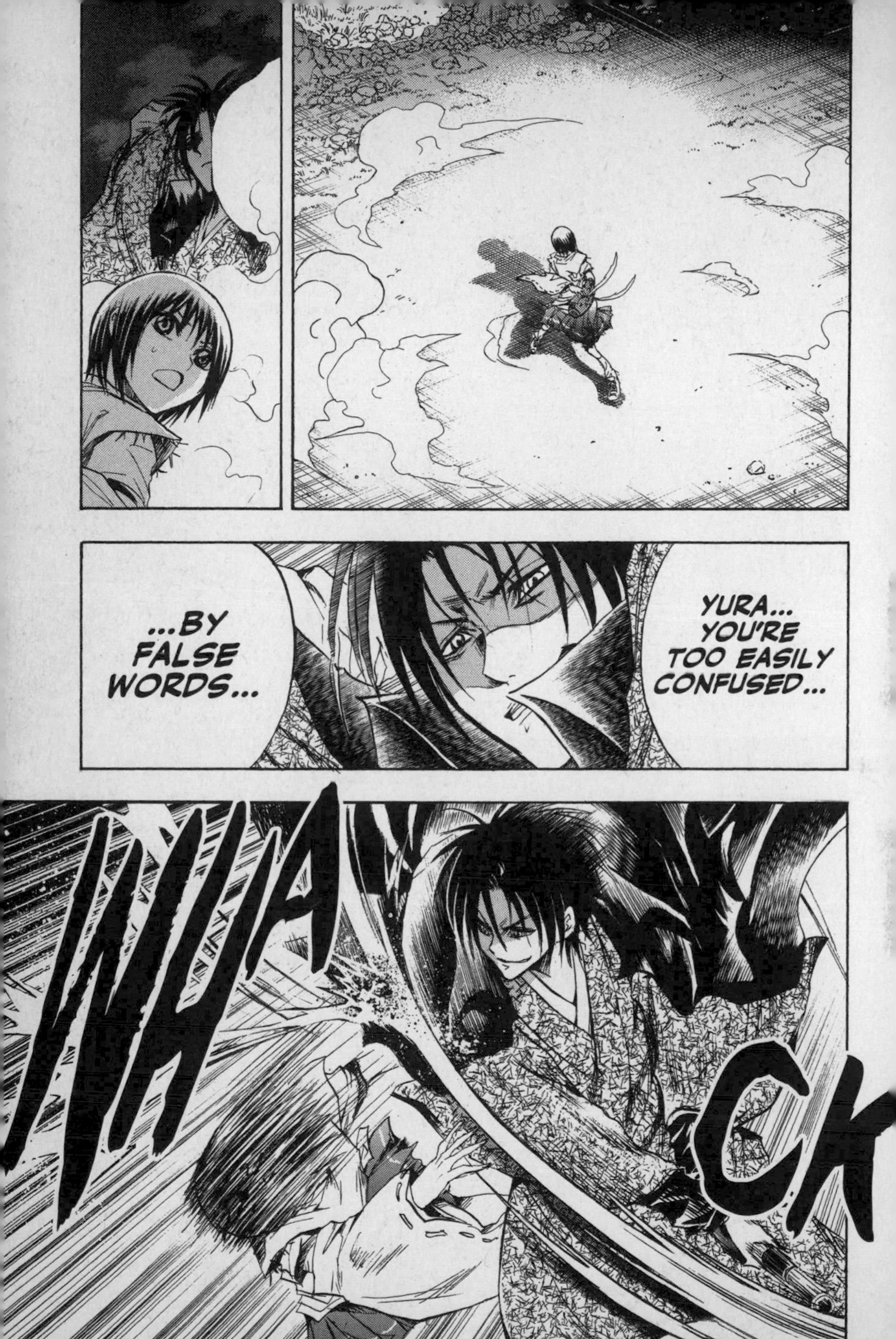
YURA... YOU'RE TOO EASILY CONFUSED...
...BY FALSE WORDS...
WHACK

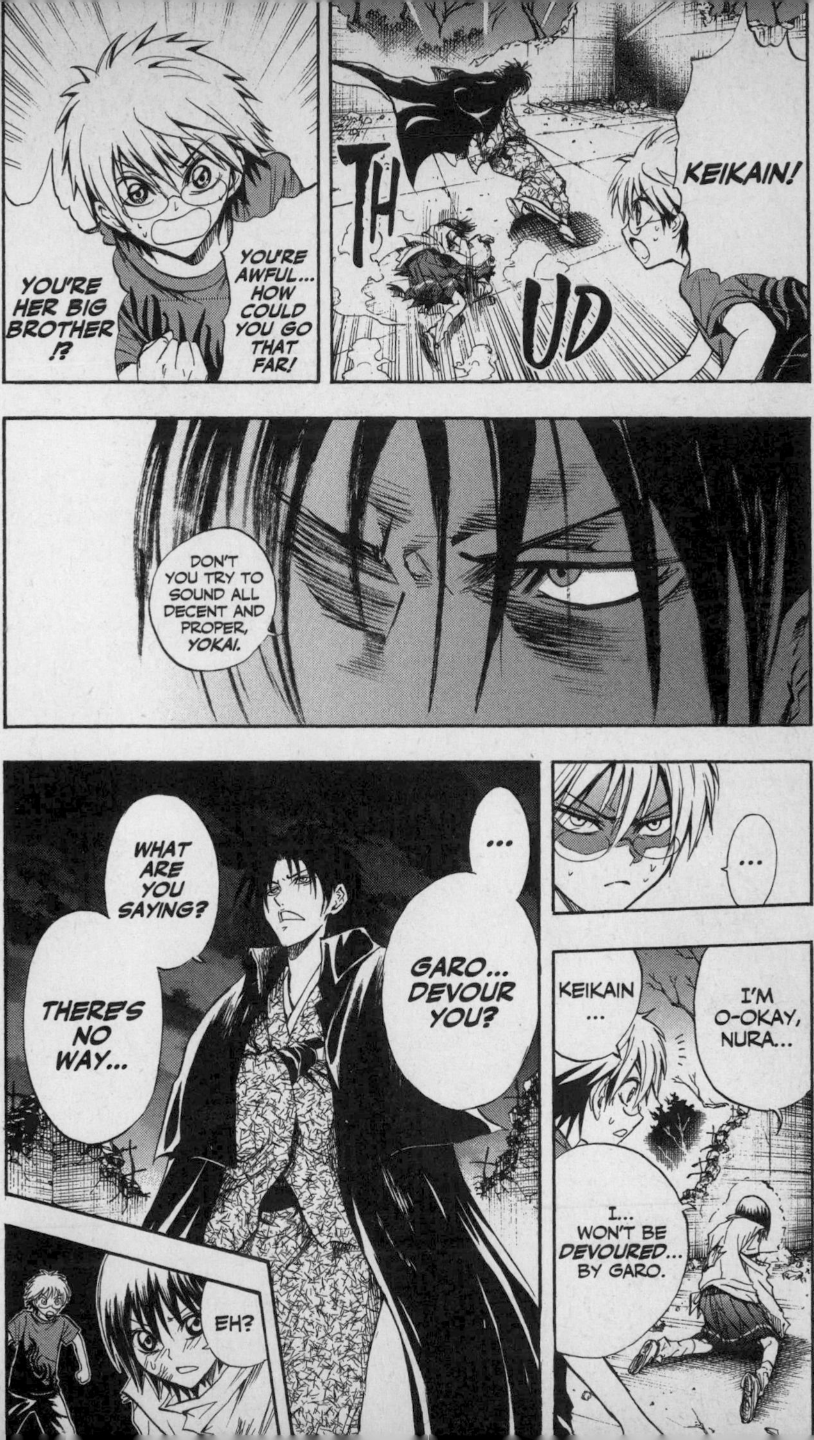

KEIKAIN!
TH
UD
YOU'RE AWFUL... HOW COULD YOU GO THAT FAR!
YOU'RE HER BIG BROTHER !?
DON'T YOU TRY TO SOUND ALL DECENT AND PROPER, YOKAI.
...
I'M O-OKAY, NURA...
KEIKAIN ...
I... WON'T BE DEVOURED... BY GARO.
...
GARO... DEVOUR YOU?
WHAT ARE YOU SAYING?
THERE'S NO WAY...
EH?

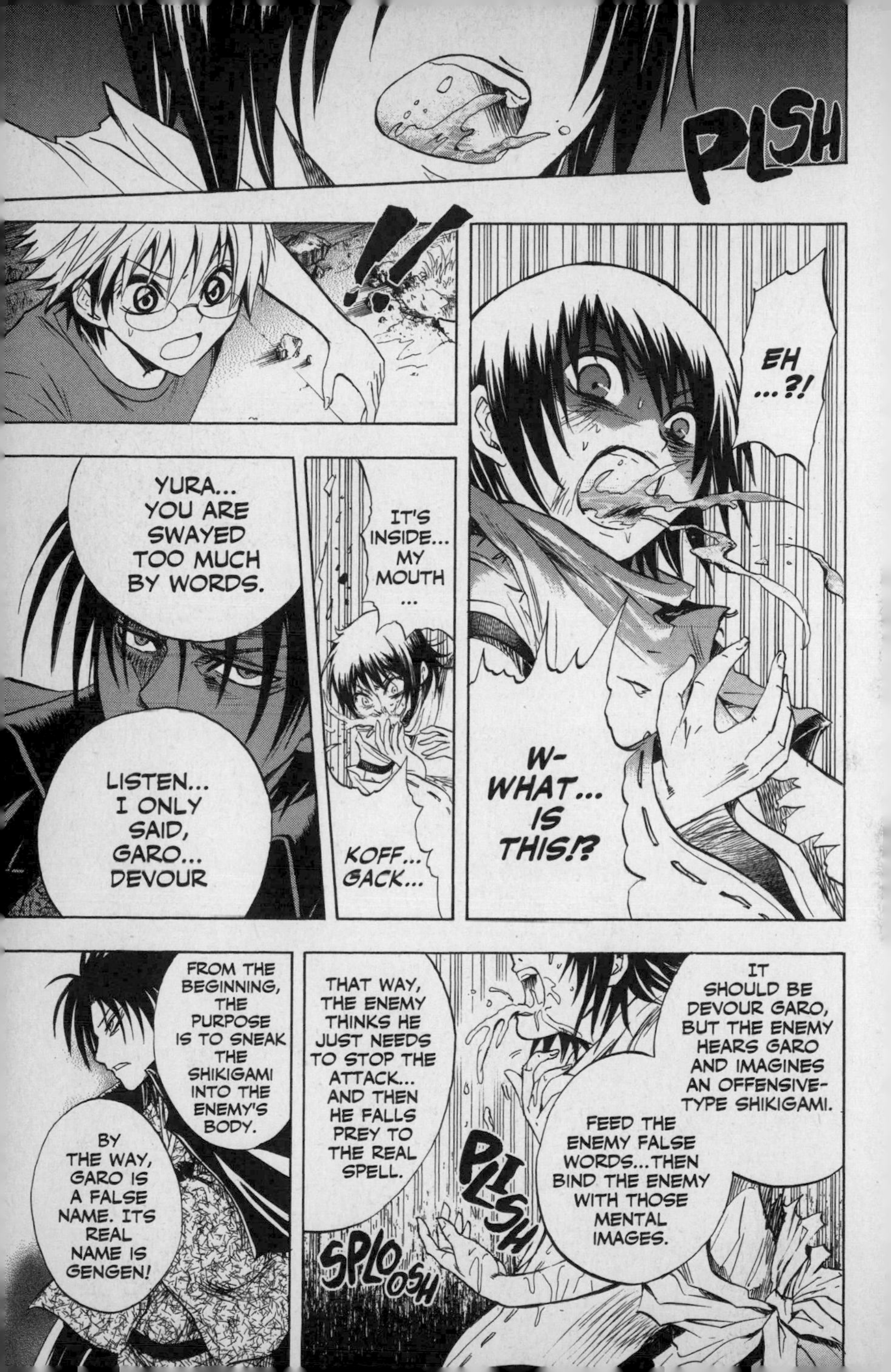
PLSH
EH ...?!
W-WHAT... IS THIS!?
!!
IT'S INSIDE... MY MOUTH ...
KOFF... GACK...
YURA... YOU ARE SWAYED TOO MUCH BY WORDS.
LISTEN... I ONLY SAID, GARO... DEVOUR
IT SHOULD BE DEVOUR GARO, BUT THE ENEMY HEARS GARO AND IMAGINES AN OFFENSIVE-TYPE SHIKIGAMI.
FEED THE ENEMY FALSE WORDS...THEN BIND THE ENEMY WITH THOSE MENTAL IMAGES.
PLSH
SPLOOSH
THAT WAY, THE ENEMY THINKS HE JUST NEEDS TO STOP THE ATTACK... AND THEN HE FALLS PREY TO THE REAL SPELL.
FROM THE BEGINNING, THE PURPOSE IS TO SNEAK THE SHIKIGAMI INTO THE ENEMY'S BODY.
BY THE WAY, GARO IS A FALSE NAME. ITS REAL NAME IS GENGEN!

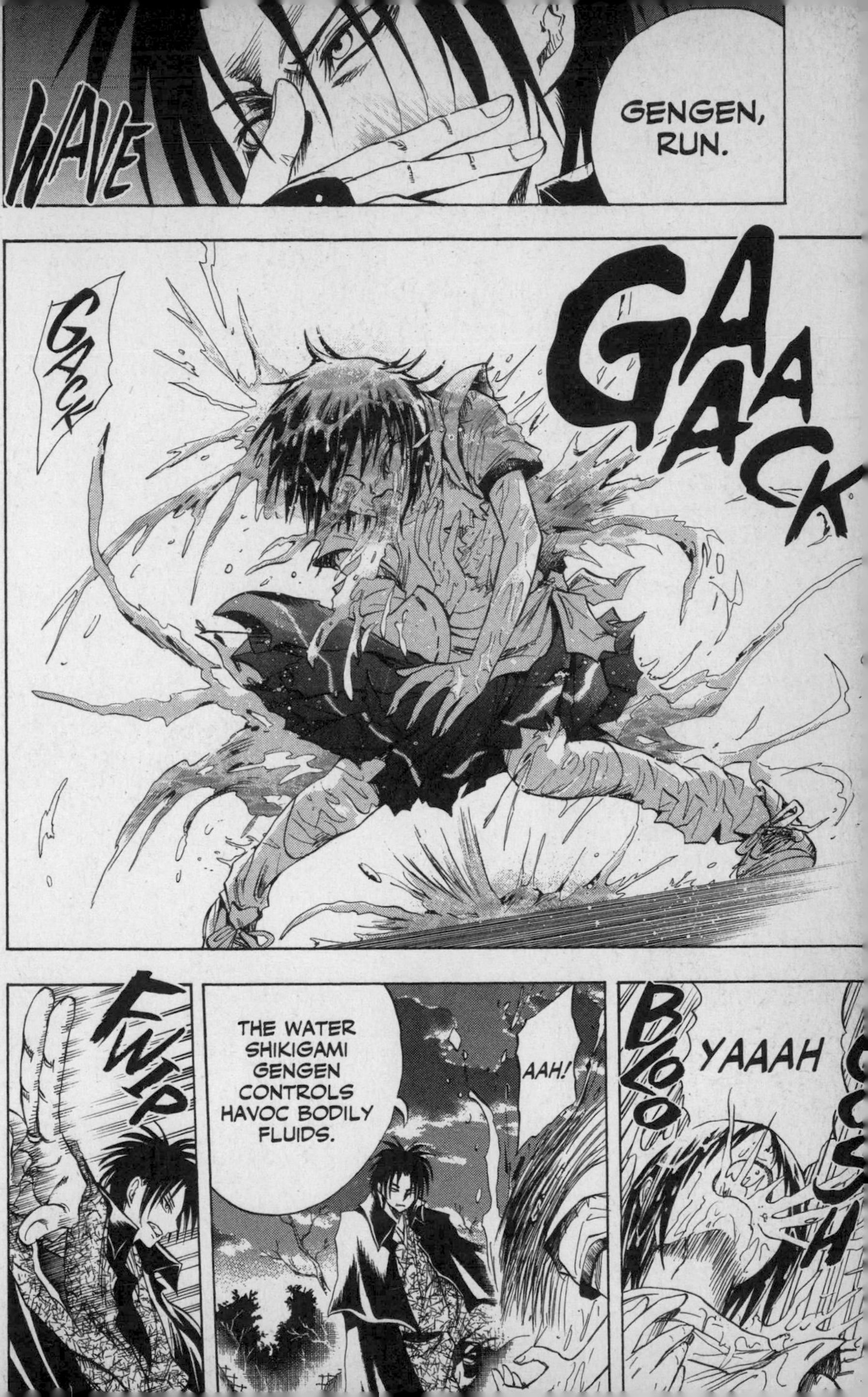
GENGEN, RUN.
WAVE
GAAACK
GACK
GUSH
YAAAH
BLOO
AAH!
THE WATER SHIKIGAMI GENGEN CONTROLS HAVOC BODILY FLUIDS.
FWIP

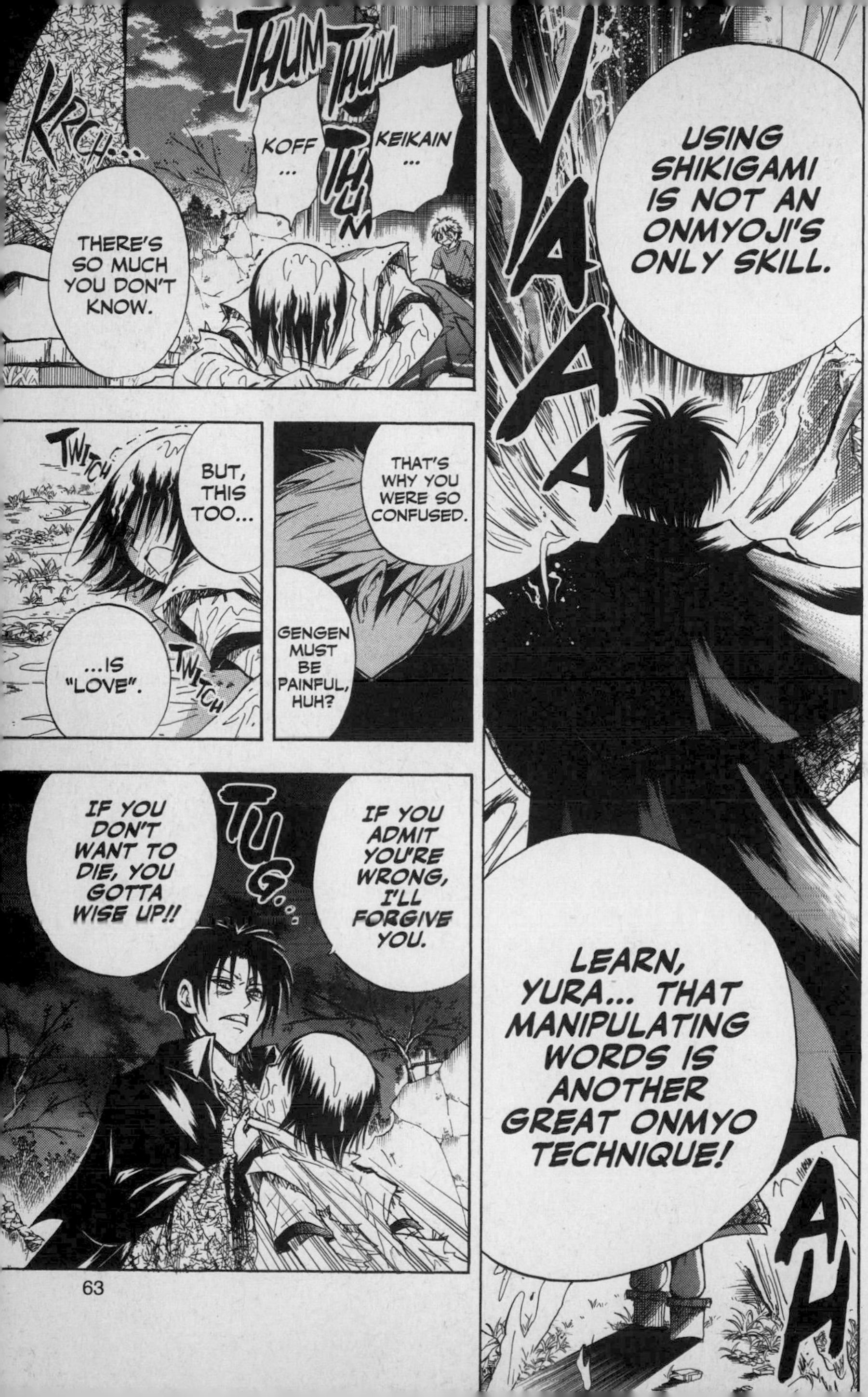
YAAAA
USING SHIKIGAMI IS NOT AN ONMYOJI'S ONLY SKILL.
LEARN, YURA... THAT MANIPULATING WORDS IS ANOTHER GREAT ONMYO TECHNIQUE!
AH
THUM THUM THUM THUM
KEIKAIN...
KOFF...
KRCH...
THERE'S SO MUCH YOU DON'T KNOW.
THAT'S WHY YOU WERE SO CONFUSED.
GENGEN MUST BE PAINFUL, HUH?
TWITCH
BUT, THIS TOO...
...IS "LOVE".
TWITCH
IF YOU ADMIT YOU'RE WRONG, I'LL FORGIVE YOU.
TUG...
IF YOU DON'T WANT TO DIE, YOU GOTTA WISE UP!!

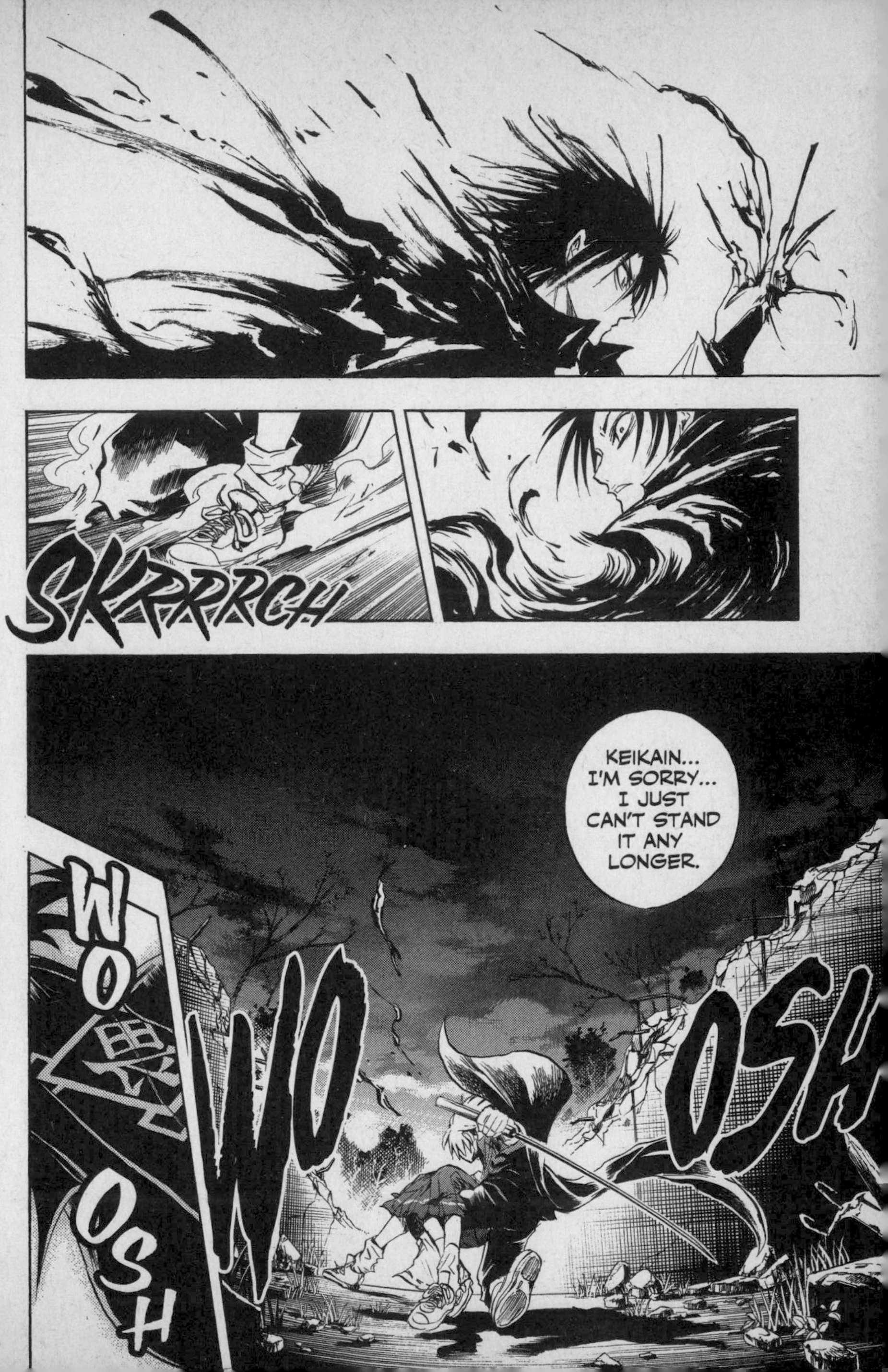
SKRRRCH
KEIKAIN... I'M SORRY... I JUST CAN'T STAND IT ANY LONGER.
WOOSH
WOOSH

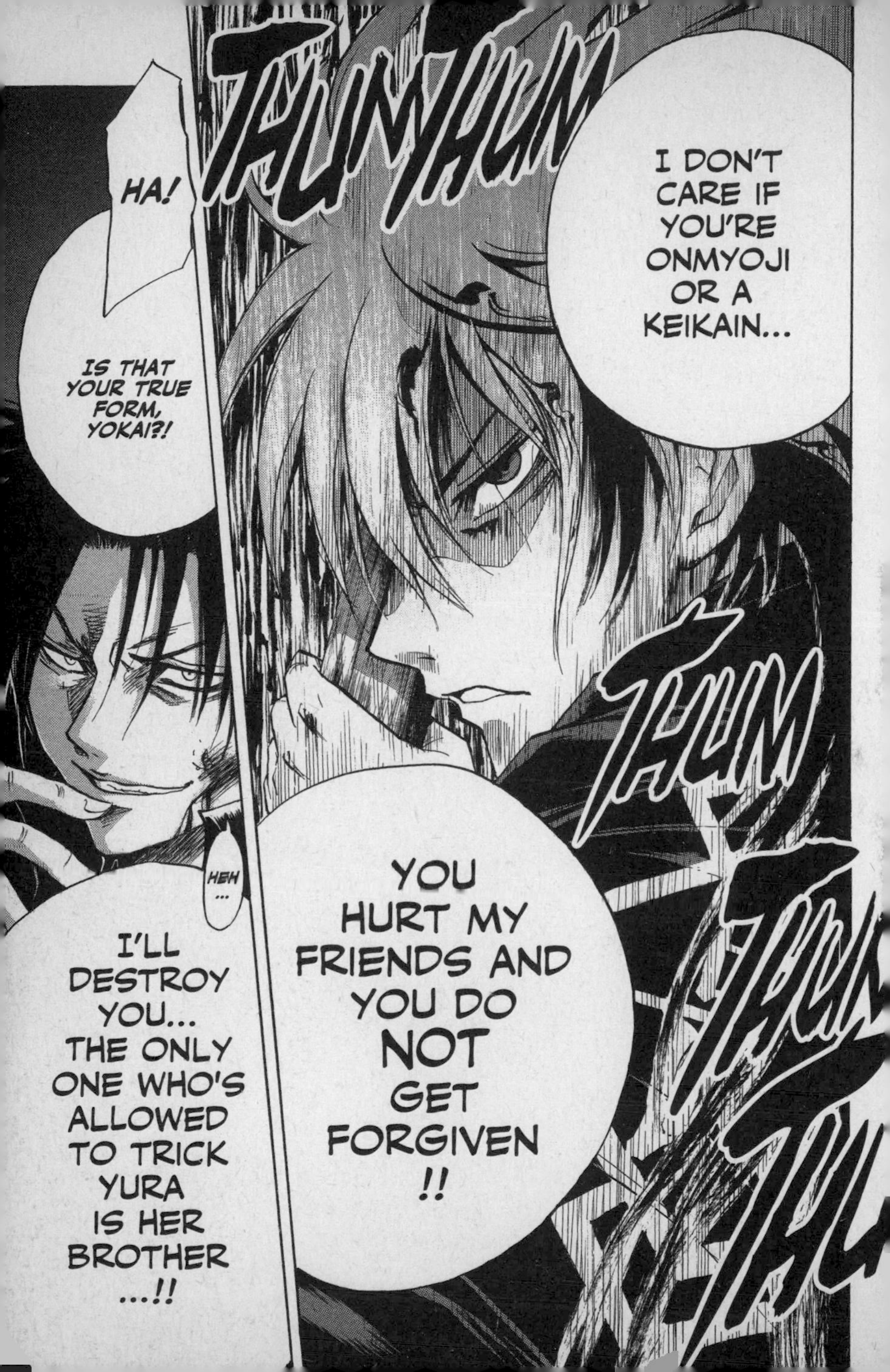

THUMTHUM
I DON'T CARE IF YOU'RE ONMYOJI OR A KEIKAIN...
THUM
YOU HURT MY FRIENDS AND YOU DO NOT GET FORGIVEN !!
HA!
IS THAT YOUR TRUE FORM, YOKAI?!
HEH ...
I'LL DESTROY YOU... THE ONLY ONE WHO'S ALLOWED TO TRICK YURA IS HER BROTHER ...!!

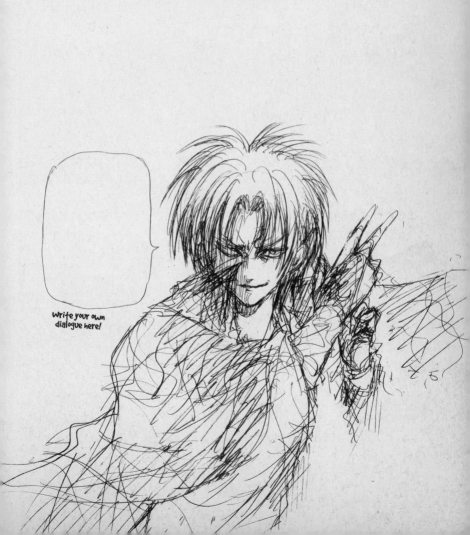

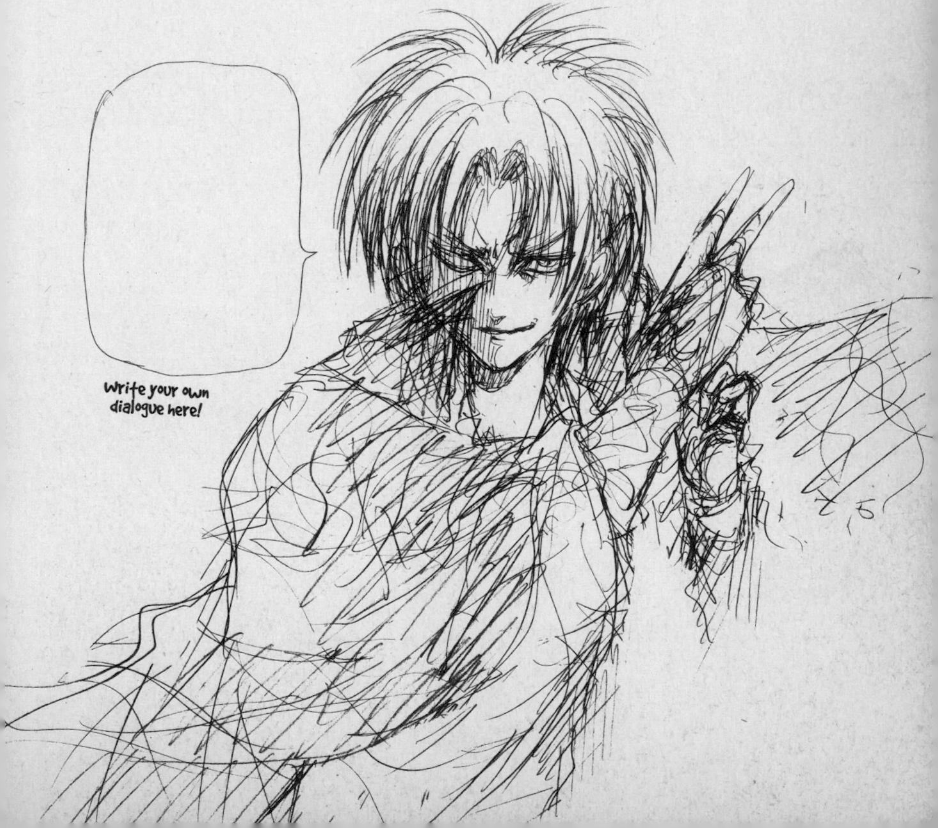
Write your own dialogue here!

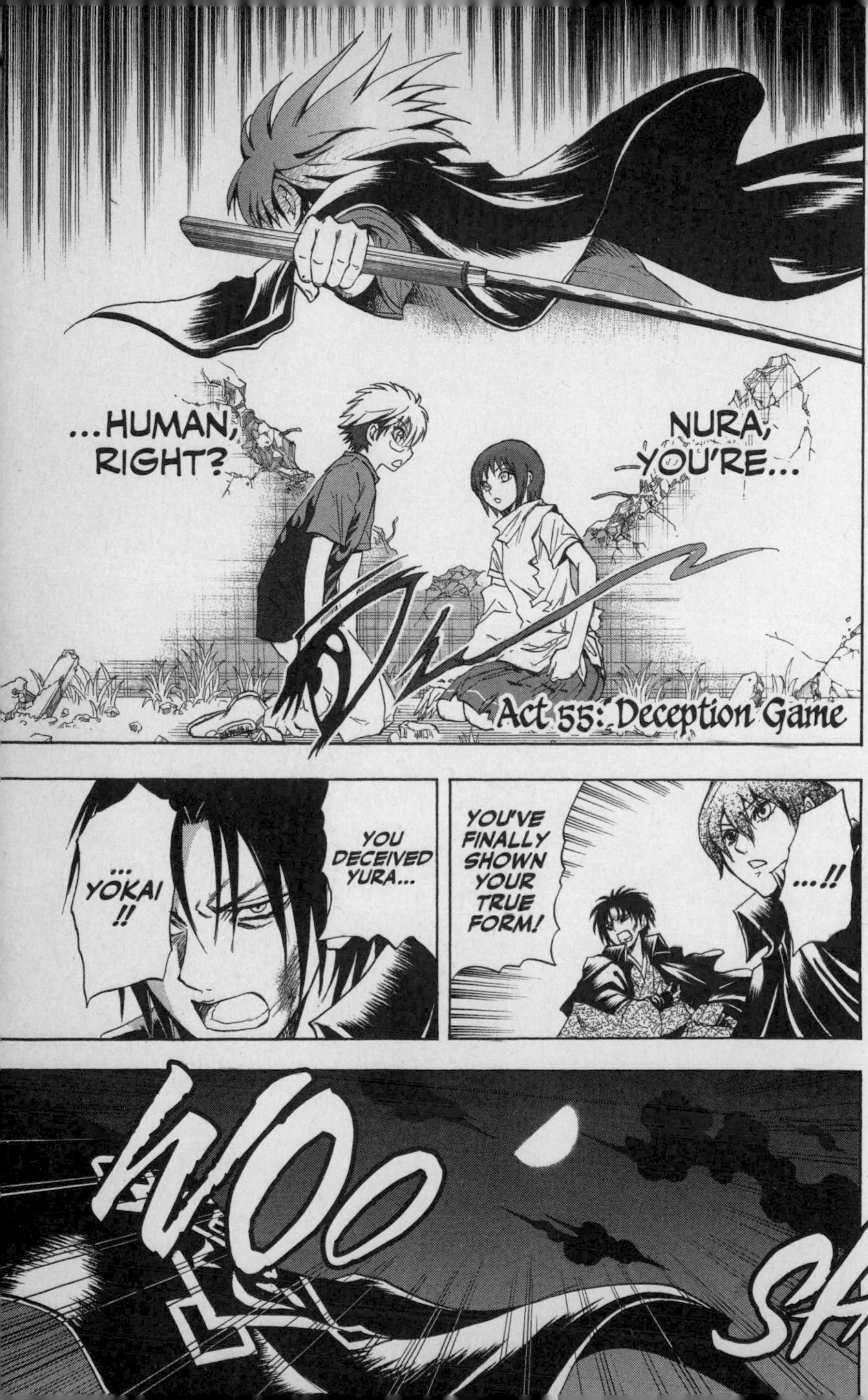
NURA, YOU'RE...
...HUMAN, RIGHT?
Act 55: Deception Game
...!!
YOU'VE FINALLY SHOWN YOUR TRUE FORM!
YOU DECEIVED YURA...
...YŌKAI!!
WOOSH

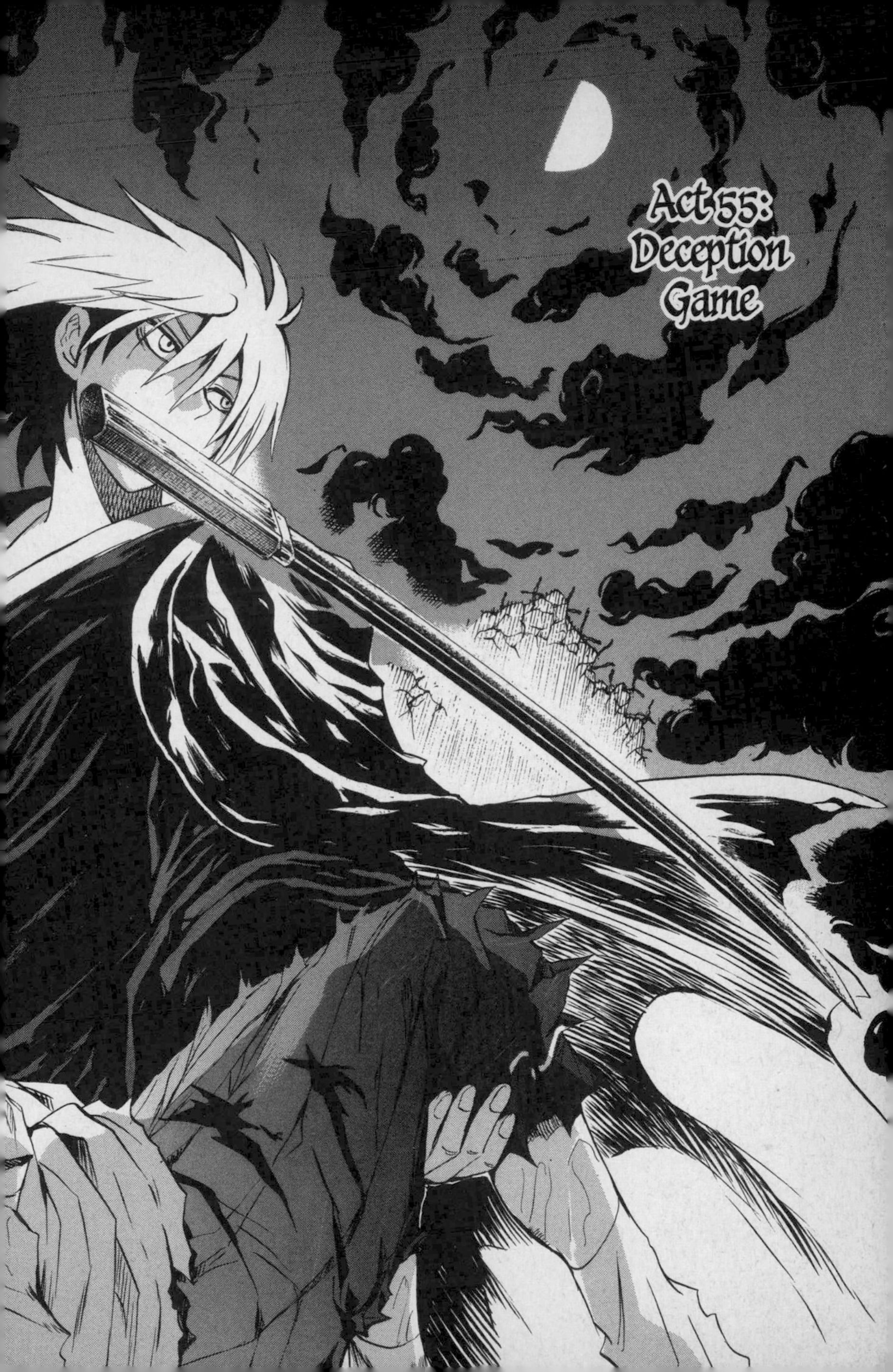
Act 55:
Deception
Game

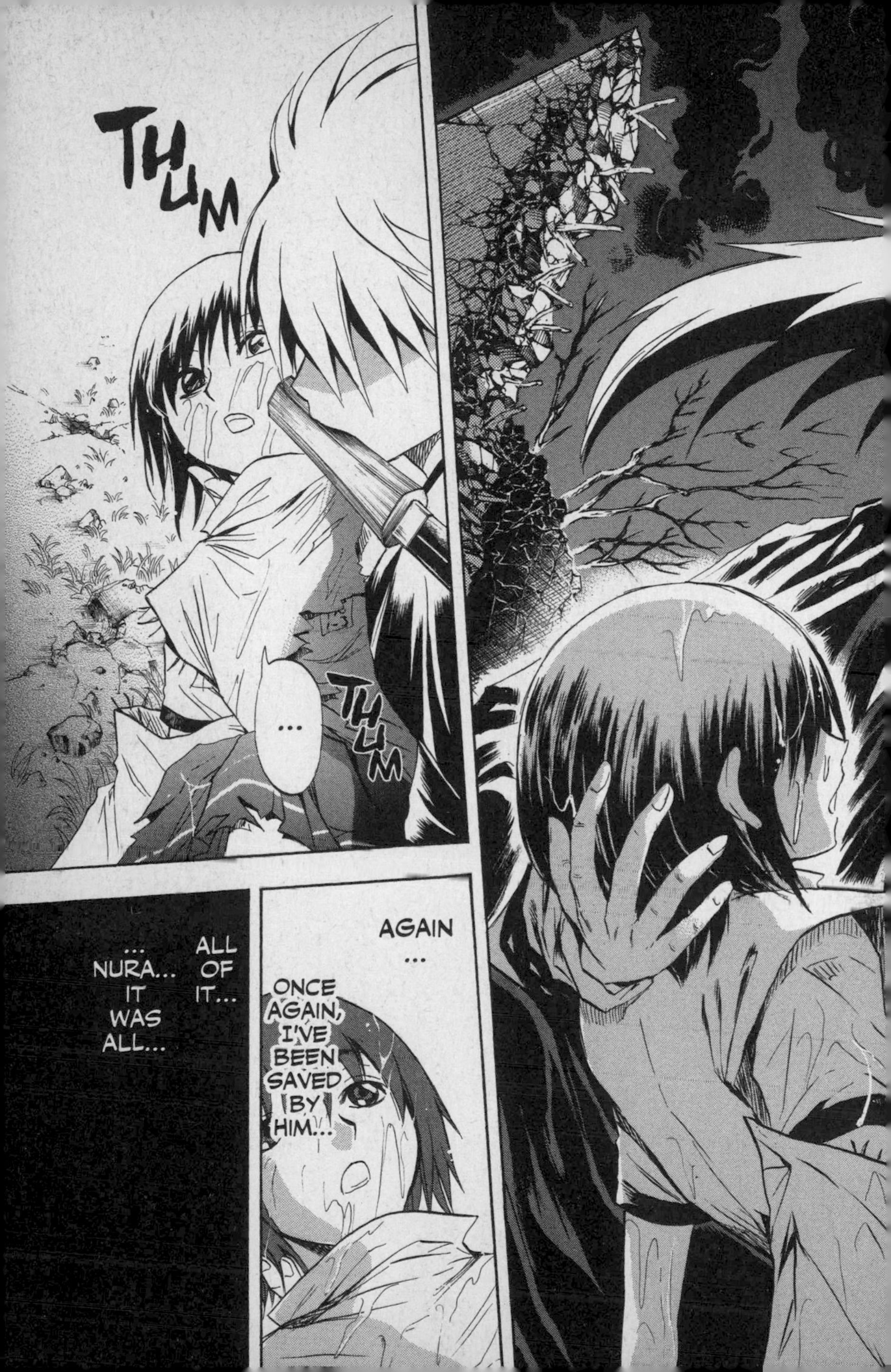
THUM
...
THUM
AGAIN...
ONCE AGAIN, I'VE BEEN SAVED BY HIM...
ALL OF IT...
...NURA... IT WAS ALL...

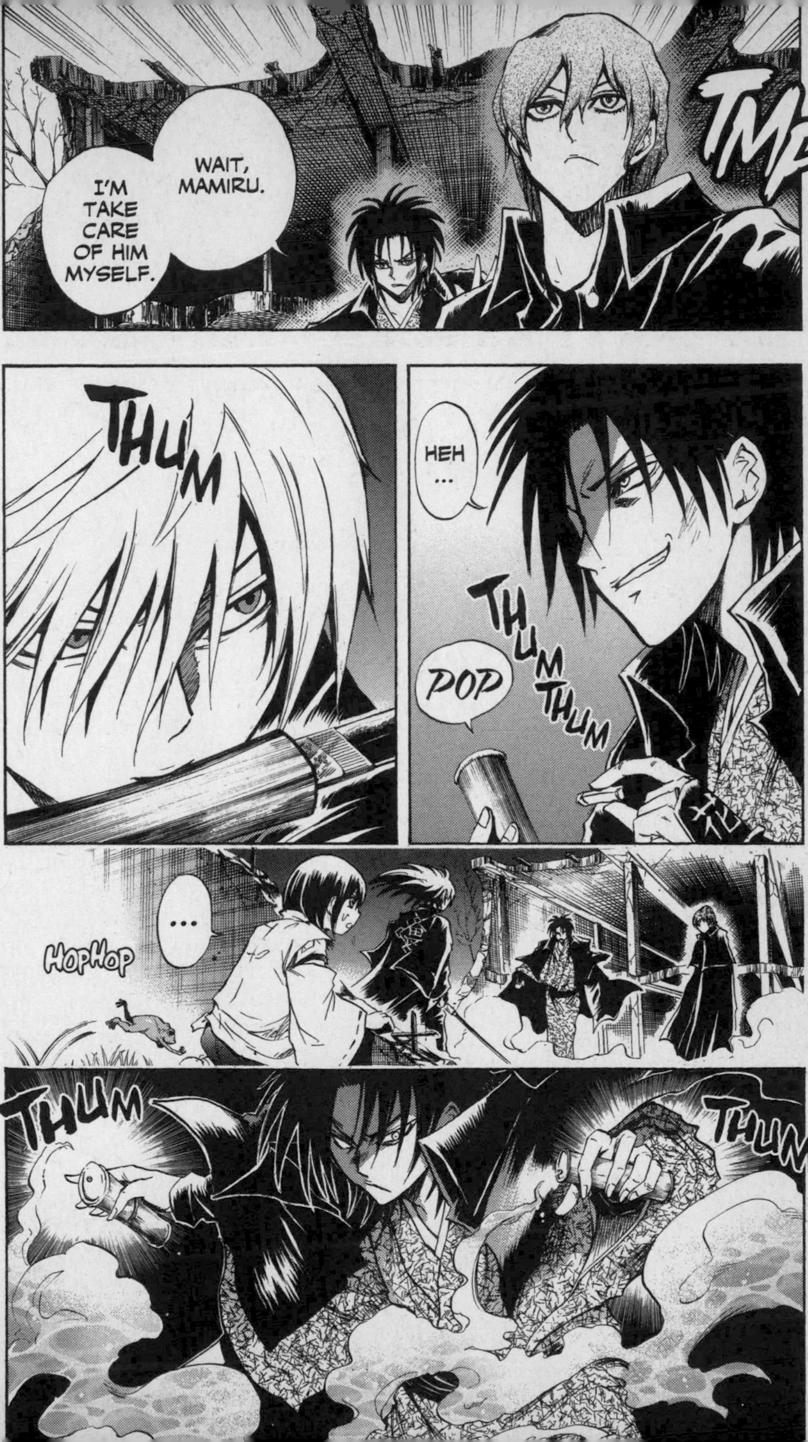
TMP
WAIT, MAMIRU.
I'M TAKE CARE OF HIM MYSELF.
HEH ...
THUM THUM THUM
POP
THUM
...
HOPHOP
THUM
THUM

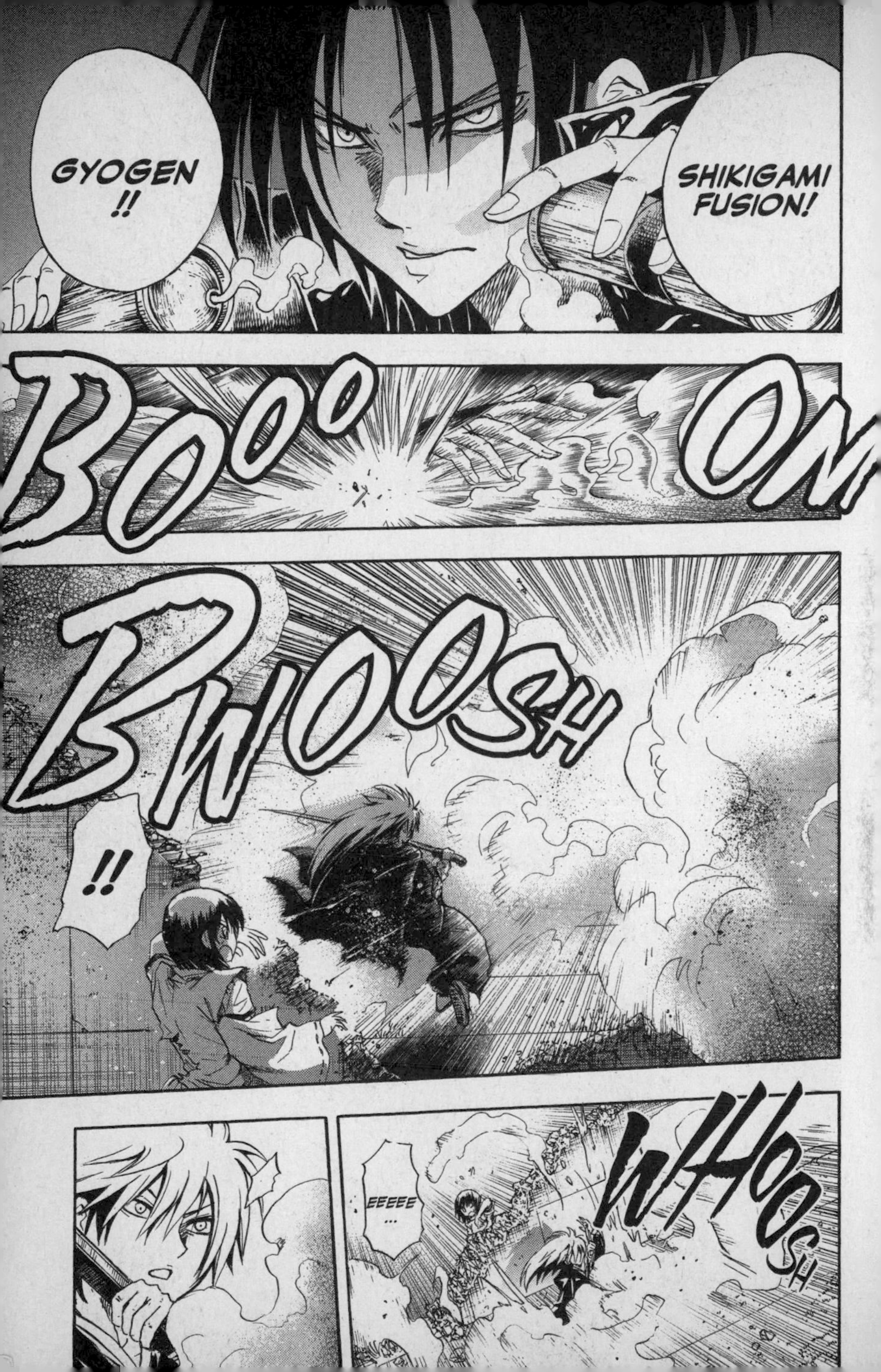
SHIKIGAMI FUSION!
GYOGEN !!
BOOOOM
BWOOSH
!!
WHOOSH
EEEEE ...

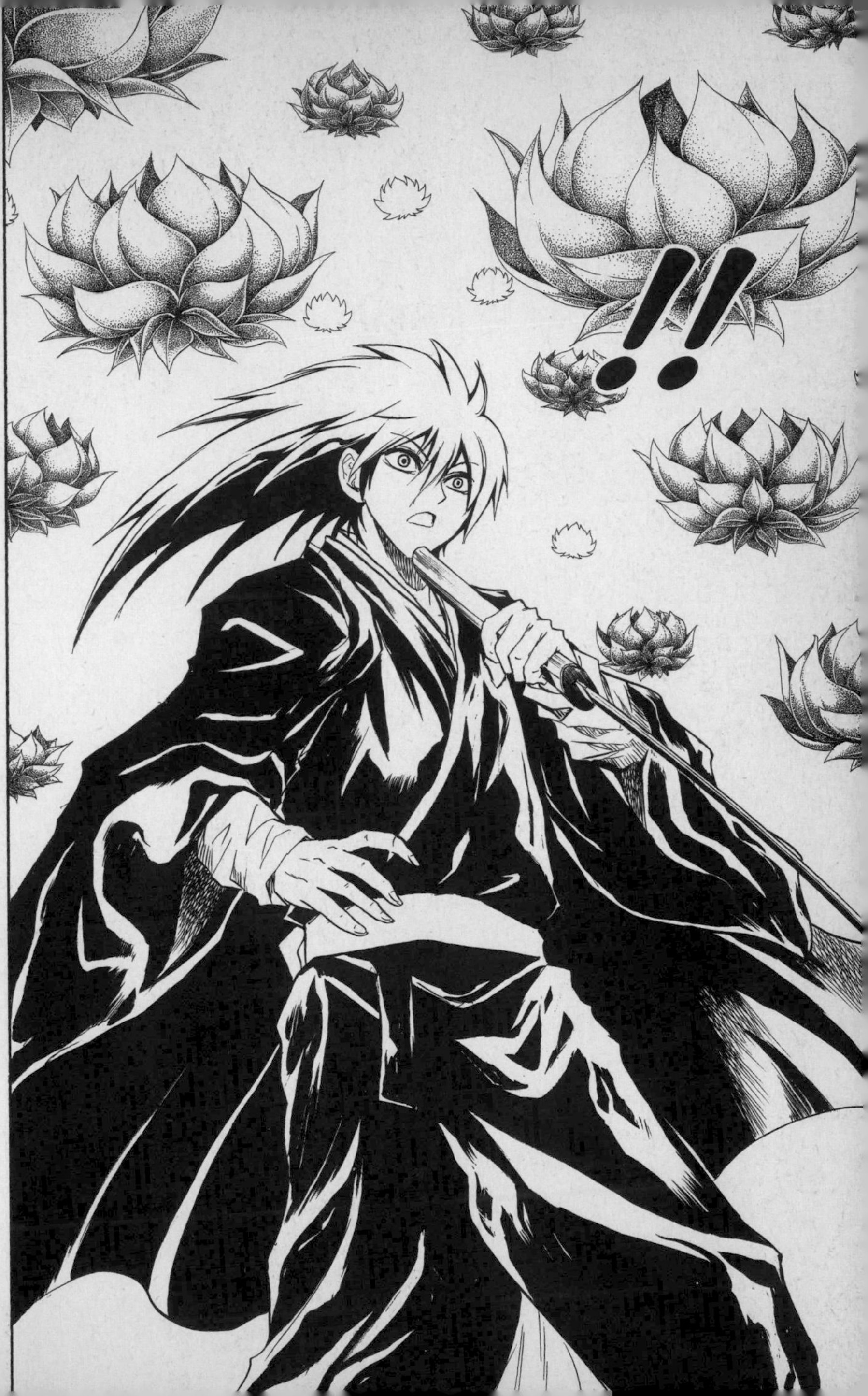
!!

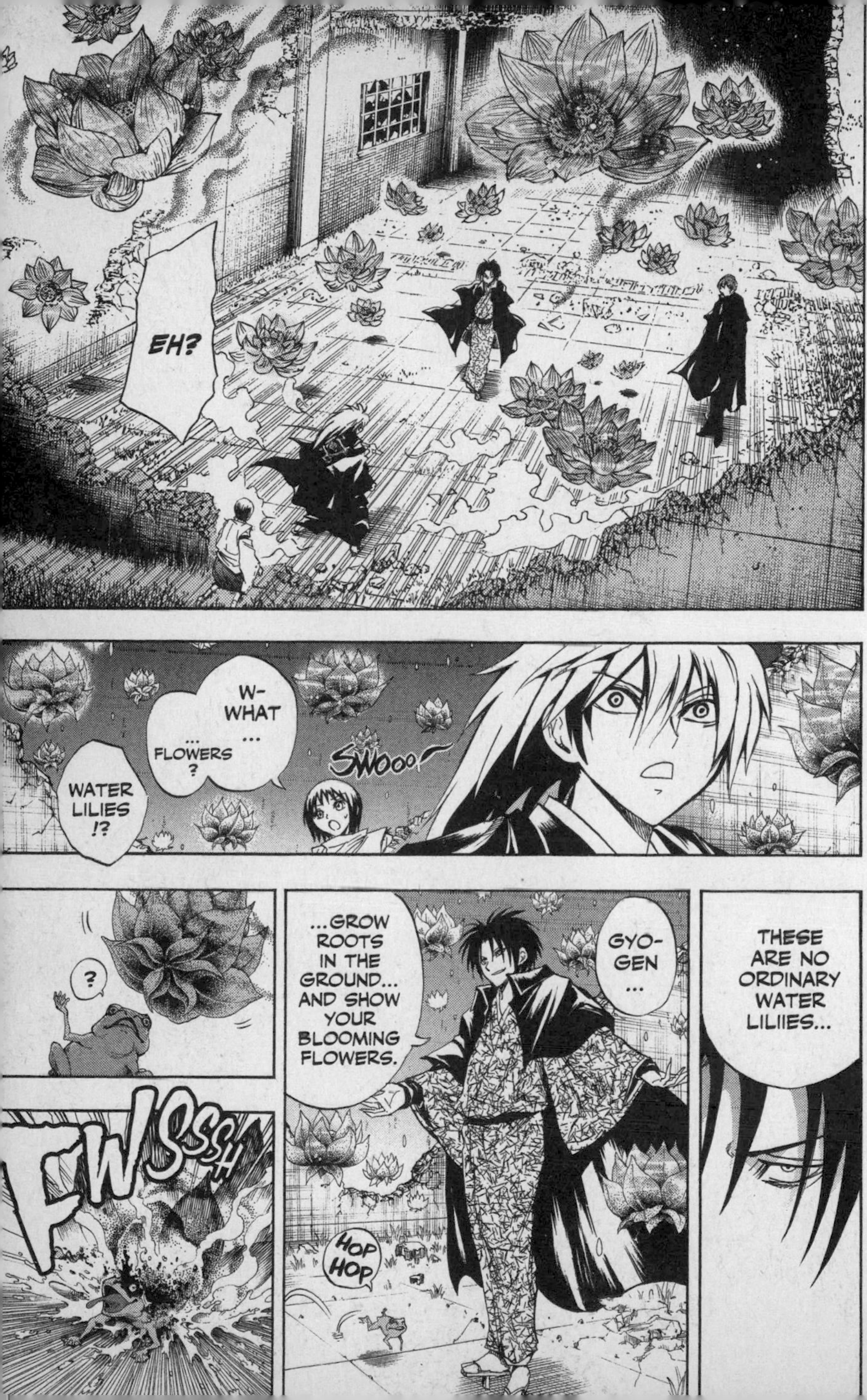
EH?
W-WHAT... FLOWERS?
SWOOO
WATER LILIES!?
THESE ARE NO ORDINARY WATER LILIIES...
GYO-GEN...
...GROW ROOTS IN THE GROUND... AND SHOW YOUR BLOOMING FLOWERS.
HOP HOP
?
FWSSSH

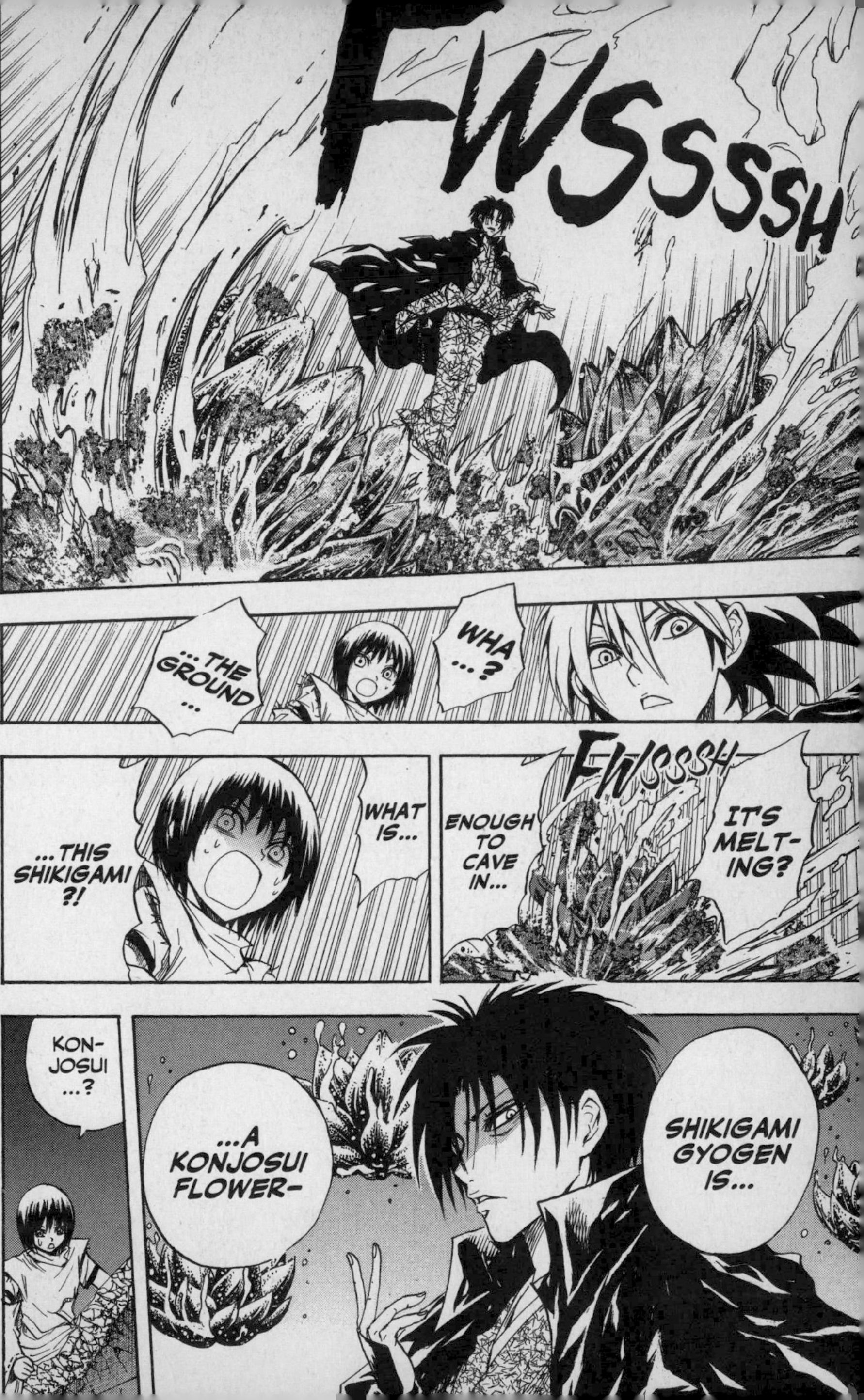
FWSSSSH
WHA...?
...THE GROUND...
FWSSSH
IT'S MELTING?
ENOUGH TO CAVE IN...
WHAT IS...
...THIS SHIKIGAMI?!
SHIKIGAMI GYOGEN IS...
...A KONJOSUI FLOWER-
KONJOSUI...?

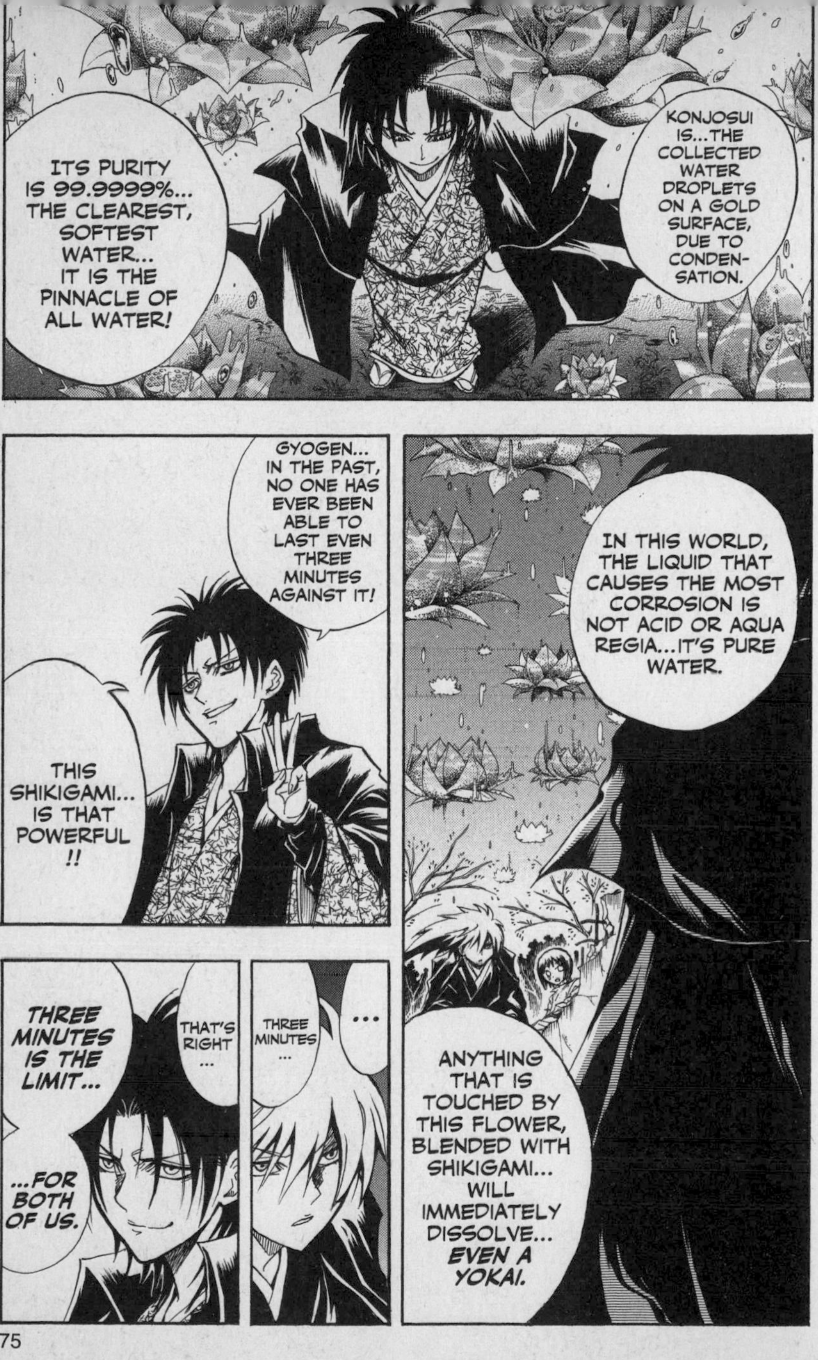
KONJOSUI IS...THE COLLECTED WATER DROPLETS ON A GOLD SURFACE, DUE TO CONDEN-SATION.
ITS PURITY IS 99.9999%... THE CLEAREST, SOFTEST WATER... IT IS THE PINNACLE OF ALL WATER!
IN THIS WORLD, THE LIQUID THAT CAUSES THE MOST CORROSION IS NOT ACID OR AQUA REGIA...IT'S PURE WATER.
ANYTHING THAT IS TOUCHED BY THIS FLOWER, BLENDED WITH SHIKIGAMI... WILL IMMEDIATELY DISSOLVE... *EVEN A YOKAI.*
GYOGEN... IN THE PAST, NO ONE HAS EVER BEEN ABLE TO LAST EVEN THREE MINUTES AGAINST IT!
THIS SHIKIGAMI... IS THAT POWERFUL !!
...
THREE MINUTES ...
THAT'S RIGHT ...
*THREE MINUTES IS THE LIMIT...*
*...FOR BOTH OF US.*

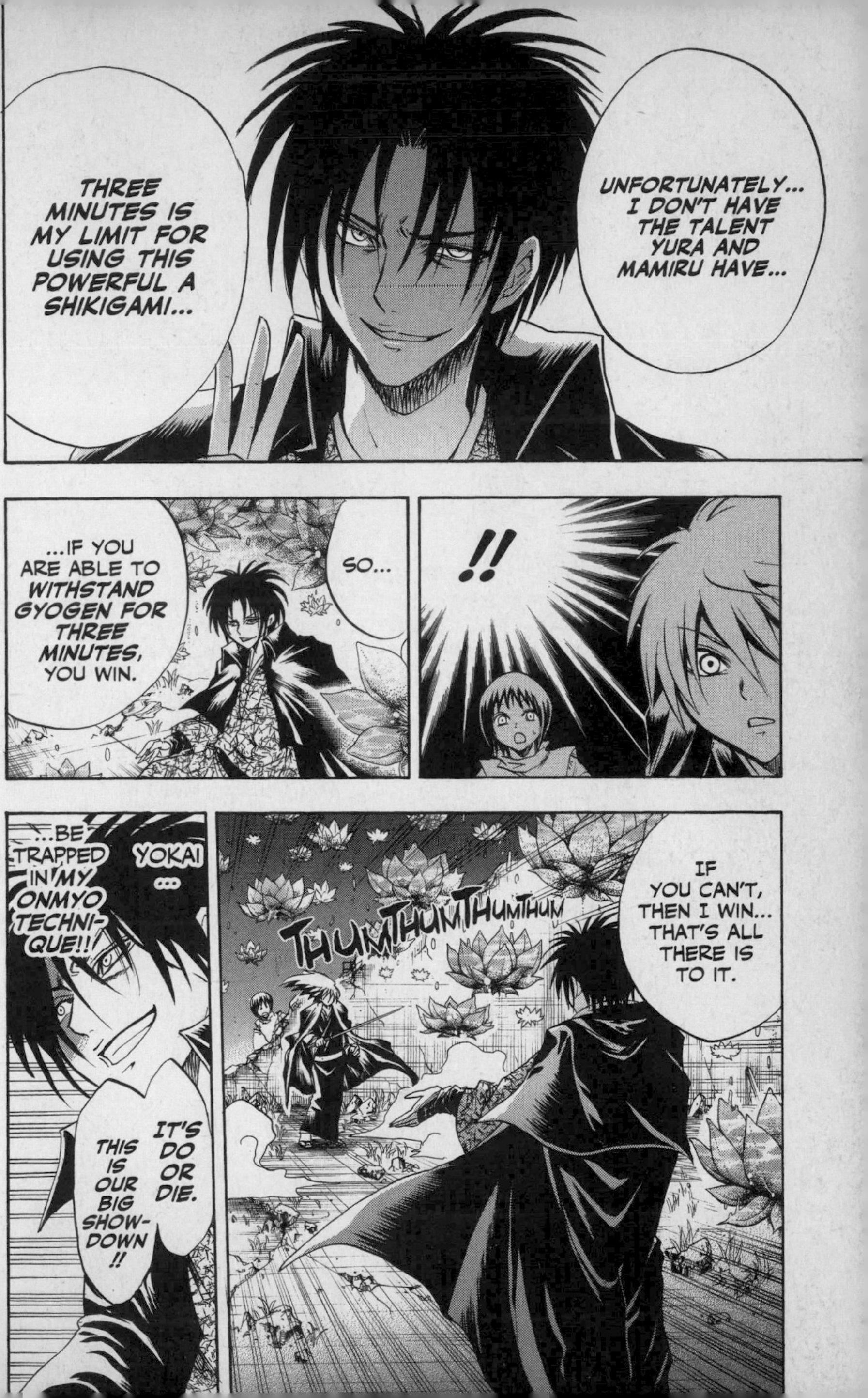
UNFORTUNATELY... I DON'T HAVE THE TALENT YURA AND MAMIRU HAVE...
THREE MINUTES IS MY LIMIT FOR USING THIS POWERFUL A SHIKIGAMI...
!!
SO...
...IF YOU ARE ABLE TO WITHSTAND GYOGEN FOR THREE MINUTES, YOU WIN.
IF YOU CAN'T, THEN I WIN... THAT'S ALL THERE IS TO IT.
THUMTHUMTHUMTHUM
YOKAI ...
...BE TRAPPED IN MY ONMYO TECHNIQUE!!
IT'S DO OR DIE.
THIS IS OUR BIG SHOWDOWN!!

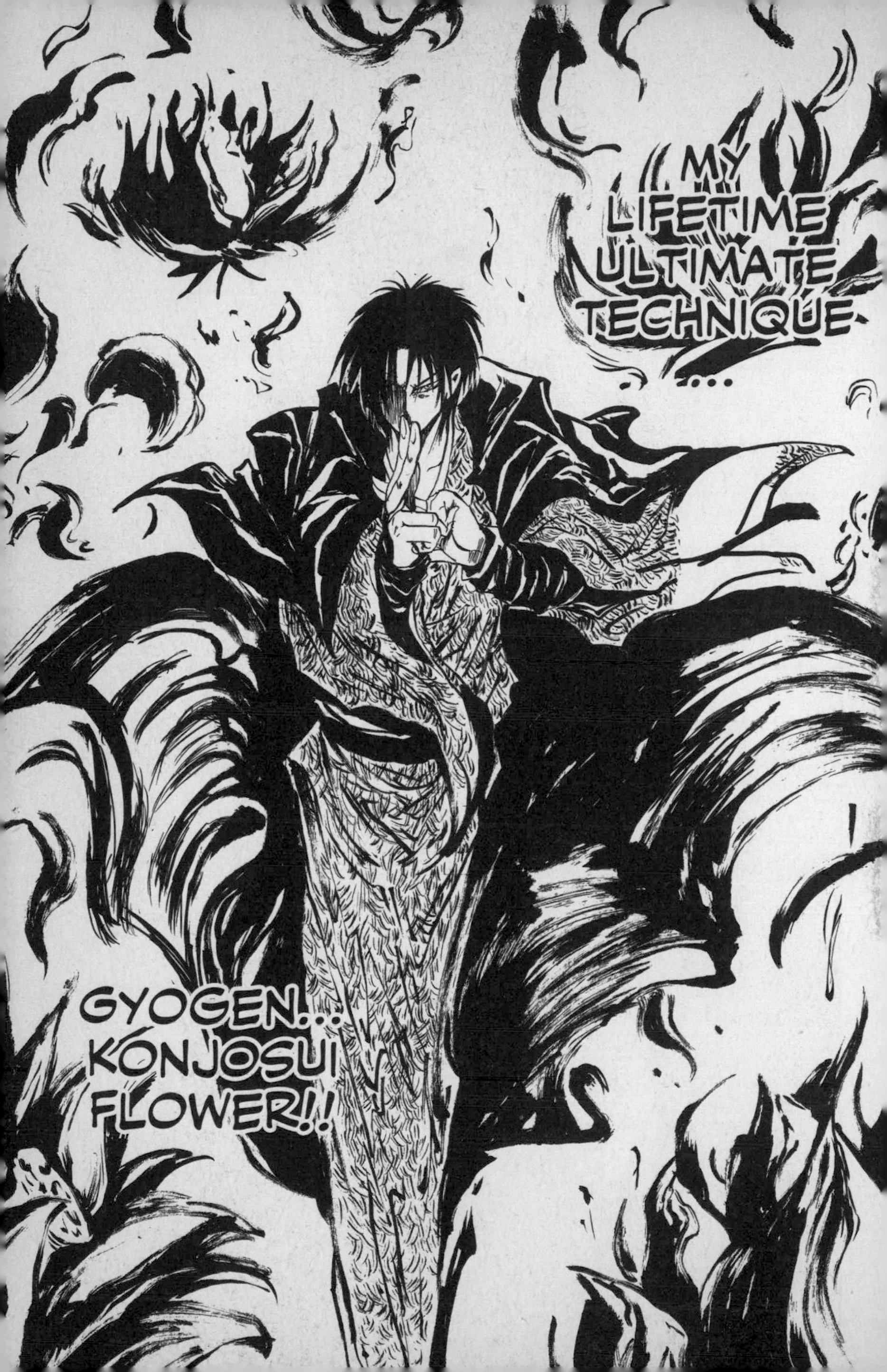
MY LIFETIME ULTIMATE TECHNIQUE...
GYOGEN... KONJOSUI FLOWER!!

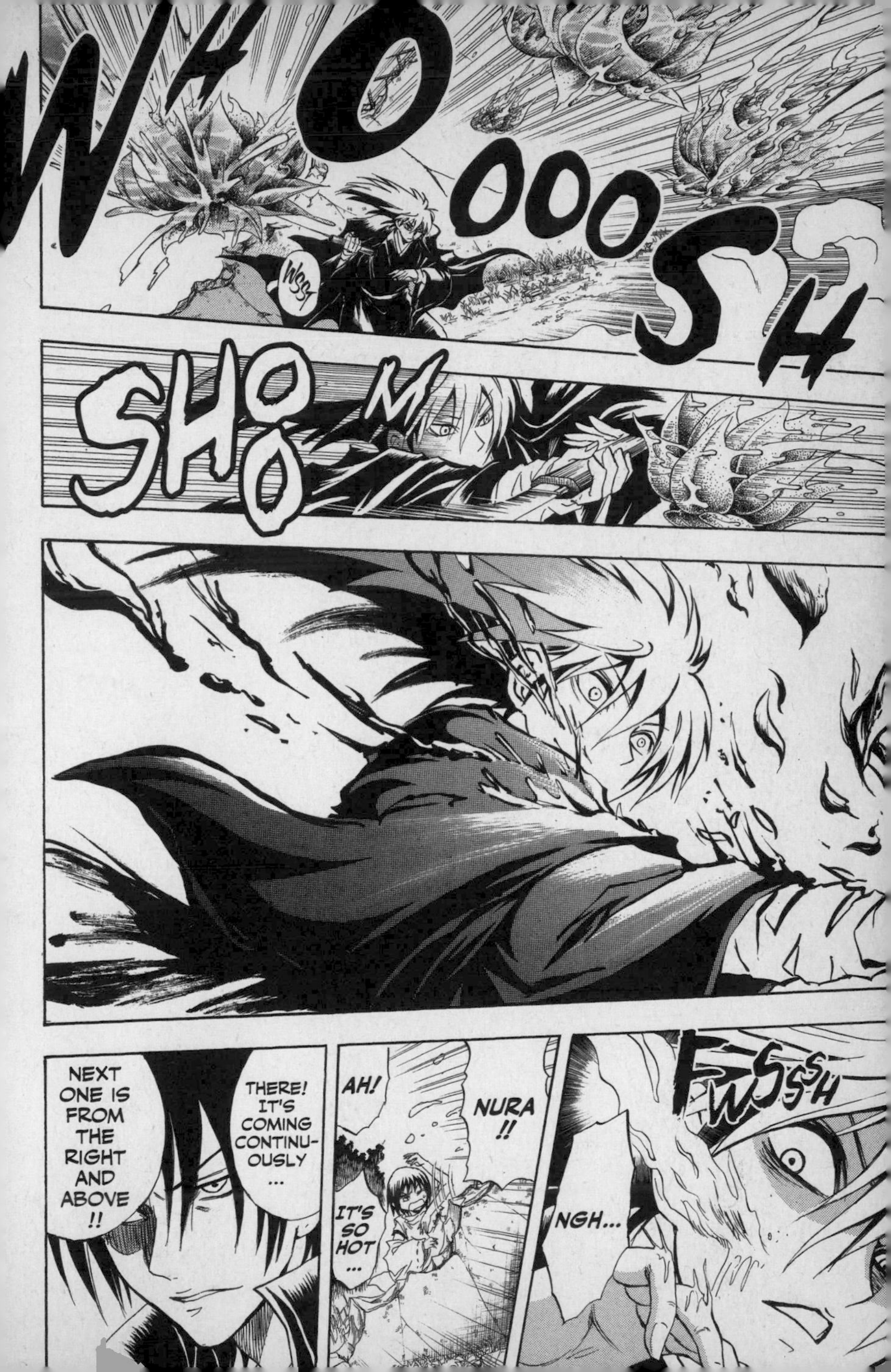
WHOOOOSH
WSSH
SHOOM
FWSSSH
NGH...
NURA!!
AH!
IT'S SO HOT...
THERE! IT'S COMING CONTINUOUSLY...
NEXT ONE IS FROM THE RIGHT AND ABOVE!!

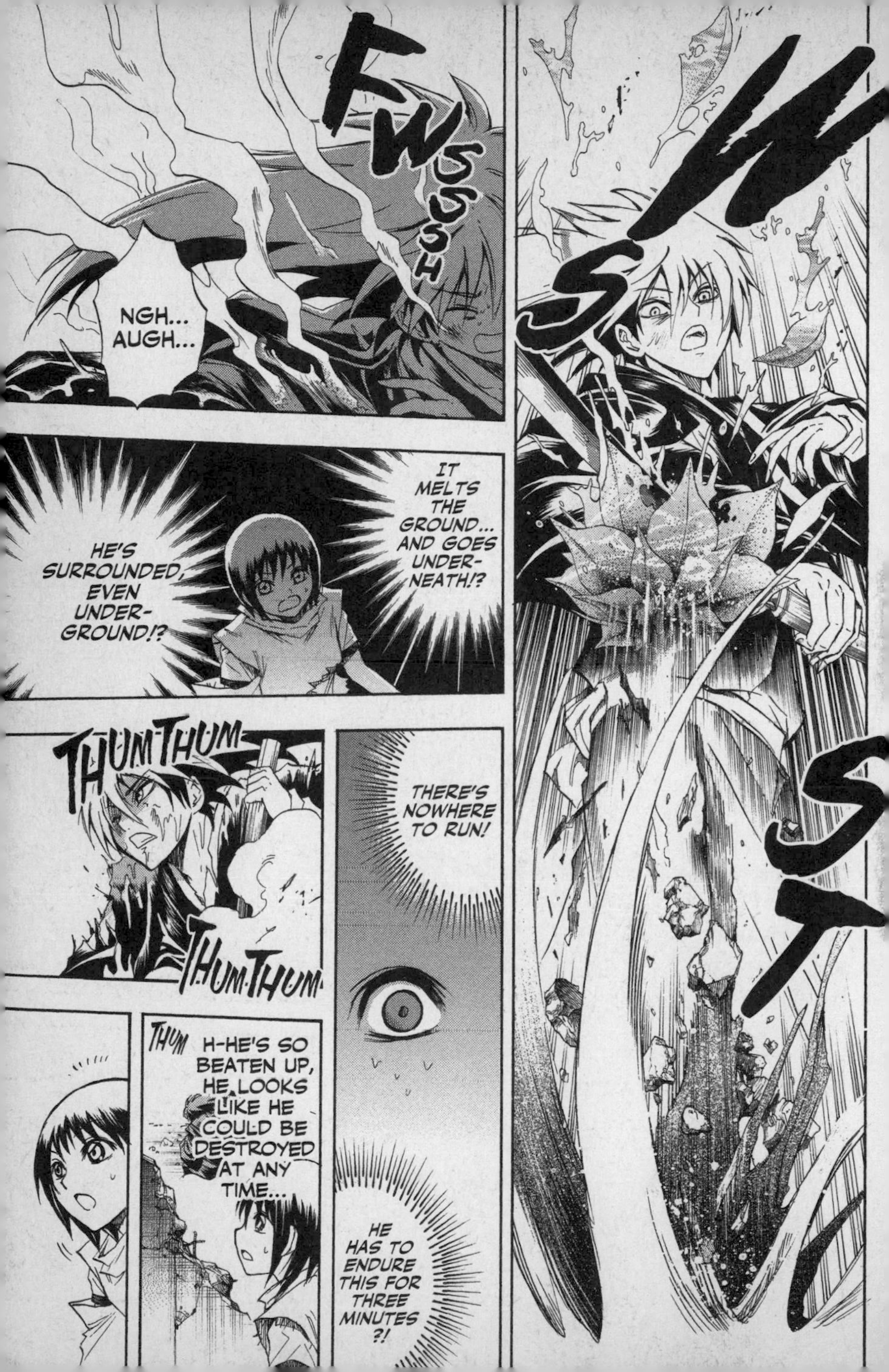
FWSSSH
NGH... AUGH...
IT MELTS THE GROUND... AND GOES UNDER-NEATH!?
HE'S SURROUNDED, EVEN UNDER-GROUND!?
THERE'S NOWHERE TO RUN!
HE HAS TO ENDURE THIS FOR THREE MINUTES?!
THUM THUM
THUM THUM
THUM
H-HE'S SO BEATEN UP, HE LOOKS LIKE HE COULD BE DESTROYED AT ANY TIME...

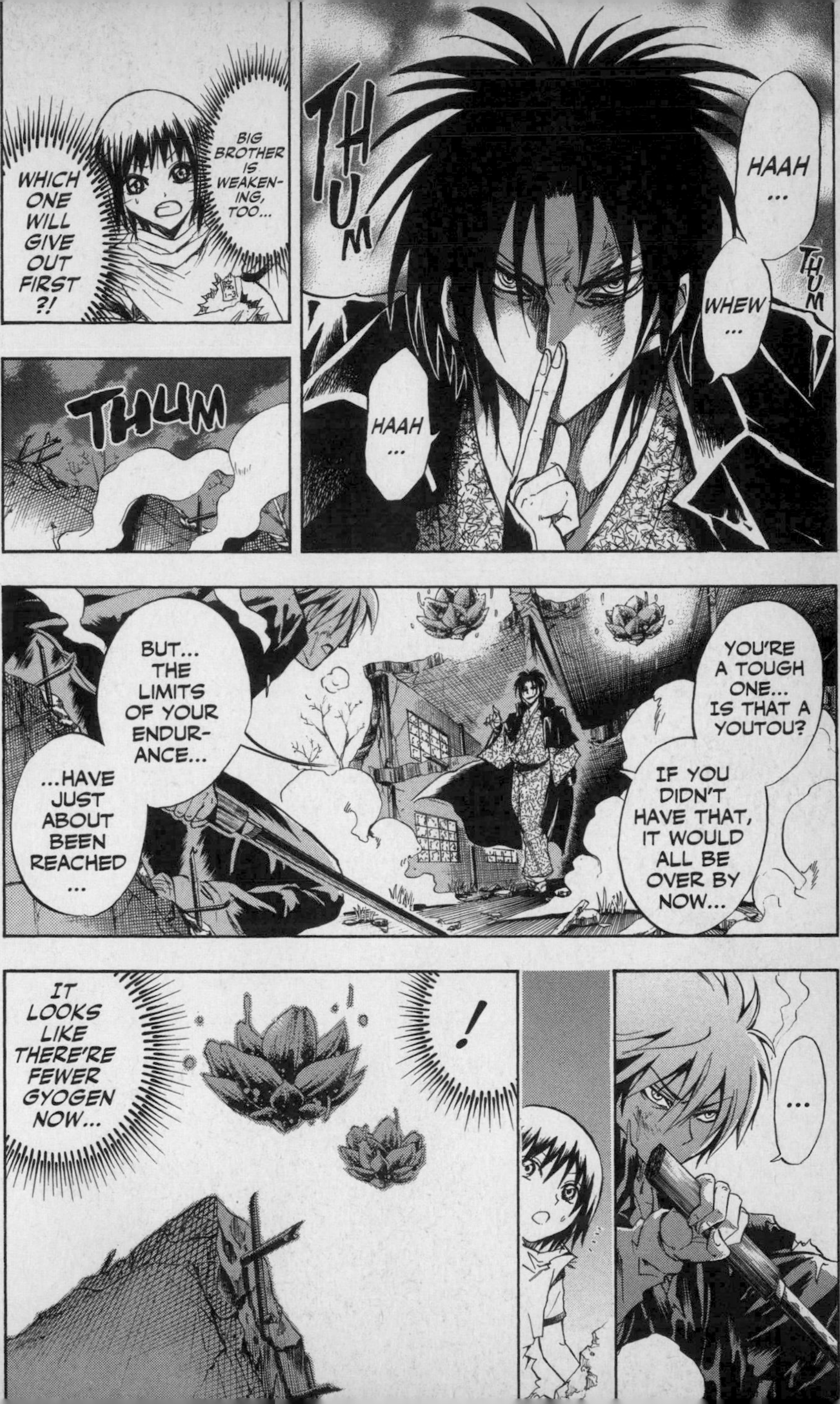
THUM
HAAH...
WHEW...
THUM
HAAH...
BIG BROTHER IS WEAKENING, TOO...
WHICH ONE WILL GIVE OUT FIRST?!
THUM
YOU'RE A TOUGH ONE... IS THAT A YOUTOU?
IF YOU DIDN'T HAVE THAT, IT WOULD ALL BE OVER BY NOW...
BUT... THE LIMITS OF YOUR ENDURANCE...
...HAVE JUST ABOUT BEEN REACHED...
...
!
IT LOOKS LIKE THERE'RE FEWER GYOGEN NOW...

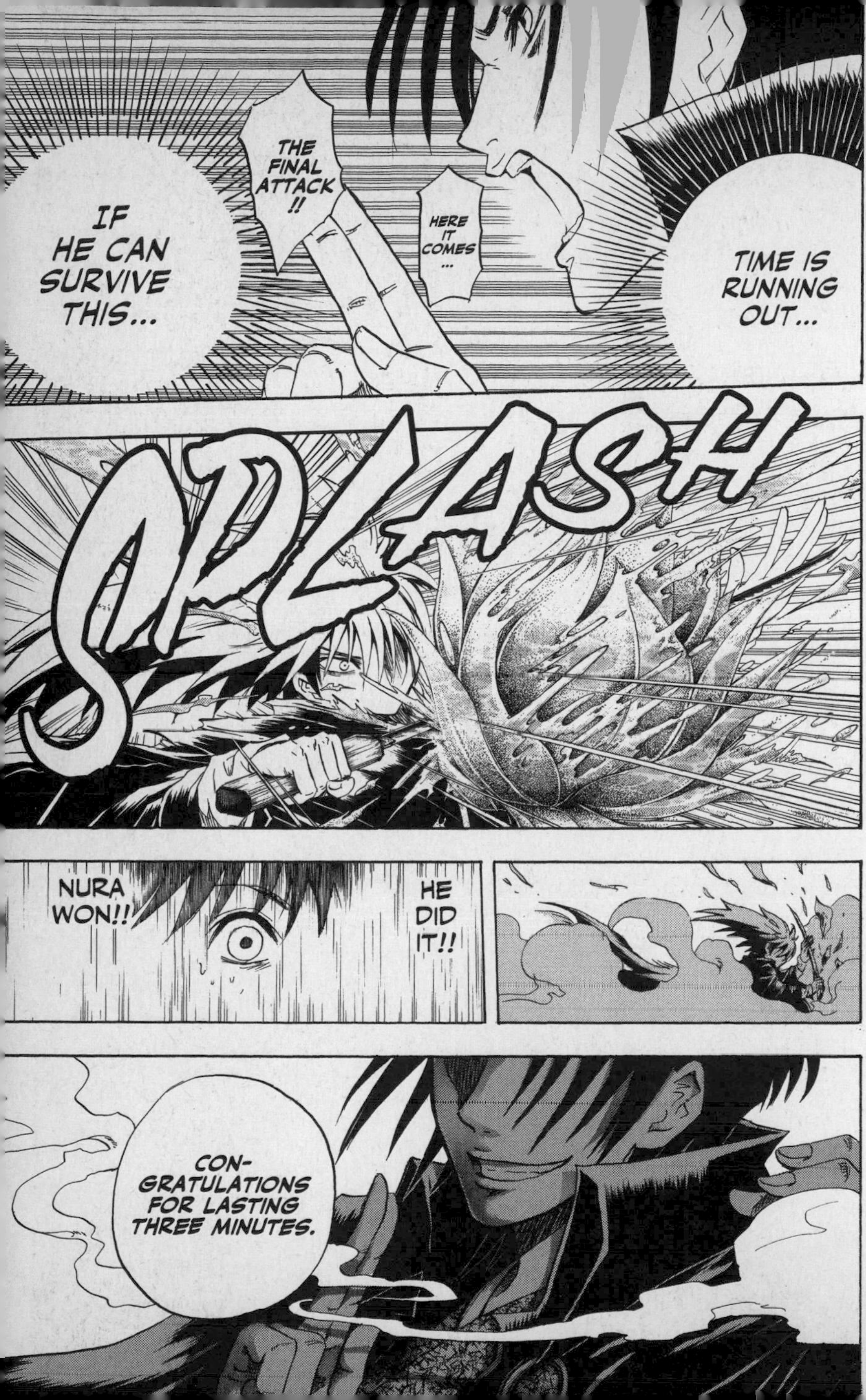
TIME IS RUNNING OUT...
HERE IT COMES...
THE FINAL ATTACK!!
IF HE CAN SURVIVE THIS...
SPLASH
HE DID IT!!
NURA WON!!
CON-GRATULATIONS FOR LASTING THREE MINUTES.

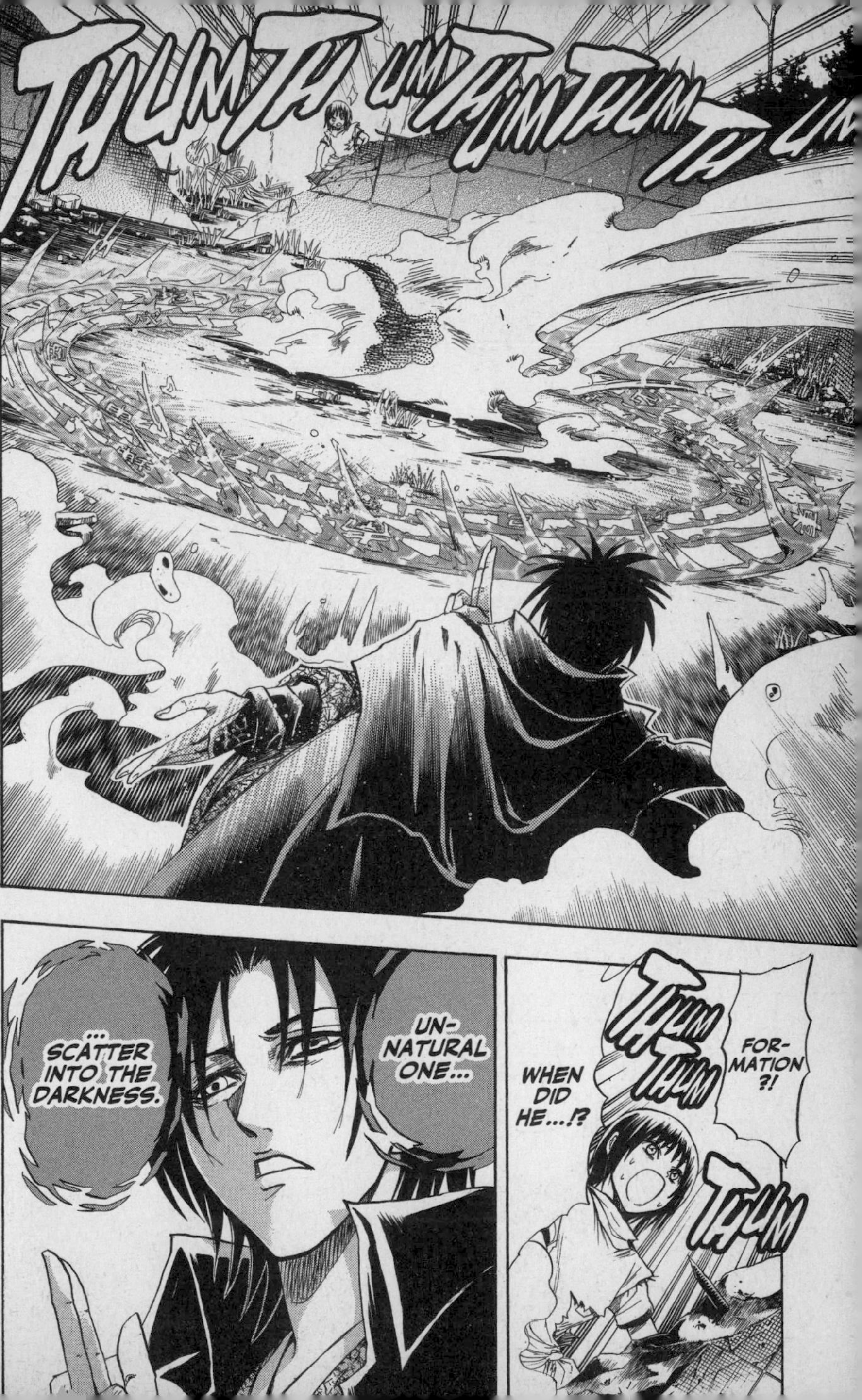
FOR-
MATION
?!
WHEN
DID
HE...!?
THUM THUM
THUM
UN-
NATURAL
ONE...
...
SCATTER
INTO THE
DARKNESS.

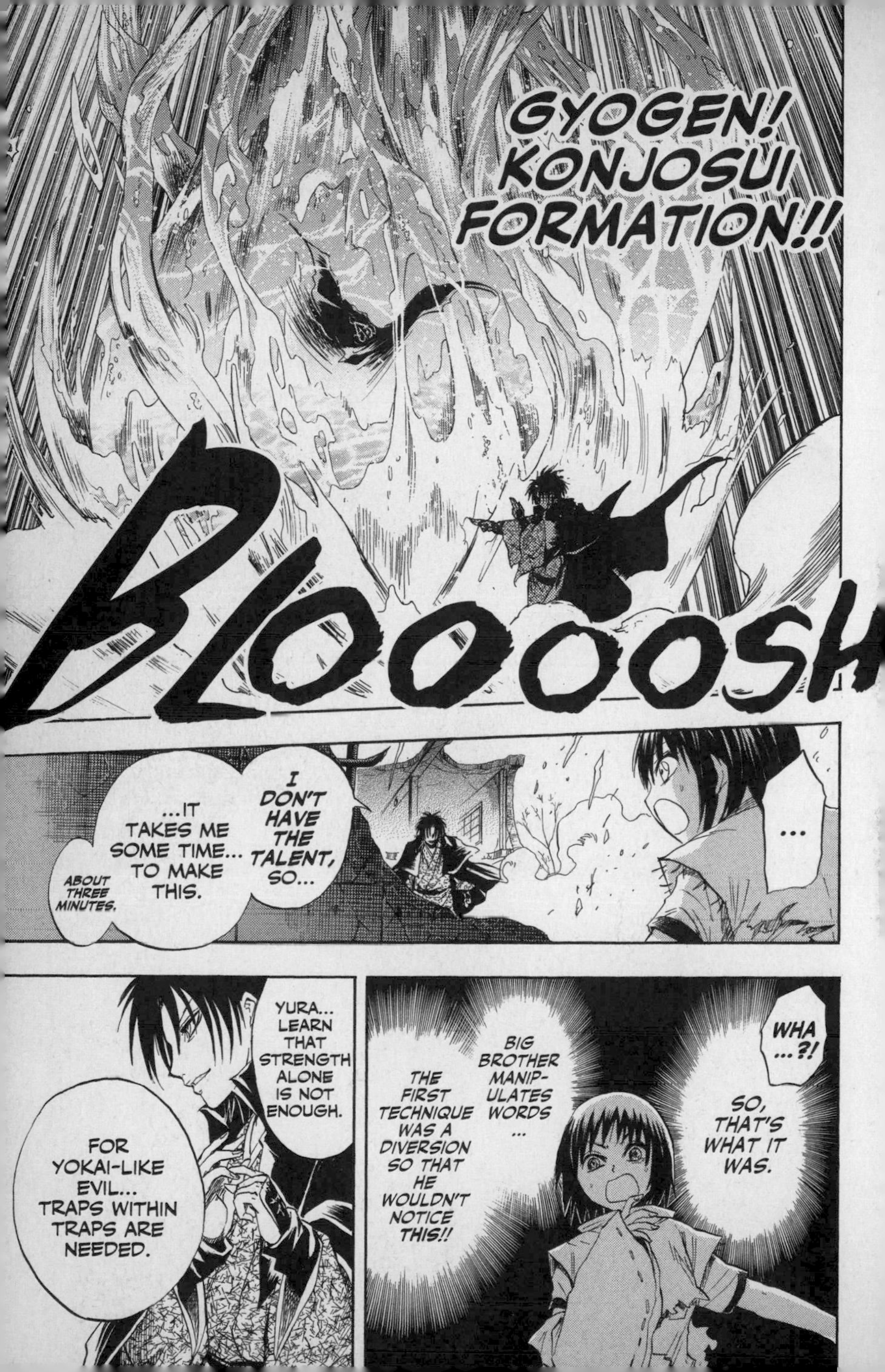
GYOGEN! KONJOSUI FORMATION!!
BLOOOOSH
...
I DON'T HAVE THE TALENT, SO...
...IT TAKES ME SOME TIME... TO MAKE THIS.
ABOUT THREE MINUTES.
WHA...?!
SO, THAT'S WHAT IT WAS.
BIG BROTHER MANIPULATES WORDS...
THE FIRST TECHNIQUE WAS A DIVERSION SO THAT HE WOULDN'T NOTICE THIS!!
YURA... LEARN THAT STRENGTH ALONE IS NOT ENOUGH.
FOR YOKAI-LIKE EVIL... TRAPS WITHIN TRAPS ARE NEEDED.

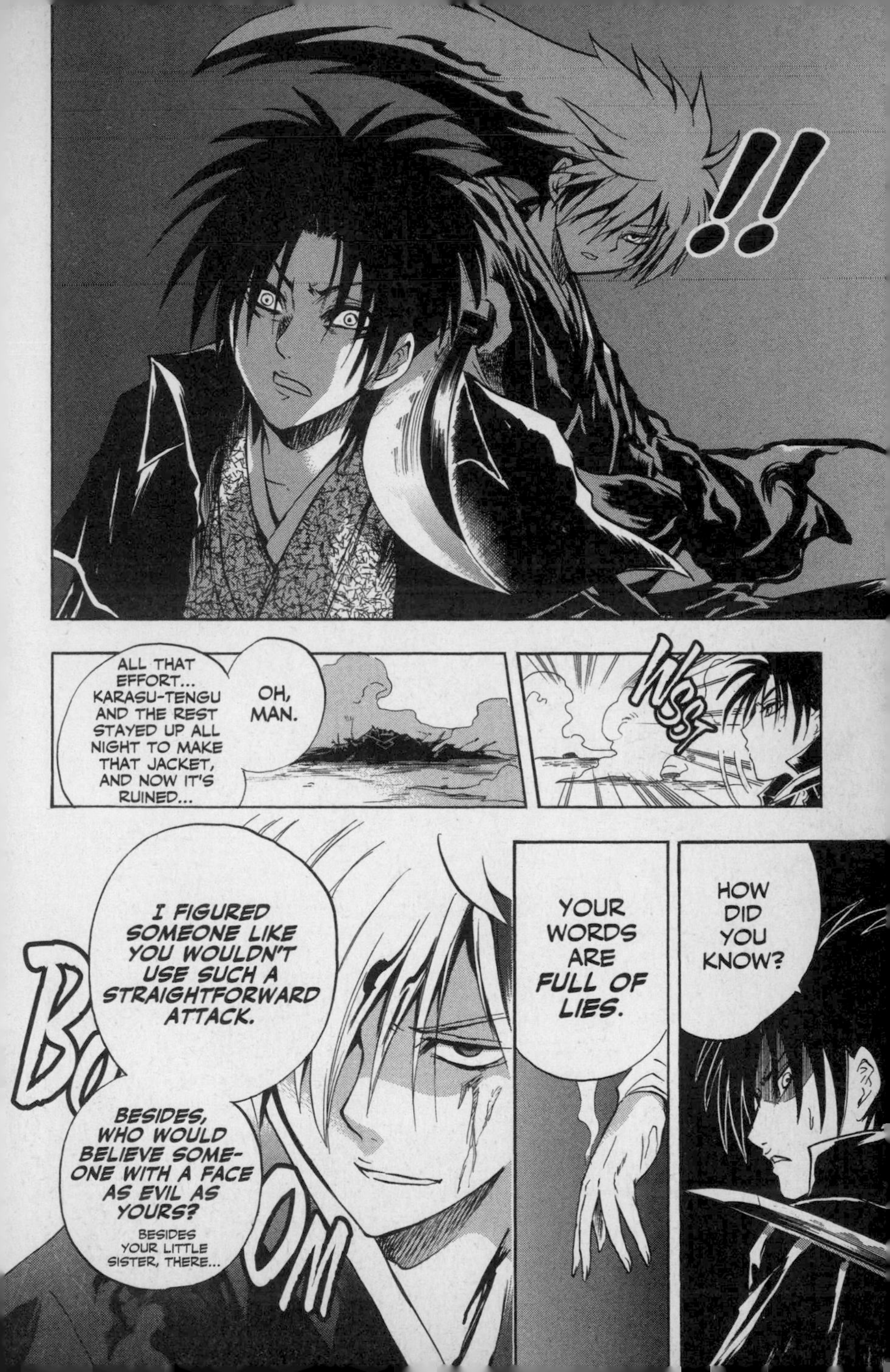
!!
OH, MAN.
ALL THAT EFFORT... KARASU-TENGU AND THE REST STAYED UP ALL NIGHT TO MAKE THAT JACKET, AND NOW IT'S RUINED...
HOW DID YOU KNOW?
YOUR WORDS ARE FULL OF LIES.
I FIGURED SOMEONE LIKE YOU WOULDN'T USE SUCH A STRAIGHTFORWARD ATTACK.
BESIDES, WHO WOULD BELIEVE SOME-ONE WITH A FACE AS EVIL AS YOURS?
BESIDES YOUR LITTLE SISTER, THERE...

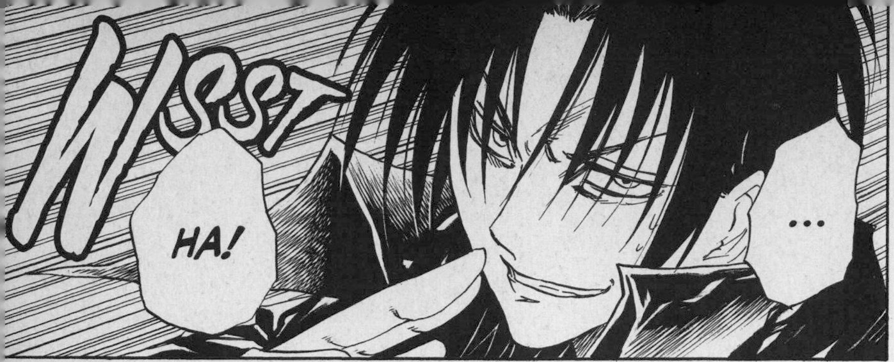
...
HA!
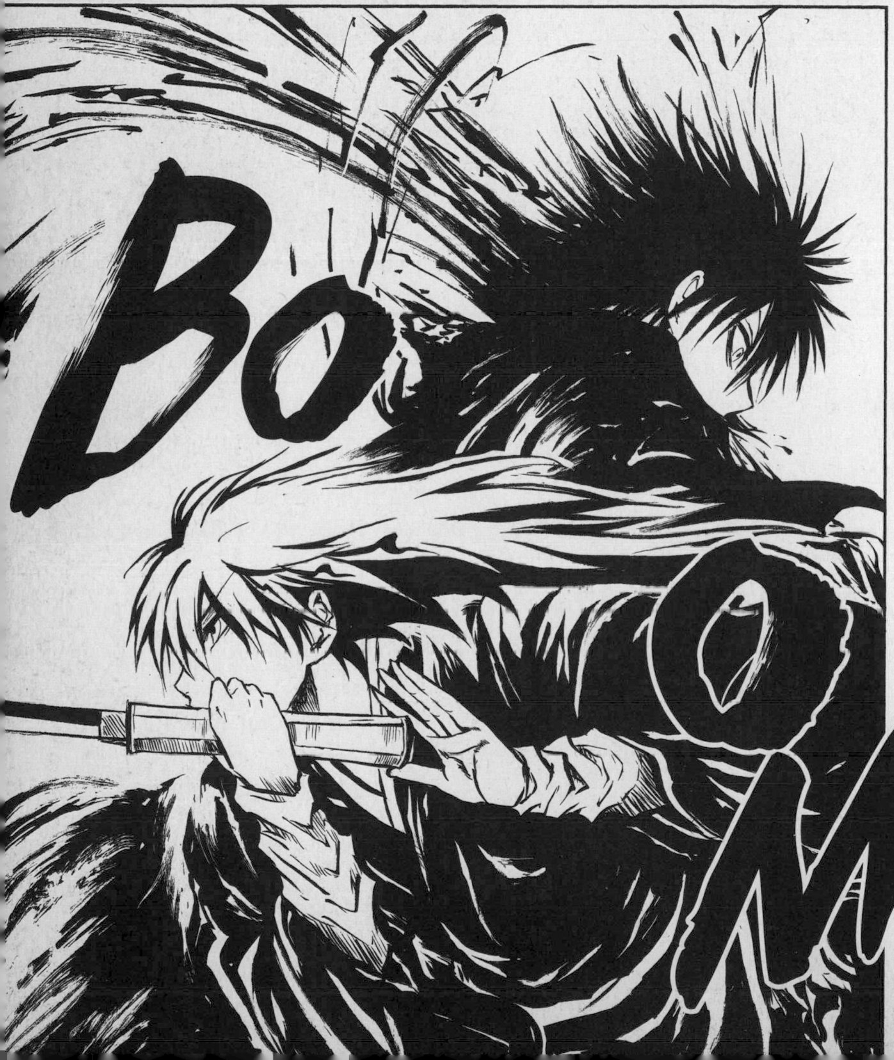
BOOM

Field Trip Edition #7 by Kiyo

# KIYOTSUGU'S YOKAI BRAIN

HEY! EVERYONE DOING OKAY OUT THERE?

KIYOTSUGU HERE!! THIS TIME AROUND, I'VE HAD ALL KINDS OF PEOPLE ANSWER YOUR QUESTIONS. OF COURSE, I WILL ANSWER SOME TOO!! YOKAI BRAIN HAS BECOME MORE CONVENIENT, AND THE KIYOJUJI PARANORMAL PATROL IS GETTING BIGGER!!

Q1: IS IT HARD FOR TSURARA TO BE AROUND FIRE WHEN SHE COOKS? ALSO, PLEASE TELL ME IF YOU HAVE A FAVORITE DISH YOU LIKE TO MAKE. *–TSERIN, GIFU PREFECTURE*

TSURARA: IT'S SO HARD BEING AROUND FIRE! (CRIES). BUT, I ENDURE IT FOR THE BENEFIT OF EVERYONE IN THE NURA CLAN. I TRY TO STAY AS FAR FROM IT AS I CAN, THOUGH! MY FAVORITE DISH IS SHAVED ICE, BUT...BASICALLY I CAN COOK ANYTHING. LATELY, I'VE BEEN MAKING CARPACCIO!

Q2: BETWEEN KUBINASHI, YUKI-ONNA AND SANBA-GARASU, WHO IS THE OLDEST? *–NASHI, IWATE PREFECTURE*

KUBINASHI: THAT WOULD BE ME. I WAS BORN DURING THE EDO PERIOD, AND I'LL TELL THAT STORY SOMEDAY. TSURARA AND THE SANBA-GARASU ARE ACTUALLY PRETTY YOUNG.

Q3: I LIKE KAPPA ♡. I SAW HIM WEARING HEADPHONES...WHAT MUSIC WAS HE LISTENING TO? *–KAPPAA, YAMAGATA PREFECTURE*

KAPPA: ANYTHING WITH A GOOD RHYTHM, BUT MOSTLY STUFF FROM OUTSIDE JAPAN.

Q4: KIYOTSUGU AND RIKUO...WHICH ONE IS MORE POPULAR AT SCHOOL? *–TADASHI SUZUKI, FUKUOKA PREFECTURE*

MAKI: I DON'T THINK EITHER OF THEM ARE...

TORII: I AGREE.

Q5: QUESTION FOR RIKUO!! OUT OF ALL THE YOKAI YOU'VE BATTLED SO FAR, WHO WAS THE HARDEST ONE TO DEFEAT? *–TSUBAS-CHAN, YAMAGATA PREFECTURE*

NIGHT RIKUO: HM? WHO WOULD IT BE...? YOSUZUME OR TAMAZUKI, PERHAPS...

Q6: WHY DOES NIGHT RIKUO ALWAYS HAVE HIS HANDS INSIDE HIS CLOTHES? IS IT BECAUSE YOUR BLOOD IS HOT? *–NORIKO FUSHIMI, SHIZUOKA PREFECTURE*

NIGHT RIKUO: ...

Q7: WHERE DOES THE KIYOJUJI PATROL MEET? *–MACHI KOBUNE, TOKYO*

KANA: WE'RE BORROWING THE SOCIAL SCIENCES PREP ROOM THAT'S NOT BEING USED!! UNTIL RECENTLY, WE USED TO MEET IN OUR CLASSROOM THOUGH. OH, BUT YURA IS USUALLY UP ON THE ROOF...I THINK?

Q8: HOW TALL ARE RYUJI AND MAMIRU? RYUJI WEARS HIGH WOODEN CLOGS, BUT THERE STILL SEEMS TO BE QUITE A DIFFERENCE... *–MIDORI, SHIZUOKA PREFECTURE*

YURA: QUITE A BIG DIFFERENCE, BUT DON'T SAY THAT IN FRONT OF BIG BROTHER. HE'LL DO SOMETHING MEAN TO YOU!!

(TO BE CONTINUED IN VOLUME 8)

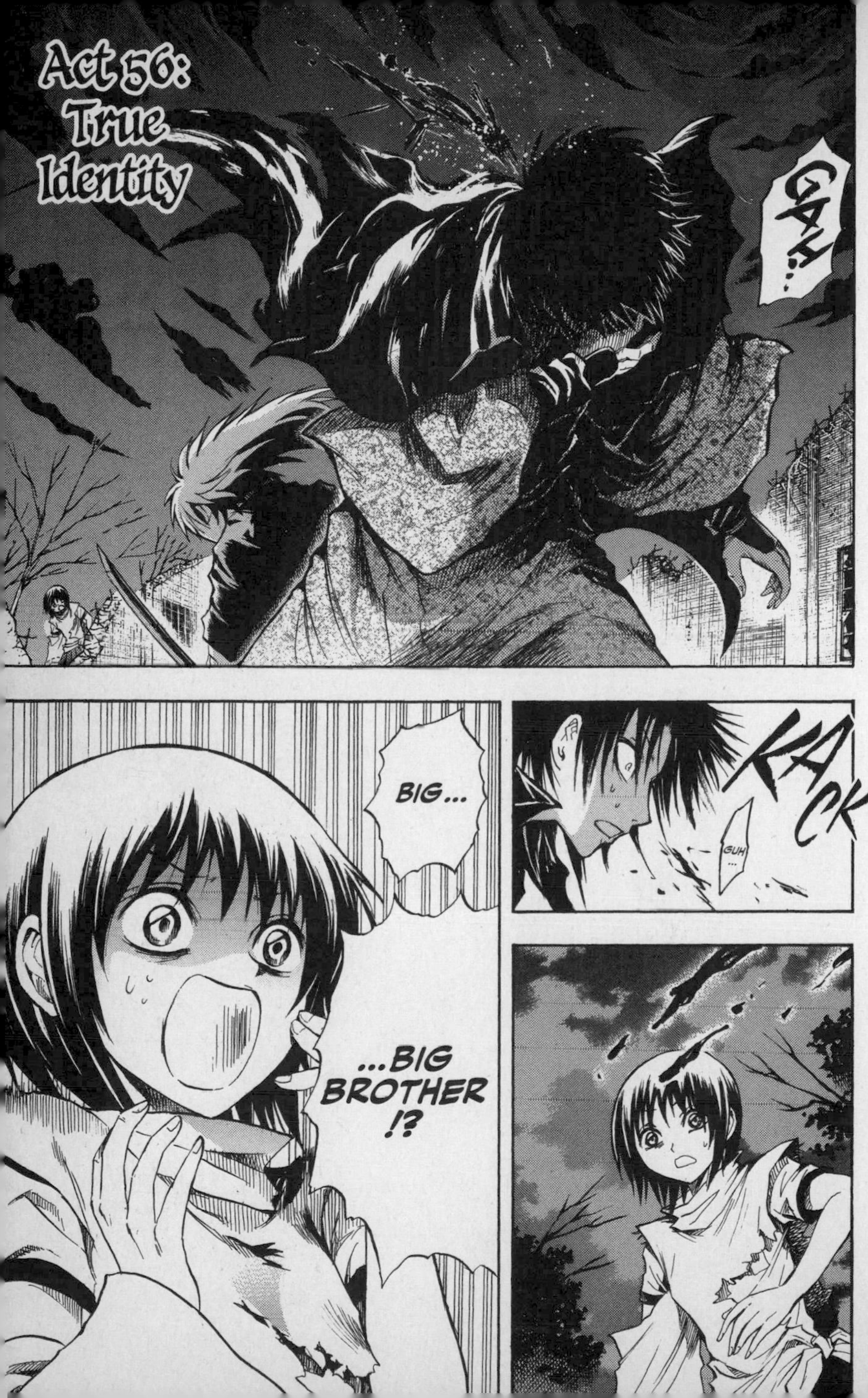
Act 56: True Identity
GAH...
KACK
GUH...
BIG...
...BIG BROTHER!?

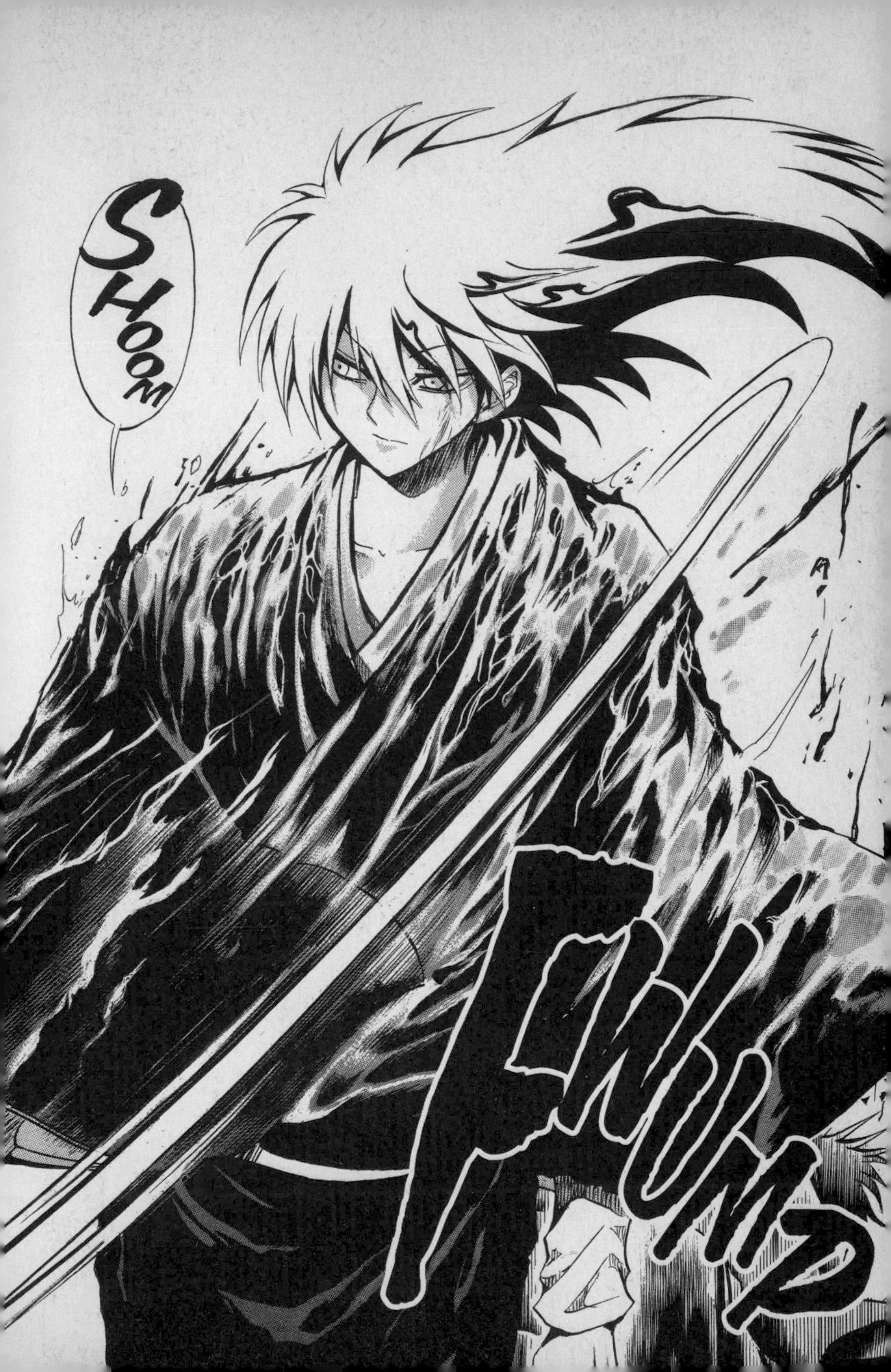
SHOOM
FWUMP

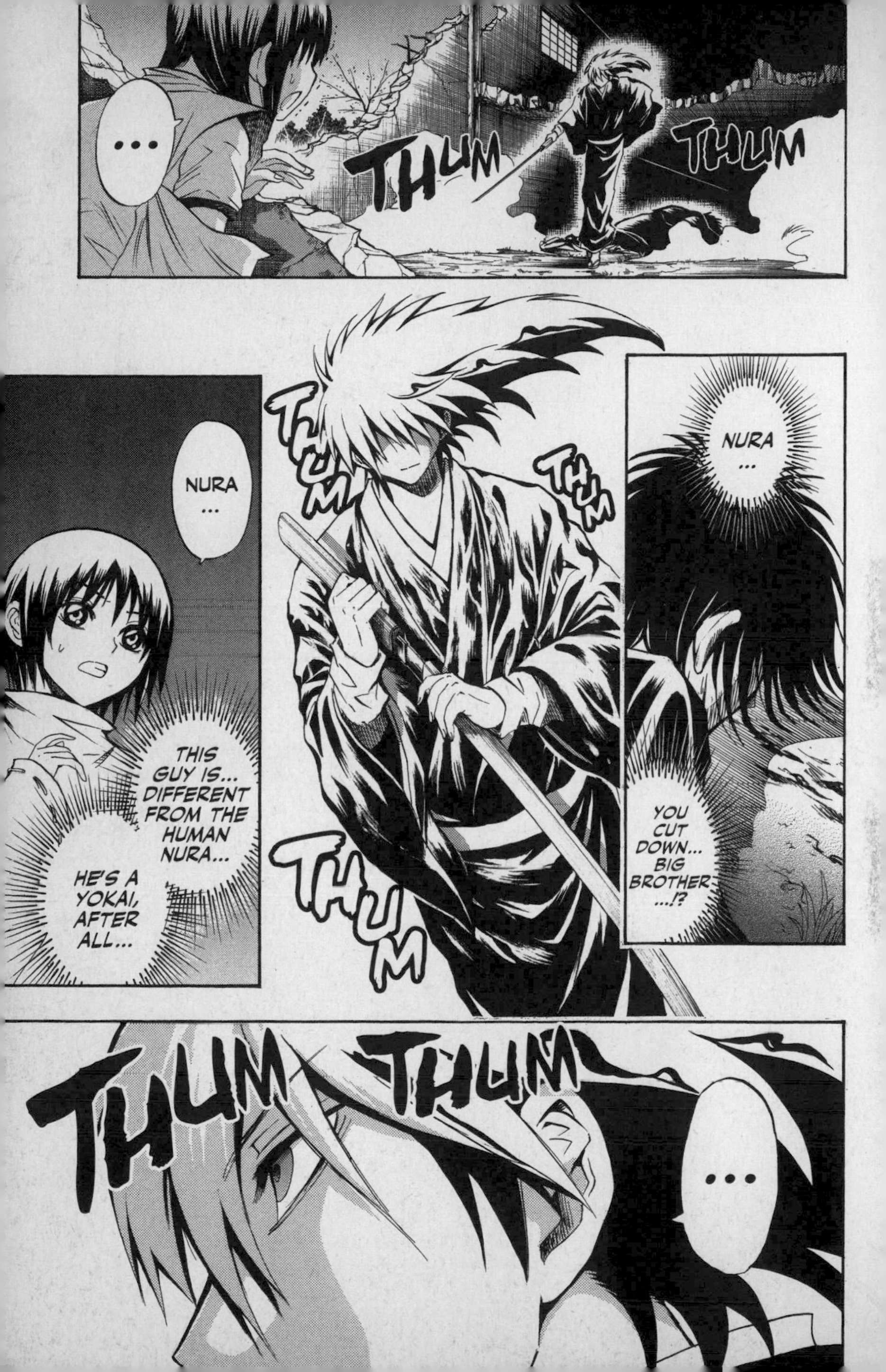
THUM
THUM
...
NURA...
YOU CUT DOWN... BIG BROTHER...!?
THUM
THUM
THUM
THUM
NURA...
THIS GUY IS... DIFFERENT FROM THE HUMAN NURA...
HE'S A YOKAI, AFTER ALL...
...
THUM
THUM

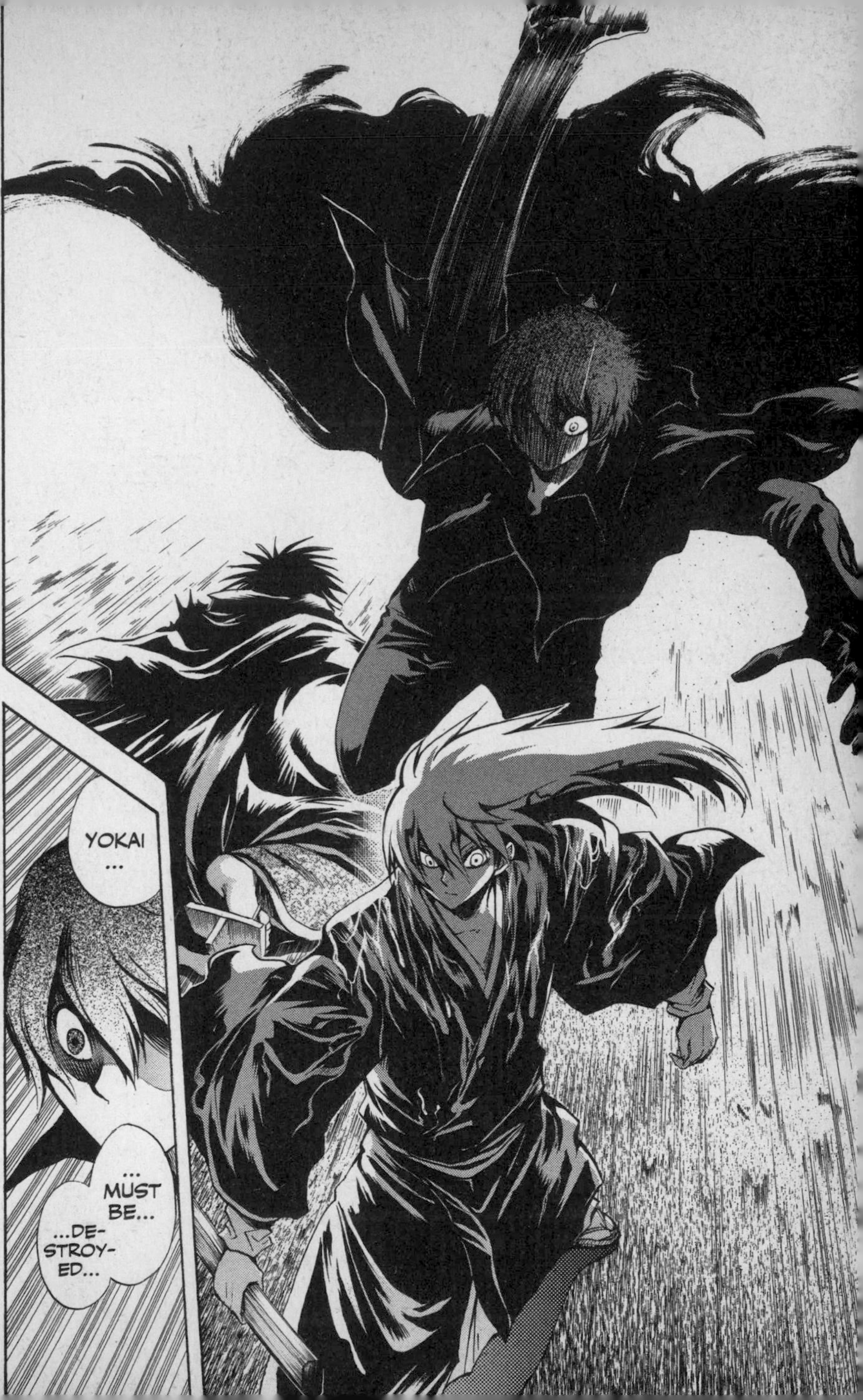
YOKAI ...
... MUST BE... ...DE-STROY-ED...

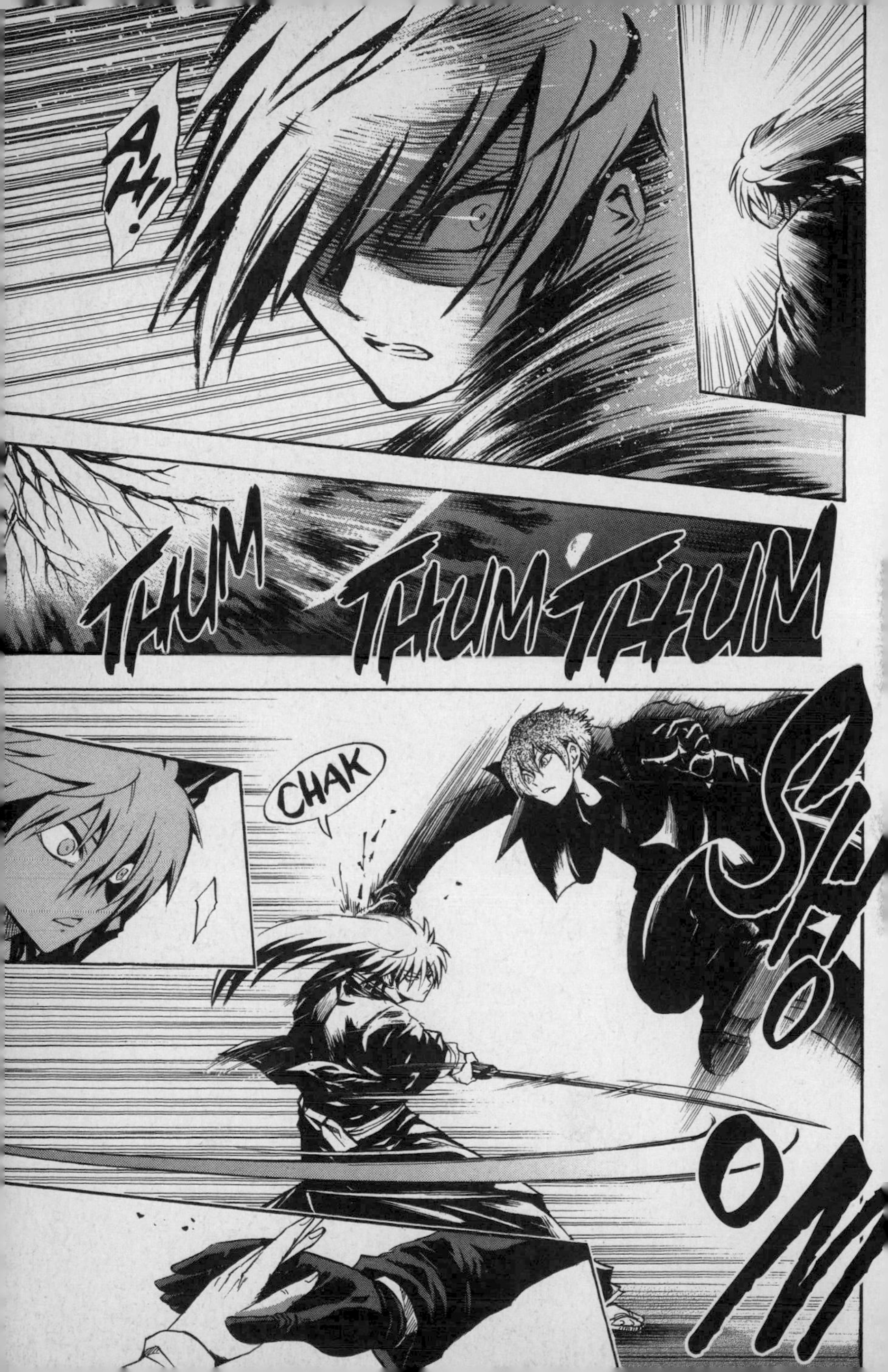
AH!
THUM
THUM THUM
CHAK
SHOOM

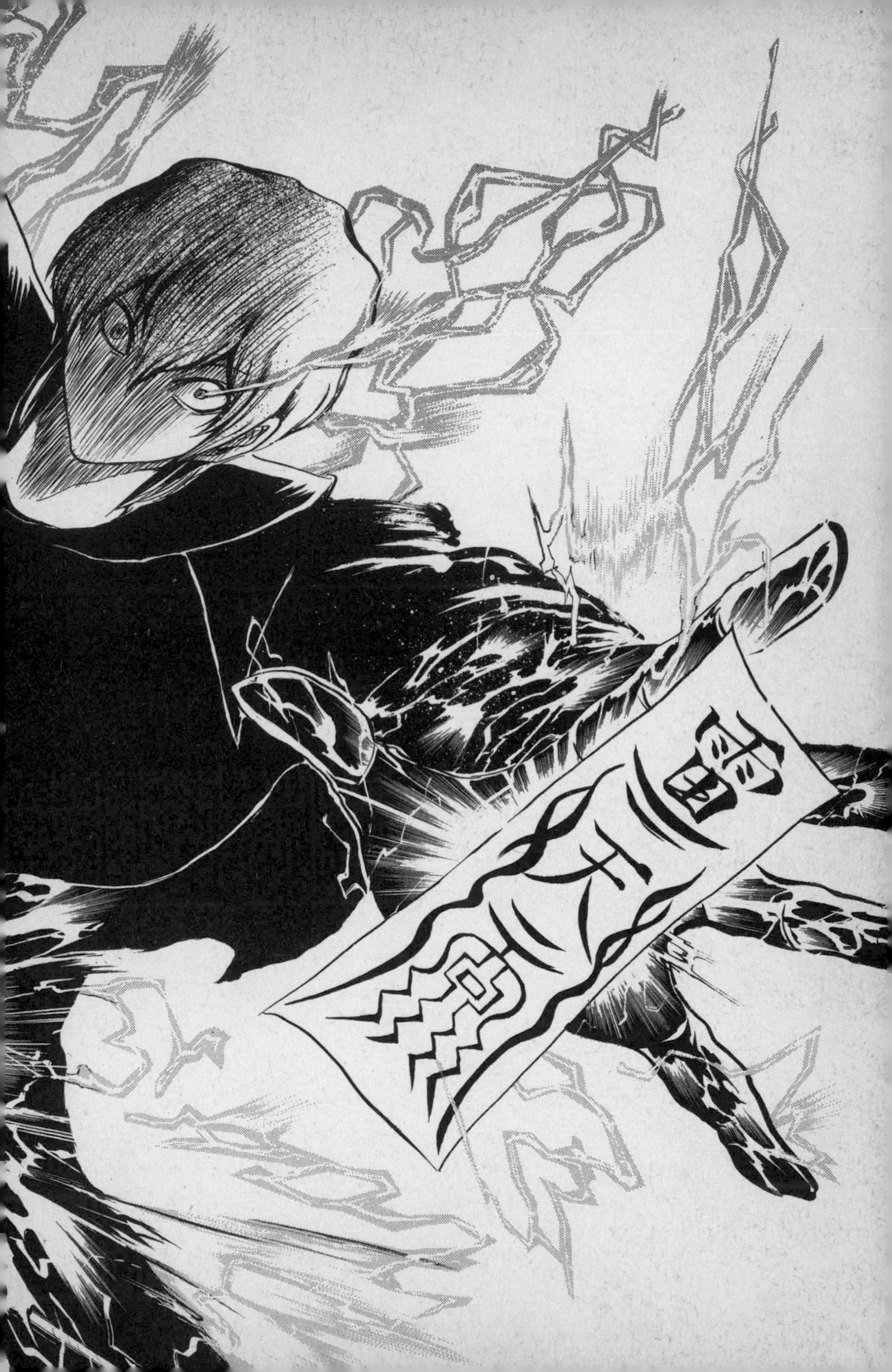

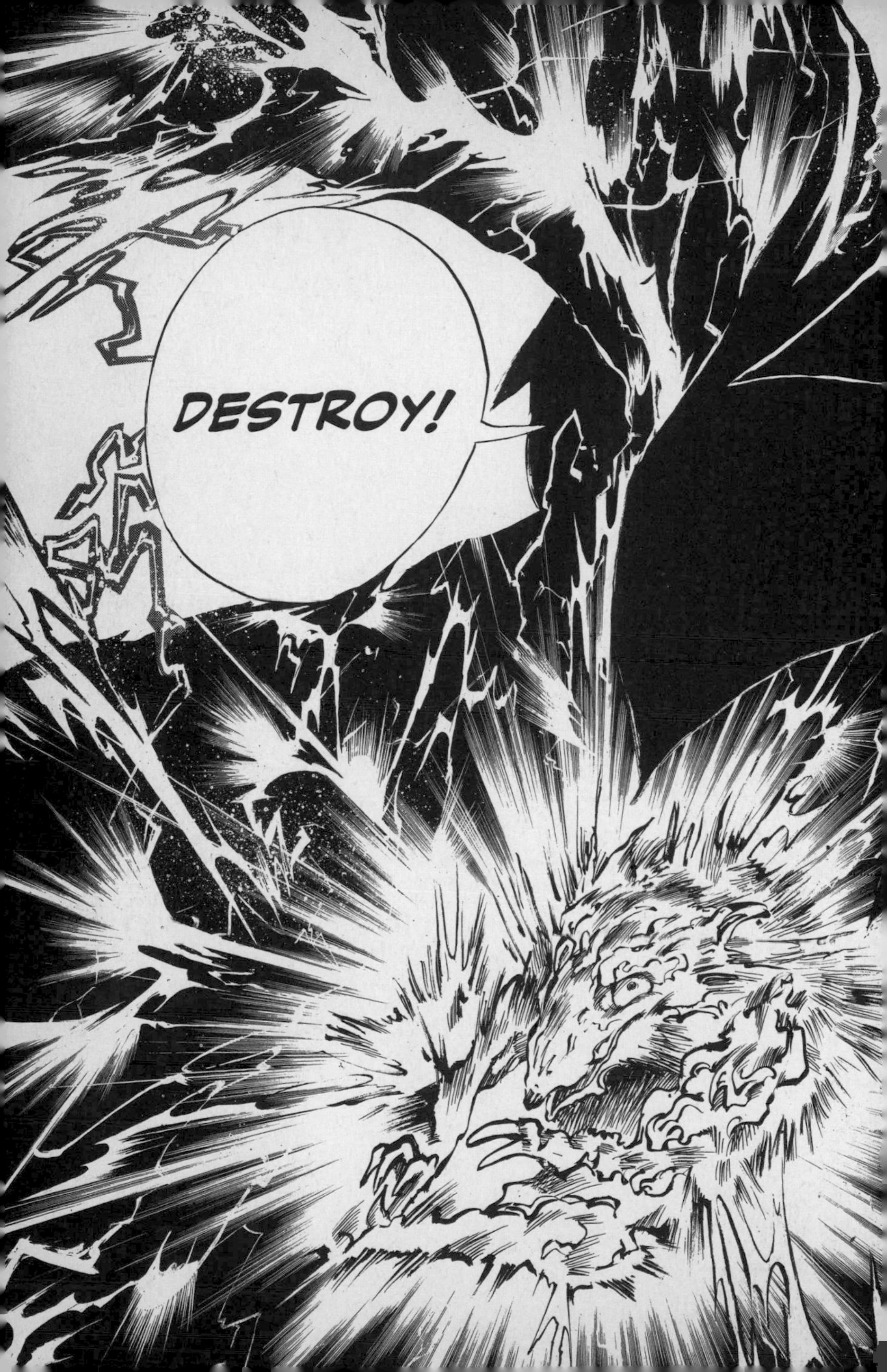
DESTROY!

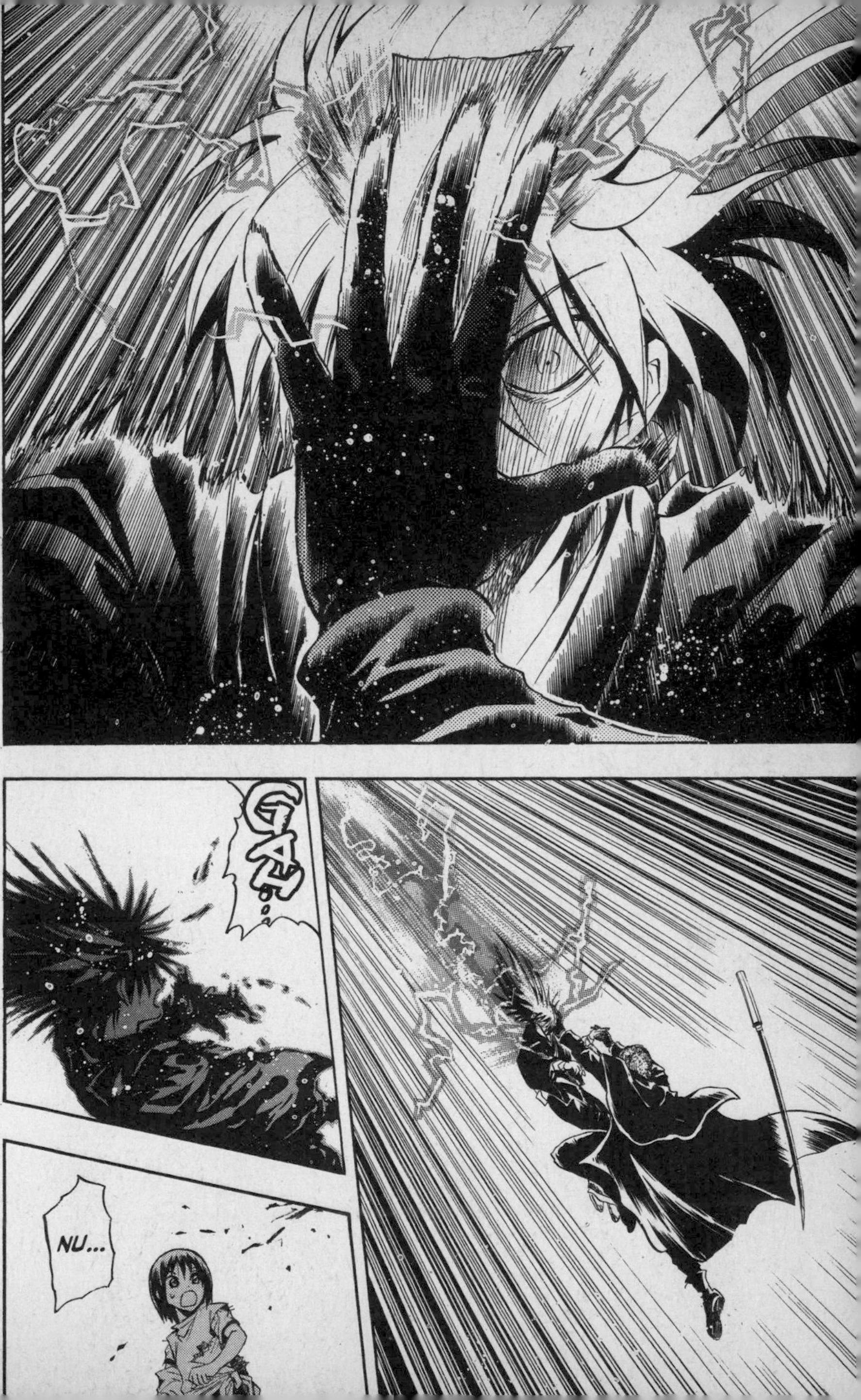
GAH...
NU...

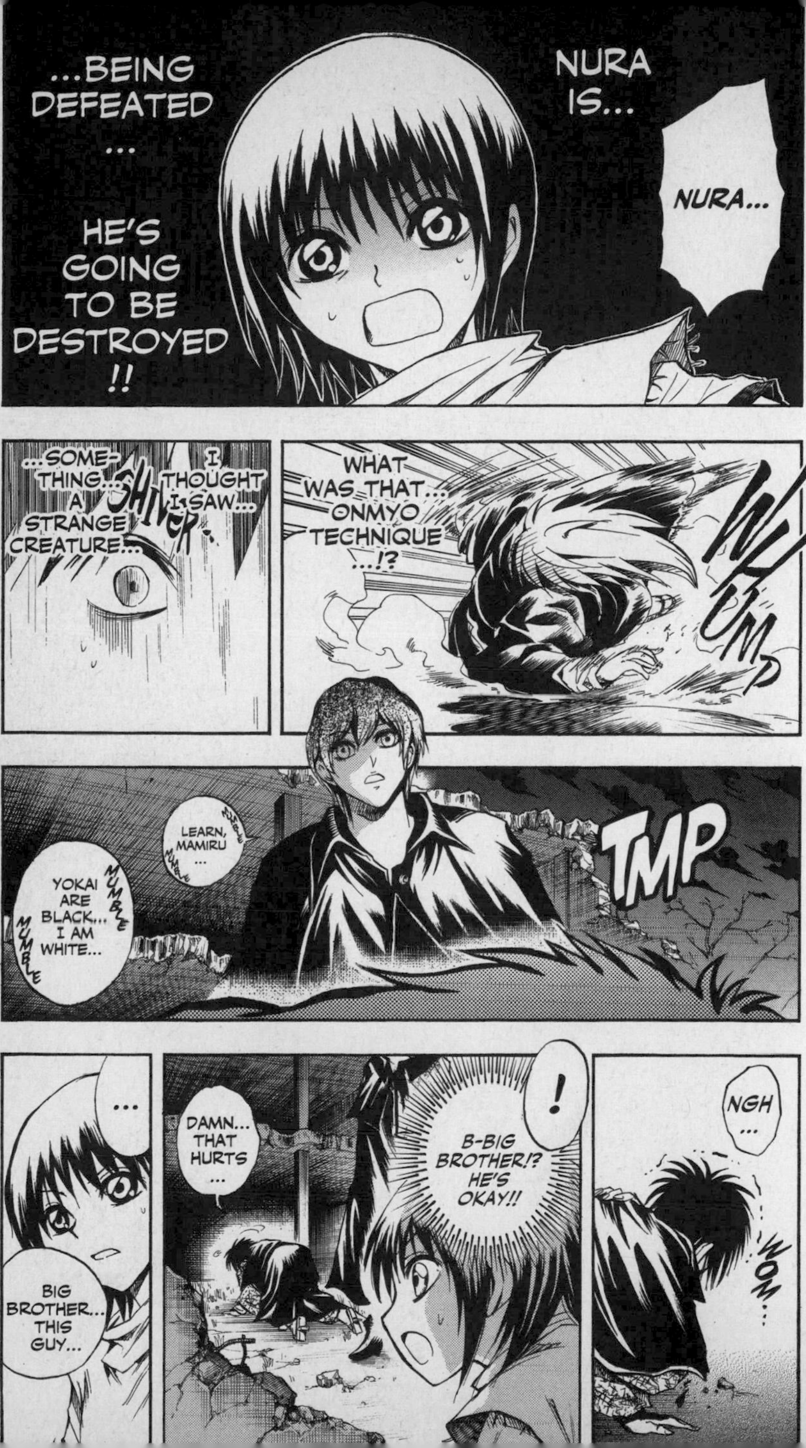
NURA IS...
NURA...
...BEING DEFEATED ...
HE'S GOING TO BE DESTROYED !!
WHUMP
WHAT WAS THAT... ONMYO TECHNIQUE ...!?
I THOUGHT I SAW...
...SOME-THING... A STRANGE CREATURE...
SHIVER
TMP
LEARN, MAMIRU ...
YOKAI ARE BLACK... I AM WHITE...
MUMBLE
MUMBLE
NGH ...
!
B-BIG BROTHER!? HE'S OKAY!!
DAMN... THAT HURTS ...
...
BIG BROTHER... THIS GUY...

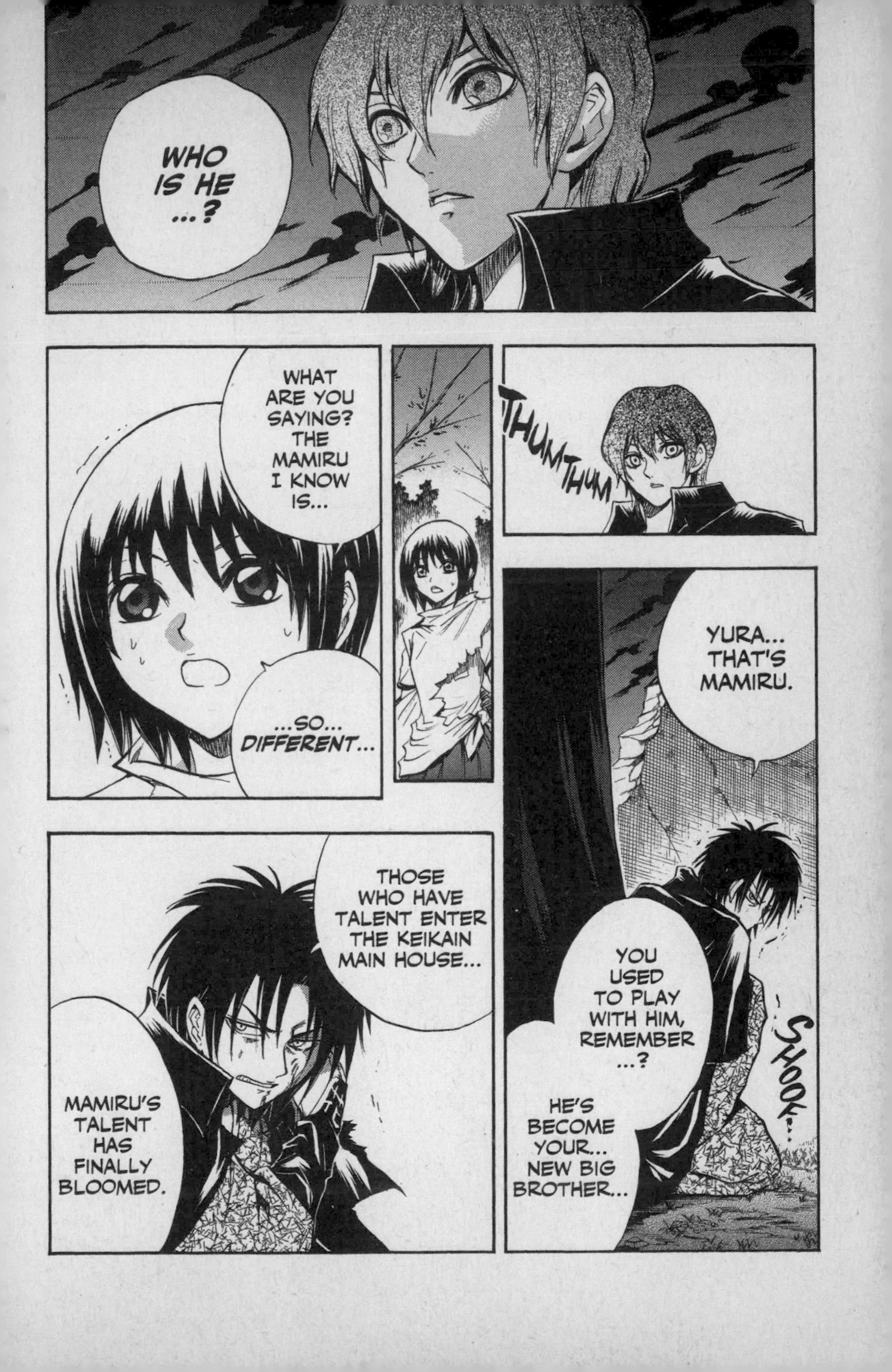
WHO IS HE ...?
THUMTHUM
WHAT ARE YOU SAYING? THE MAMIRU I KNOW IS...
...SO... DIFFERENT...
YURA... THAT'S MAMIRU.
YOU USED TO PLAY WITH HIM, REMEMBER ...?
HE'S BECOME YOUR... NEW BIG BROTHER...
SHOOK...
THOSE WHO HAVE TALENT ENTER THE KEIKAIN MAIN HOUSE...
MAMIRU'S TALENT HAS FINALLY BLOOMED.

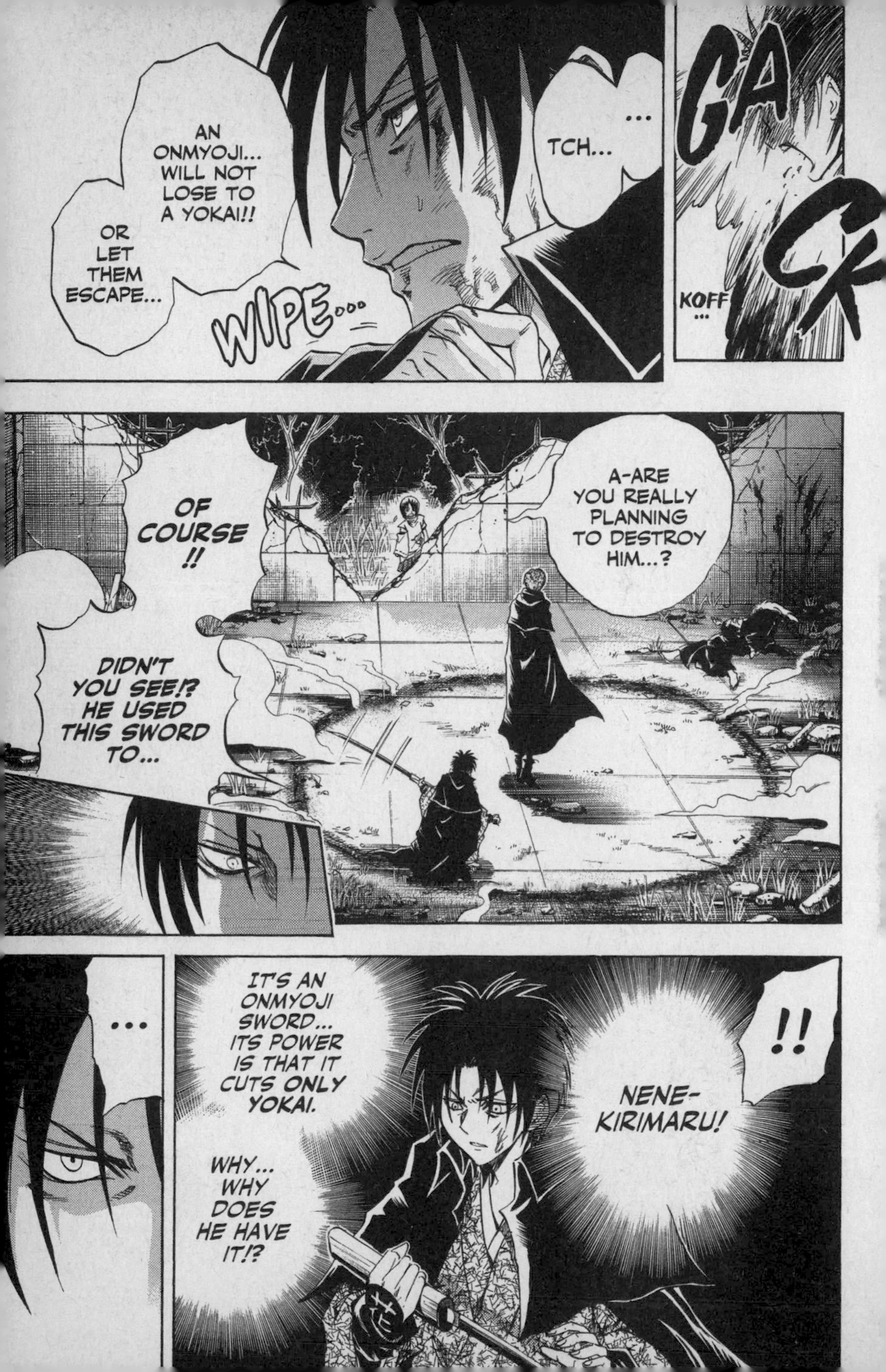
GACK
KOFF...
... TCH...
AN ONMYOJI... WILL NOT LOSE TO A YOKAI!!
OR LET THEM ESCAPE...
WIPE...
A-ARE YOU REALLY PLANNING TO DESTROY HIM...?
OF COURSE!!
DIDN'T YOU SEE!? HE USED THIS SWORD TO...
!!
NENE-KIRIMARU!
IT'S AN ONMYOJI SWORD... ITS POWER IS THAT IT CUTS ONLY YOKAI.
WHY... WHY DOES HE HAVE IT!?
...

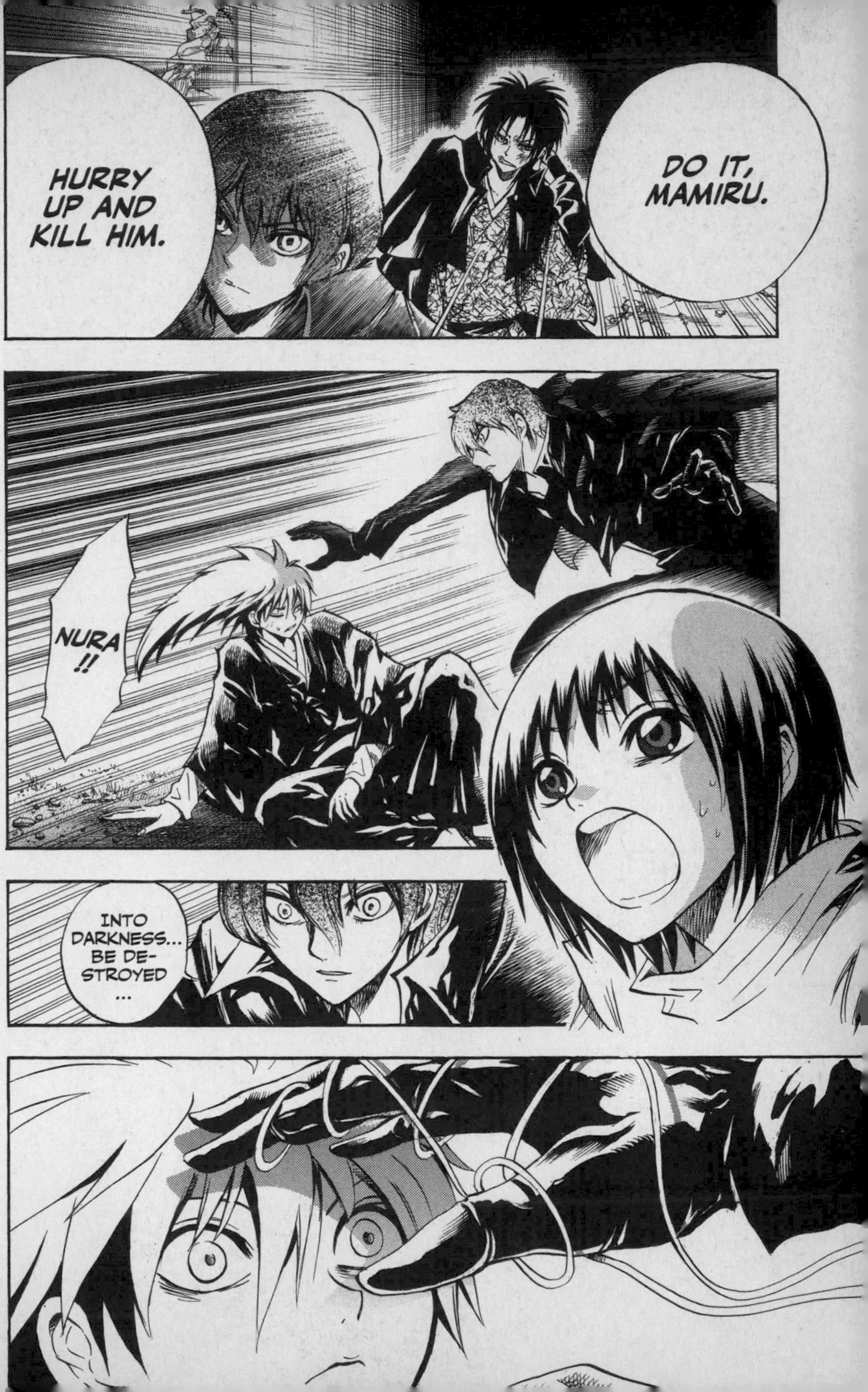
DO IT, MAMIRU.
HURRY UP AND KILL HIM.
NURA!!
INTO DARKNESS... BE DE-STROYED...

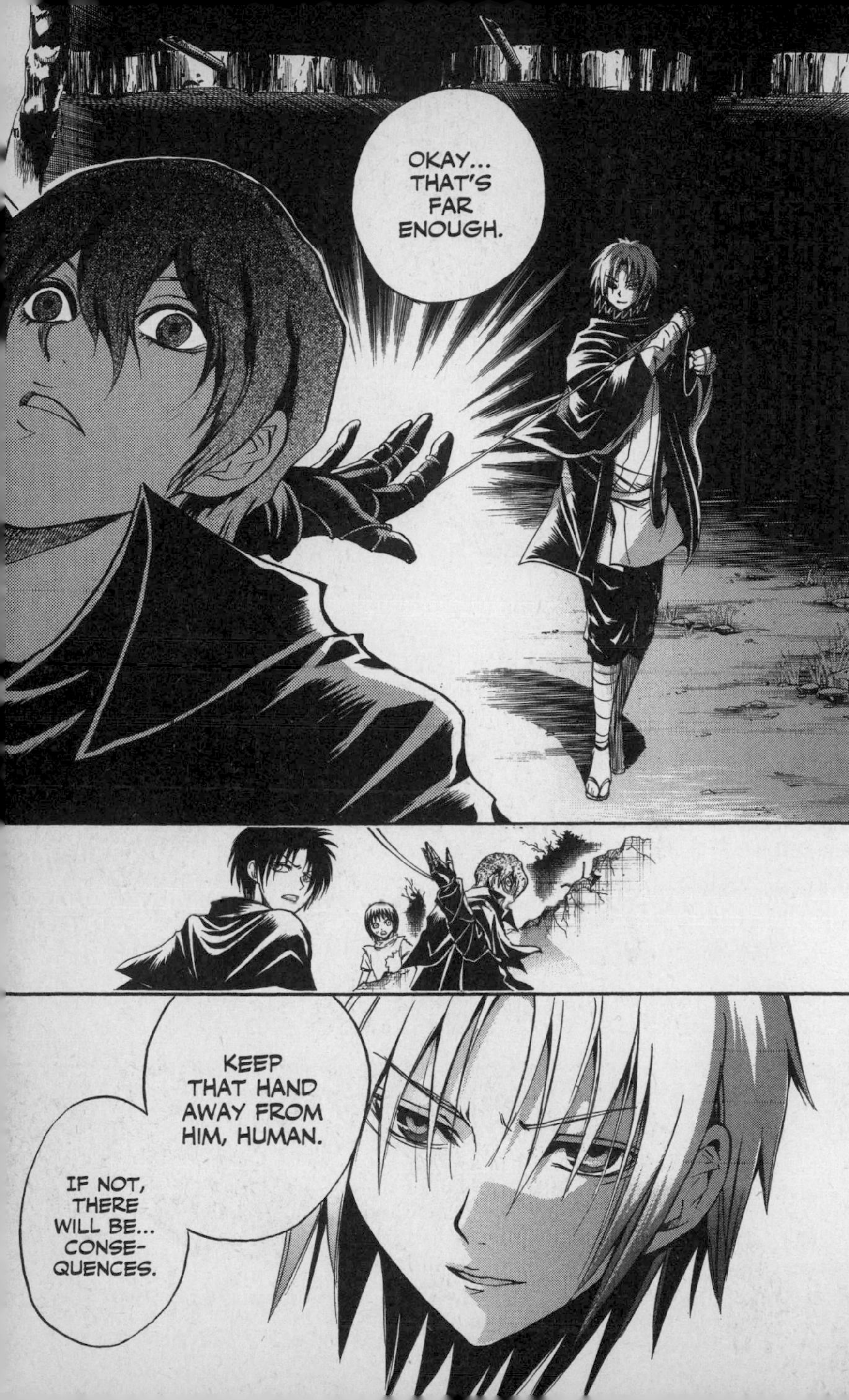
OKAY... THAT'S FAR ENOUGH.
KEEP THAT HAND AWAY FROM HIM, HUMAN.
IF NOT, THERE WILL BE... CONSE-QUENCES.

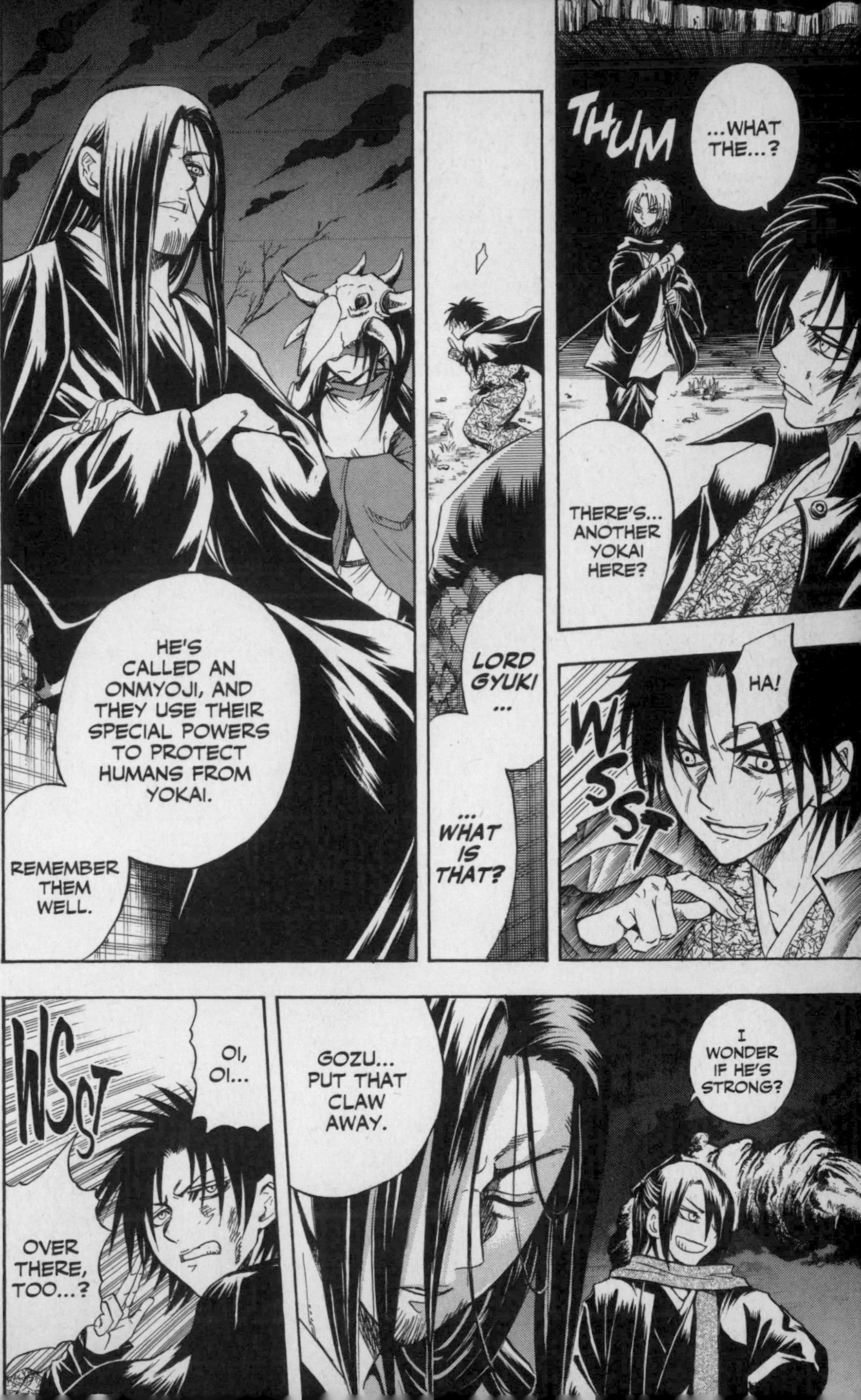
THUM
...WHAT THE...?
THERE'S... ANOTHER YOKAI HERE?
HA!
WISSST
LORD GYUKI...
...WHAT IS THAT?
HE'S CALLED AN ONMYOJI, AND THEY USE THEIR SPECIAL POWERS TO PROTECT HUMANS FROM YOKAI.
REMEMBER THEM WELL.
I WONDER IF HE'S STRONG?
GOZU... PUT THAT CLAW AWAY.
WSST
OI, OI...
OVER THERE, TOO...?

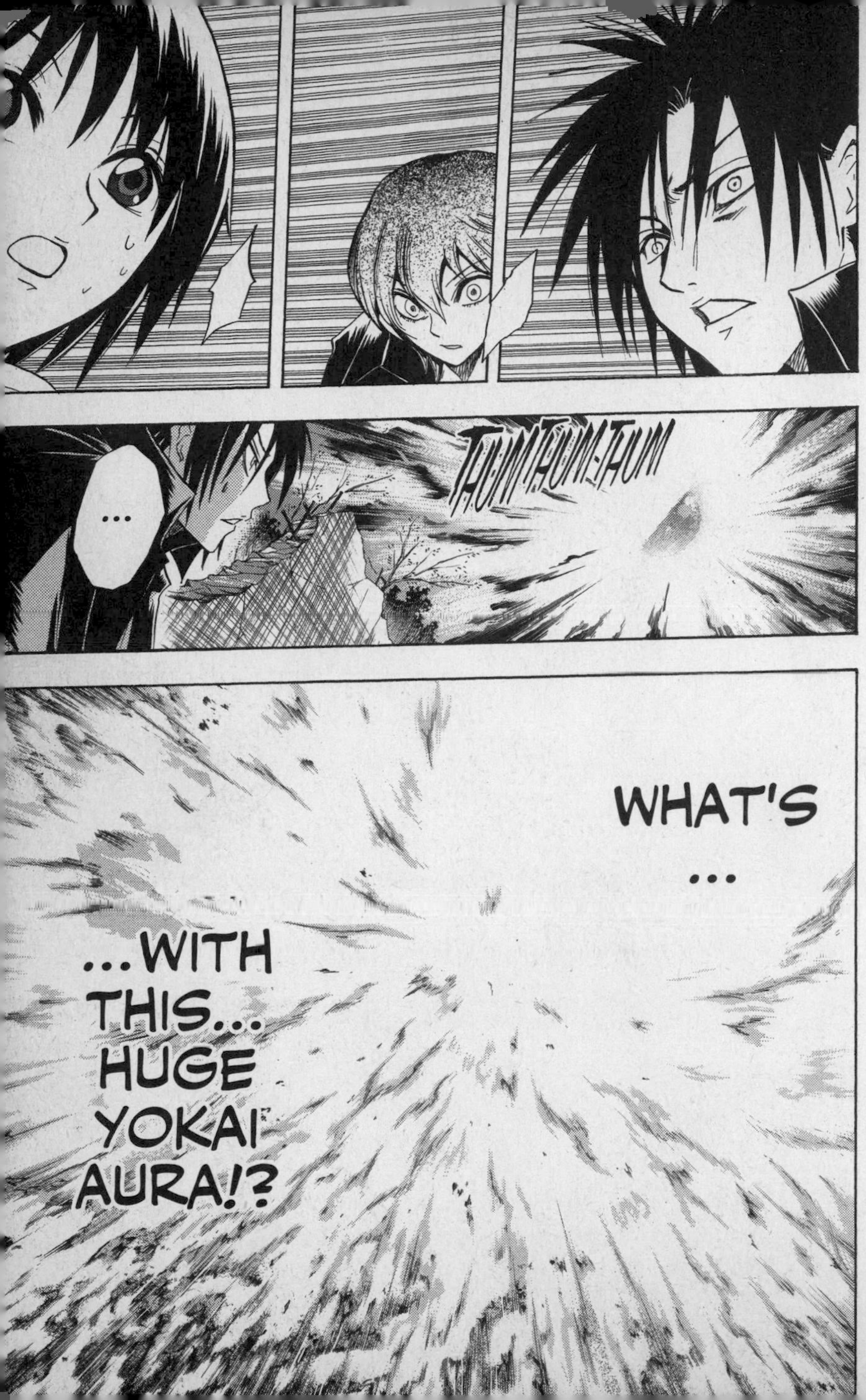
THUM THUM THUM
...
WHAT'S ...
...WITH THIS... HUGE YOKAI AURA!?

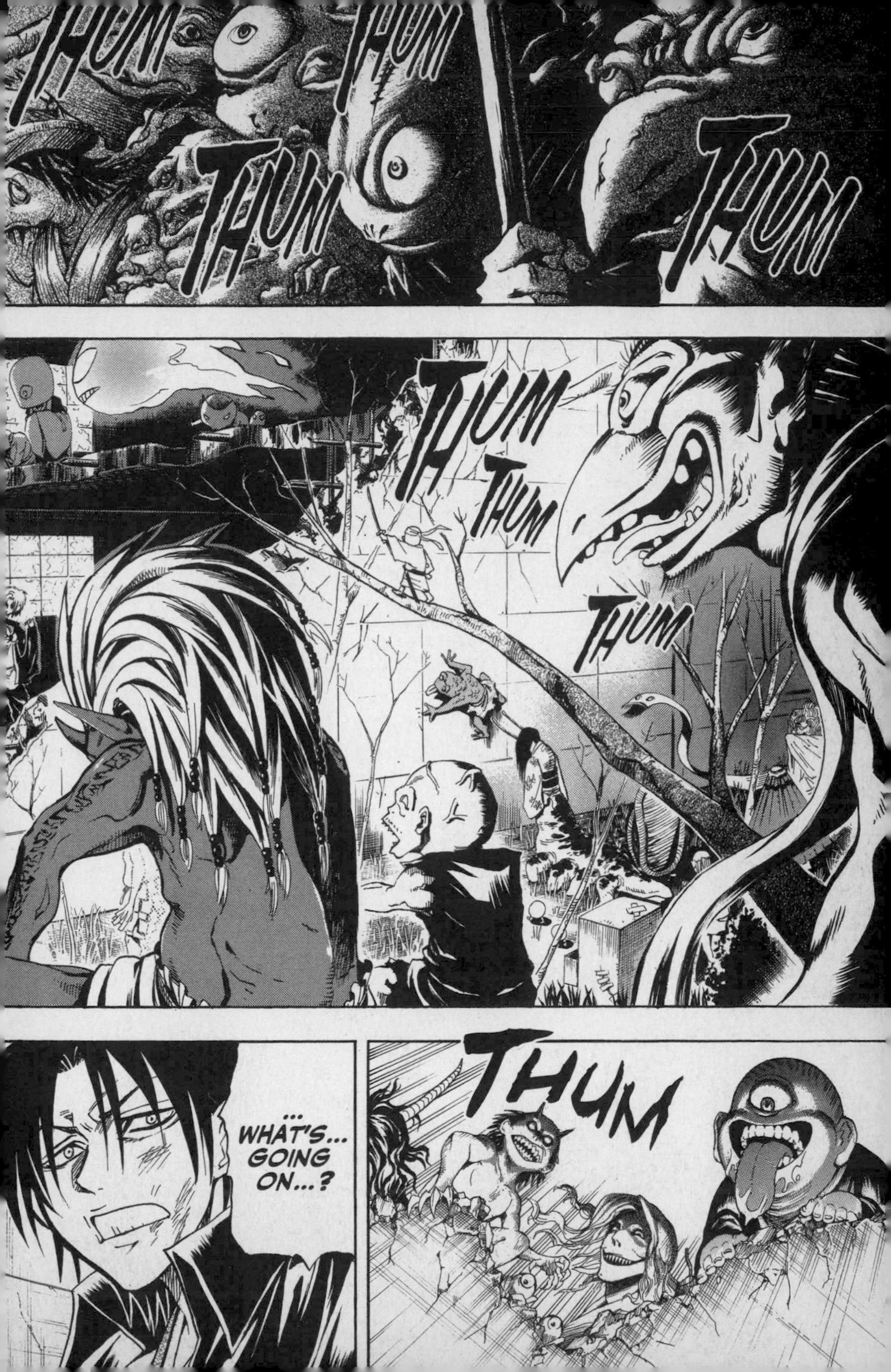
THUM
THUM
THUM
THUM
THUM
THUM
THUM
THUM
THUM
... WHAT'S... GOING ON...?

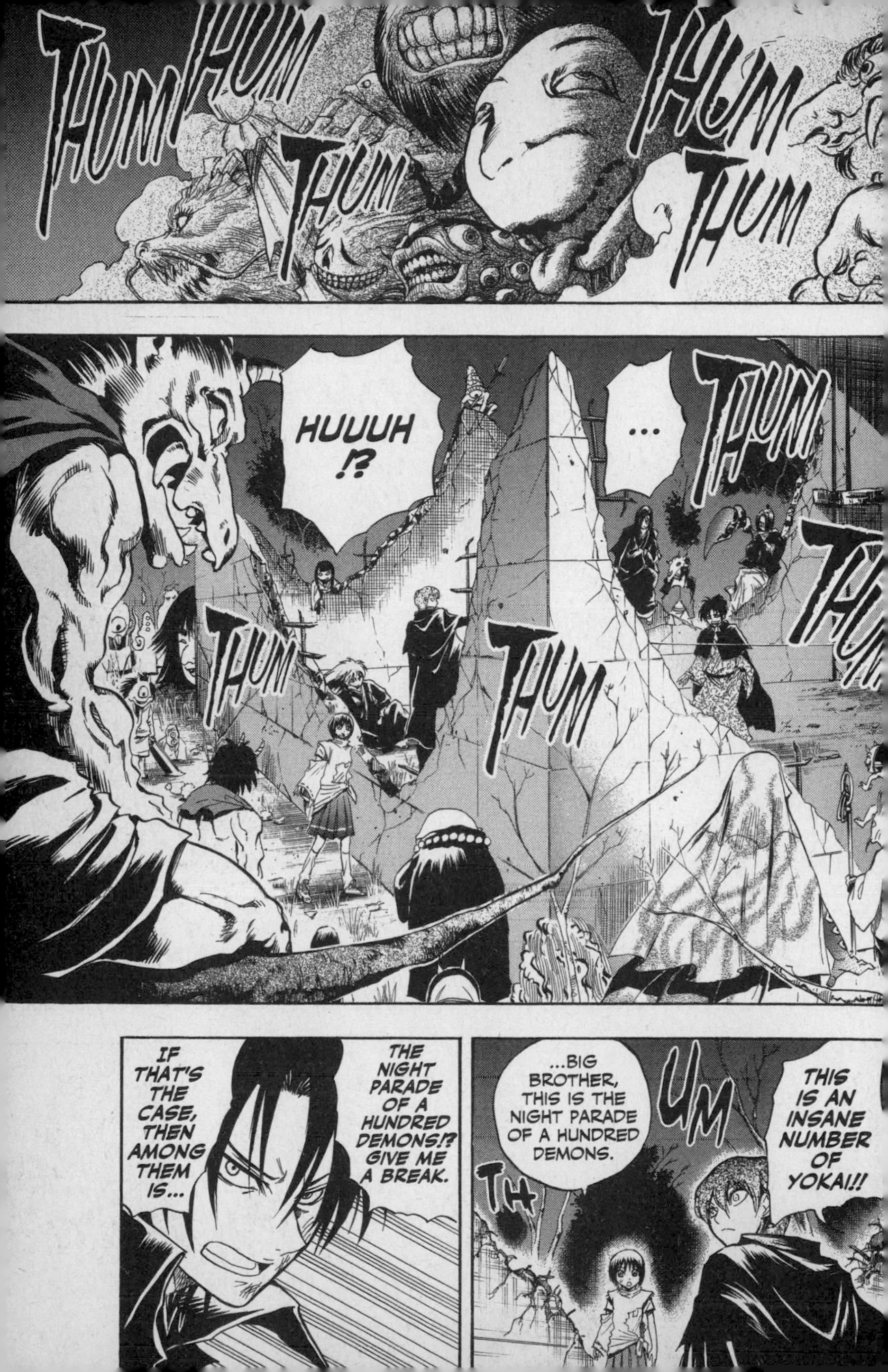
HUM
THUM
THUM
HUM
THUM
THUM
THUM
...
THUM
HUUUH !?
THUM
THIS IS AN INSANE NUMBER OF YOKAI!!
UM
...BIG BROTHER, THIS IS THE NIGHT PARADE OF A HUNDRED DEMONS.
TH
THE NIGHT PARADE OF A HUNDRED DEMONS!? GIVE ME A BREAK.
IF THAT'S THE CASE, THEN AMONG THEM IS...

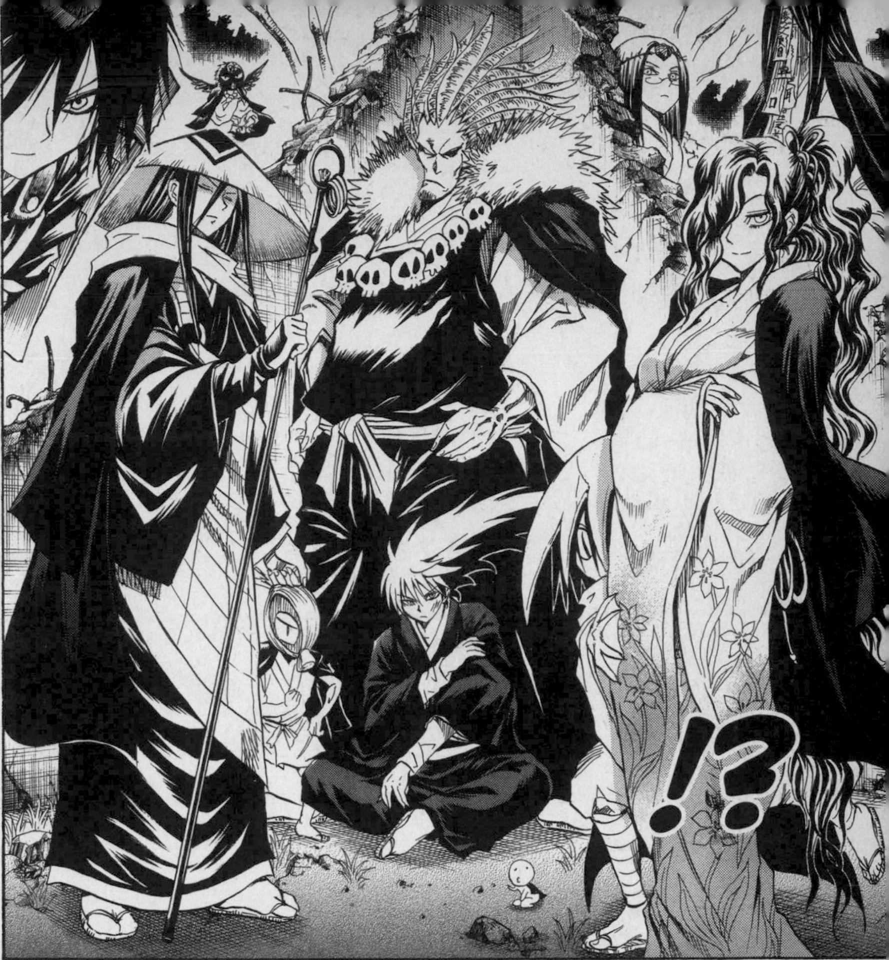
!?
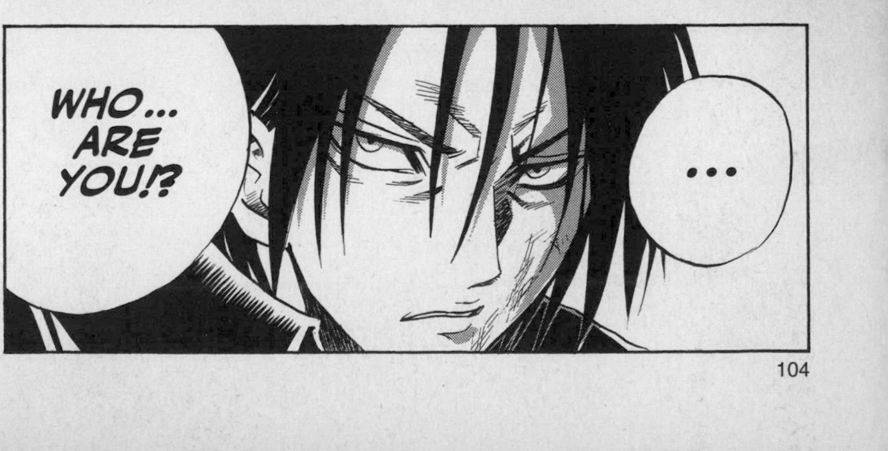
...
WHO... ARE YOU!?

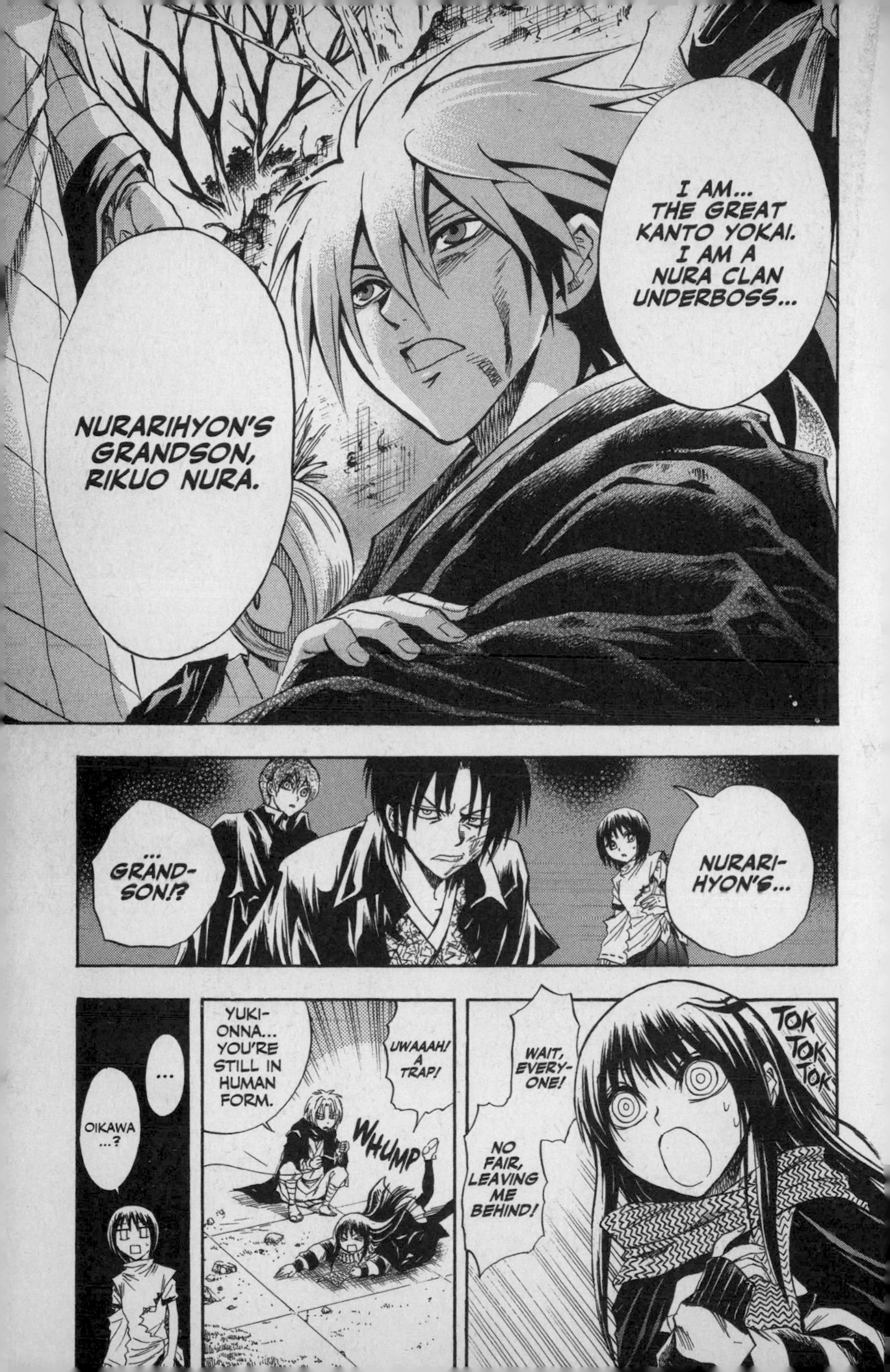
I AM... THE GREAT KANTO YOKAI. I AM A NURA CLAN UNDERBOSS...
NURARIHYON'S GRANDSON, RIKUO NURA.
NURARI-HYON'S...
...GRÄND-SON!?
TOK TOK TOK
WAIT, EVERY-ONE!
NO FAIR, LEAVING ME BEHIND!
UWAAAH! A TRAP!
WHUMP
YUKI-ONNA... YOU'RE STILL IN HUMAN FORM.
...
OIKAWA ...?

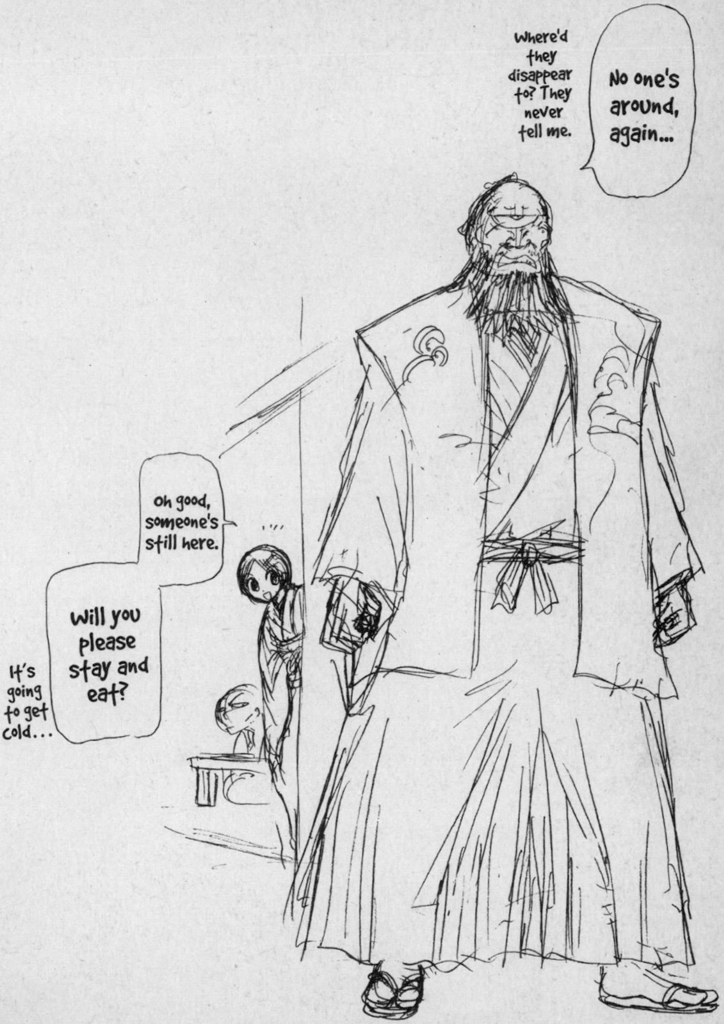
No one's around, again...
Where'd they disappear to? They never tell me.
Oh good, someone's still here.
Will you please stay and eat?
It's going to get cold...

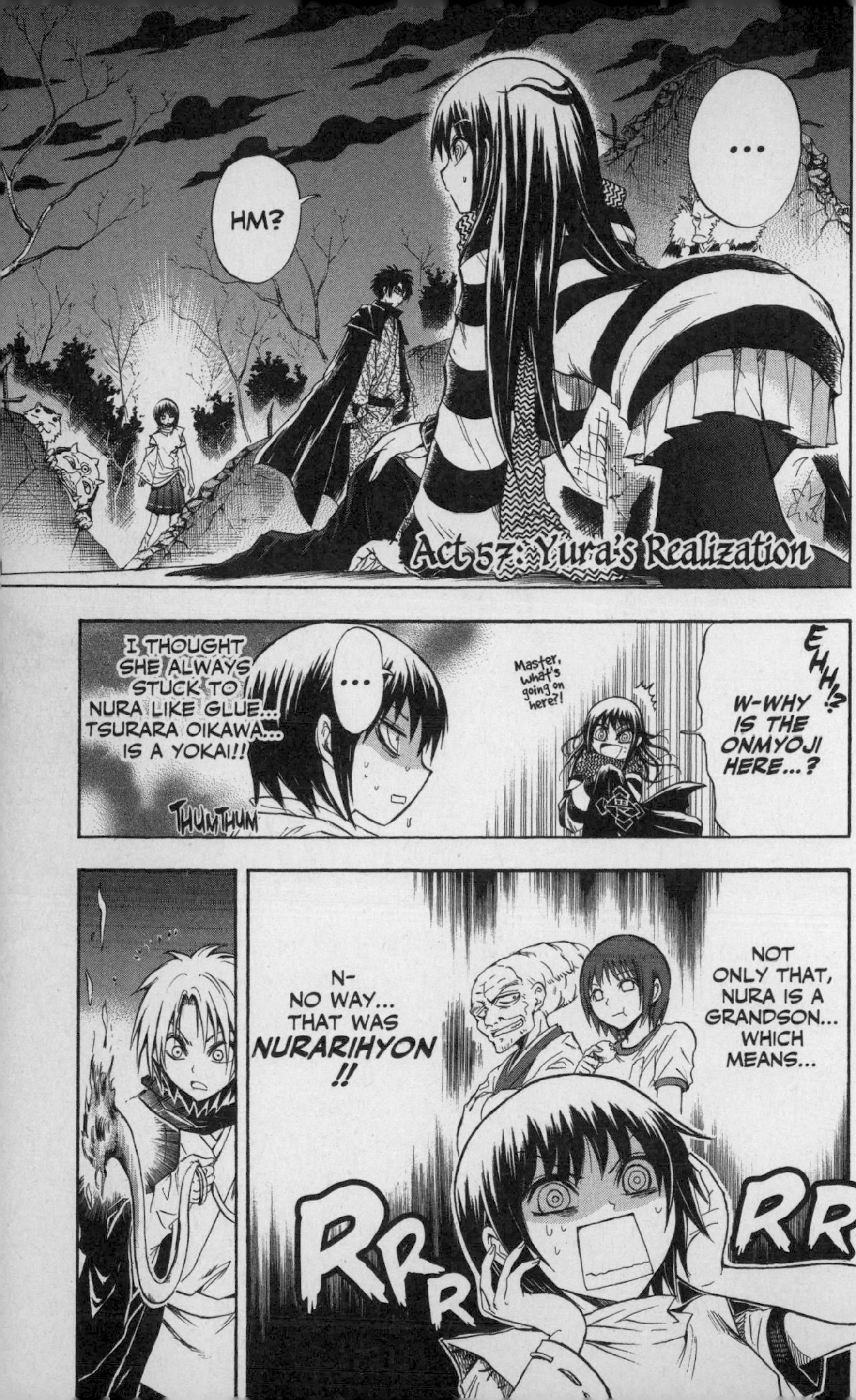
...
HM?
Act 57: Yura's Realization
EHH!?
W-WHY IS THE ONMYOJI HERE...?
Master, what's going on here?!
...
I THOUGHT SHE ALWAYS STUCK TO NURA LIKE GLUE... TSURARA OIKAWA... IS A YOKAI!!
THUMTHUM
NOT ONLY THAT, NURA IS A GRANDSON... WHICH MEANS...
N- NO WAY... THAT WAS NURARIHYON!!
RRRRR

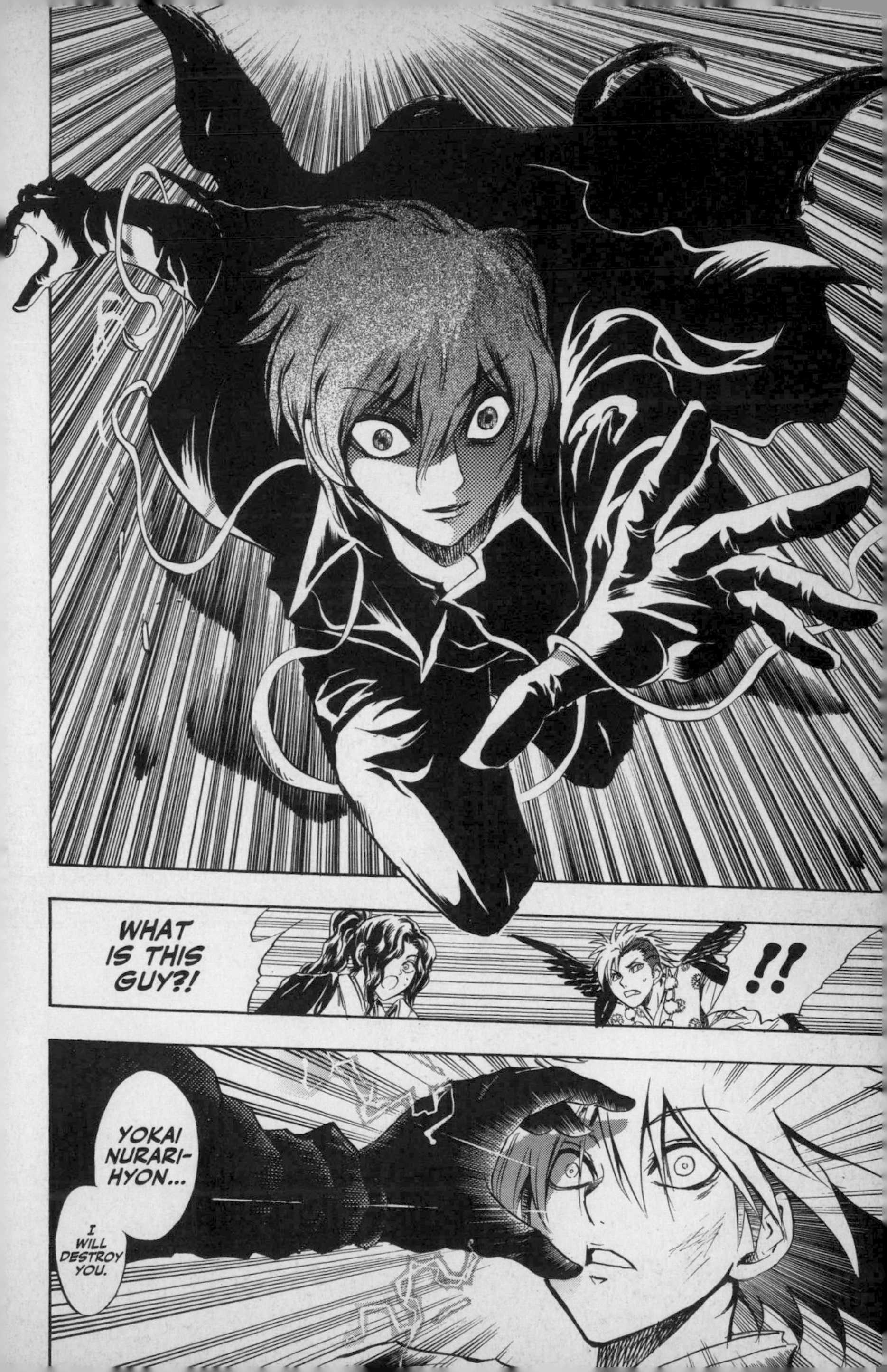
!!
WHAT IS THIS GUY?!
YOKAI NURARI-HYON...
I WILL DESTROY YOU.

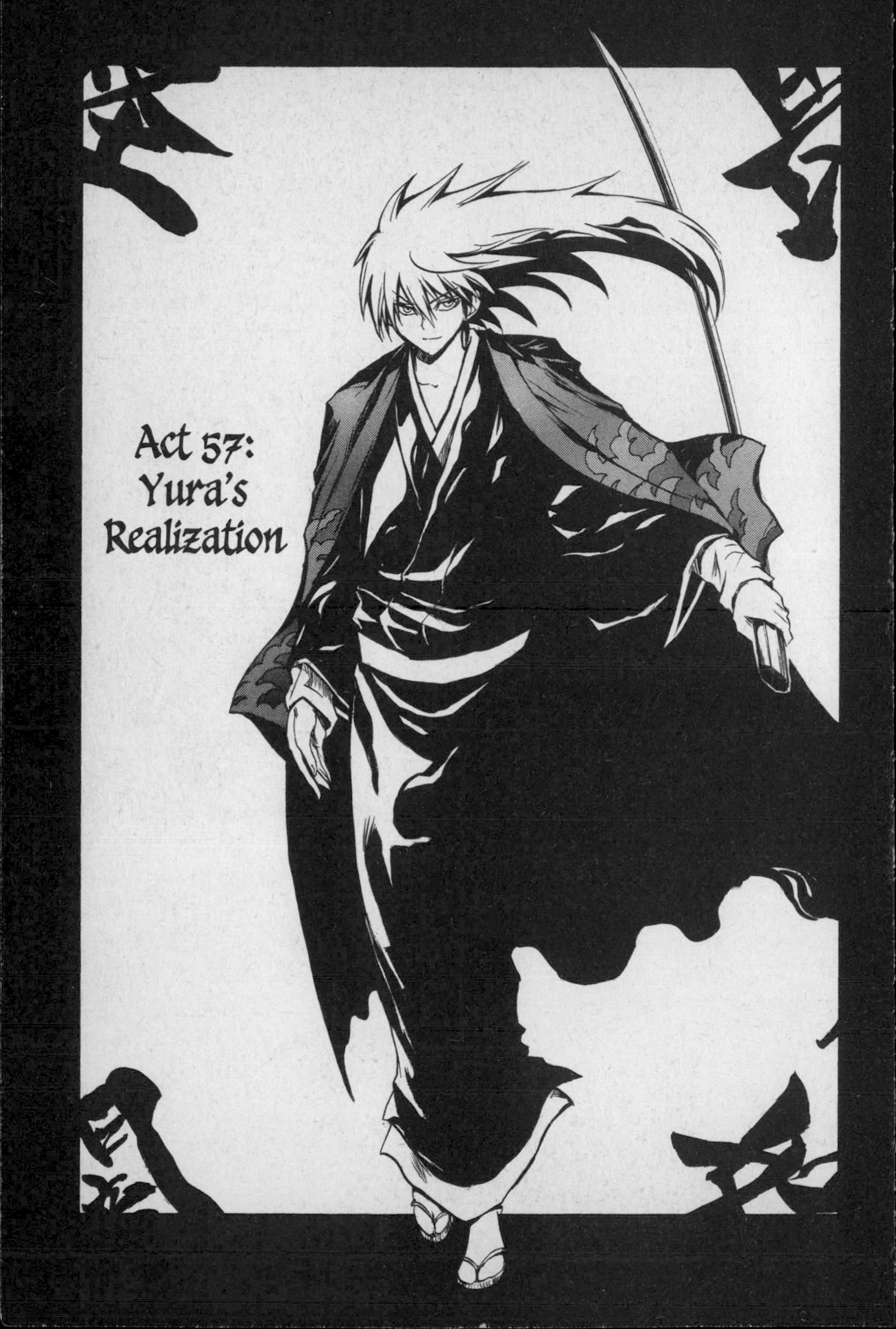
Act 57:
Yura's
Realization

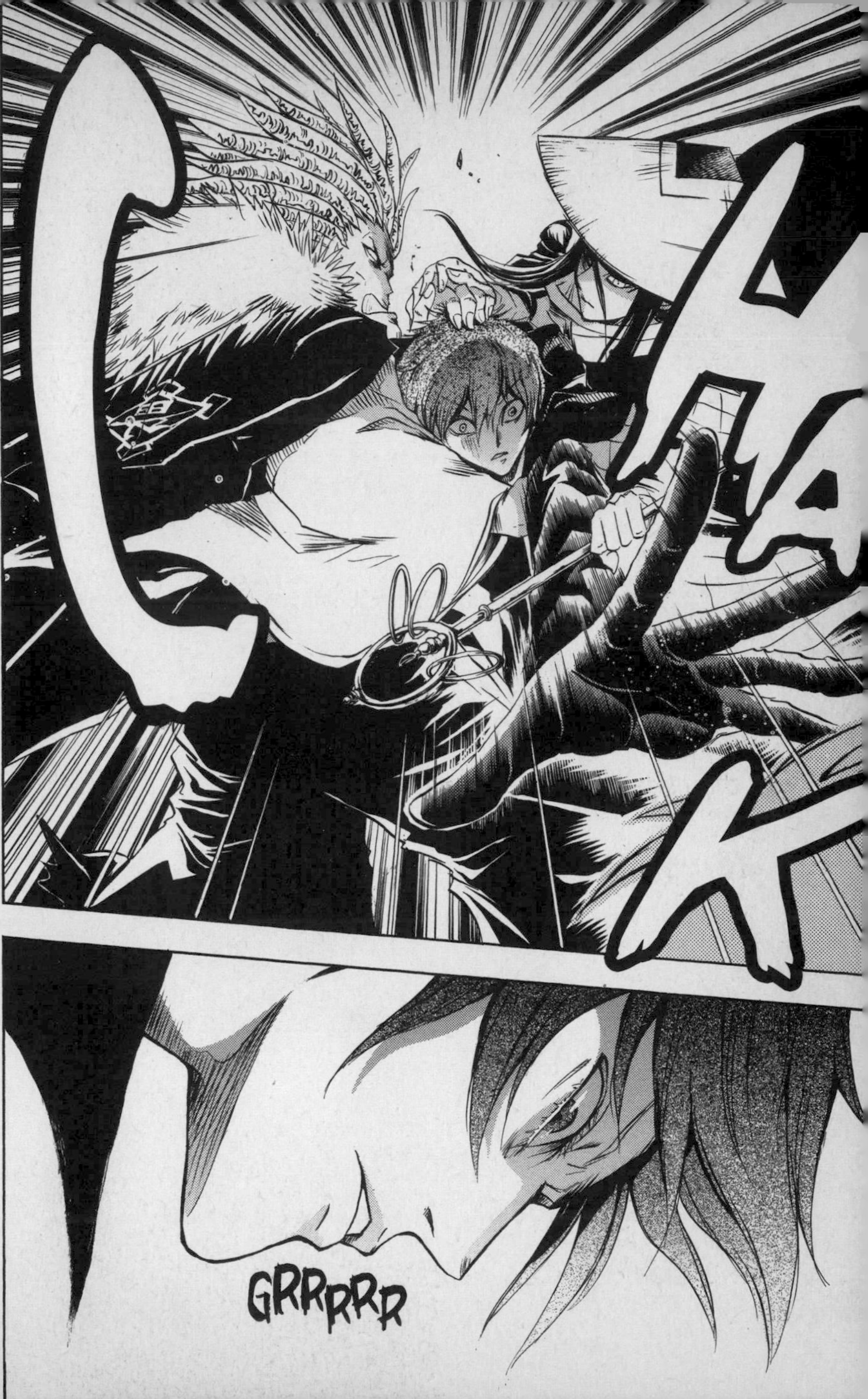
GRRRRR

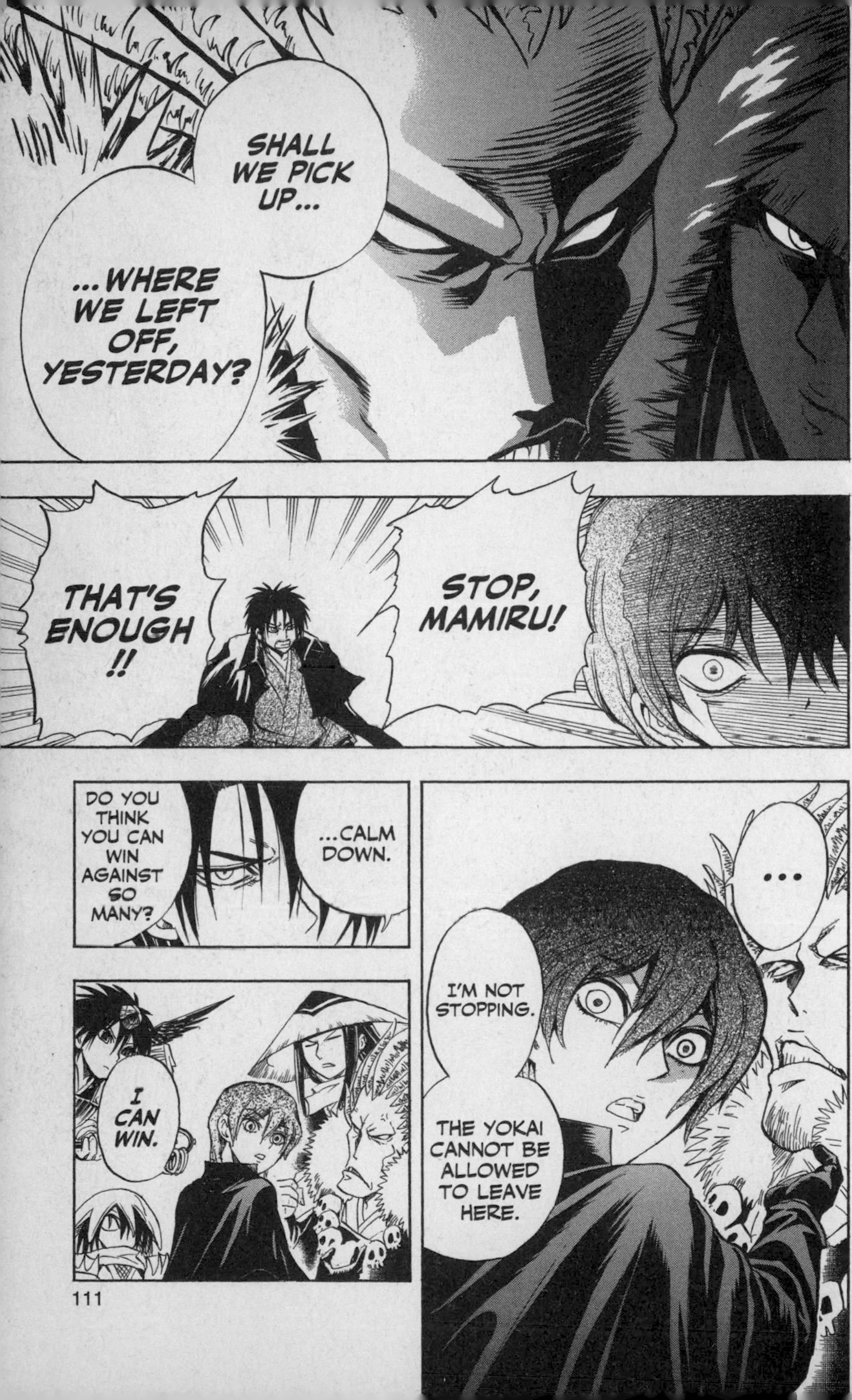
SHALL WE PICK UP...
...WHERE WE LEFT OFF, YESTERDAY?
STOP, MAMIRU!
THAT'S ENOUGH!!
...
I'M NOT STOPPING.
THE YOKAI CANNOT BE ALLOWED TO LEAVE HERE.
...CALM DOWN.
DO YOU THINK YOU CAN WIN AGAINST SO MANY?
I CAN WIN.

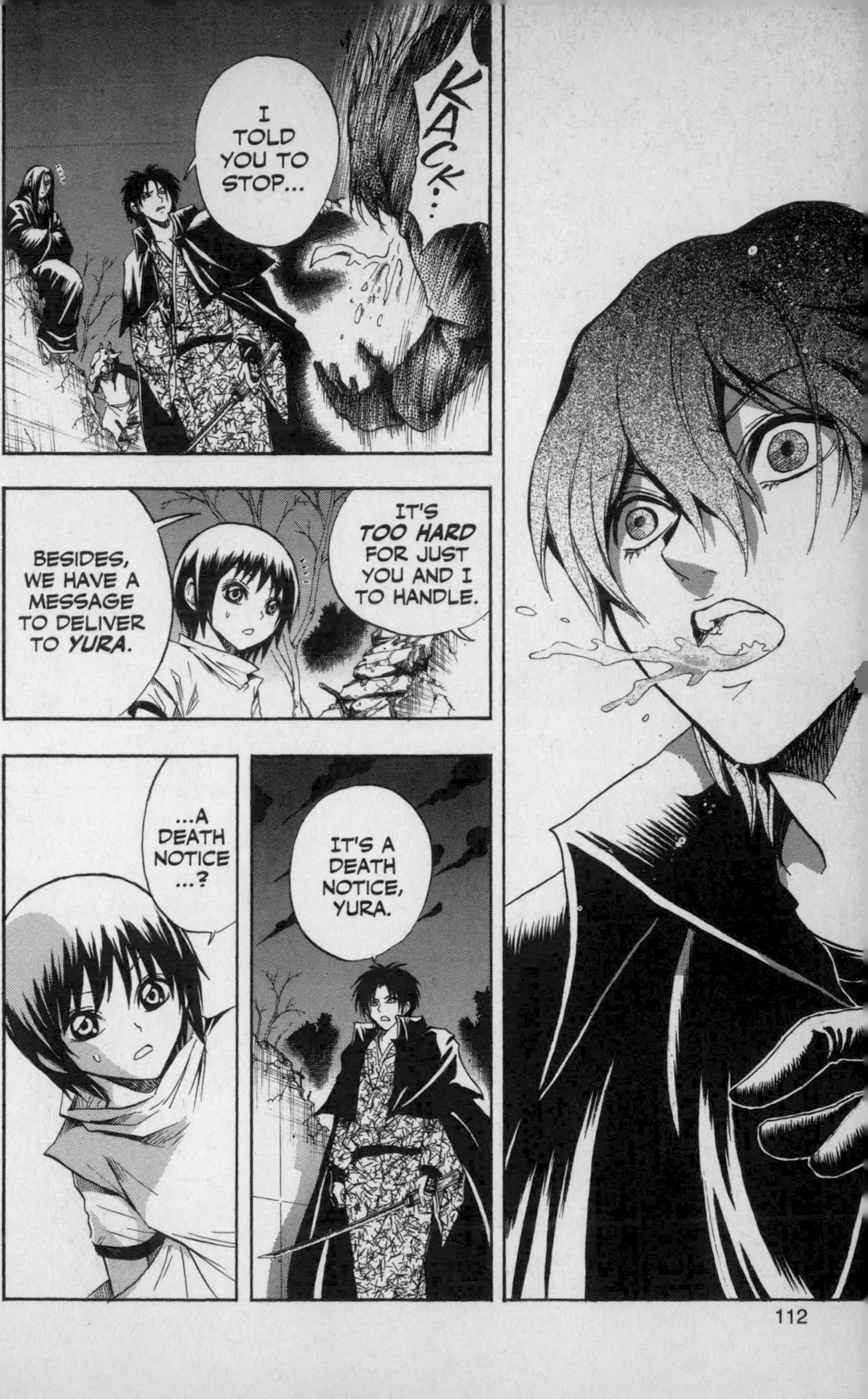
KACK...
I TOLD YOU TO STOP...
IT'S TOO HARD FOR JUST YOU AND I TO HANDLE.
BESIDES, WE HAVE A MESSAGE TO DELIVER TO YURA.
IT'S A DEATH NOTICE, YURA.
...A DEATH NOTICE ...?

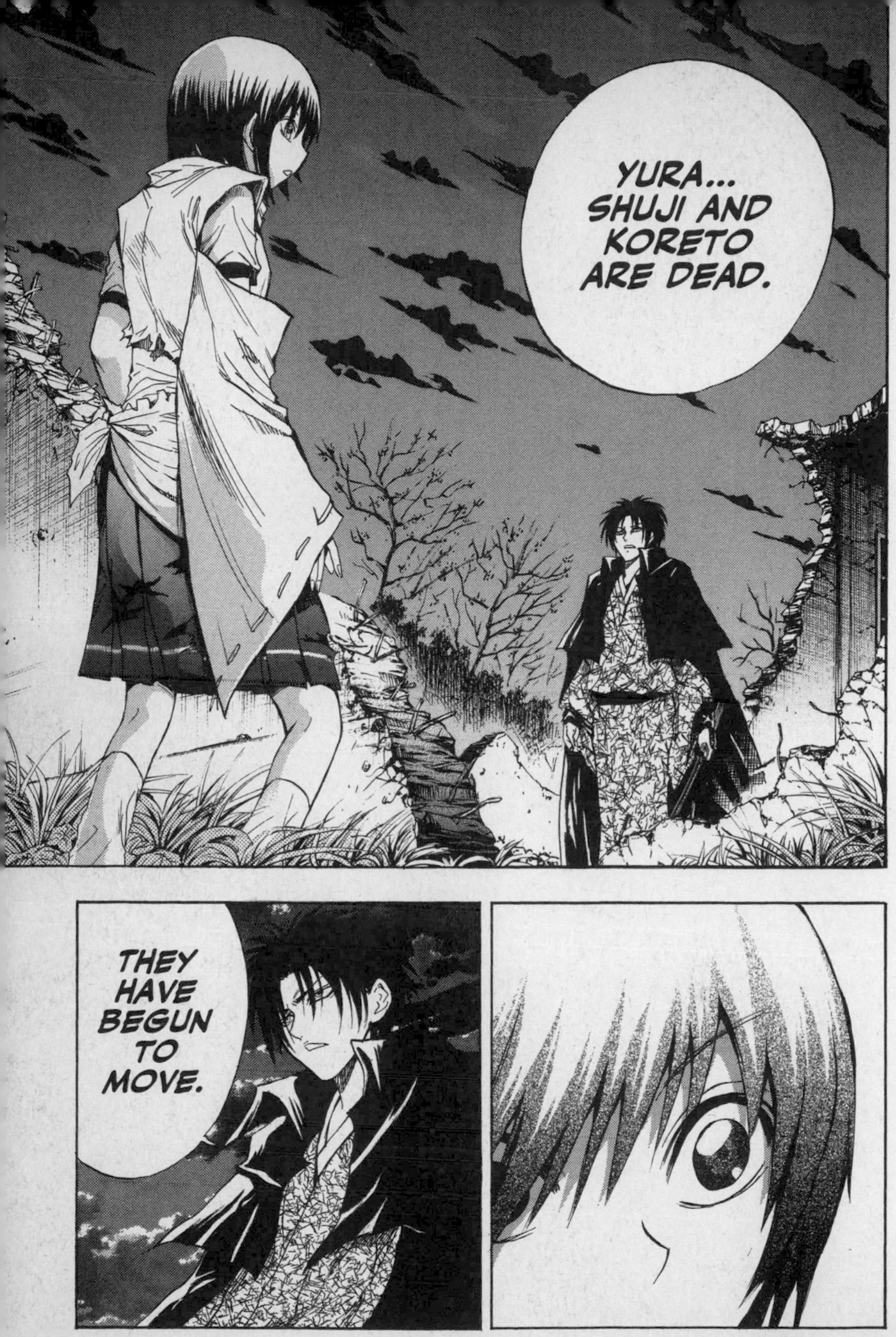
YURA... SHUJI AND KORETO ARE DEAD.
THEY HAVE BEGUN TO MOVE.

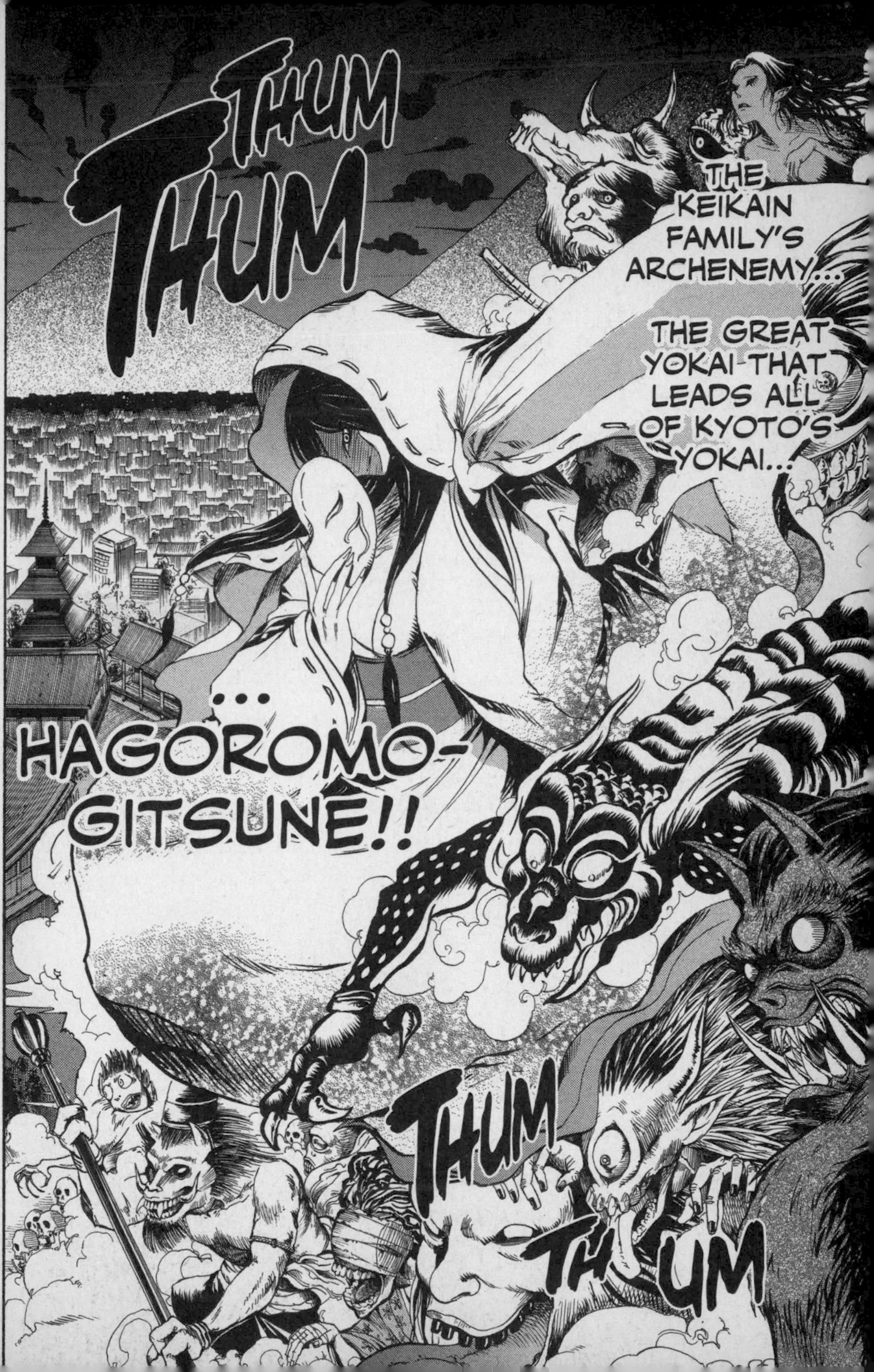

THUM THUM
THE KEIKAIN FAMILY'S ARCHENEMY...
THE GREAT YOKAI THAT LEADS ALL OF KYOTO'S YOKAI...
... HAGOROMO-GITSUNE!!
THUM THUM

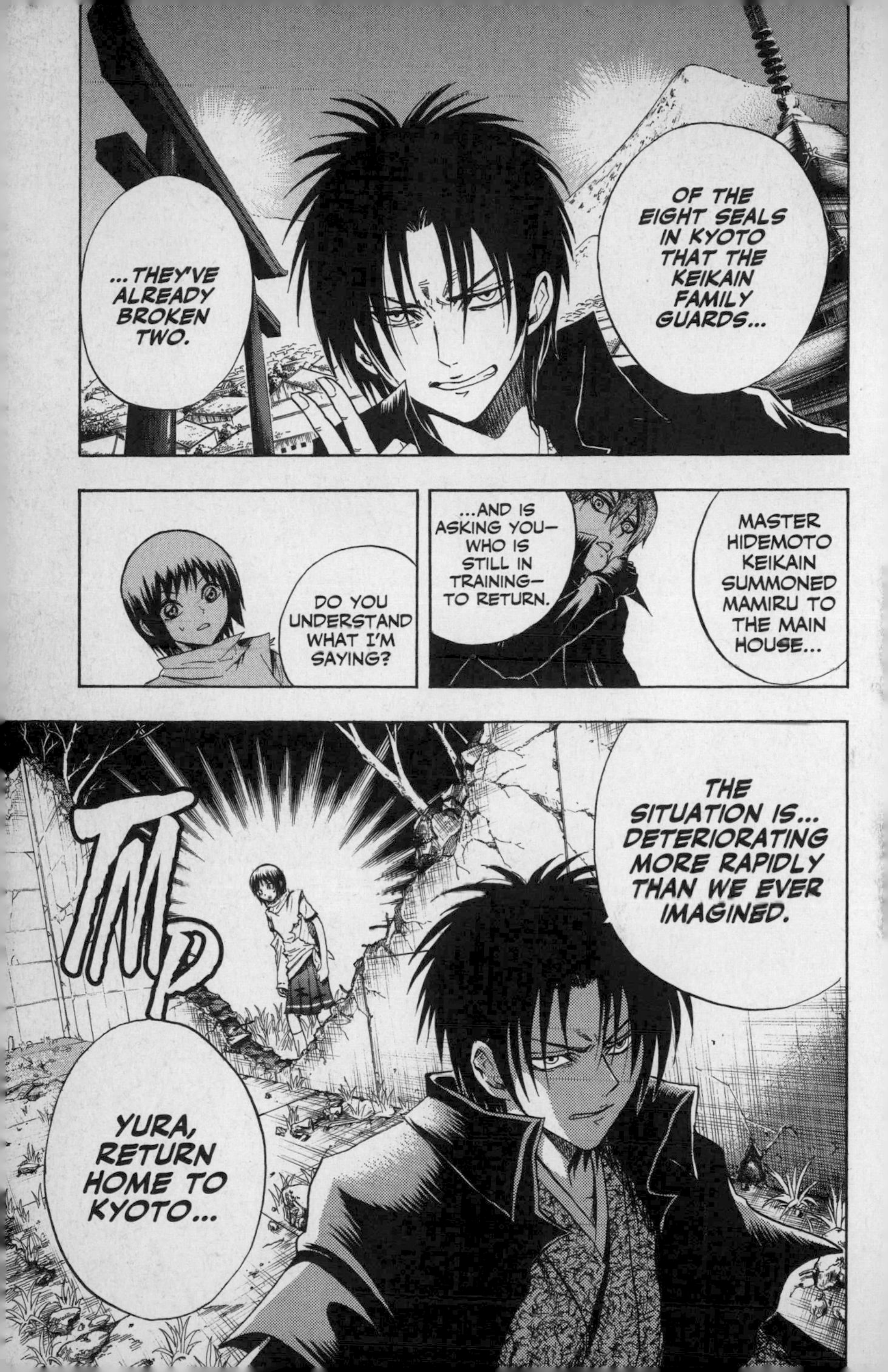
OF THE EIGHT SEALS IN KYOTO THAT THE KEIKAIN FAMILY GUARDS...
...THEY'VE ALREADY BROKEN TWO.
MASTER HIDEMOTO KEIKAIN SUMMONED MAMIRU TO THE MAIN HOUSE...
...AND IS ASKING YOU—WHO IS STILL IN TRAINING—TO RETURN.
DO YOU UNDERSTAND WHAT I'M SAYING?
THE SITUATION IS... DETERIORATING MORE RAPIDLY THAN WE EVER IMAGINED.
TMP
YURA, RETURN HOME TO KYOTO...

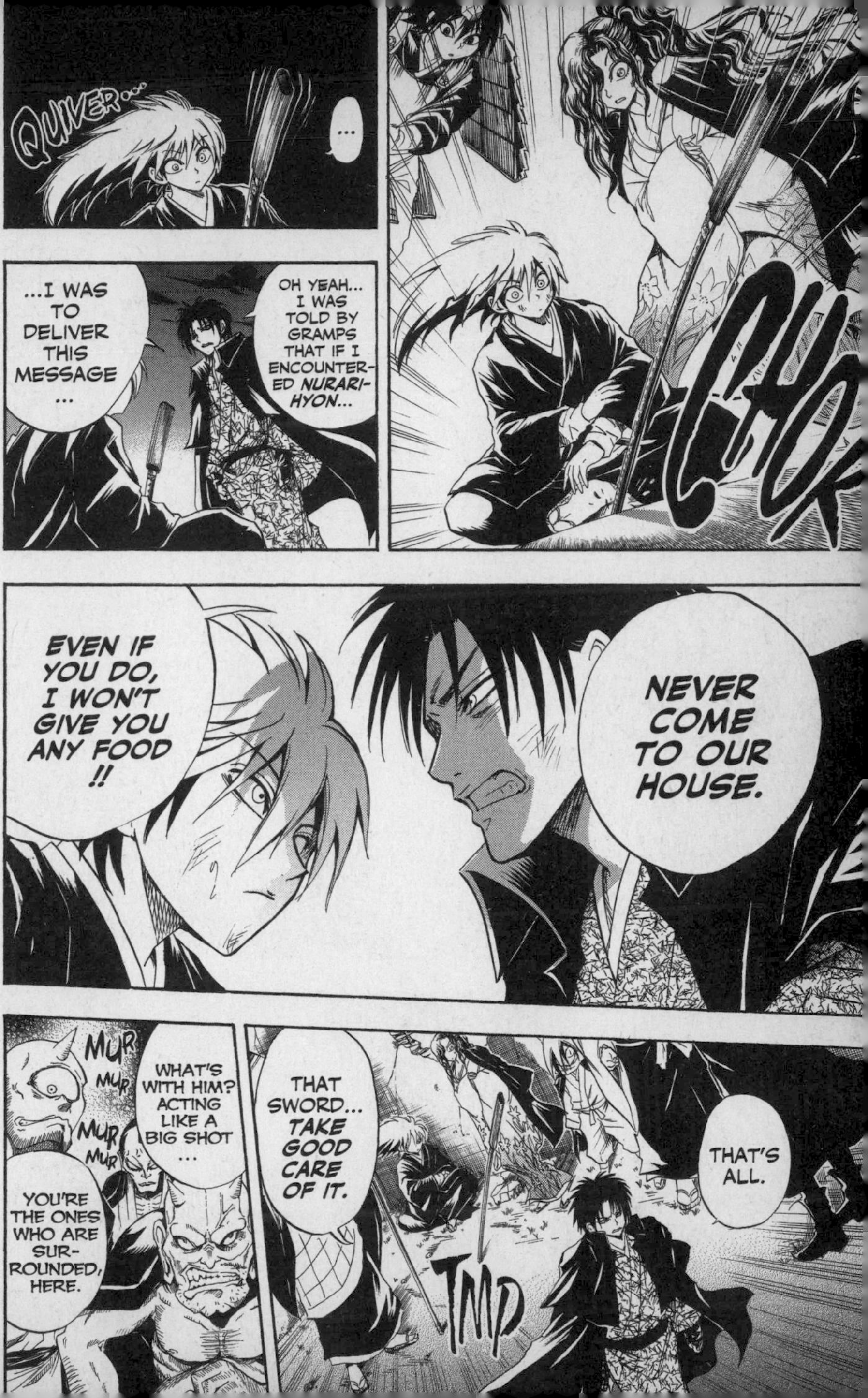
CHOK
QUIVER...
...
OH YEAH... I WAS TOLD BY GRAMPS THAT IF I ENCOUNTERED NURARIHYON...
...I WAS TO DELIVER THIS MESSAGE...
NEVER COME TO OUR HOUSE.
EVEN IF YOU DO, I WON'T GIVE YOU ANY FOOD!!
THAT'S ALL.
TMP
THAT SWORD... TAKE GOOD CARE OF IT.
WHAT'S WITH HIM? ACTING LIKE A BIG SHOT...
MUR MUR MUR MUR
YOU'RE THE ONES WHO ARE SURROUNDED, HERE.

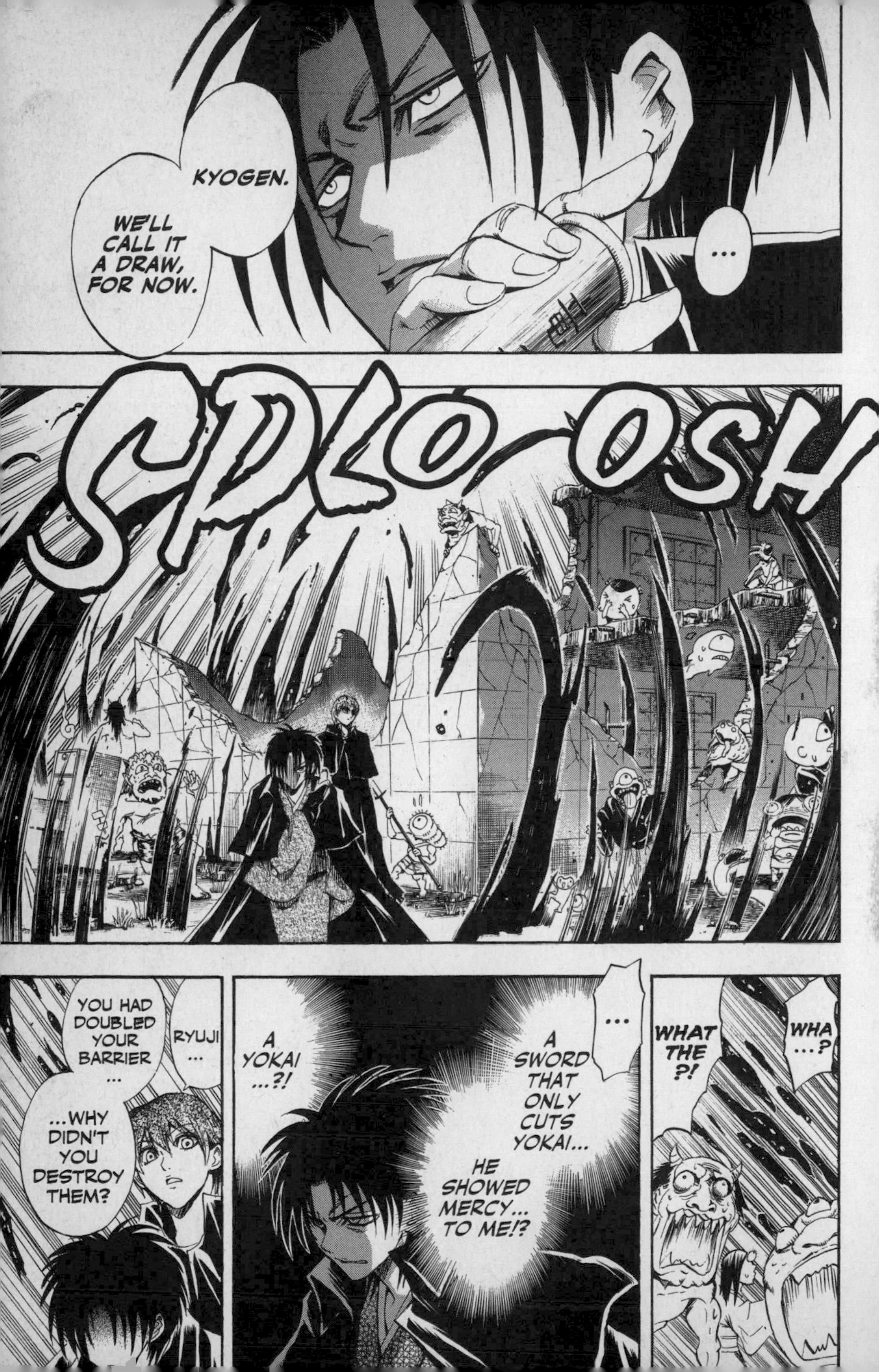
KYOGEN.
WE'LL CALL IT A DRAW, FOR NOW.
...
SPLO-OSH
WHA...?
WHAT THE?!
...
A SWORD THAT ONLY CUTS YOKAI...
HE SHOWED MERCY... TO ME!?
A YOKAI...?!
RYUJI...
YOU HAD DOUBLED YOUR BARRIER...
...WHY DIDN'T YOU DESTROY THEM?

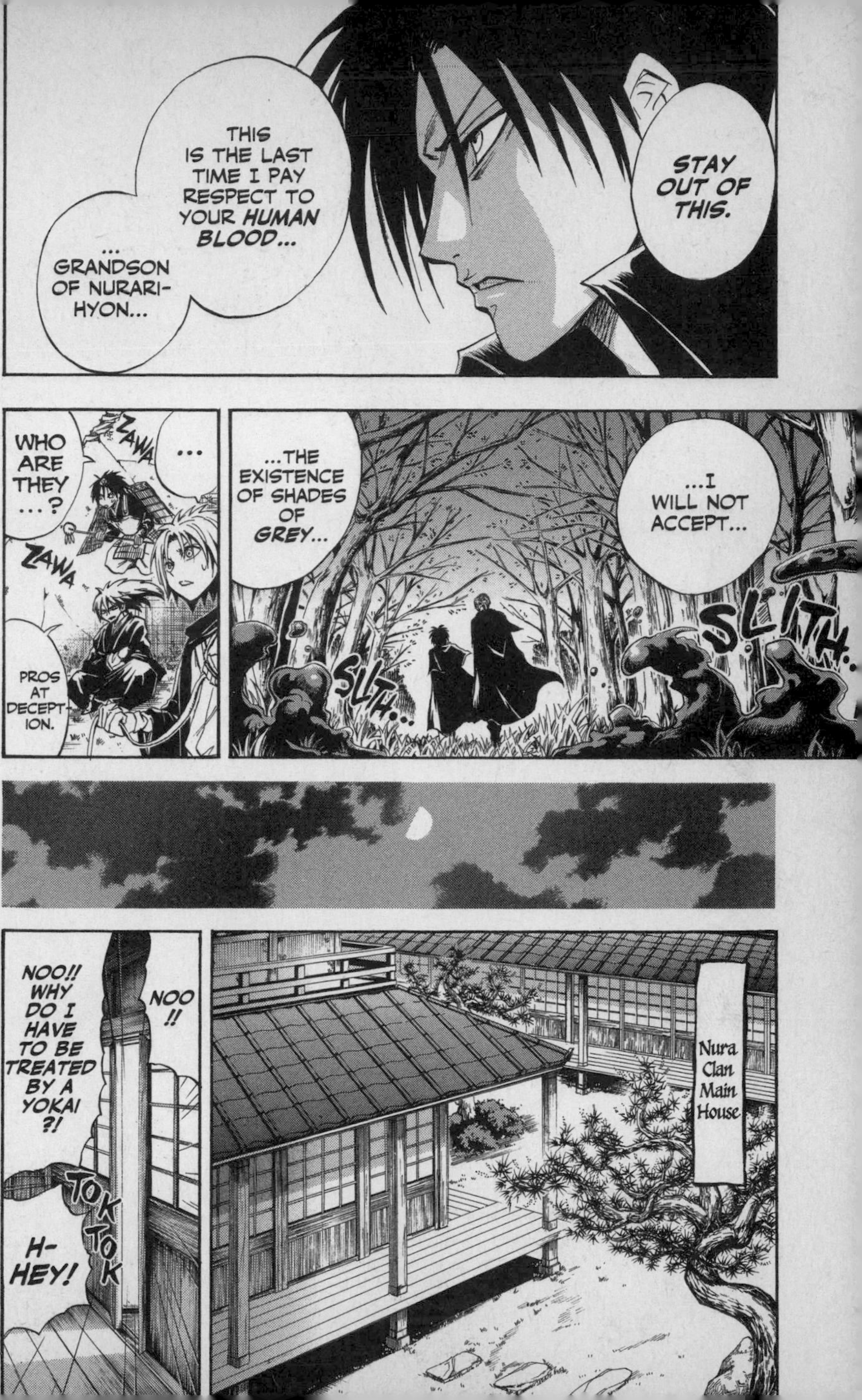
STAY OUT OF THIS.
THIS IS THE LAST TIME I PAY RESPECT TO YOUR HUMAN BLOOD...
...GRANDSON OF NURARI-HYON...
...I WILL NOT ACCEPT...
SLITH...
...THE EXISTENCE OF SHADES OF GREY...
SLITH...
...
ZAWA
WHO ARE THEY...?
ZAWA
PROS AT DECEPTION.
Nura Clan Main House
NOO!!
NOO!! WHY DO I HAVE TO BE TREATED BY A YOKAI?!
TOK TOK
H-HEY!

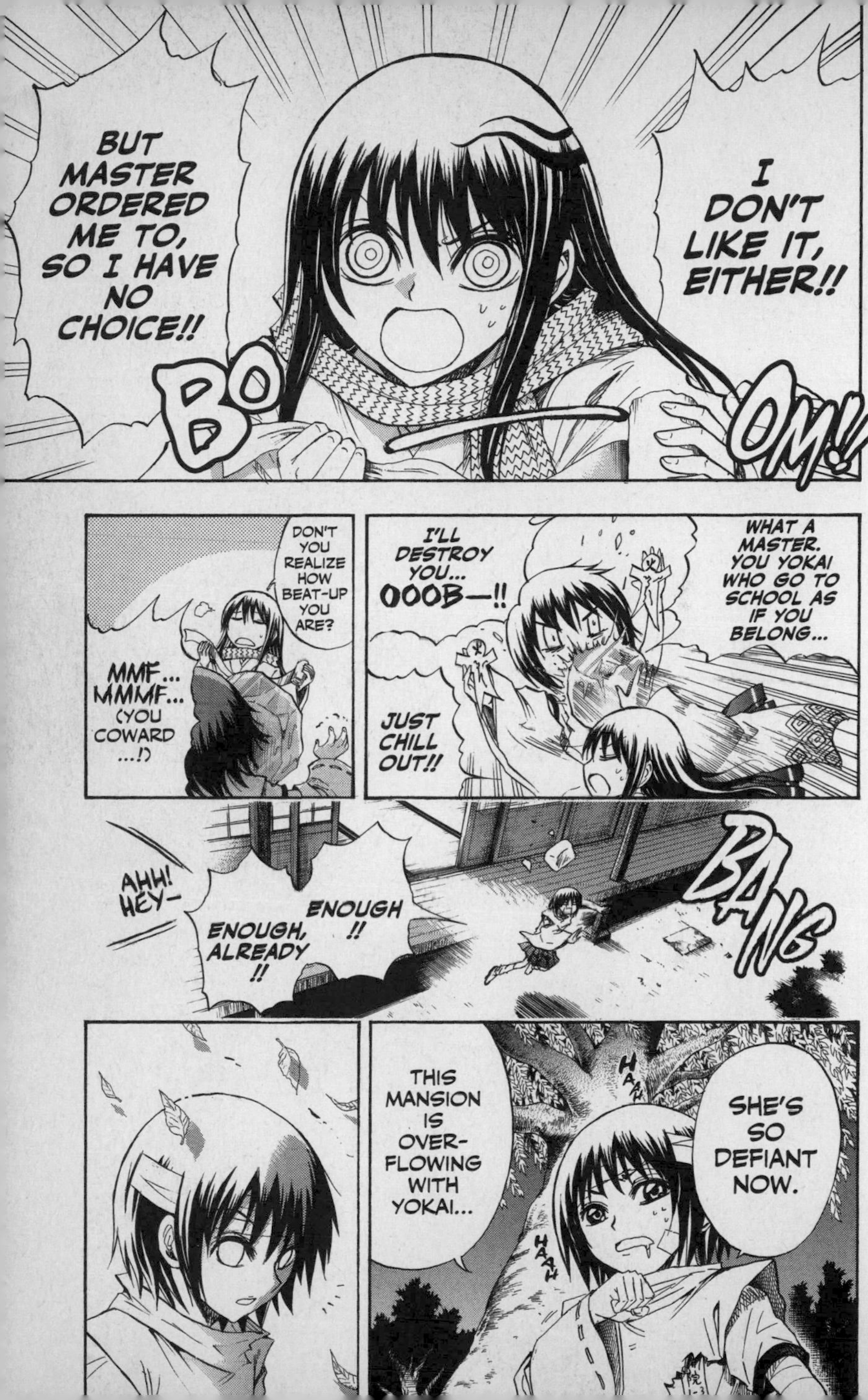
I DON'T LIKE IT, EITHER!!
BUT MASTER ORDERED ME TO, SO I HAVE NO CHOICE!!
BOOM!!
WHAT A MASTER. YOU YOKAI WHO GO TO SCHOOL AS IF YOU BELONG...
I'LL DESTROY YOU... OOOB—!!
JUST CHILL OUT!!
DON'T YOU REALIZE HOW BEAT-UP YOU ARE?
MMF... MMMF... (YOU COWARD ...!)
BANG
ENOUGH !!
ENOUGH, ALREADY !!
AHH! HEY-
SHE'S SO DEFIANT NOW.
HAAH
THIS MANSION IS OVER-FLOWING WITH YOKAI...
HAAH

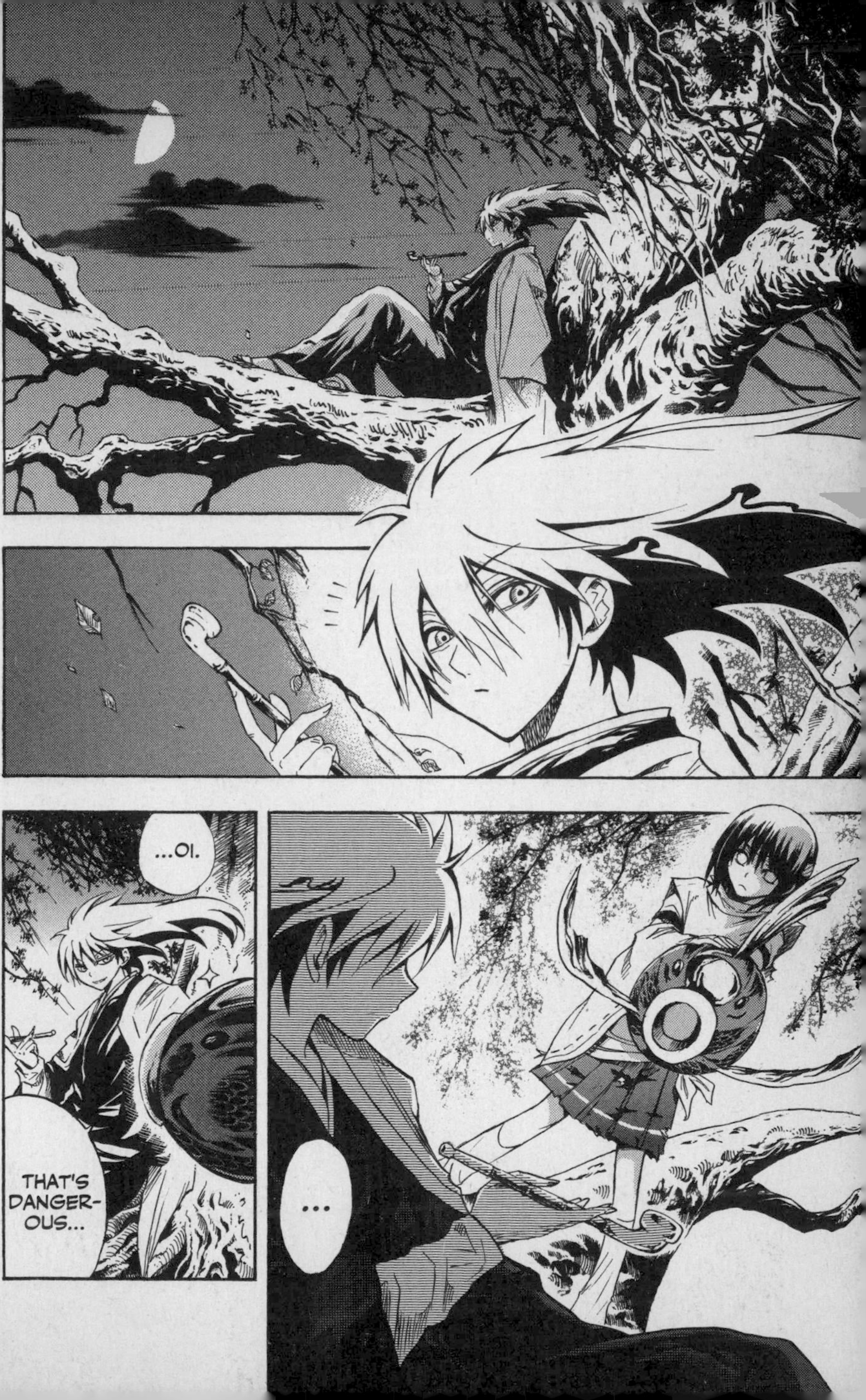
...
...OI.
THAT'S DANGER-OUS...

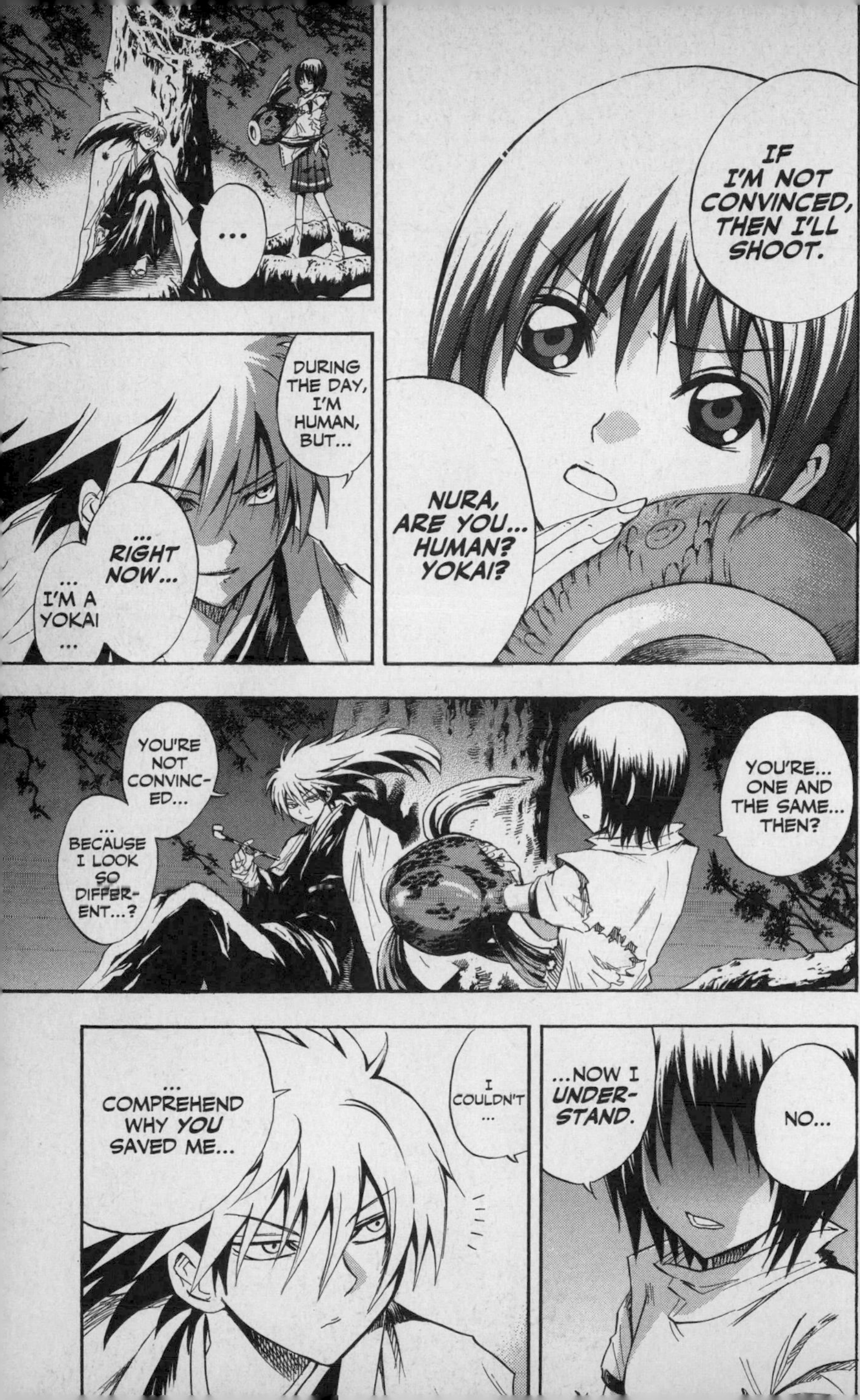
IF I'M NOT CONVINCED, THEN I'LL SHOOT.
NURA, ARE YOU... HUMAN? YOKAI?
...
DURING THE DAY, I'M HUMAN, BUT...
... RIGHT NOW...
... I'M A YOKAI ...
YOU'RE... ONE AND THE SAME... THEN?
YOU'RE NOT CONVINCED...
... BECAUSE I LOOK SO DIFFERENT...?
NO...
...NOW I UNDERSTAND.
I COULDN'T ...
... COMPREHEND WHY YOU SAVED ME...

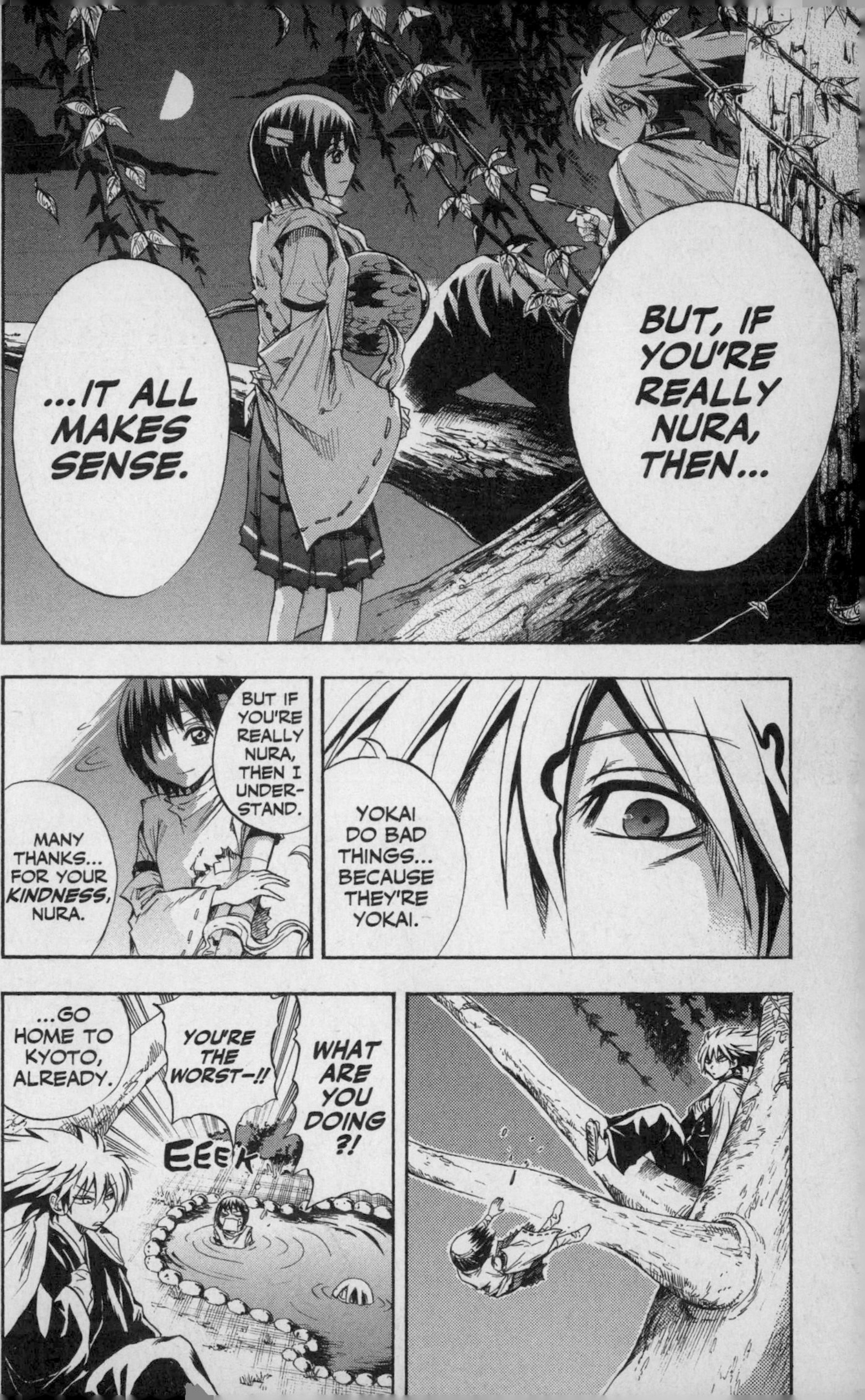
BUT, IF YOU'RE REALLY NURA, THEN...
...IT ALL MAKES SENSE.
YOKAI DO BAD THINGS... BECAUSE THEY'RE YOKAI.
BUT IF YOU'RE REALLY NURA, THEN I UNDERSTAND.
MANY THANKS... FOR YOUR *KINDNESS*, NURA.
WHAT ARE YOU DOING?!
YOU'RE THE WORST-!!
EEEK
...GO HOME TO KYOTO, ALREADY.

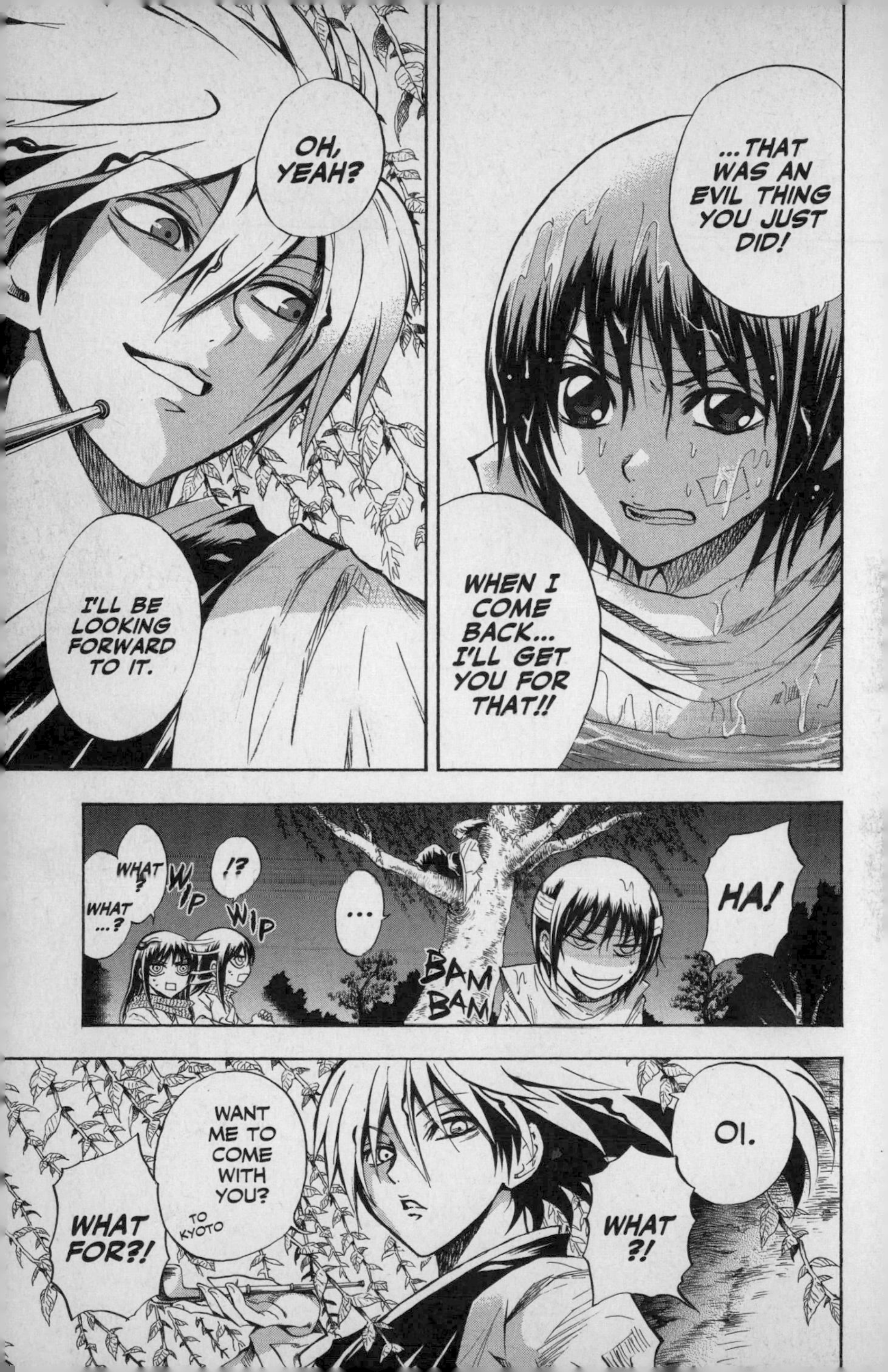
...THAT WAS AN EVIL THING YOU JUST DID!
WHEN I COME BACK... I'LL GET YOU FOR THAT!!
OH, YEAH?
I'LL BE LOOKING FORWARD TO IT.
HA!
BAM BAM
...
!?
WIP WIP
WHAT?
WHAT...?
OI.
WHAT?!
WANT ME TO COME WITH YOU?
TO KYOTO
WHAT FOR?!

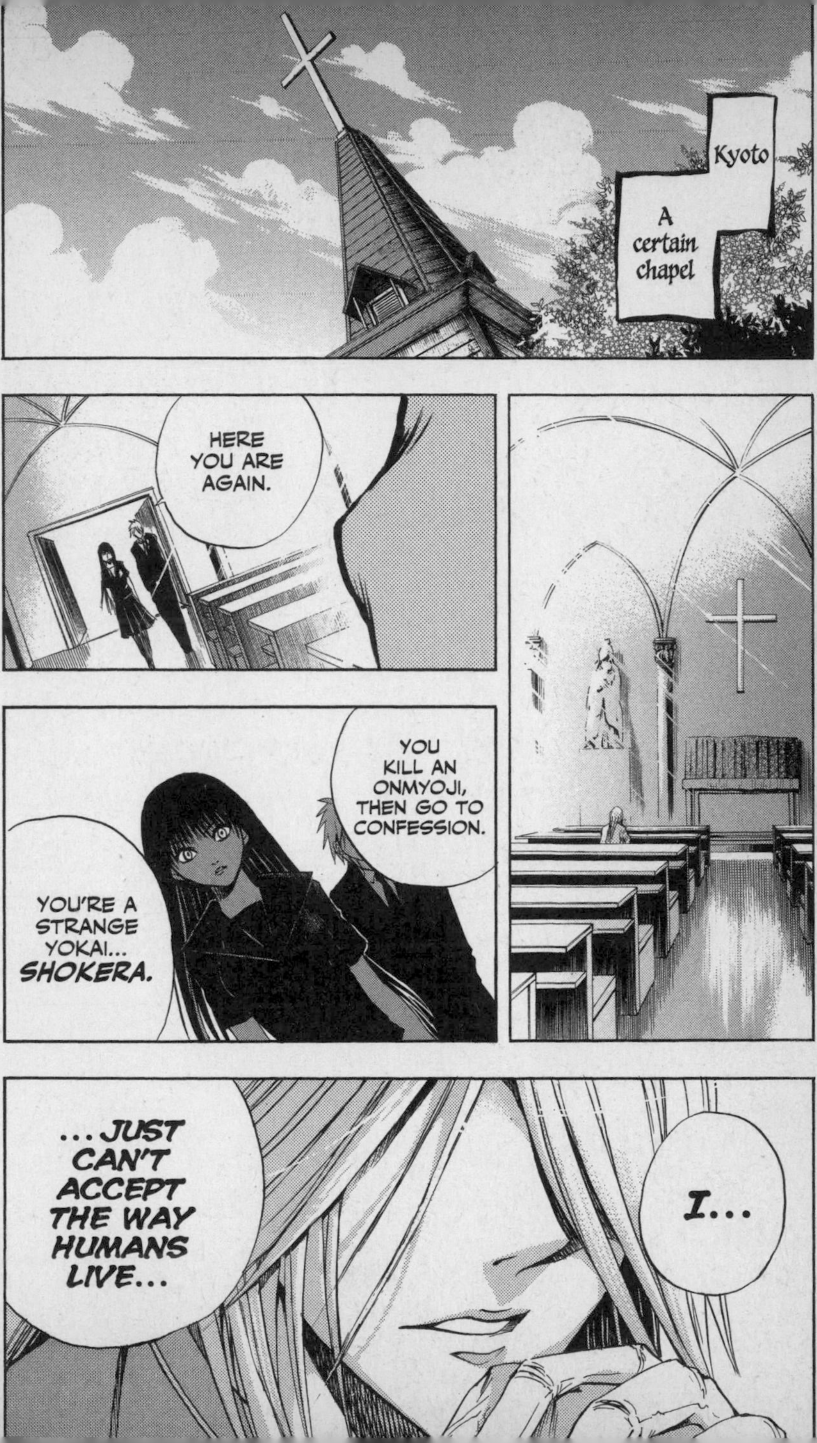
Kyoto
A certain chapel
HERE YOU ARE AGAIN.
YOU KILL AN ONMYOJI, THEN GO TO CONFESSION.
YOU'RE A STRANGE YOKAI... SHOKERA.
I...
...JUST CAN'T ACCEPT THE WAY HUMANS LIVE...

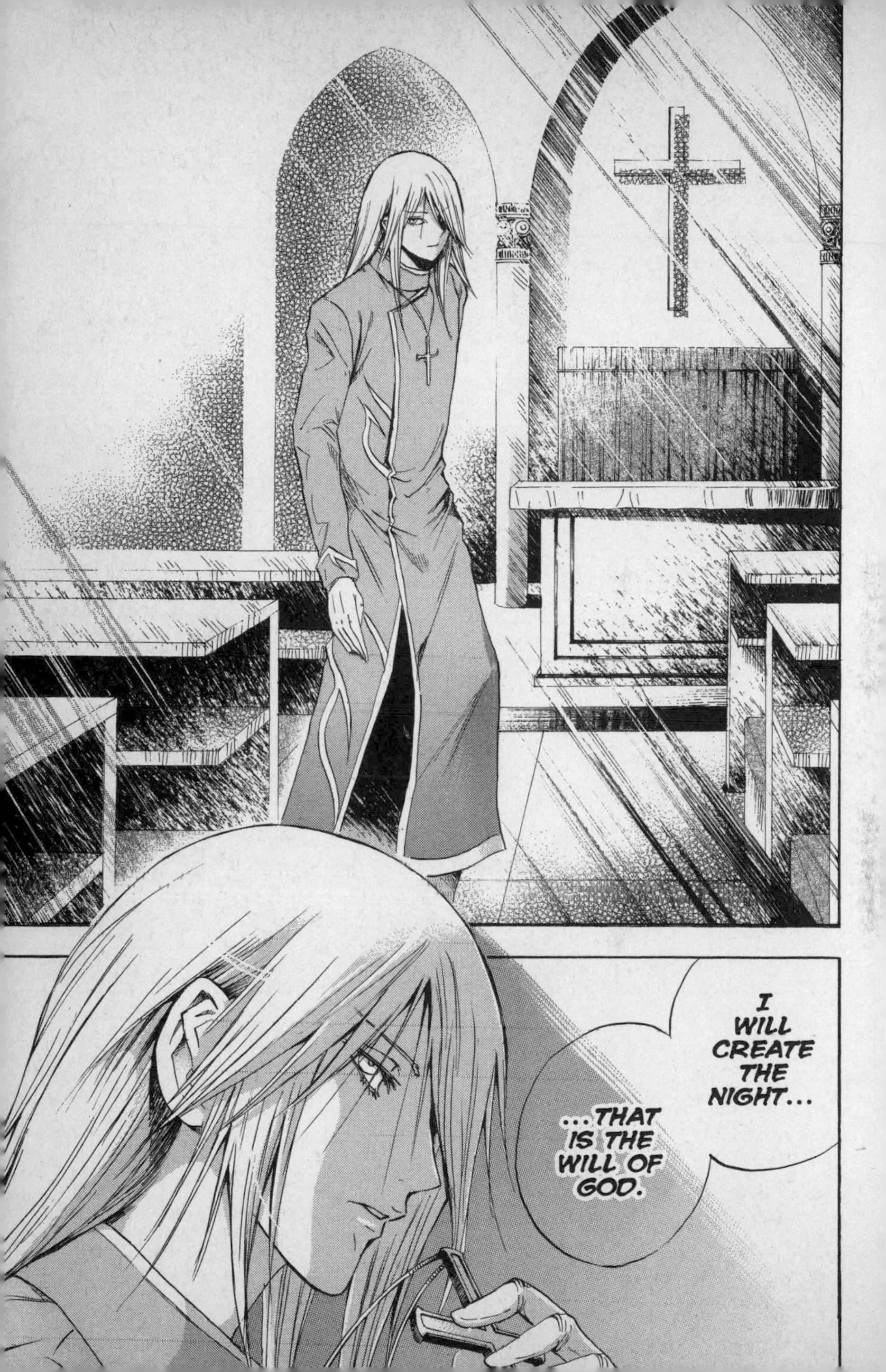
I WILL CREATE THE NIGHT...
...THAT IS THE WILL OF GOD.

NURA: RISE OF THE YOKAI CLAN

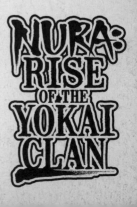

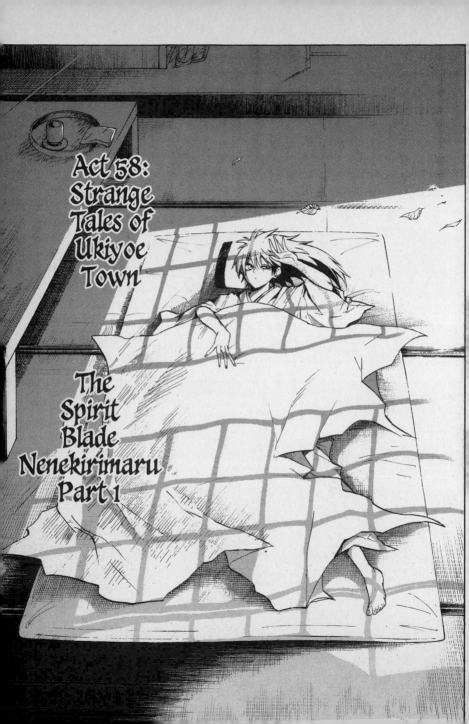

Act 58:
Strange
Tales of
Ukiyoe
Town

The
Spirit
Blade
Nenekirimaru
Part 1

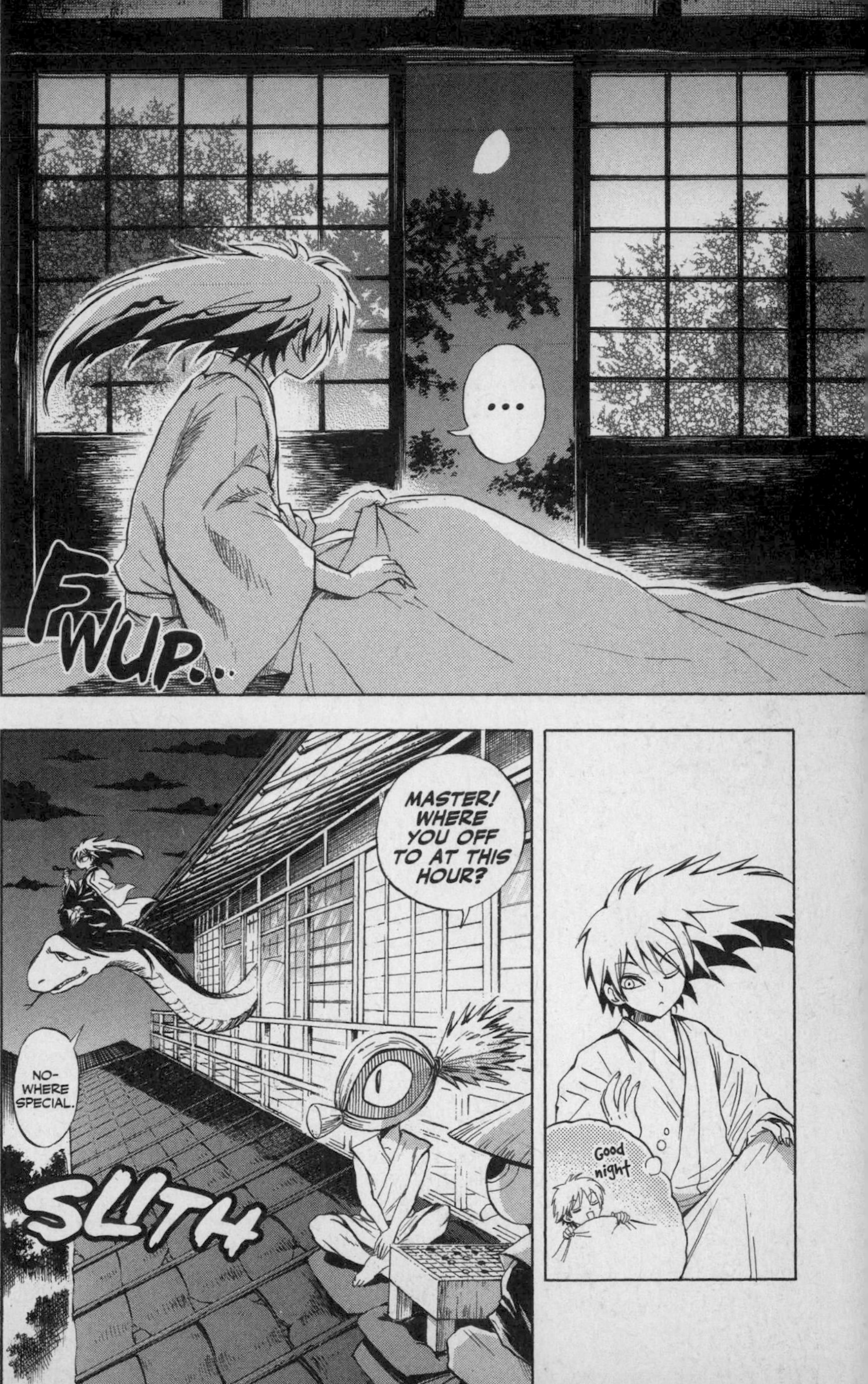
...
FWUP...
Good night
MASTER! WHERE YOU OFF TO AT THIS HOUR?
NO-WHERE SPECIAL.
SLITH

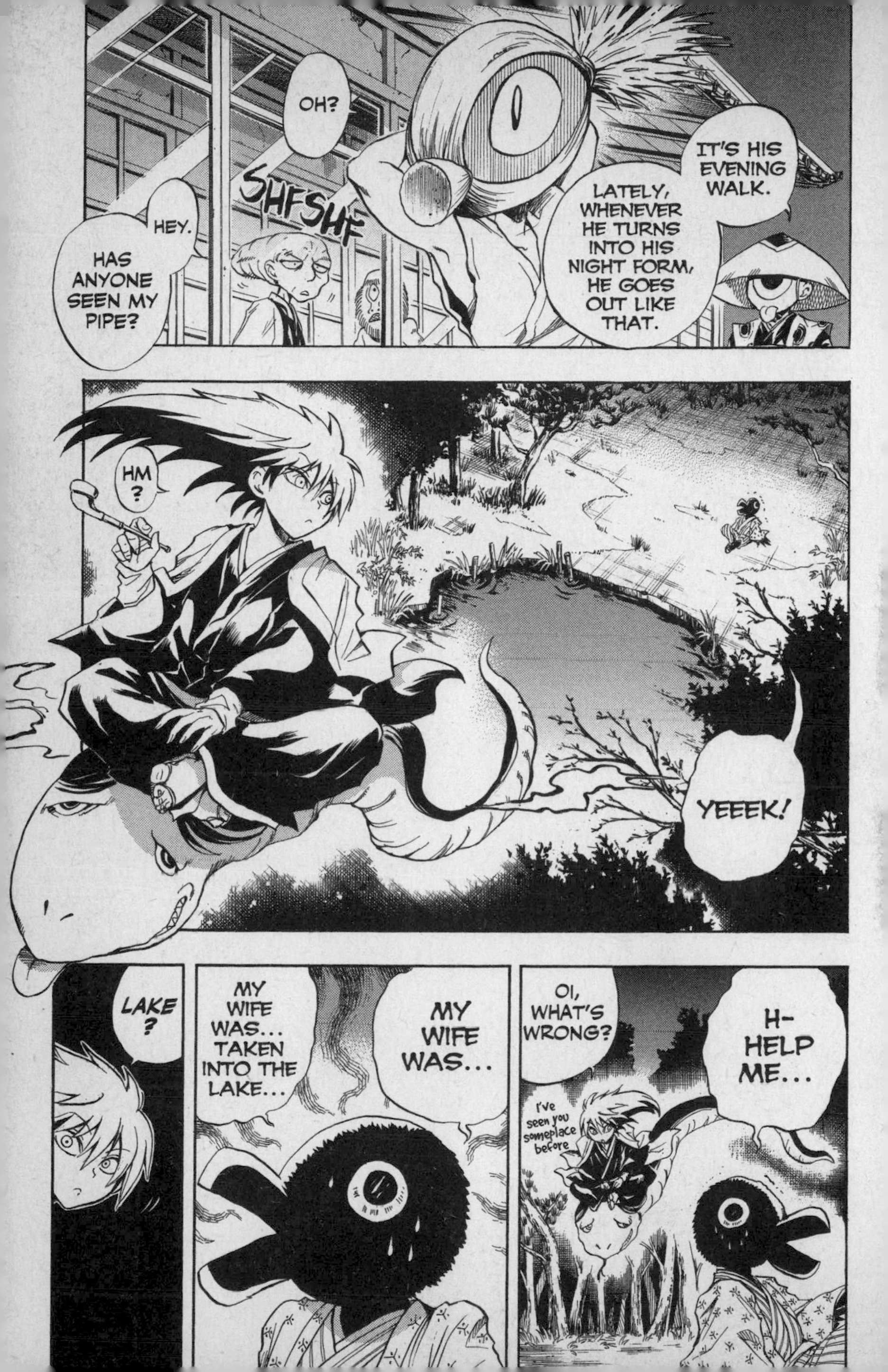
IT'S HIS EVENING WALK.
LATELY, WHENEVER HE TURNS INTO HIS NIGHT FORM, HE GOES OUT LIKE THAT.
OH?
SHFSHF
HEY.
HAS ANYONE SEEN MY PIPE?
YEEEK!
HM?
H- HELP ME...
OI, WHAT'S WRONG?
I've seen you someplace before
MY WIFE WAS...
MY WIFE WAS... TAKEN INTO THE LAKE...
LAKE?

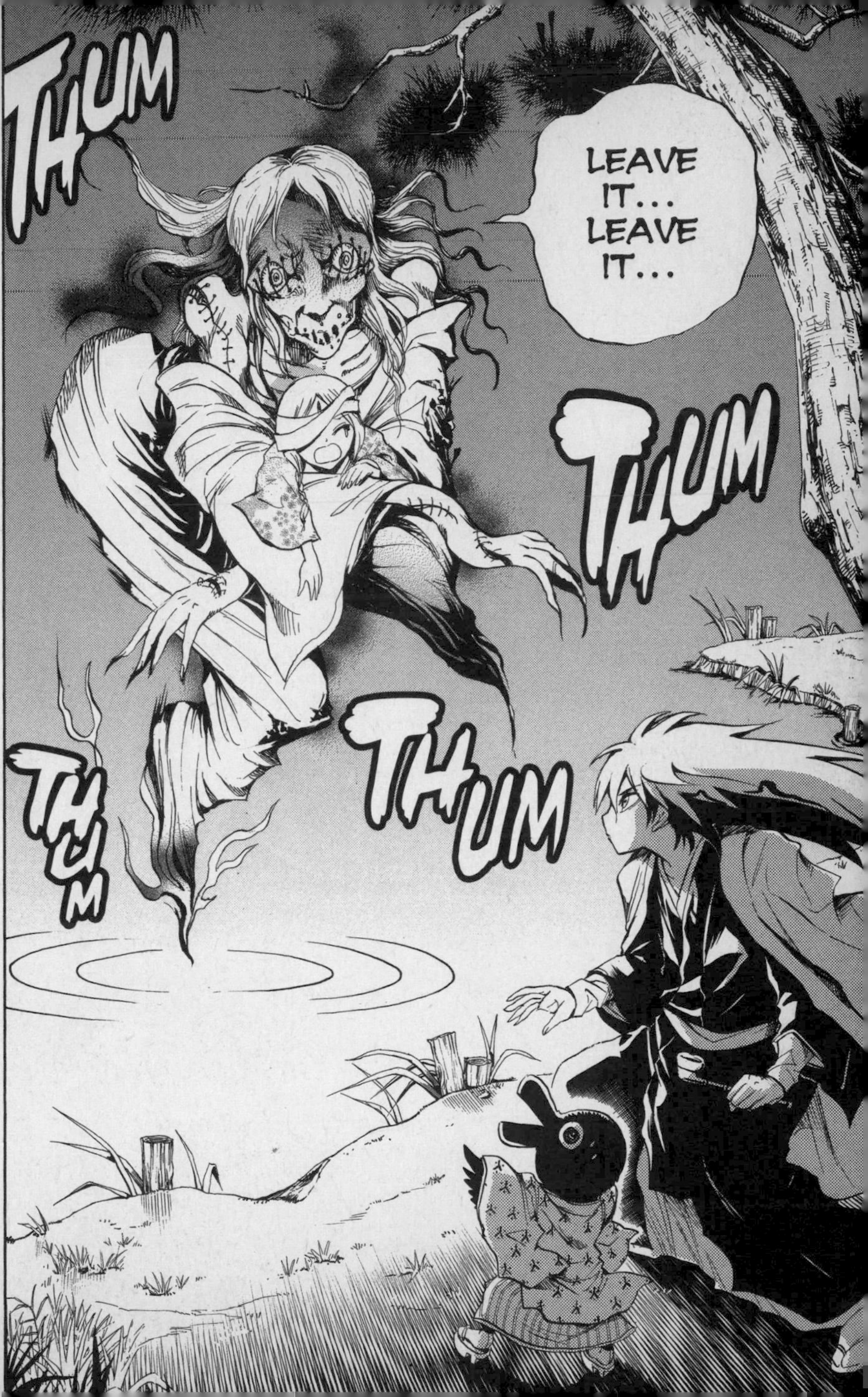

LEAVE IT... LEAVE IT...
THUM
THUM
THUM
THUM

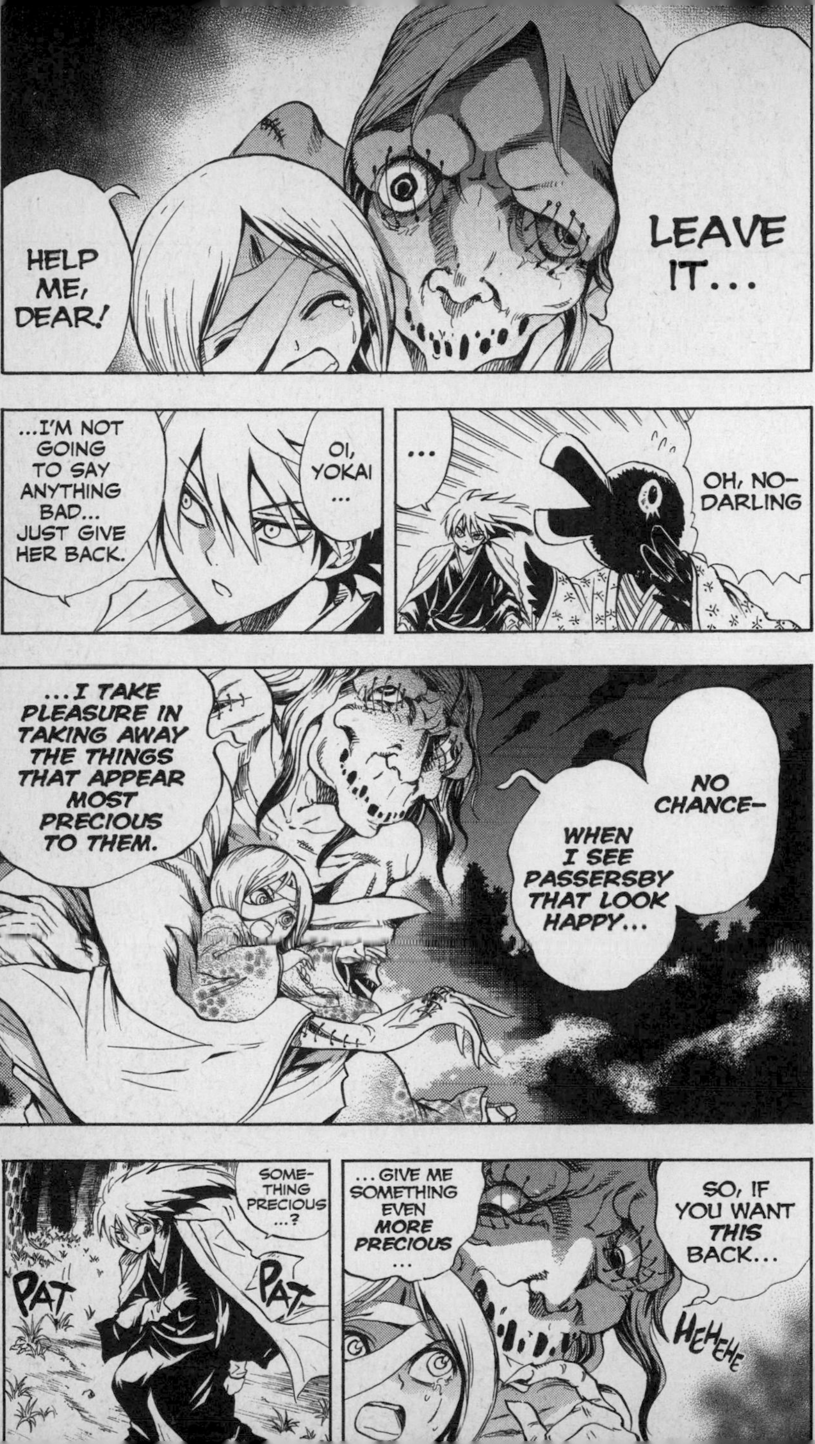
LEAVE IT...
HELP ME, DEAR!
OH, NO— DARLING
...
OI, YOKAI ...
...I'M NOT GOING TO SAY ANYTHING BAD... JUST GIVE HER BACK.
NO CHANCE— WHEN I SEE PASSERSBY THAT LOOK HAPPY...
...I TAKE PLEASURE IN TAKING AWAY THE THINGS THAT APPEAR MOST PRECIOUS TO THEM.
SO, IF YOU WANT THIS BACK...
HEHEHE
...GIVE ME SOMETHING EVEN MORE PRECIOUS ...
SOME-THING PRECIOUS ...?
PAT
PAT

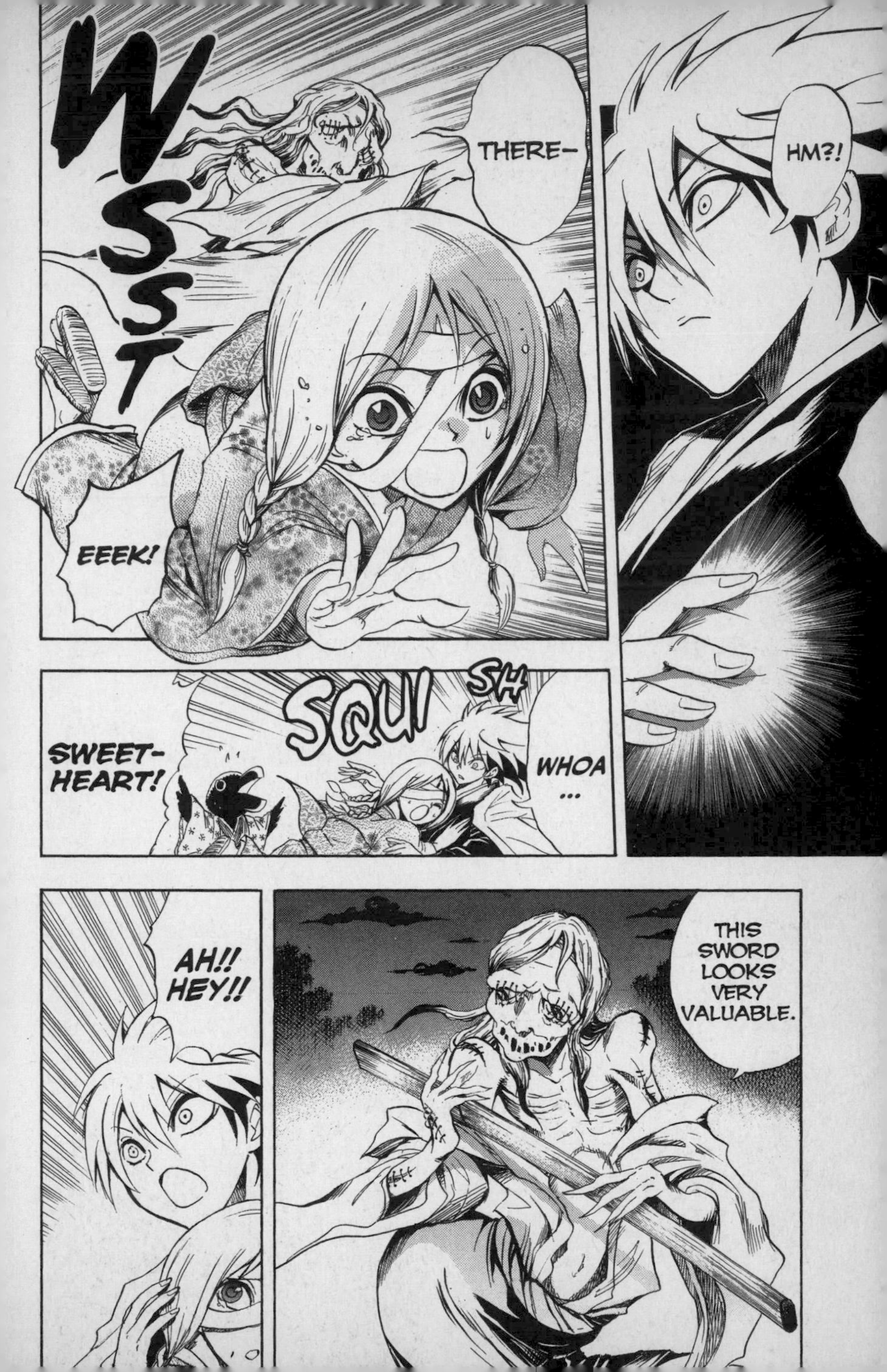

HM?!
THERE-
WSST
EEEK!
WHOA ...
SQUISH
SWEET-HEART!
THIS SWORD LOOKS VERY VALUABLE.
AH!! HEY!!

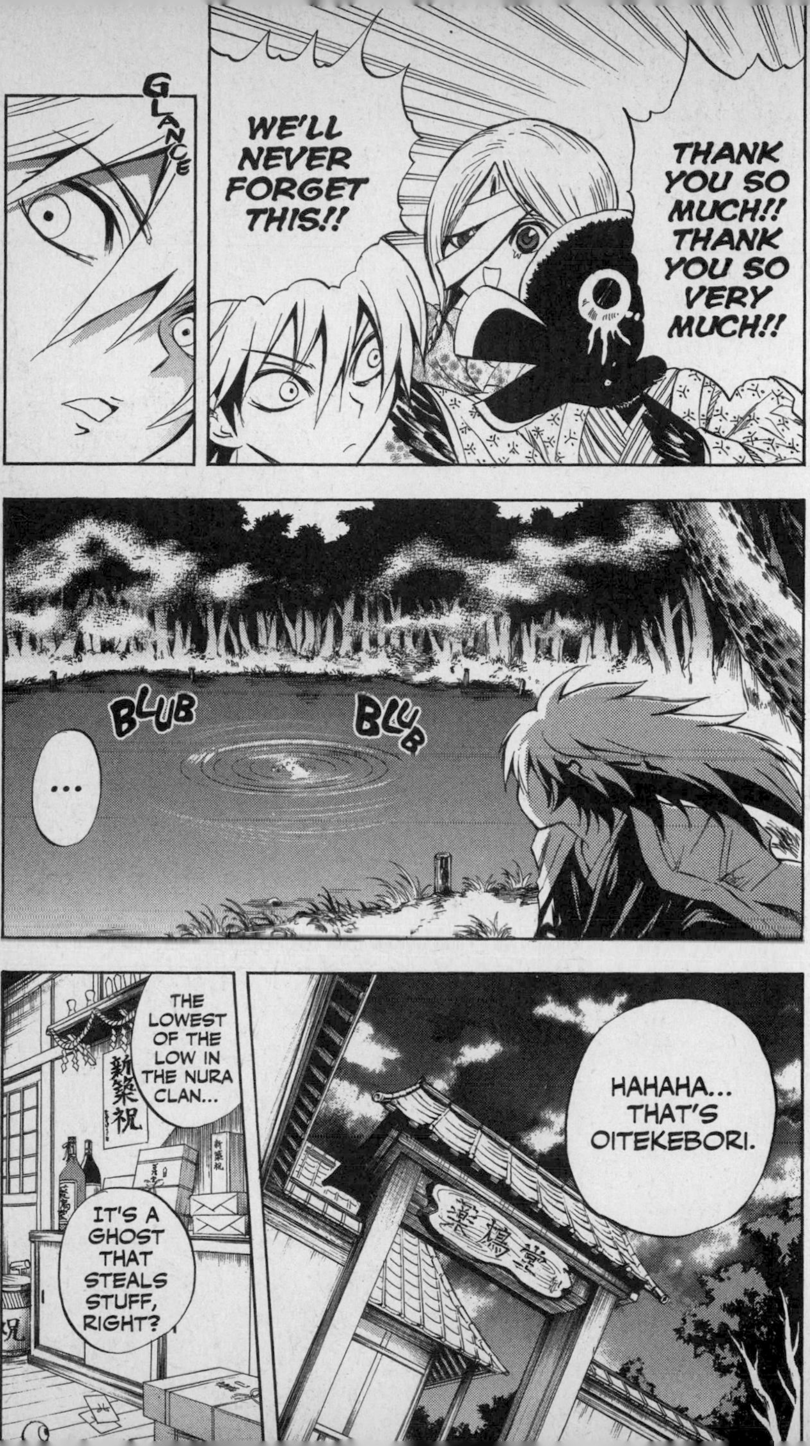
THANK YOU SO MUCH!! THANK YOU SO VERY MUCH!!
WE'LL NEVER FORGET THIS!!
GLANCE
BLUB
BLUB
...
HAHAHA... THAT'S OITEKEBORI.
THE LOWEST OF THE LOW IN THE NURA CLAN...
IT'S A GHOST THAT STEALS STUFF, RIGHT?

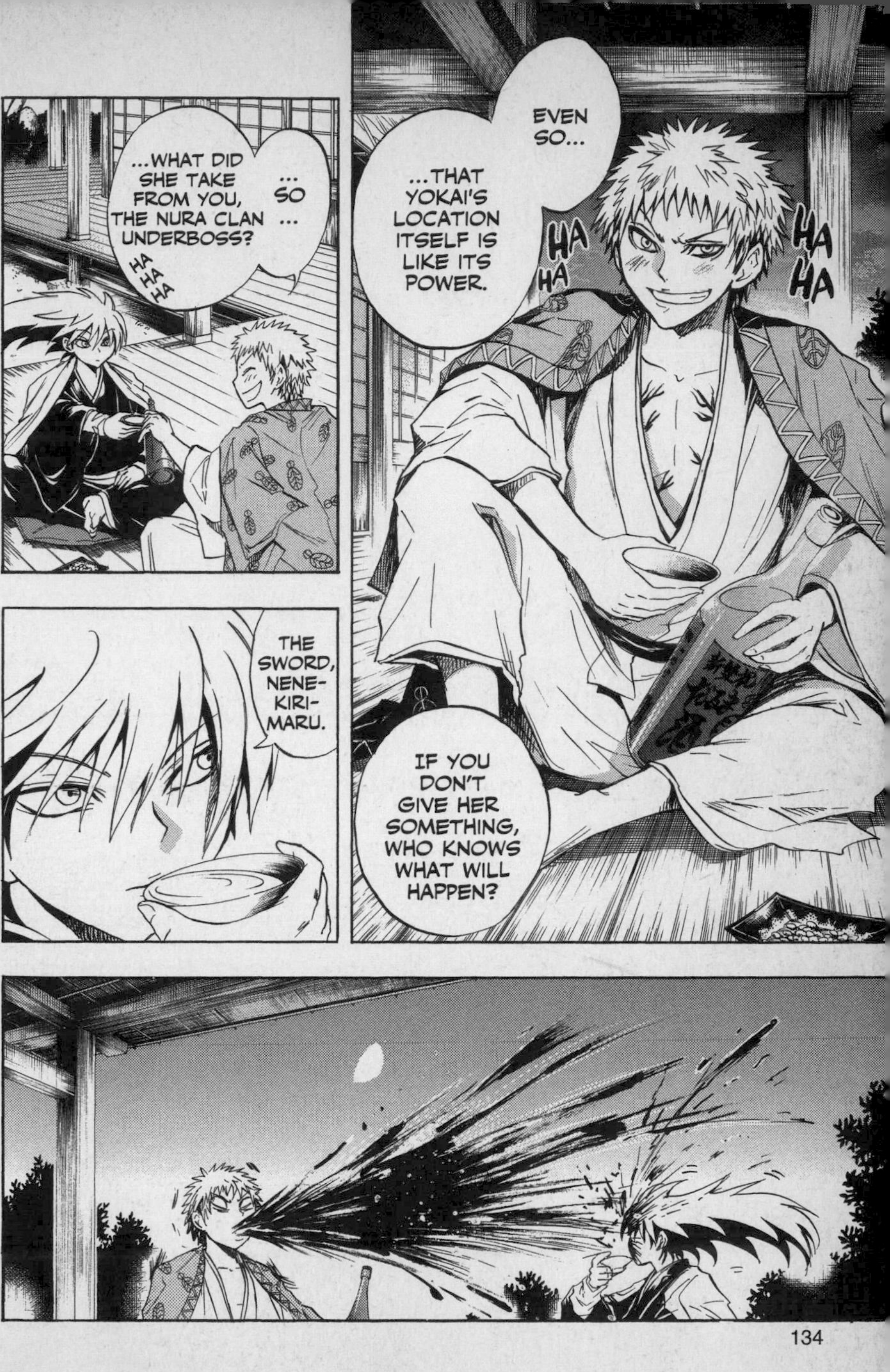
HA HA
EVEN SO...
...THAT YOKAI'S LOCATION ITSELF IS LIKE ITS POWER.
HA HA
IF YOU DON'T GIVE HER SOMETHING, WHO KNOWS WHAT WILL HAPPEN?
... SO ...
...WHAT DID SHE TAKE FROM YOU, THE NURA CLAN UNDERBOSS?
HA HA HA
THE SWORD, NENE-KIRI-MARU.

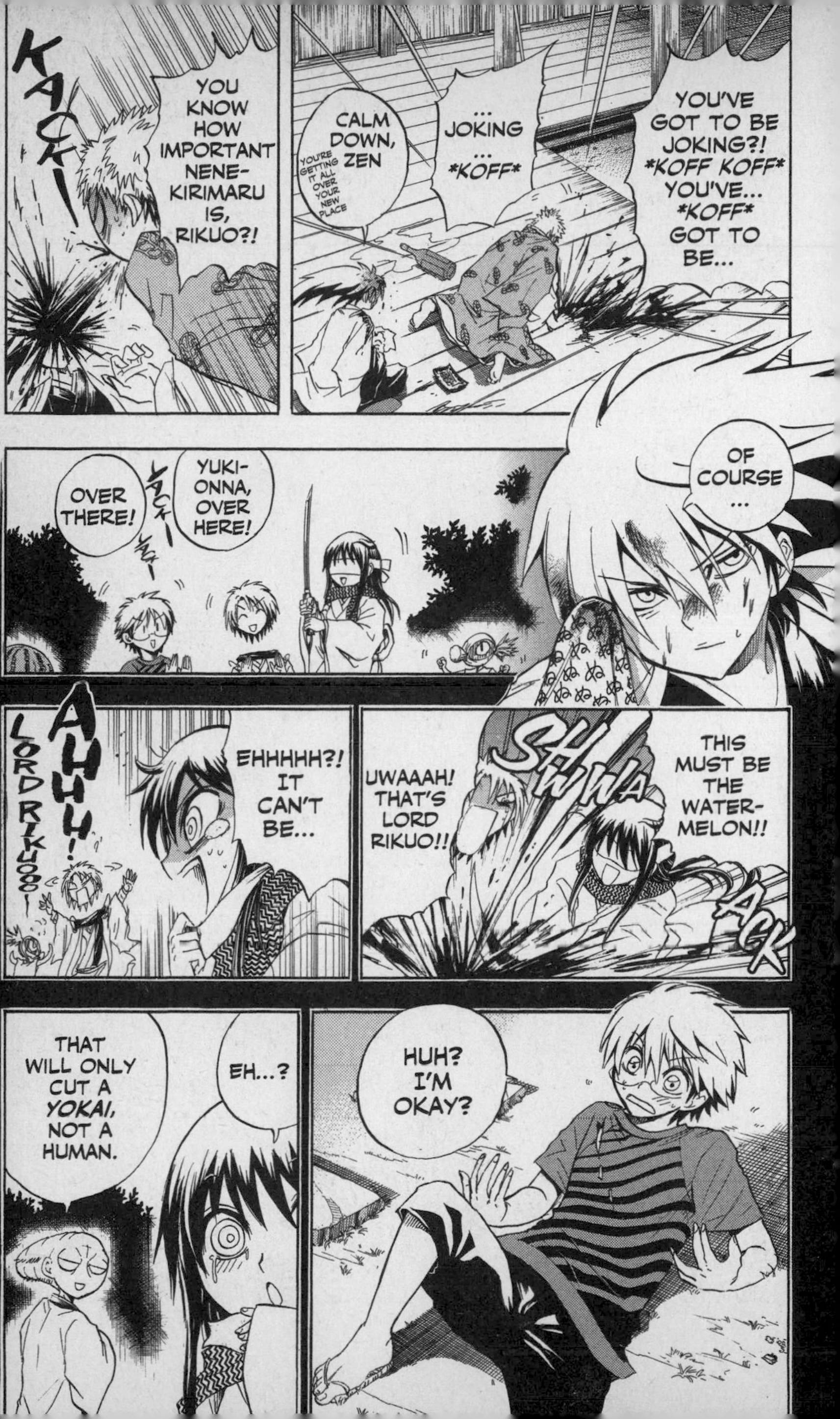
YOU'VE GOT TO BE JOKING?! *KOFF KOFF* YOU'VE... *KOFF* GOT TO BE...
... JOKING ... *KOFF*
CALM DOWN, ZEN
YOU'RE GETTING IT ALL OVER YOUR NEW PLACE
KACK!
YOU KNOW HOW IMPORTANT NENE-KIRIMARU IS, RIKUO?!
OF COURSE ...
YUKI-ONNA, OVER HERE!
OVER THERE!
THIS MUST BE THE WATER-MELON!!
SHWA
ACK
UWAAAH! THAT'S LORD RIKUO!!
EHHHHH?! IT CAN'T BE...
AHHH!
LORD RIKUOOO!
HUH? I'M OKAY?
EH...?
THAT WILL ONLY CUT A *YOKAI*, NOT A HUMAN.

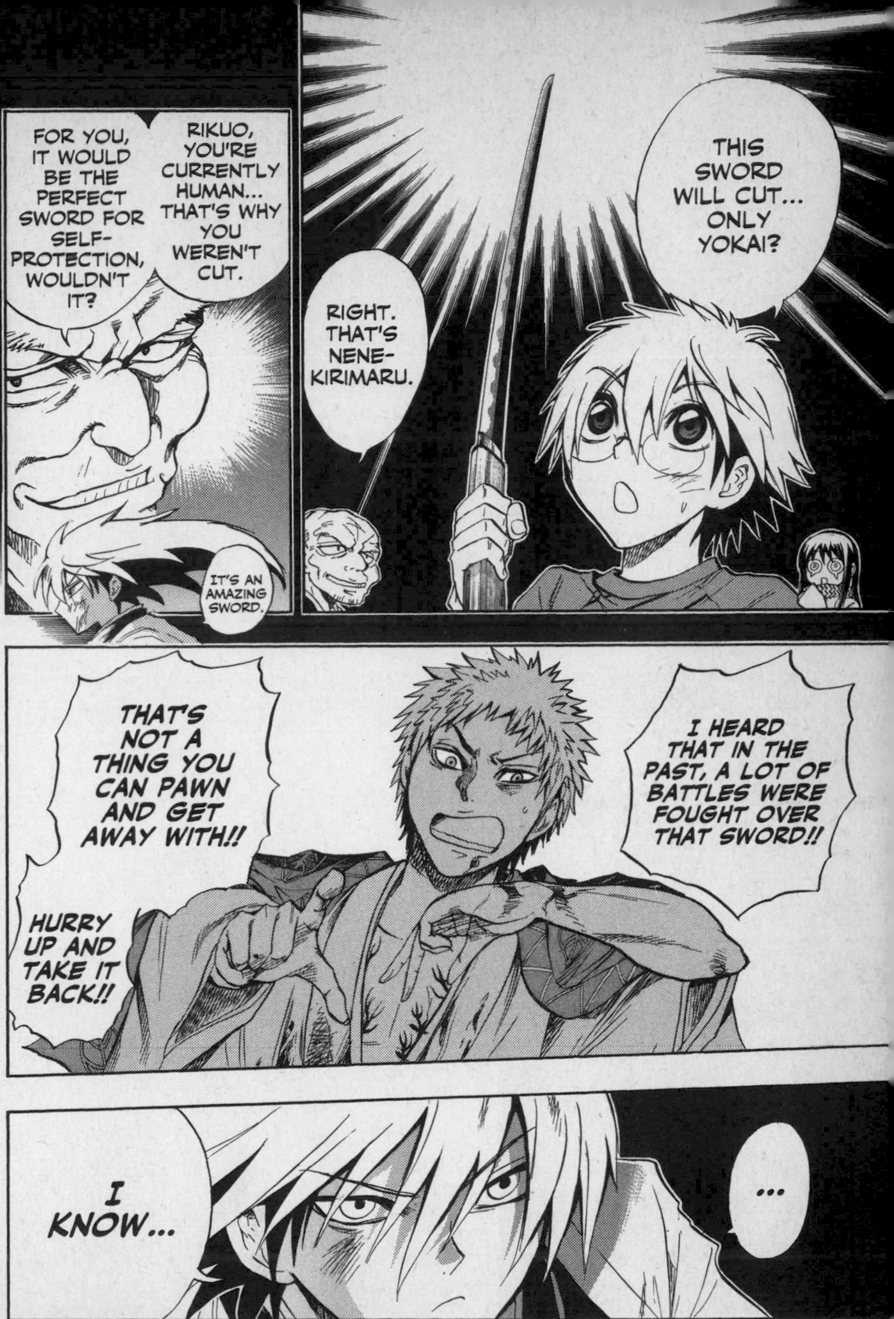
THIS SWORD WILL CUT... ONLY YOKAI?
RIGHT. THAT'S NENE-KIRIMARU.
RIKUO, YOU'RE CURRENTLY HUMAN... THAT'S WHY YOU WEREN'T CUT.
FOR YOU, IT WOULD BE THE PERFECT SWORD FOR SELF-PROTECTION, WOULDN'T IT?
IT'S AN AMAZING SWORD.
I HEARD THAT IN THE PAST, A LOT OF BATTLES WERE FOUGHT OVER THAT SWORD!!
THAT'S NOT A THING YOU CAN PAWN AND GET AWAY WITH!!
HURRY UP AND TAKE IT BACK!!
...
I KNOW...

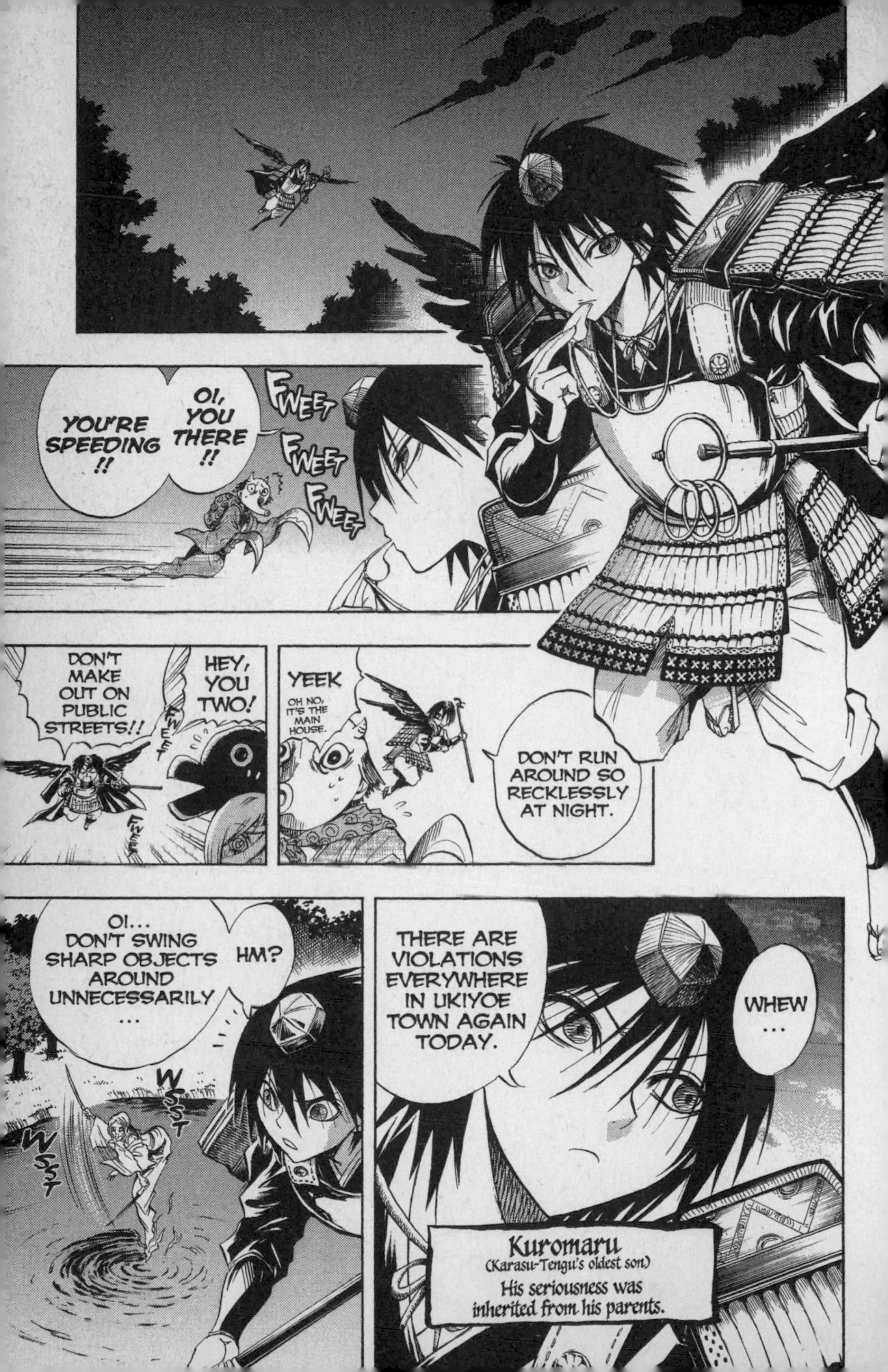
OI, YOU THERE!!
YOU'RE SPEEDING!!
FWEET
FWEET
FWEET
DON'T RUN AROUND SO RECKLESSLY AT NIGHT.
YEEK
OH NO, IT'S THE MAIN HOUSE.
HEY, YOU TWO!
DON'T MAKE OUT ON PUBLIC STREETS!!
FWEET
FWEET
WHEW...
THERE ARE VIOLATIONS EVERYWHERE IN UKIYOE TOWN AGAIN TODAY.
Kuromaru
(Karasu-Tengu's oldest son)
His seriousness was inherited from his parents.
HM?
OI... DON'T SWING SHARP OBJECTS AROUND UNNECESSARILY...
WSSST
WSSST

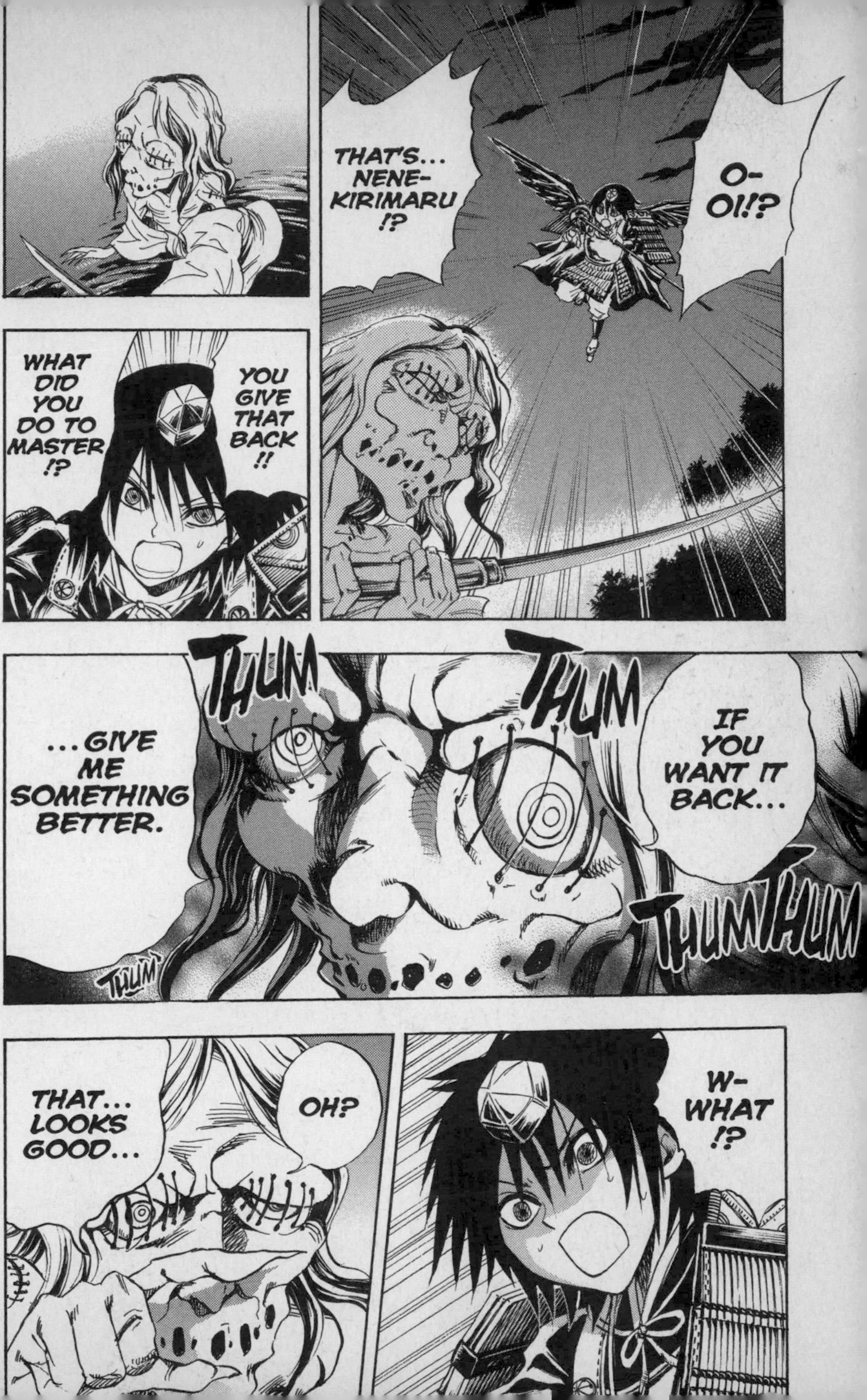
O-OI!?
THAT'S... NENE-KIRIMARU!?
YOU GIVE THAT BACK!!
WHAT DID YOU DO TO MASTER!?
IF YOU WANT IT BACK...
THUM
THUM
THUMTHUM
...GIVE ME SOMETHING BETTER.
THUM
W-WHAT!?
OH?
THAT... LOOKS GOOD...

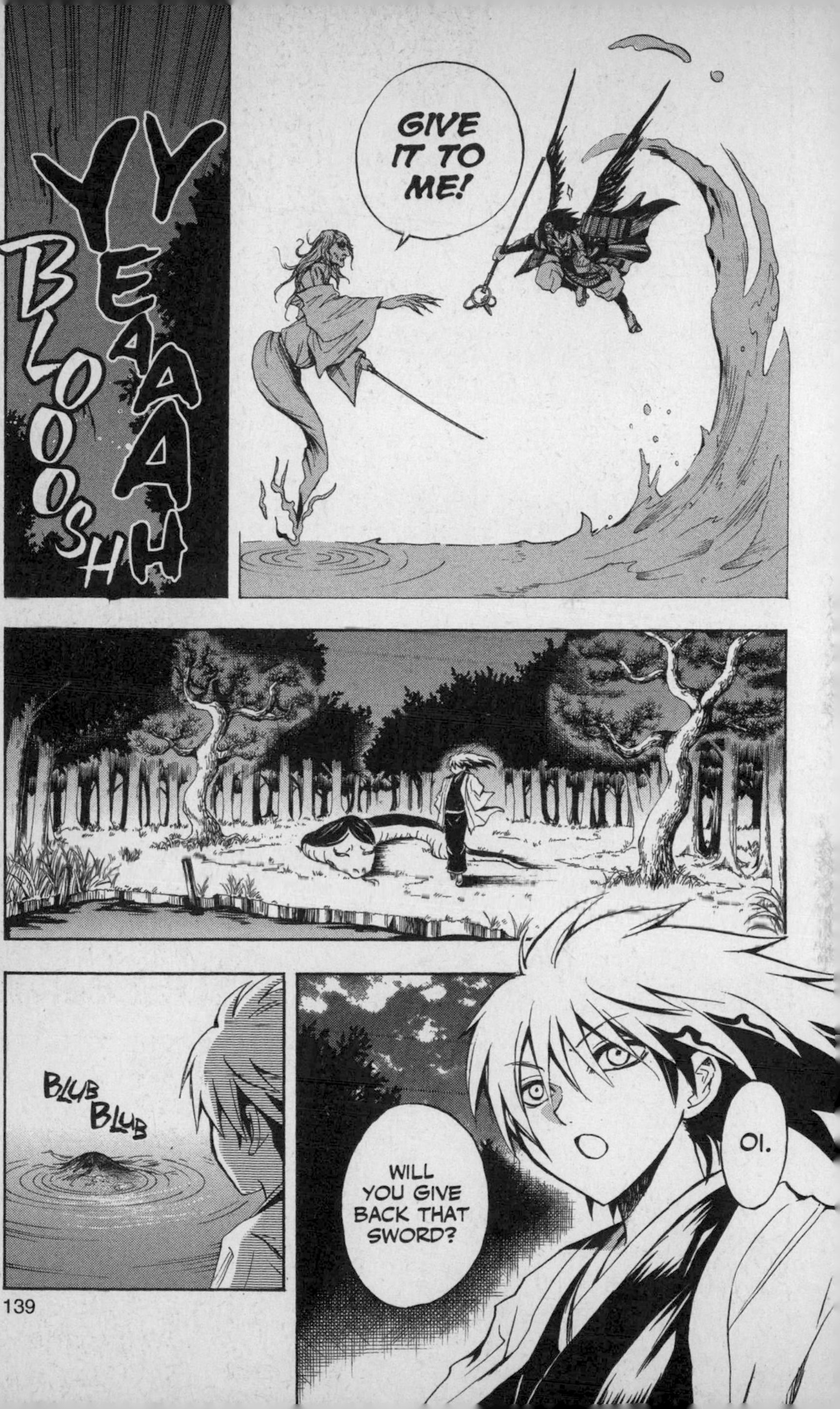
GIVE IT TO ME!
YYEAAAH
BLOOOSH
OI.
WILL YOU GIVE BACK THAT SWORD?
BLUB BLUB

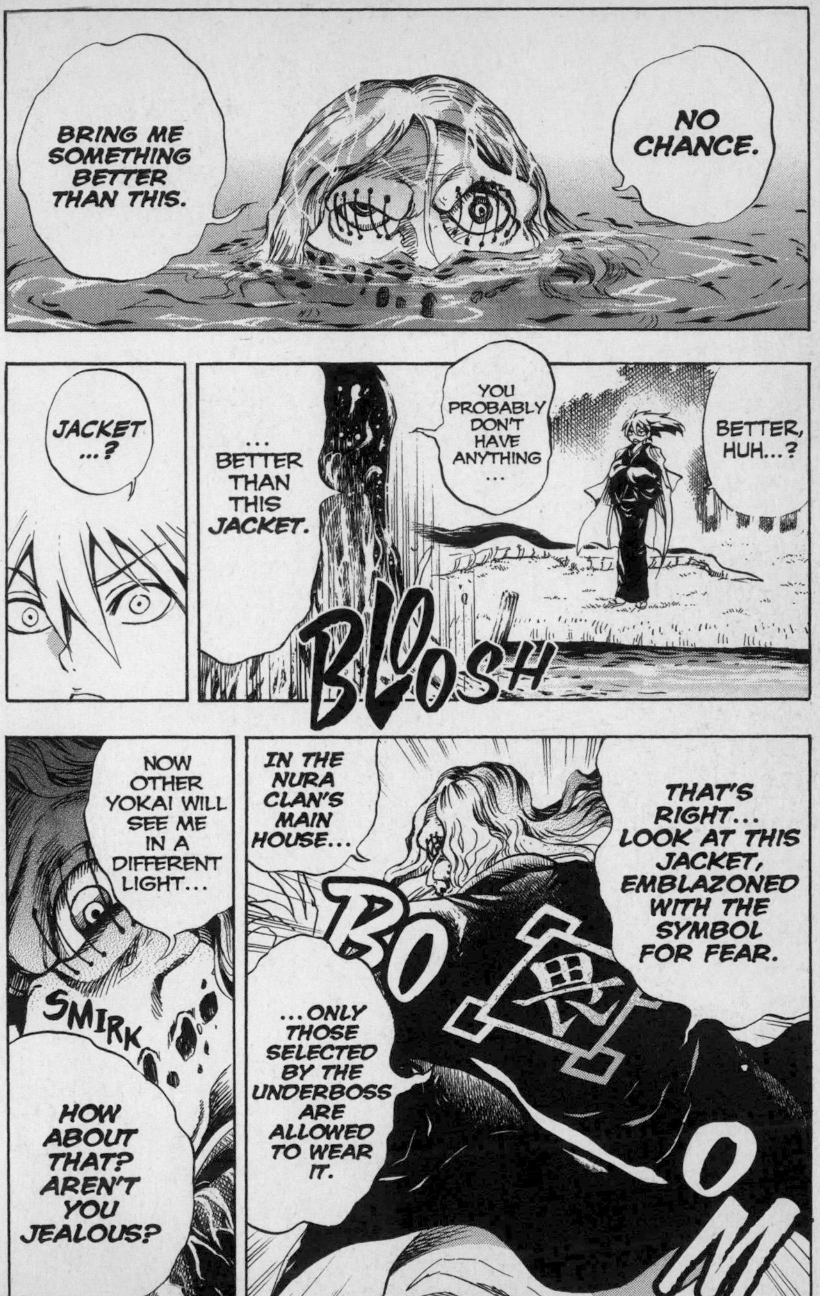
NO CHANCE.
BRING ME SOMETHING BETTER THAN THIS.
BETTER, HUH...?
YOU PROBABLY DON'T HAVE ANYTHING...
...BETTER THAN THIS JACKET.
BLOOSH
JACKET...?
THAT'S RIGHT... LOOK AT THIS JACKET, EMBLAZONED WITH THE SYMBOL FOR FEAR.
IN THE NURA CLAN'S MAIN HOUSE...
...ONLY THOSE SELECTED BY THE UNDERBOSS ARE ALLOWED TO WEAR IT.
BOOM
NOW OTHER YOKAI WILL SEE ME IN A DIFFERENT LIGHT...
SMIRK
HOW ABOUT THAT? AREN'T YOU JEALOUS?

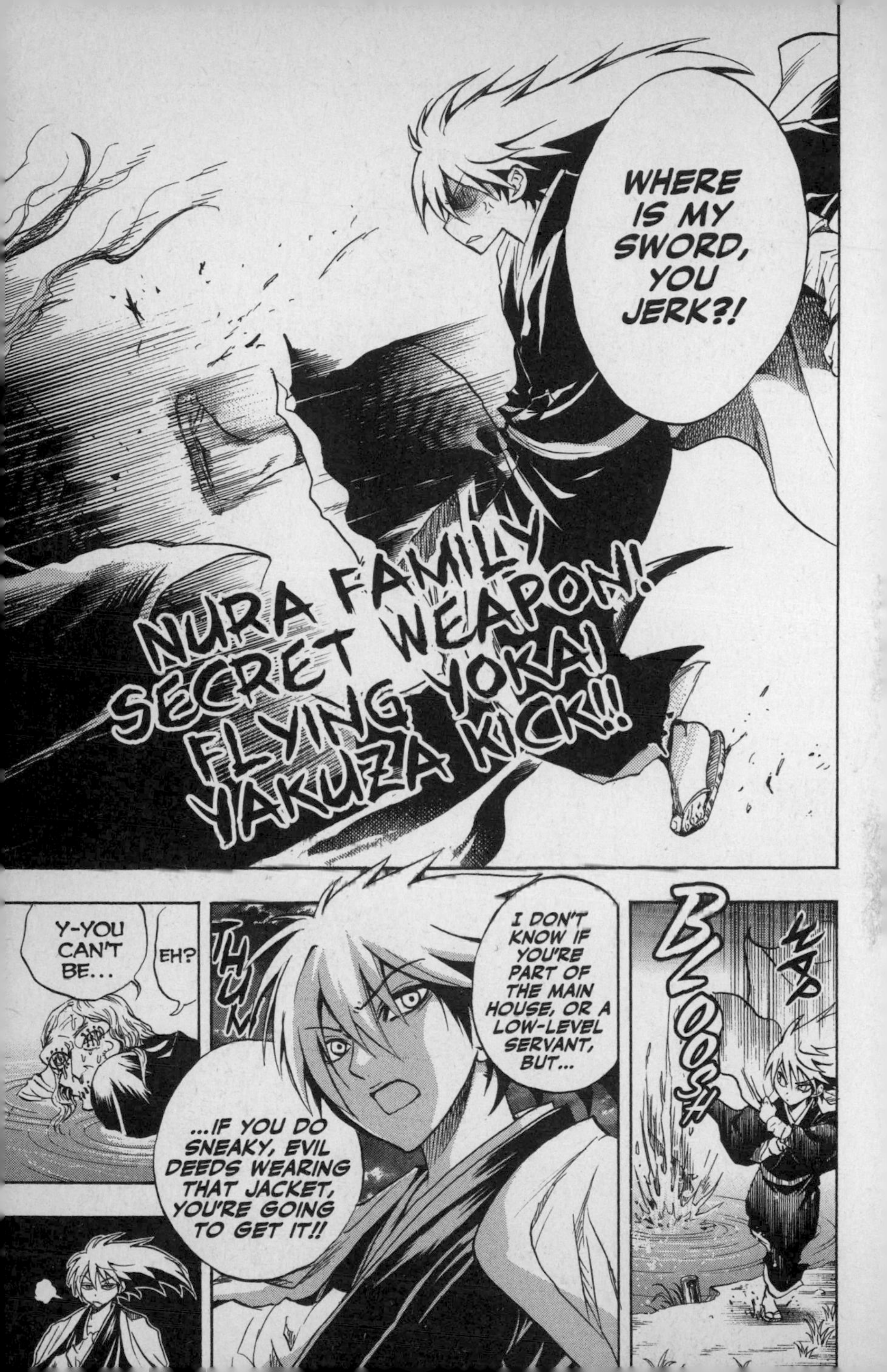

WHERE IS MY SWORD, YOU JERK?!
NURA FAMILY SECRET WEAPON! FLYING YOKAI YAKUZA KICK!!
BLOOOSH
WAP
THUM
I DON'T KNOW IF YOU'RE PART OF THE MAIN HOUSE, OR A LOW-LEVEL SERVANT, BUT...
...IF YOU DO SNEAKY, EVIL DEEDS WEARING THAT JACKET, YOU'RE GOING TO GET IT!!
EH?
Y-YOU CAN'T BE...

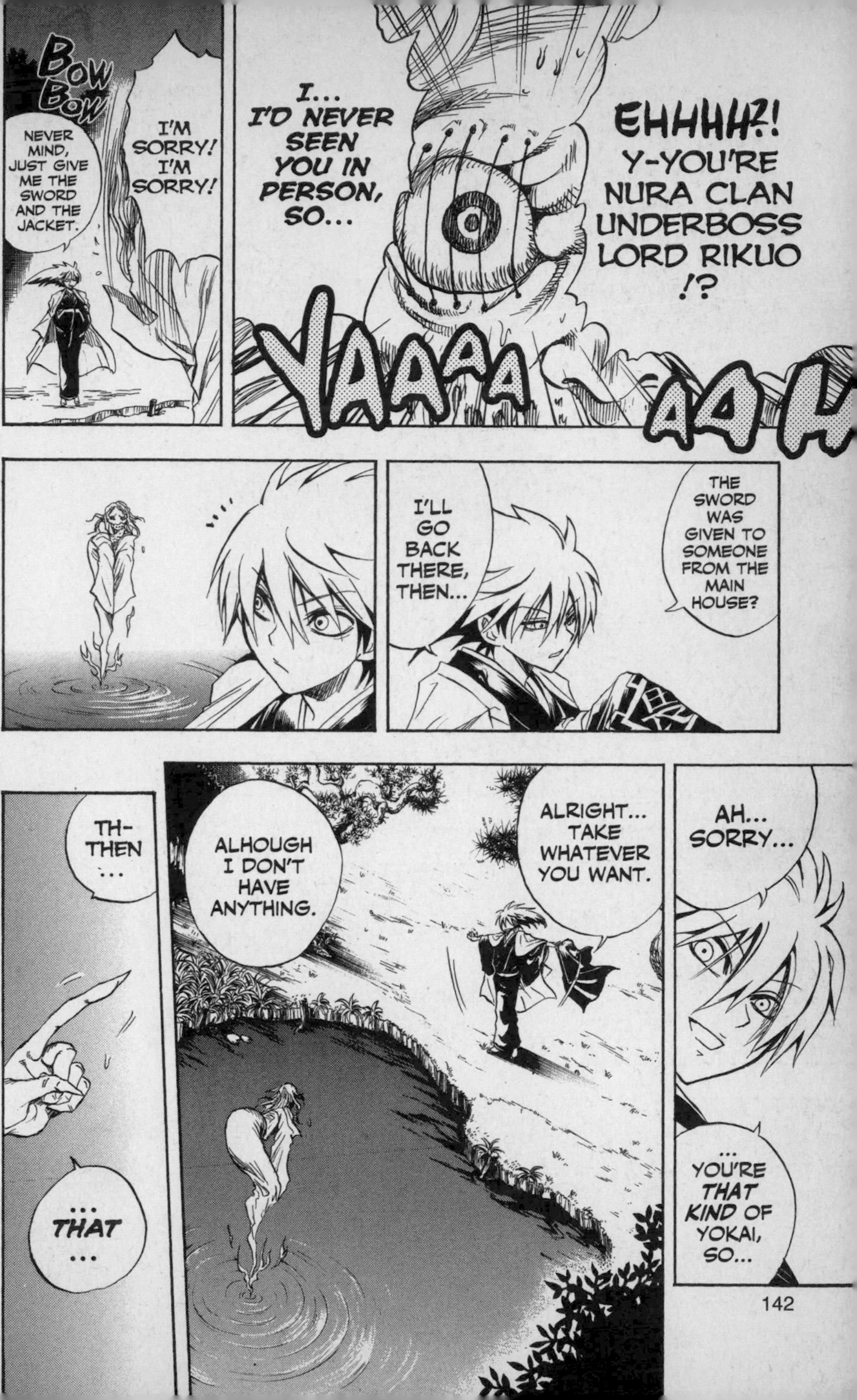
EHHHH?! Y-YOU'RE NURA CLAN UNDERBOSS LORD RIKUO !?
I... I'D NEVER SEEN YOU IN PERSON, SO...
YAAAA AAH
I'M SORRY! I'M SORRY!
NEVER MIND, JUST GIVE ME THE SWORD AND THE JACKET.
BOW BOW
THE SWORD WAS GIVEN TO SOMEONE FROM THE MAIN HOUSE?
I'LL GO BACK THERE, THEN...
AH... SORRY...
... YOU'RE *THAT KIND* OF YOKAI, SO...
ALRIGHT... TAKE WHATEVER YOU WANT.
ALHOUGH I DON'T HAVE ANYTHING.
TH-THEN ...
... *THAT* ...

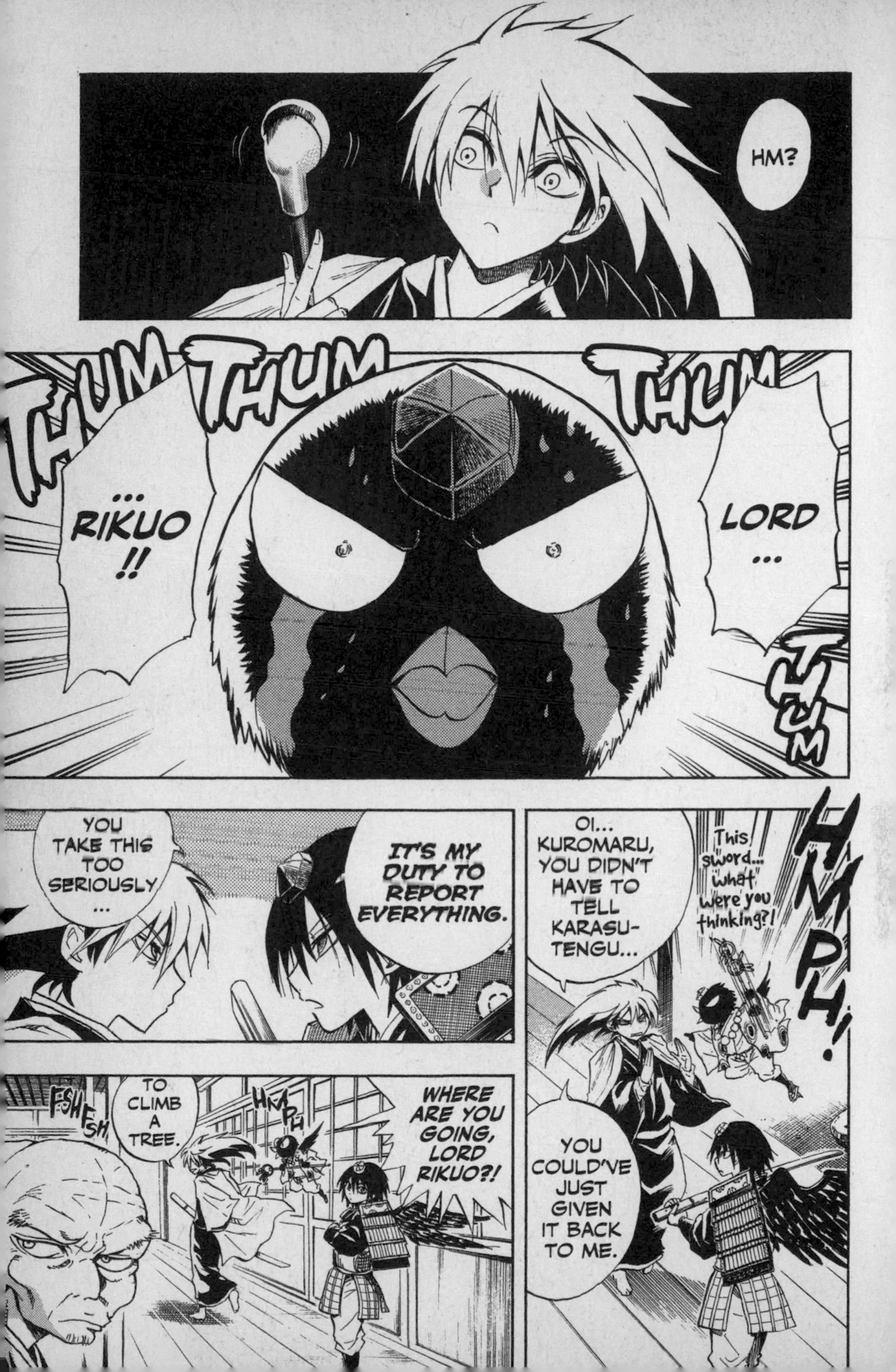
HM?
THUM
THUM
THUM
THUM THUM
LORD ...
... RIKUO !!
HMPH!
This sword... what were you thinking?!
OI... KUROMARU, YOU DIDN'T HAVE TO TELL KARASU-TENGU...
YOU COULD'VE JUST GIVEN IT BACK TO ME.
IT'S MY DUTY TO REPORT EVERYTHING.
YOU TAKE THIS TOO SERIOUSLY ...
WHERE ARE YOU GOING, LORD RIKUO?!
HMPH
TO CLIMB A TREE.
FSH FSH

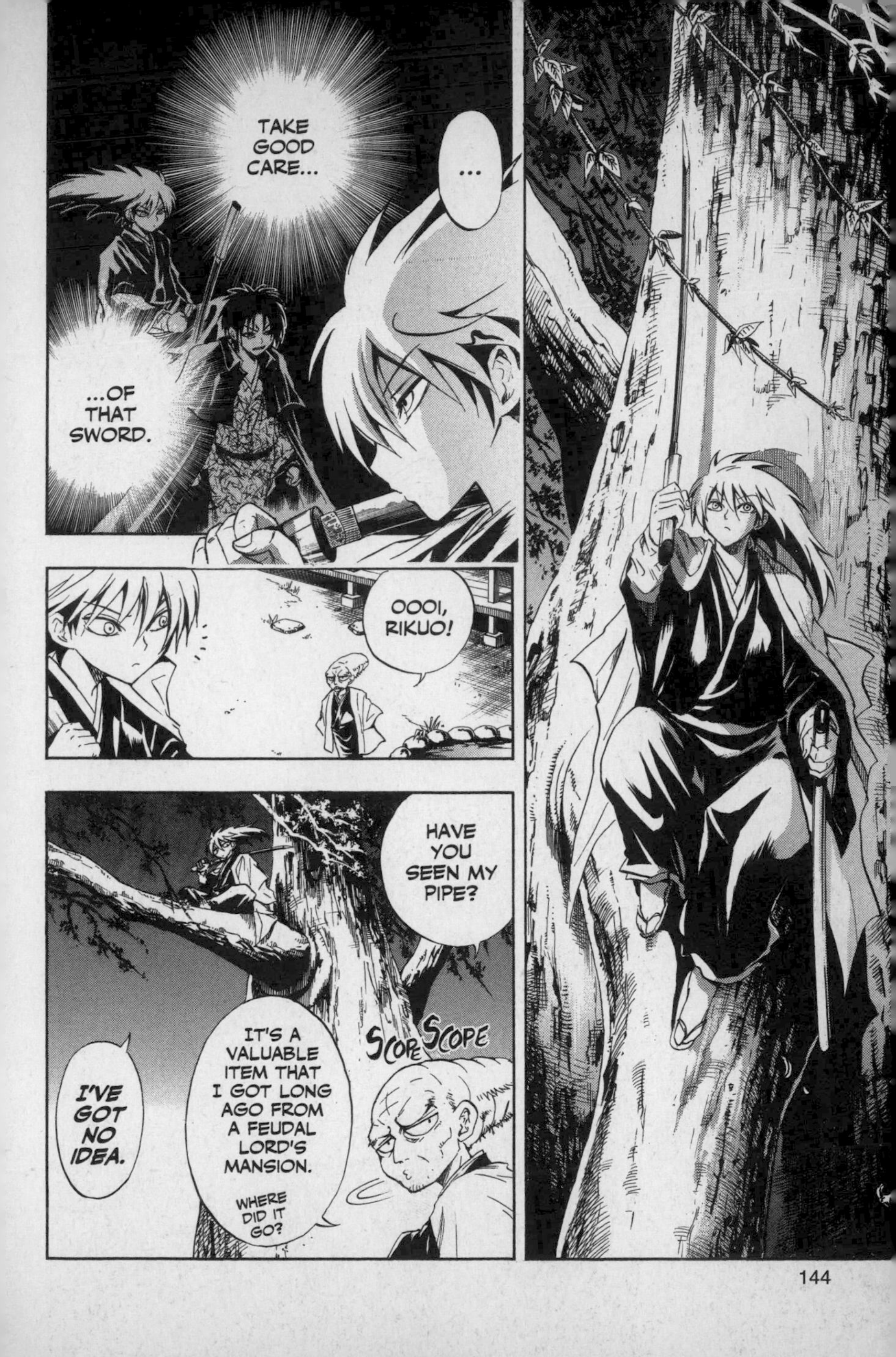
TAKE GOOD CARE...
...OF THAT SWORD.
...
OOOI, RIKUO!
HAVE YOU SEEN MY PIPE?
SCOPE SCOPE
IT'S A VALUABLE ITEM THAT I GOT LONG AGO FROM A FEUDAL LORD'S MANSION.
WHERE DID IT GO?
I'VE GOT NO IDEA.

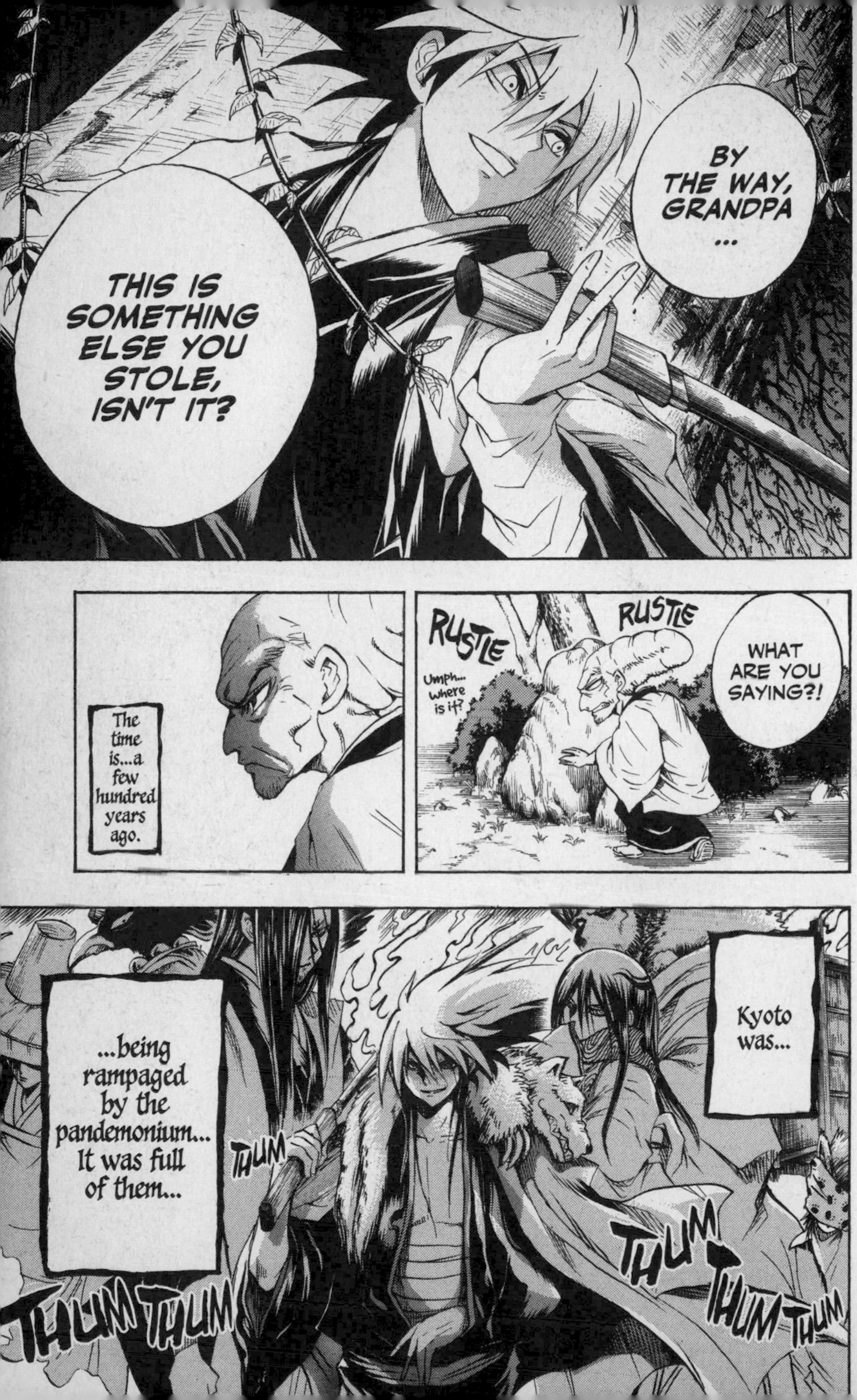
BY THE WAY, GRANDPA...
THIS IS SOMETHING ELSE YOU STOLE, ISN'T IT?
RUSTLE
WHAT ARE YOU SAYING?!
RUSTLE
Umph... where is it?
The time is...a few hundred years ago.
Kyoto was...
...being rampaged by the pandemonium... It was full of them...
THUM
THUM
THUM
THUM THUM
THUM THUM

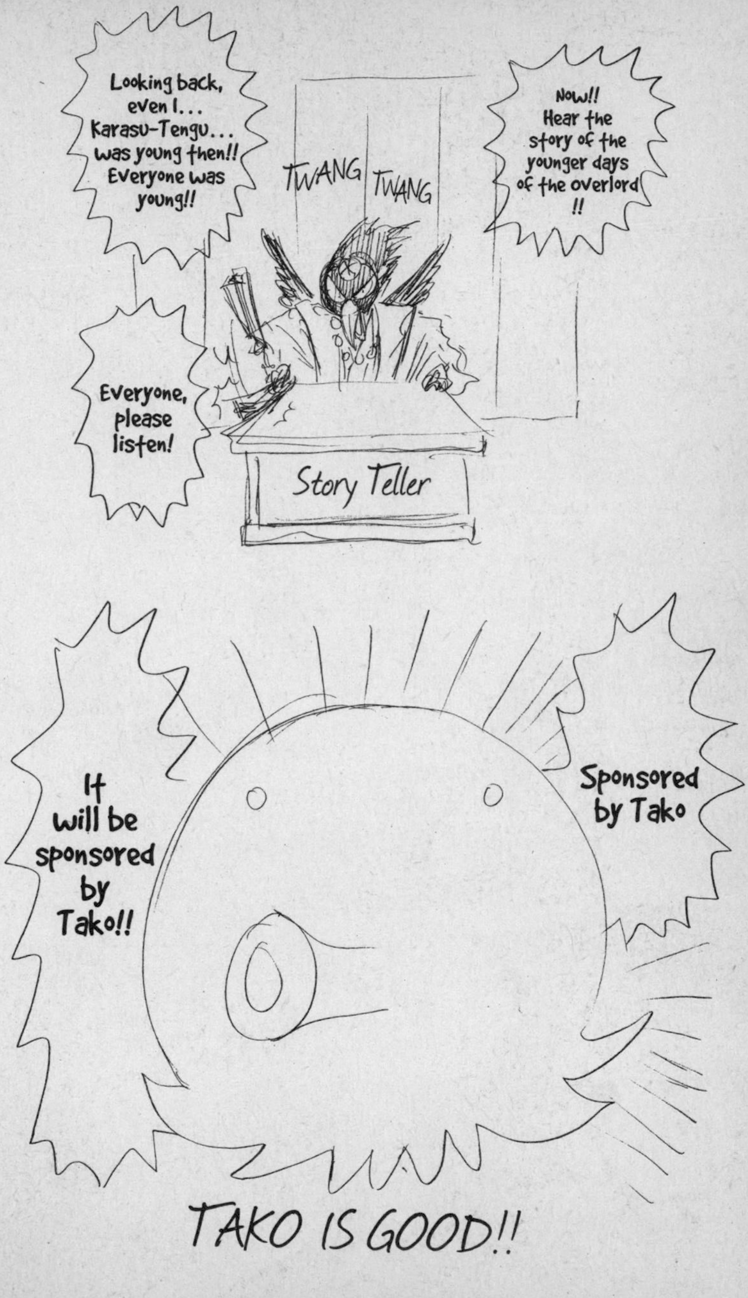
Now!! Hear the story of the younger days of the overlord!!
TWANG TWANG
Looking back, even I... Karasu-Tengu... was young then!! Everyone was young!!
Everyone, please listen!
Story Teller
Sponsored by Tako
It will be sponsored by Tako!!
TAKO IS GOOD!!

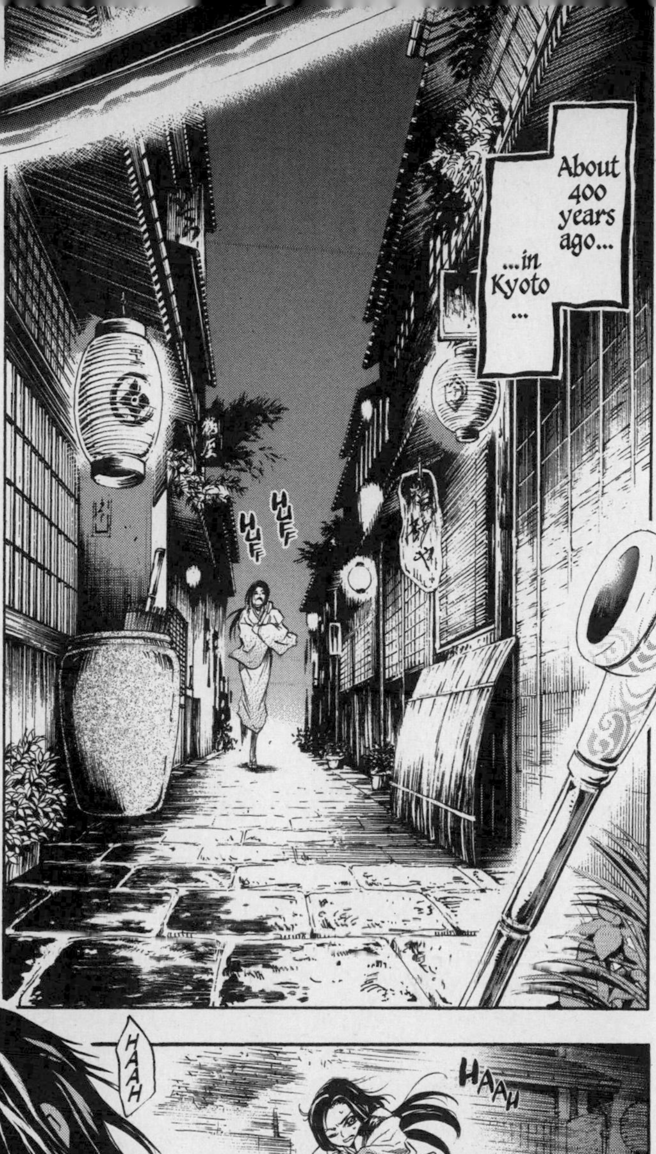
About 400 years ago...
...in Kyoto ...
HUFF HUFF

# Act 59: The Sword and the Pipe

## The Spirit Blade Nenekirimaru, Part 2

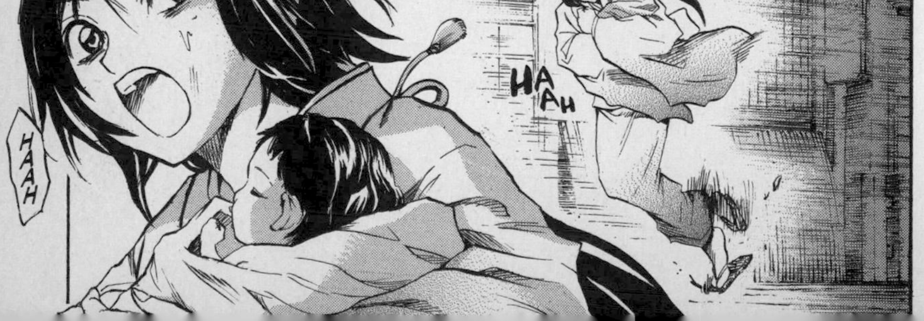
HAAH
HAAH
HAAH
HAAH

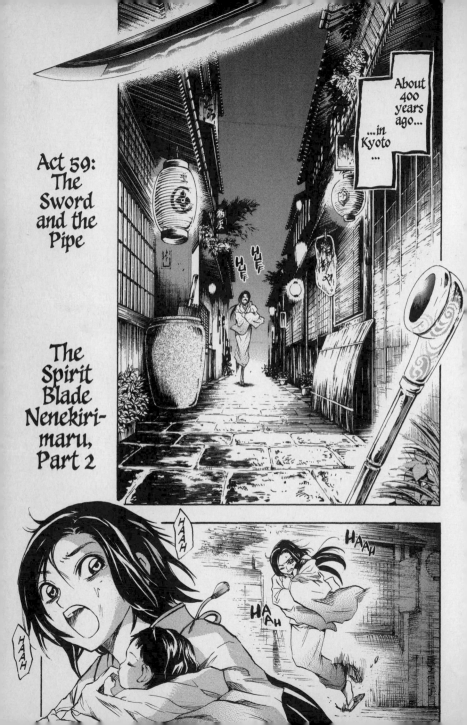

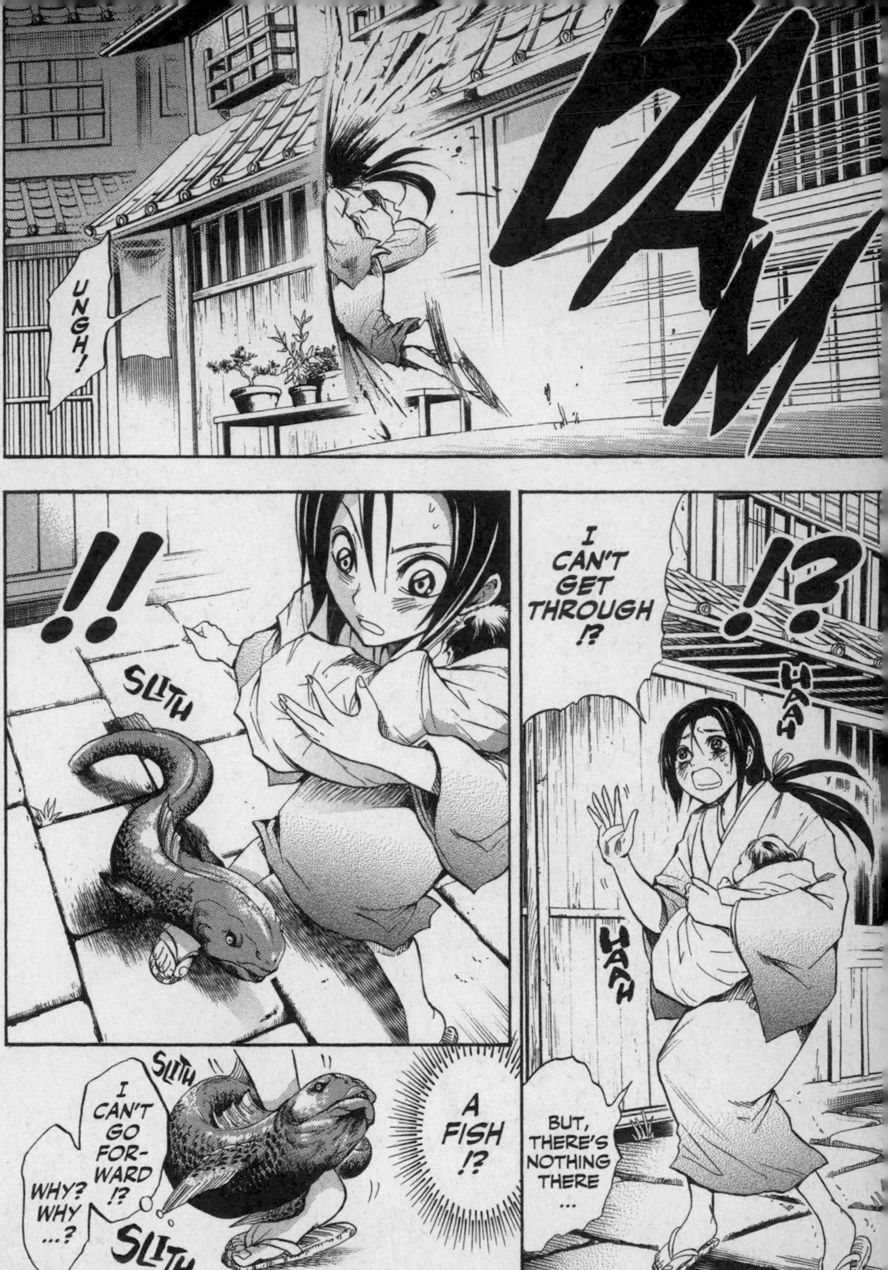
DAM
UNGH!
!?
I CAN'T GET THROUGH !?
HAAH
HAAH
BUT, THERE'S NOTHING THERE ...
!!
SLITH
A FISH !?
SLITH
I CAN'T GO FOR-WARD !?
WHY? WHY ...?
SLITH

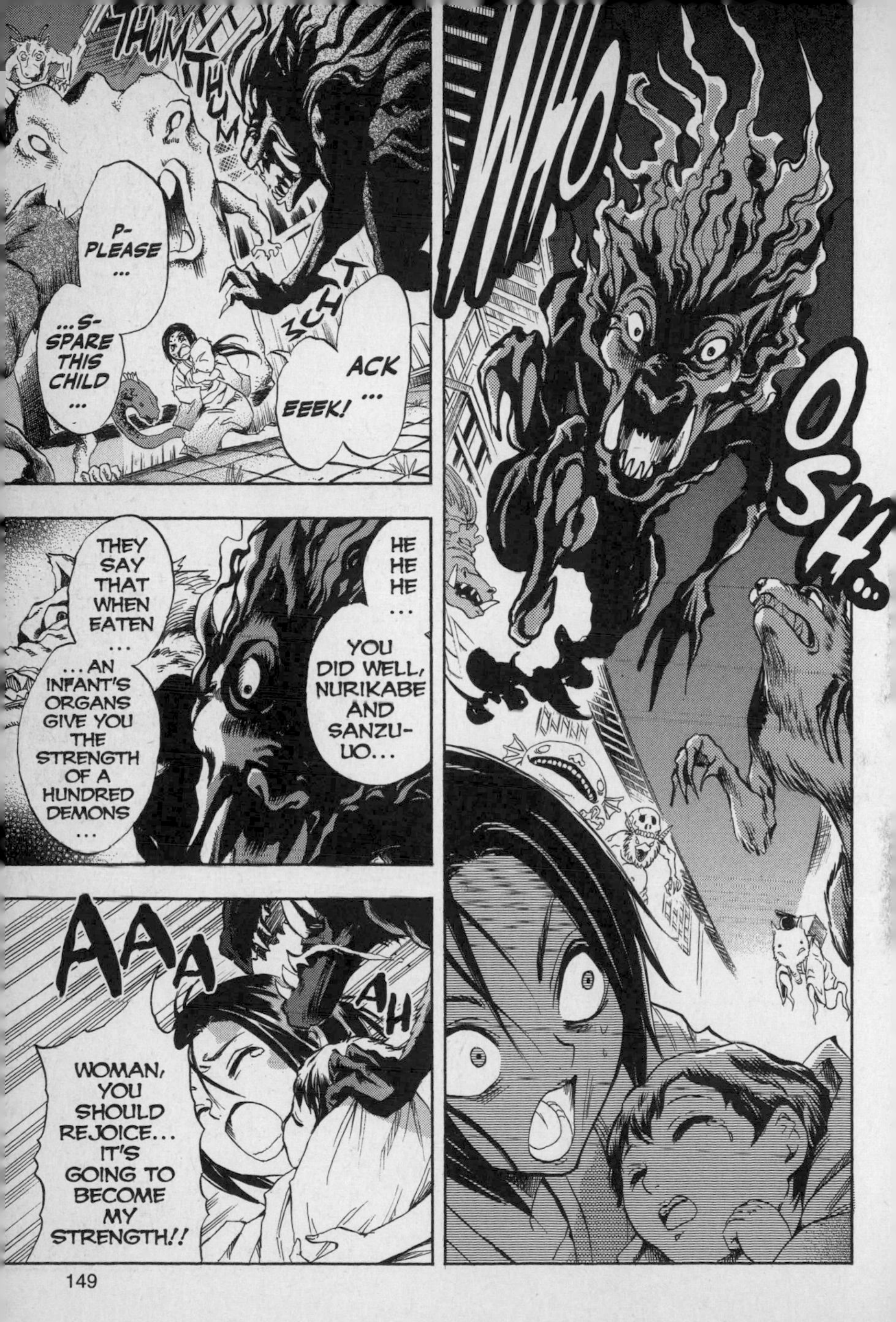
WHO
OSH...
THUM THUM
THUMP
ACK... EEEK!
P-PLEASE...
...S-SPARE THIS CHILD...
HE HE HE...
YOU DID WELL, NURIKABE AND SANZU-UO...
THEY SAY THAT WHEN EATEN...
...AN INFANT'S ORGANS GIVE YOU THE STRENGTH OF A HUNDRED DEMONS...
AAAAH
WOMAN, YOU SHOULD REJOICE... IT'S GOING TO BECOME MY STRENGTH!!

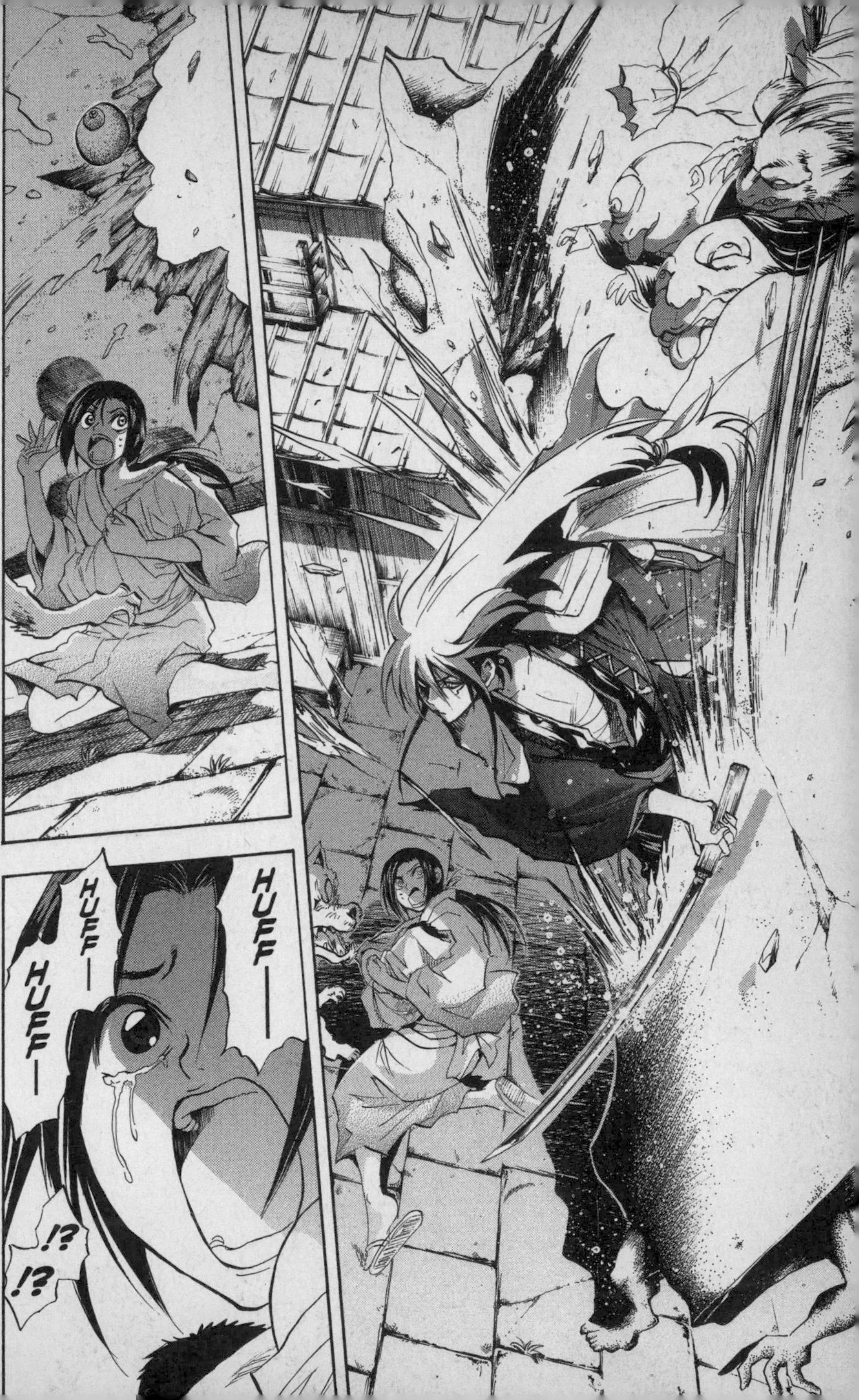
HUFF—
HUFF—
HUFF—
!?
!?

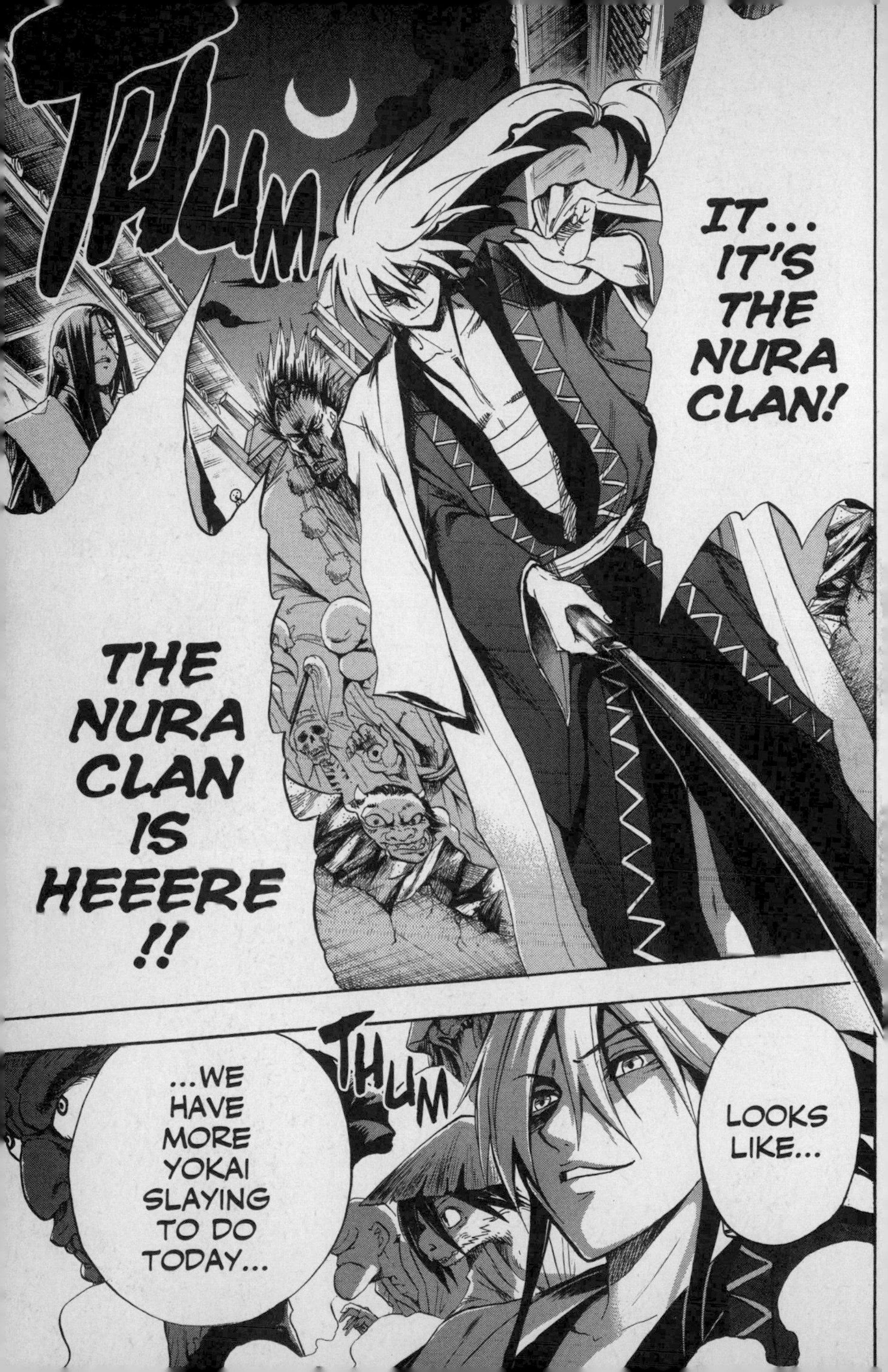
IT... IT'S THE NURA CLAN!
THUM
THE NURA CLAN IS HEEERE!!
LOOKS LIKE...
THUM
...WE HAVE MORE YOKAI SLAYING TO DO TODAY...

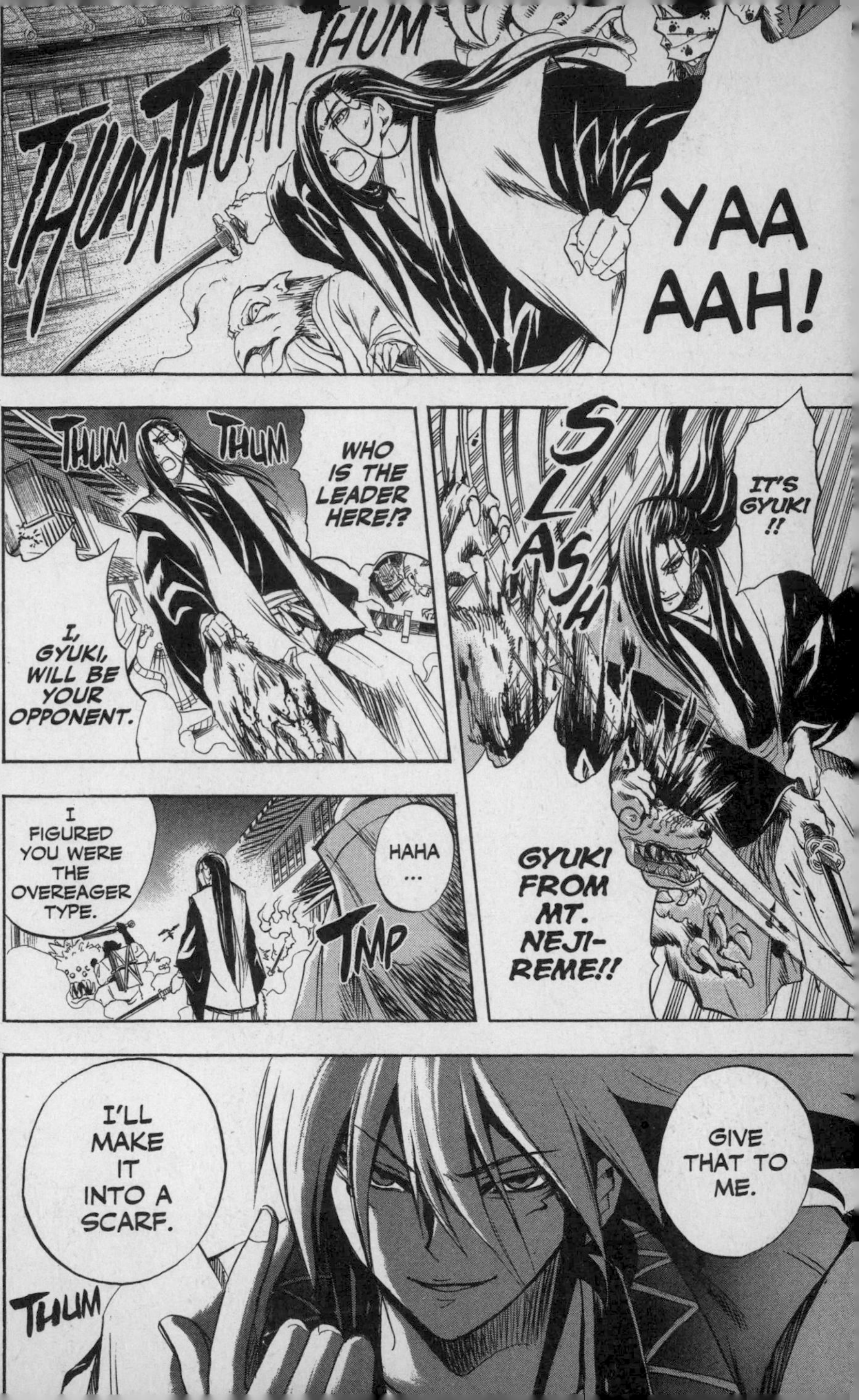
THUM THUM THUM
YAA AAH!
IT'S GYUKI!!
SLASH
GYUKI FROM MT. NEJI-REME!!
THUM THUM
WHO IS THE LEADER HERE!?
I, GYUKI, WILL BE YOUR OPPONENT.
HAHA...
I FIGURED YOU WERE THE OVEREAGER TYPE.
TMP
GIVE THAT TO ME.
I'LL MAKE IT INTO A SCARF.
THUM

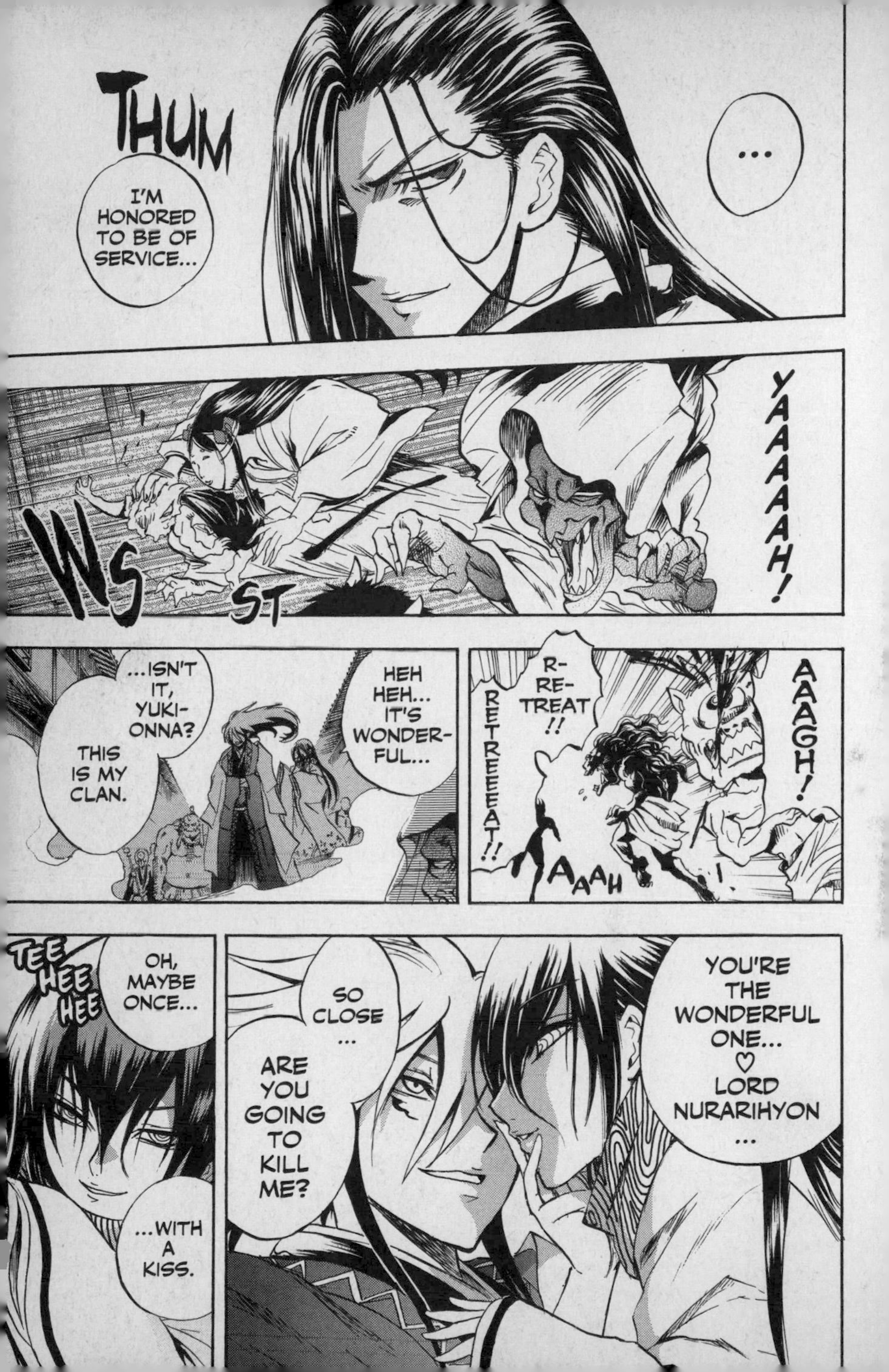
...
THUM
I'M HONORED TO BE OF SERVICE...
YAAAAAAH!
WSST
AAAGH!
R-RE-TREAT!!
RETREEEAT!!
AAAH
HEH HEH... IT'S WONDERFUL...
...ISN'T IT, YUKI-ONNA?
THIS IS MY CLAN.
YOU'RE THE WONDERFUL ONE... ♡ LORD NURARIHYON...
SO CLOSE...
ARE YOU GOING TO KILL ME?
TEE HEE HEE
OH, MAYBE ONCE...
...WITH A KISS.

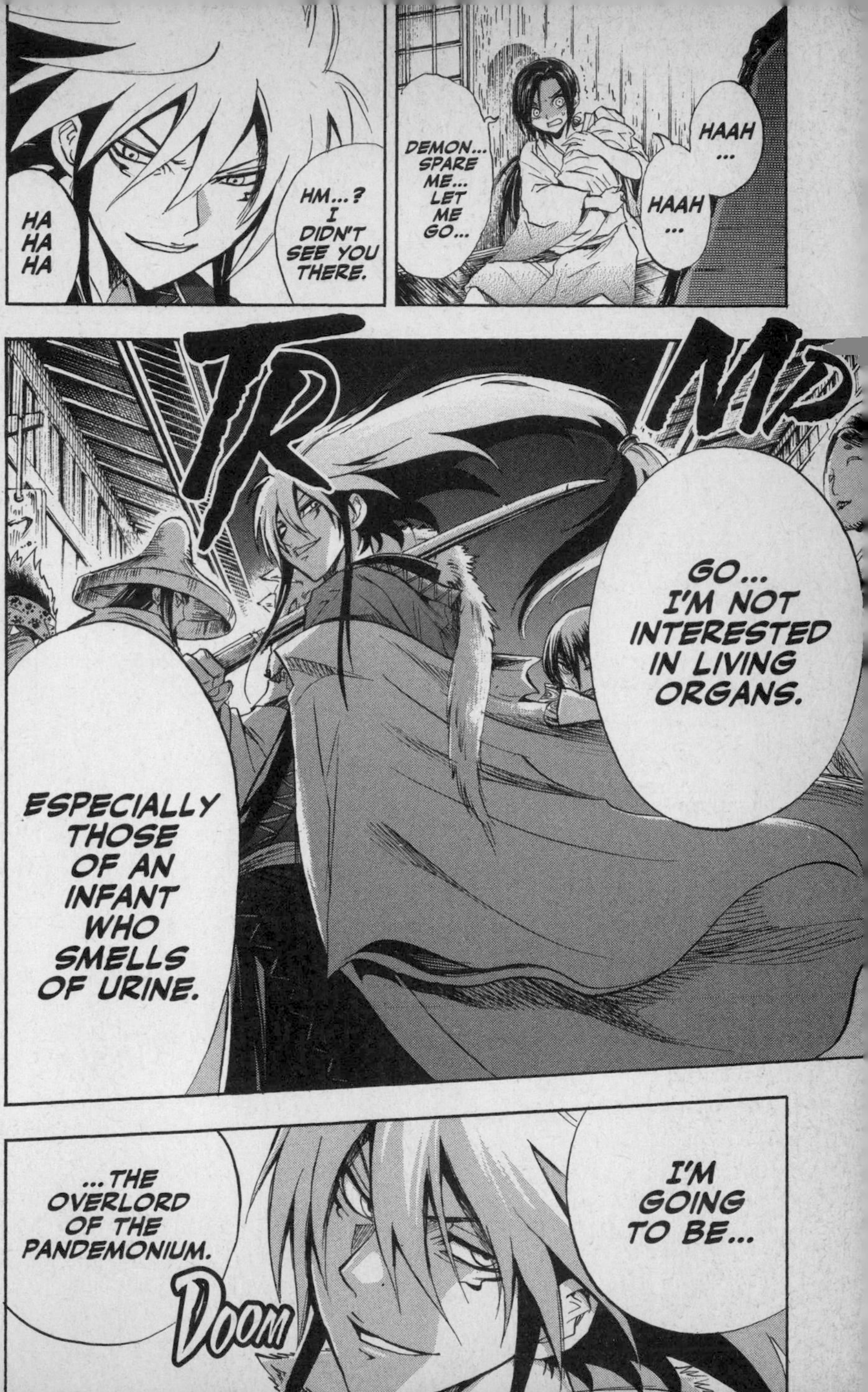
HAAH ...
HAAH ...
DEMON... SPARE ME... LET ME GO...
HM...? I DIDN'T SEE YOU THERE.
HA HA HA
TMP
GO... I'M NOT INTERESTED IN LIVING ORGANS.
ESPECIALLY THOSE OF AN INFANT WHO SMELLS OF URINE.
I'M GOING TO BE...
...THE OVERLORD OF THE PANDEMONIUM.
DOOM

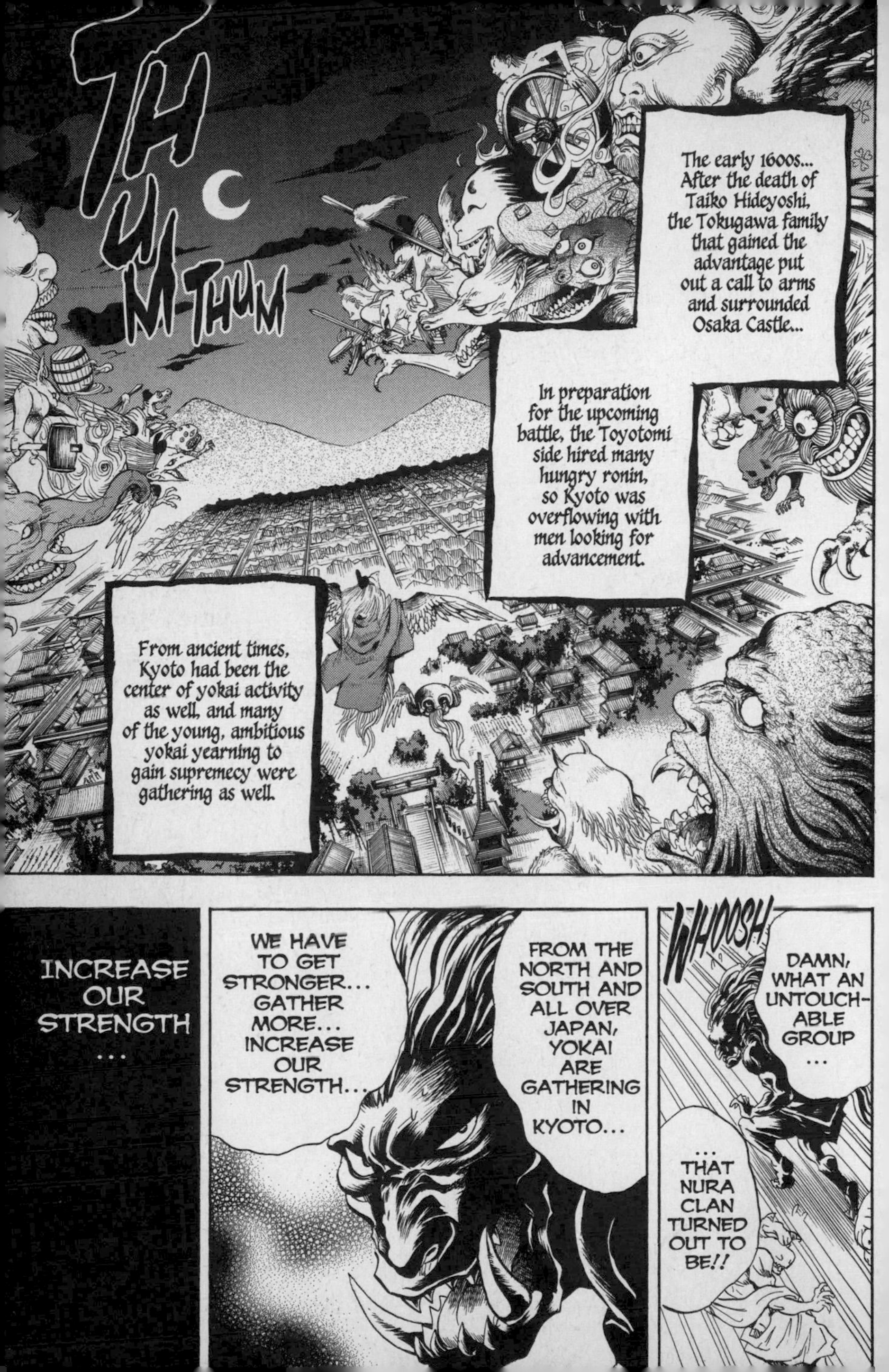
The early 1600s... After the death of Taiko Hideyoshi, the Tokugawa family that gained the advantage put out a call to arms and surrounded Osaka Castle...
THUM THUM
In preparation for the upcoming battle, the Toyotomi side hired many hungry ronin, so Kyoto was overflowing with men looking for advancement.
From ancient times, Kyoto had been the center of yokai activity as well, and many of the young, ambitious yokai yearning to gain supremecy were gathering as well.
WHOOSH
DAMN, WHAT AN UNTOUCH-ABLE GROUP...
...THAT NURA CLAN TURNED OUT TO BE!!
FROM THE NORTH AND SOUTH AND ALL OVER JAPAN, YOKAI ARE GATHERING IN KYOTO...
WE HAVE TO GET STRONGER... GATHER MORE... INCREASE OUR STRENGTH...
INCREASE OUR STRENGTH...

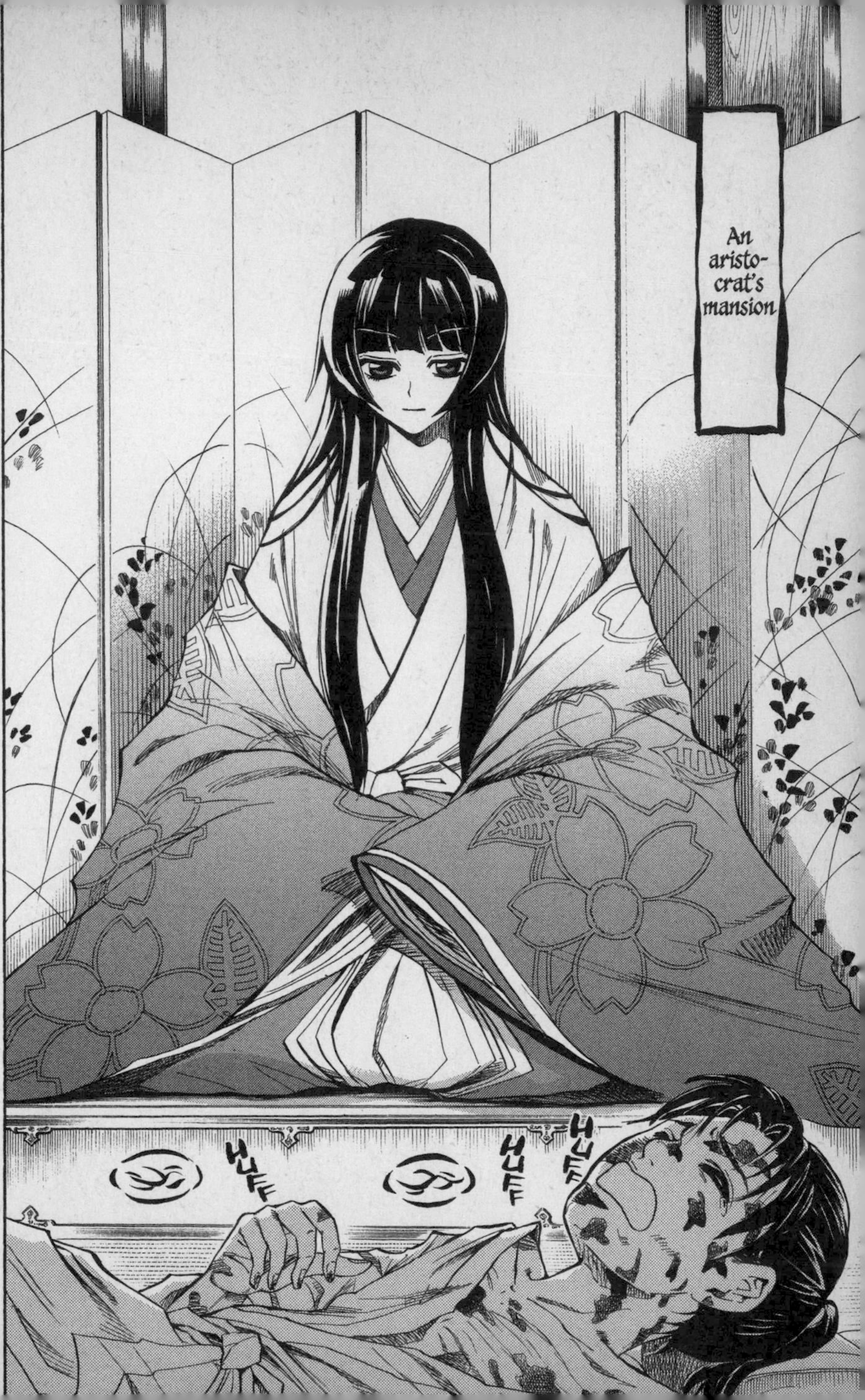
An aristo-crat's mansion
HUFF
HUFF
HUFF

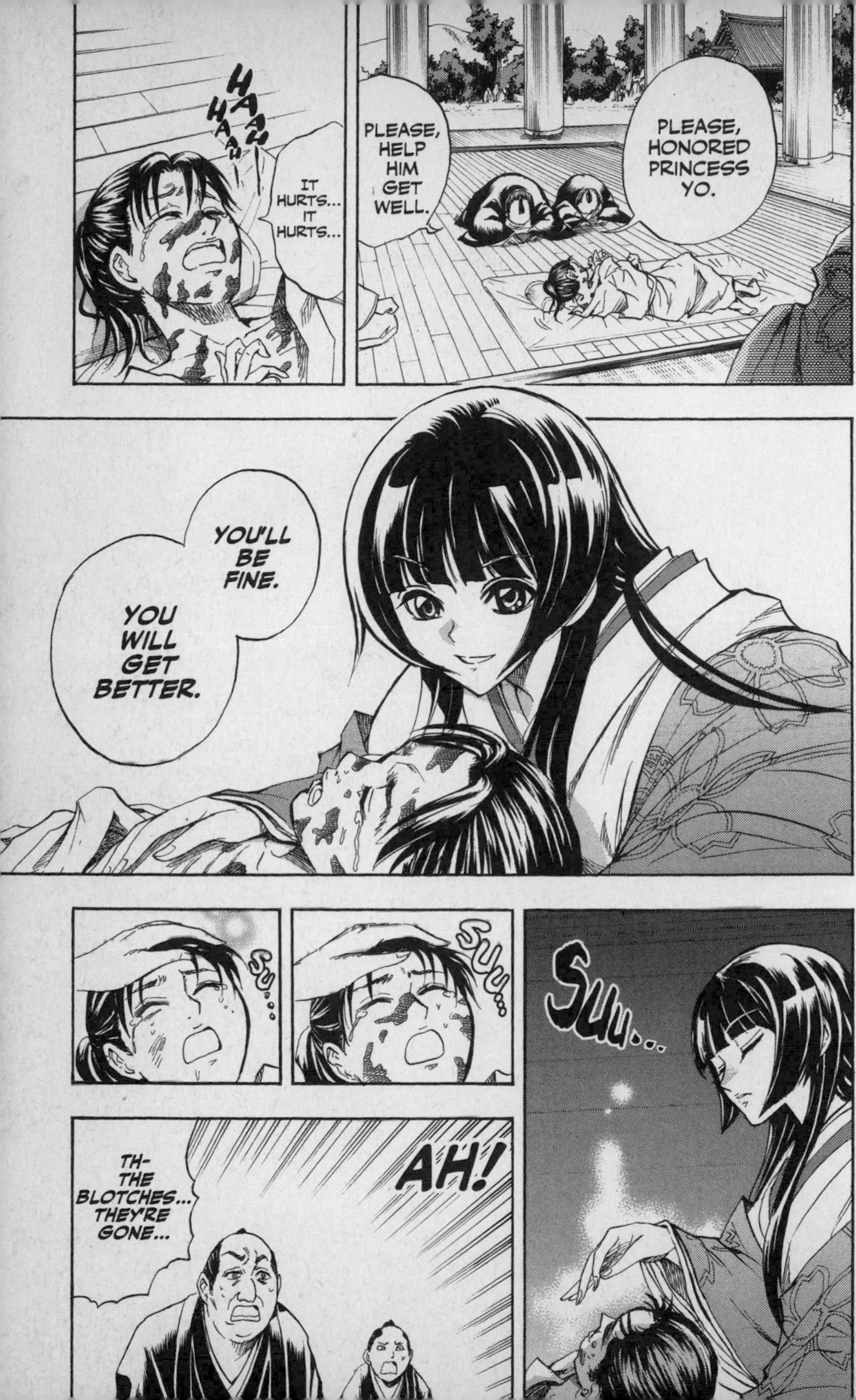
PLEASE, HONORED PRINCESS YO.
PLEASE, HELP HIM GET WELL.
HAAH
HAAH
IT HURTS... IT HURTS...
YOU'LL BE FINE.
YOU WILL GET BETTER.
SUU...
SUU...
SU...
AH!
TH- THE BLOTCHES... THEY'RE GONE...

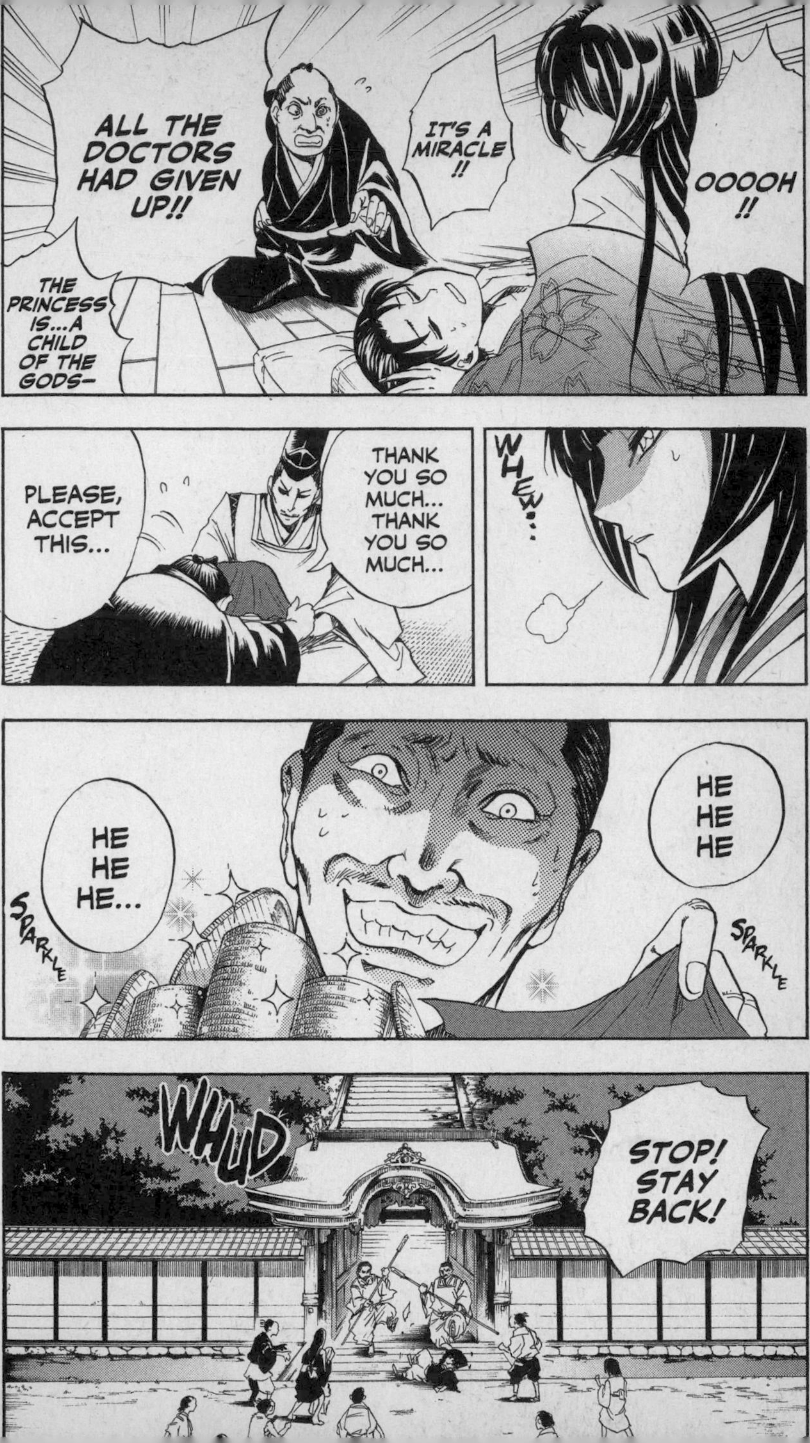
OOOOH !!
IT'S A MIRACLE !!
ALL THE DOCTORS HAD GIVEN UP!!
THE PRINCESS IS...A CHILD OF THE GODS–
WHEW...
THANK YOU SO MUCH... THANK YOU SO MUCH...
PLEASE, ACCEPT THIS...
HE HE HE
SPARKLE
HE HE HE...
SPARKLE
STOP! STAY BACK!
WHUD

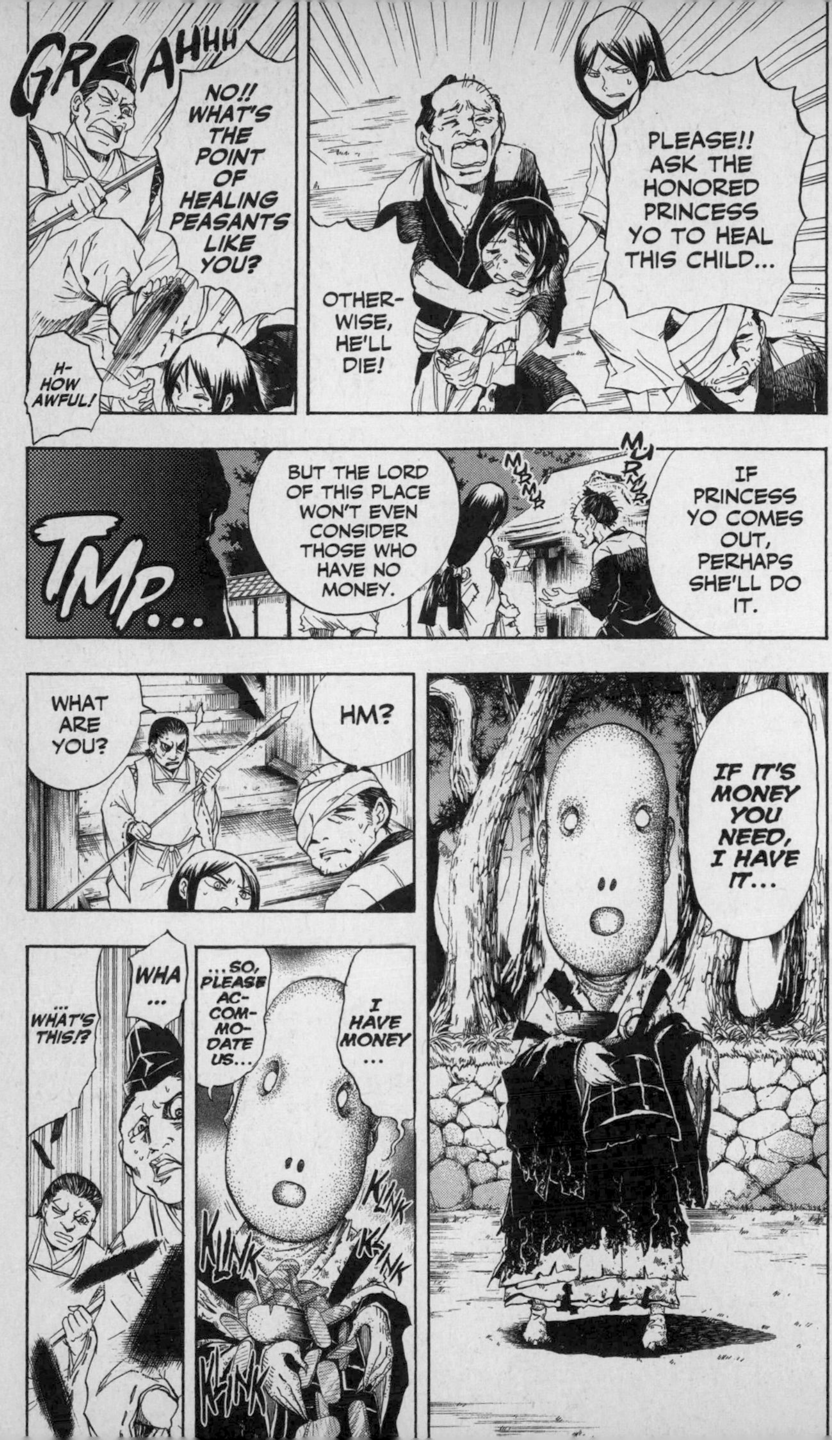
PLEASE!! ASK THE HONORED PRINCESS YO TO HEAL THIS CHILD...
OTHER-WISE, HE'LL DIE!
GRAAHHH
NO!! WHAT'S THE POINT OF HEALING PEASANTS LIKE YOU?
H-HOW AWFUL!
MURMUR MURMUR
IF PRINCESS YO COMES OUT, PERHAPS SHE'LL DO IT.
BUT THE LORD OF THIS PLACE WON'T EVEN CONSIDER THOSE WHO HAVE NO MONEY.
TMP...
IF IT'S MONEY YOU NEED, I HAVE IT...
HM?
WHAT ARE YOU?
I HAVE MONEY...
...SO, PLEASE AC-COM-MO-DATE US...
KLINK
KLINK
KLINK
KLINK
WHA...
...WHAT'S THIS!?

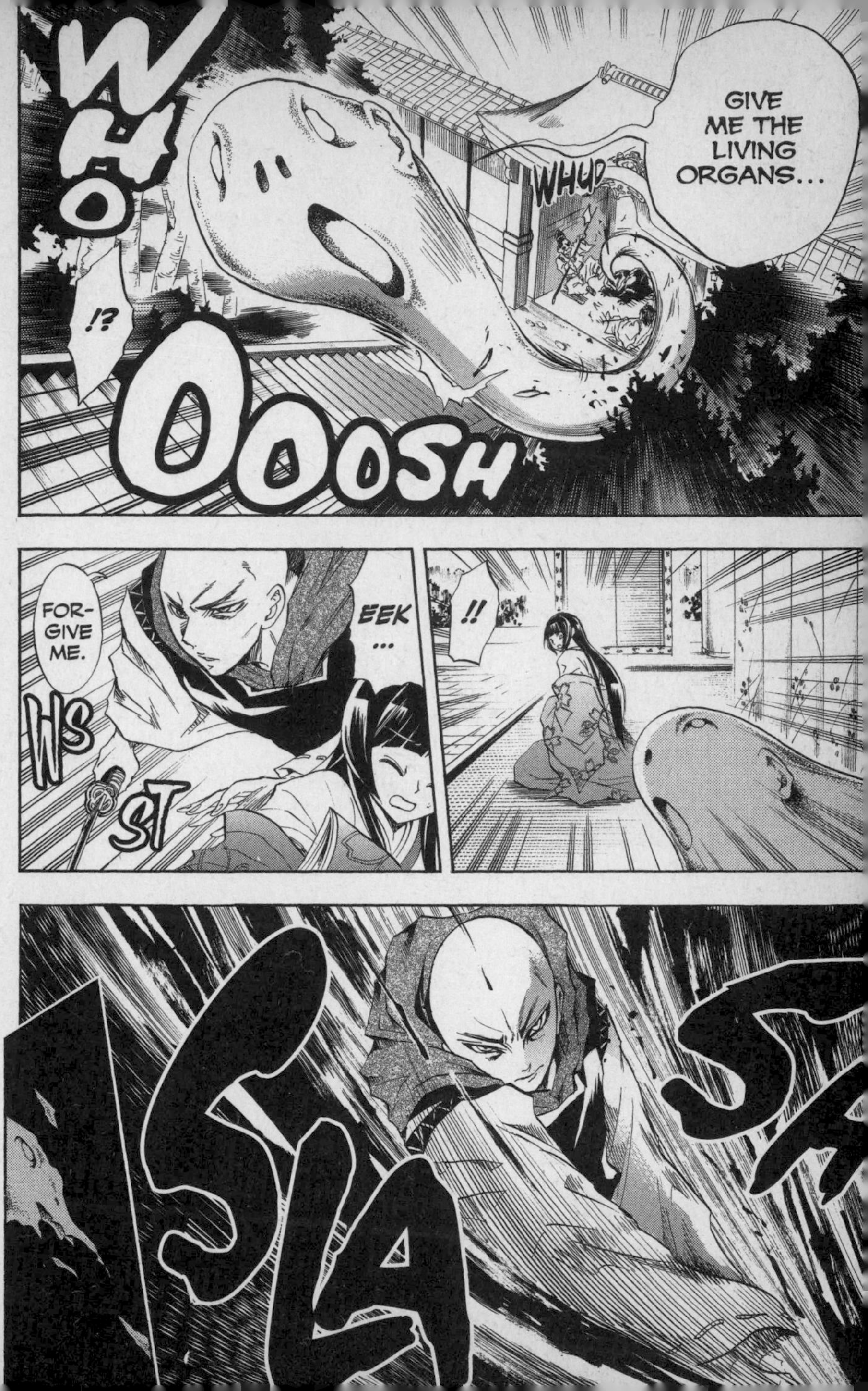
GIVE ME THE LIVING ORGANS...
WHUD
WHO
OOOSH
!?
!!
EEK ...
FOR-GIVE ME.
WS
W ST
SH
SLA

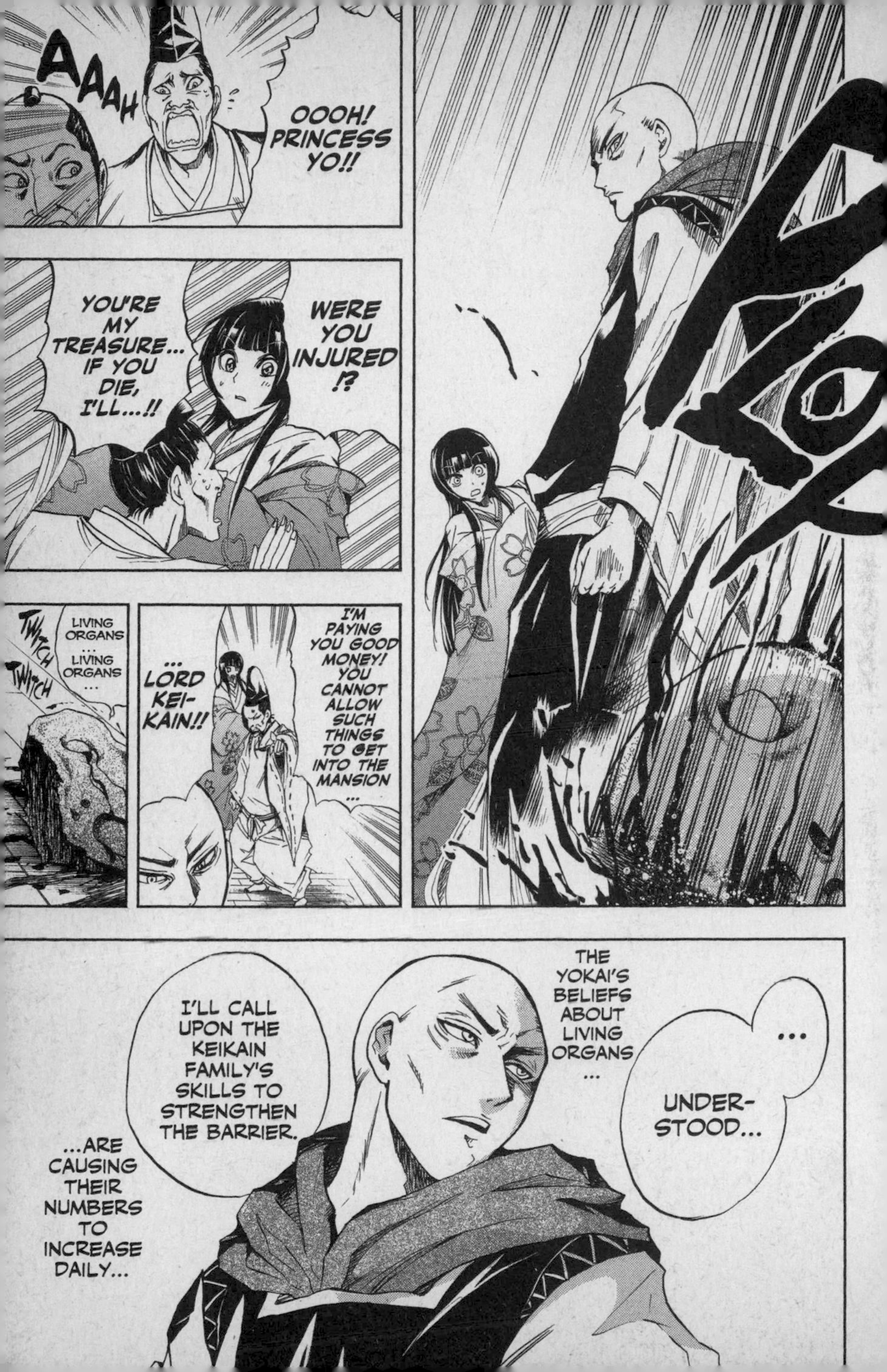
AAAH
OOOH! PRINCESS YO!!
WERE YOU INJURED!?
YOU'RE MY TREASURE... IF YOU DIE, I'LL...!!
I'M PAYING YOU GOOD MONEY! YOU CANNOT ALLOW SUCH THINGS TO GET INTO THE MANSION...
...LORD KEI-KAIN!!
TWITCH TWITCH
LIVING ORGANS ... LIVING ORGANS ...
...
UNDERSTOOD...
THE YOKAI'S BELIEFS ABOUT LIVING ORGANS ...
...ARE CAUSING THEIR NUMBERS TO INCREASE DAILY...
I'LL CALL UPON THE KEIKAIN FAMILY'S SKILLS TO STRENGTHEN THE BARRIER.

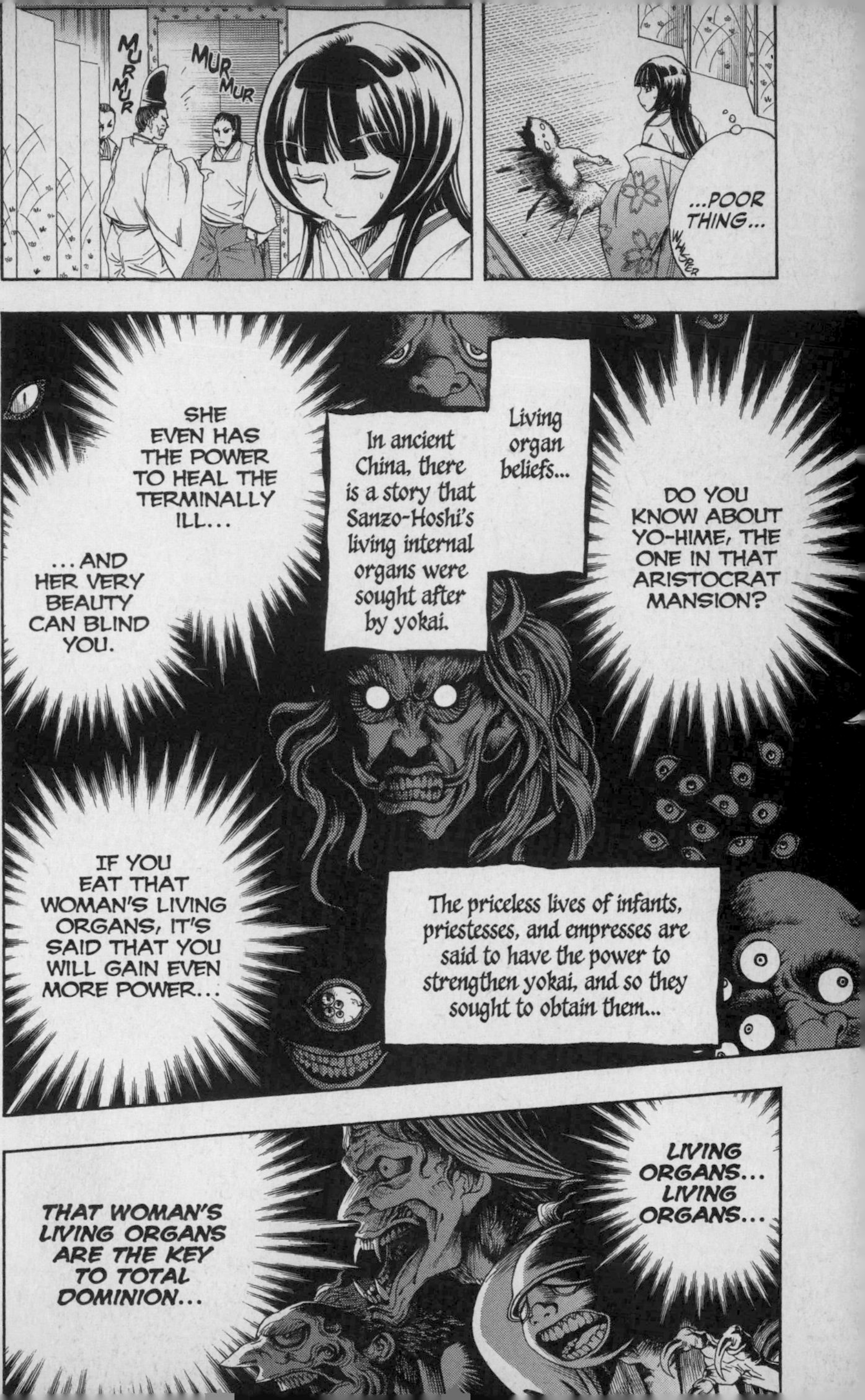
...POOR THING...
WHISPER
MURMUR
MUR MUR
DO YOU KNOW ABOUT YO-HIME, THE ONE IN THAT ARISTOCRAT MANSION?
Living organ beliefs...
In ancient China, there is a story that Sanzo-Hoshi's living internal organs were sought after by yokai.
SHE EVEN HAS THE POWER TO HEAL THE TERMINALLY ILL...
...AND HER VERY BEAUTY CAN BLIND YOU.
The priceless lives of infants, priestesses, and empresses are said to have the power to strengthen yokai, and so they sought to obtain them...
IF YOU EAT THAT WOMAN'S LIVING ORGANS, IT'S SAID THAT YOU WILL GAIN EVEN MORE POWER...
LIVING ORGANS... LIVING ORGANS...
THAT WOMAN'S LIVING ORGANS ARE THE KEY TO TOTAL DOMINION...

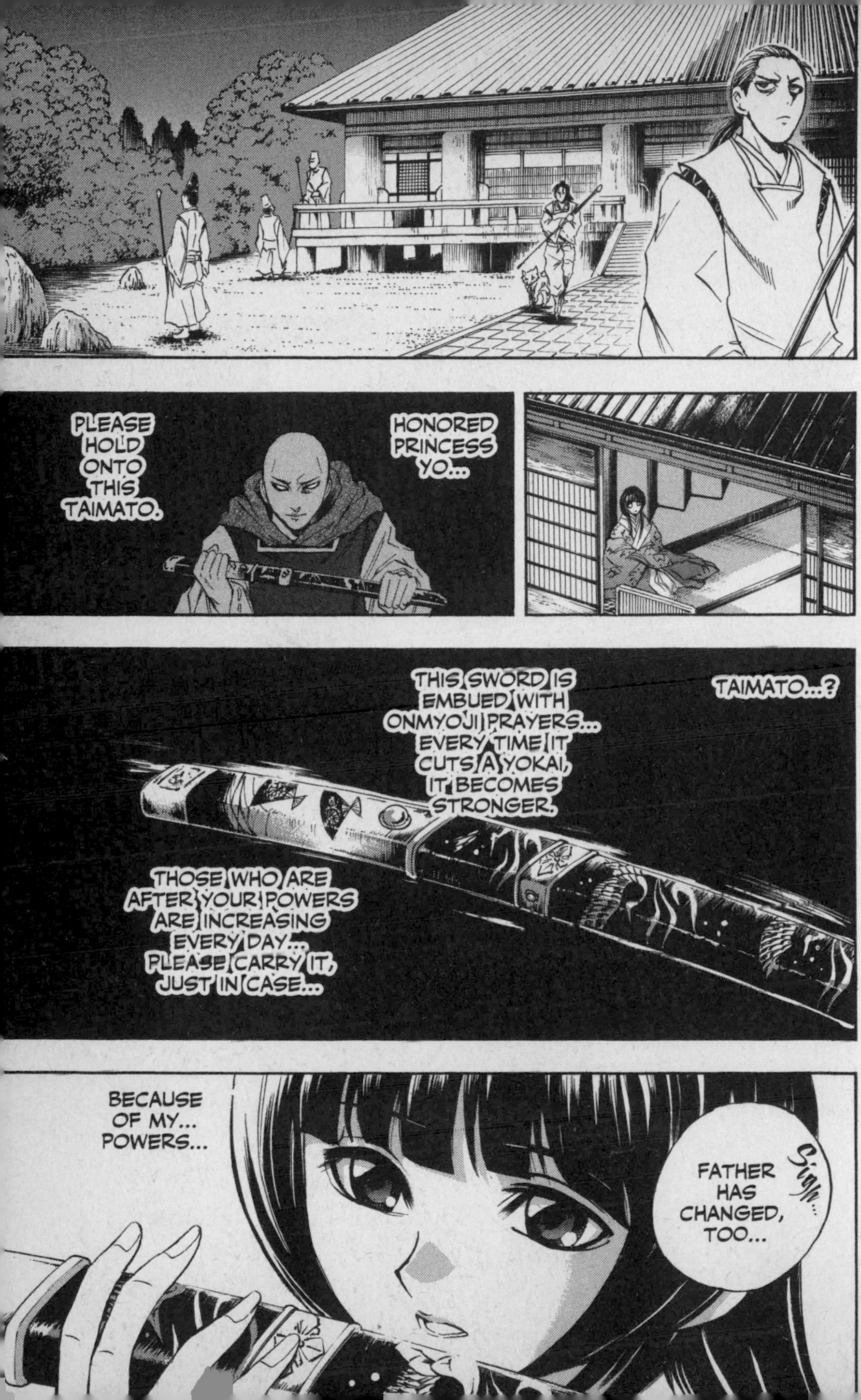
HONORED PRINCESS YO...
PLEASE HOLD ONTO THIS TAIMATO.
TAIMATO...?
THIS SWORD IS EMBUED WITH ONMYOJI PRAYERS... EVERY TIME IT CUTS A YOKAI, IT BECOMES STRONGER.
THOSE WHO ARE AFTER YOUR POWERS ARE INCREASING EVERY DAY... PLEASE CARRY IT, JUST IN CASE...
Sigh...
FATHER HAS CHANGED, TOO...
BECAUSE OF MY... POWERS...

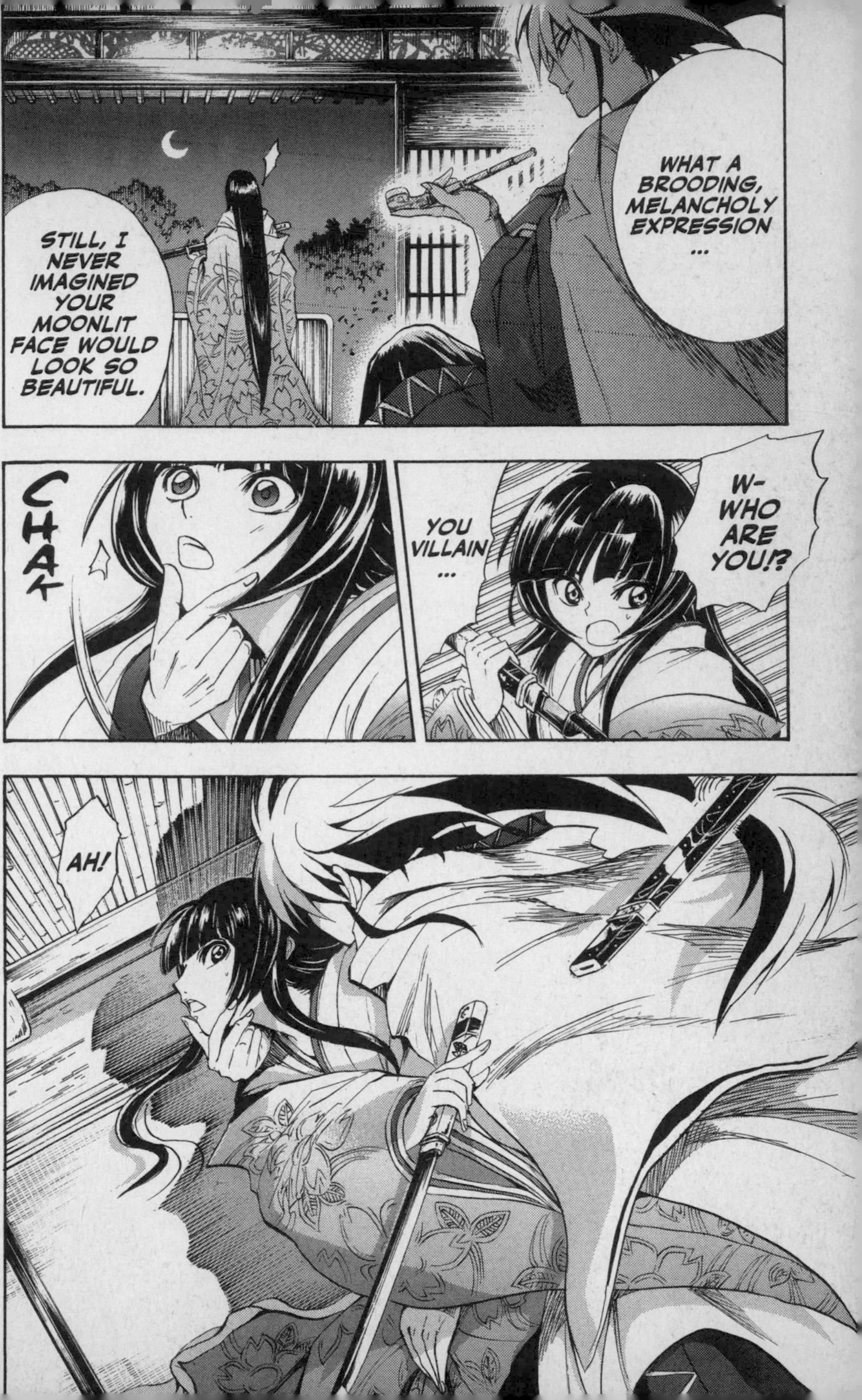
WHAT A BROODING, MELANCHOLY EXPRESSION ...
STILL, I NEVER IMAGINED YOUR MOONLIT FACE WOULD LOOK SO BEAUTIFUL.
W-WHO ARE YOU!?
YOU VILLAIN ...
CHAK
AH!

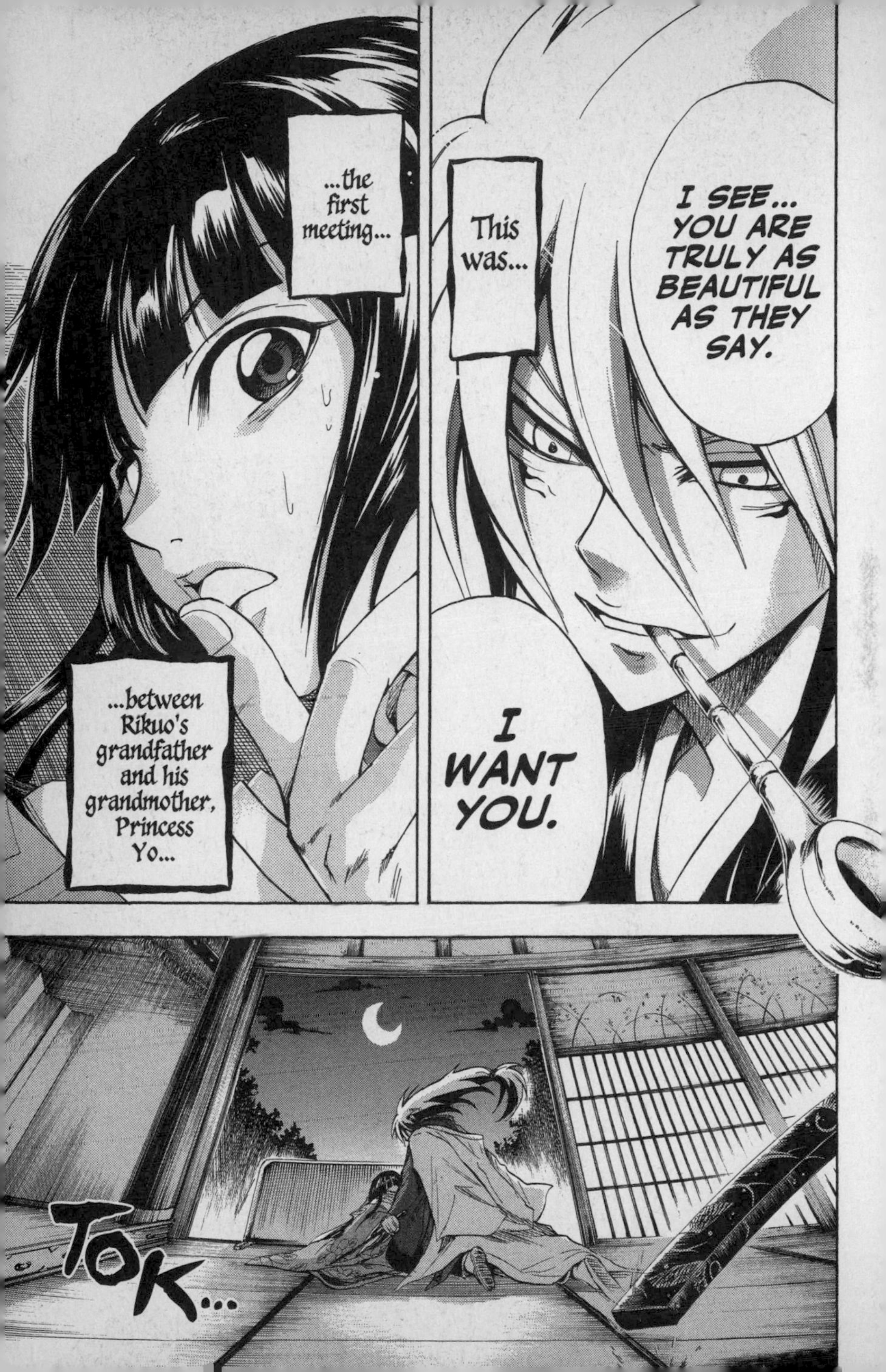
I SEE... YOU ARE TRULY AS BEAUTIFUL AS THEY SAY.
This was...
I WANT YOU.
...the first meeting...
...between Rikuo's grandfather and his grandmother, Princess Yo...
TOK...

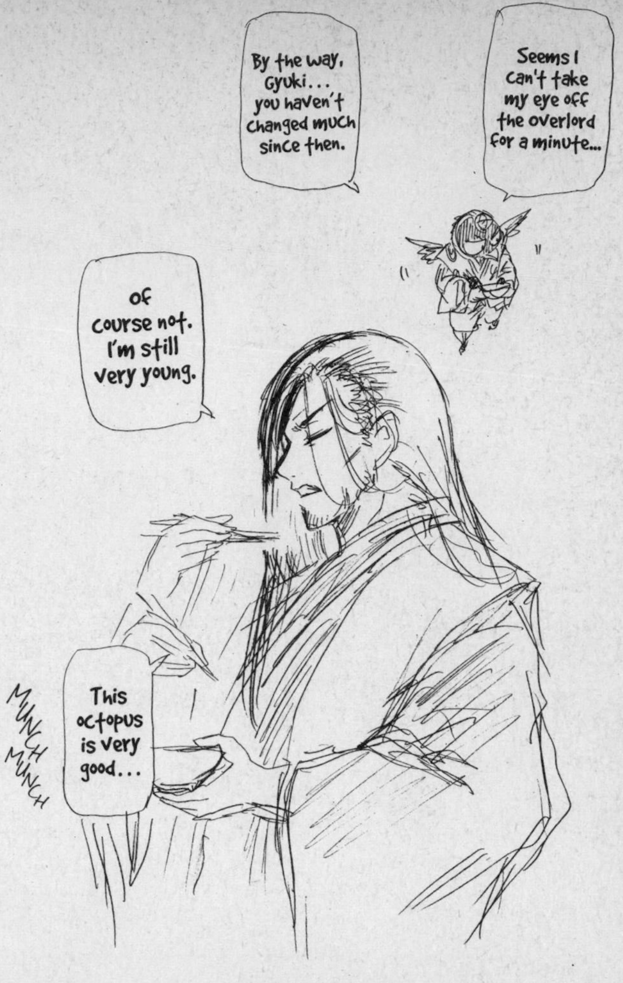
Seems I can't take my eye off the overlord for a minute...
By the way, Gyuki... you haven't changed much since then.
of course not. I'm still very young.
This octopus is very good...
MUNCH MUNCH

**PLEASE KEEP SENDING US YOUR QUESTIONS AND ILLUSTRATIONS!!**

| | |
|---|---|
| MAILING ADDRESS: | NURA EDITOR<br>VIZ MEDIA<br>P.O. BOX 77010<br>SAN FRANCISCO, CA 94107 |

*PLEASE INCLUDE YOUR NAME, AGE, ADDRESS AND PHONE NUMBER IN THE LETTER. IF YOU DO NOT WANT TO INCLUDE YOUR NAME, PLEASE USE A HANDLE OR NICKNAME. LETTERS AND ILLUSTRATIONS MAILED TO US WILL BE STORED FOR A CERTAIN PERIOD, BUT THEN LATER DISCARDED. IF YOU WISH TO KEEP A COPY, PLEASE MAKE ONE YOURSELF BEFORE MAILING IT IN. IF YOU'D LIKE TO HAVE YOUR NAME AND ADDRESS REMAIN ANONYMOUS, PLEASE INDICATE THAT IN YOUR LETTER.

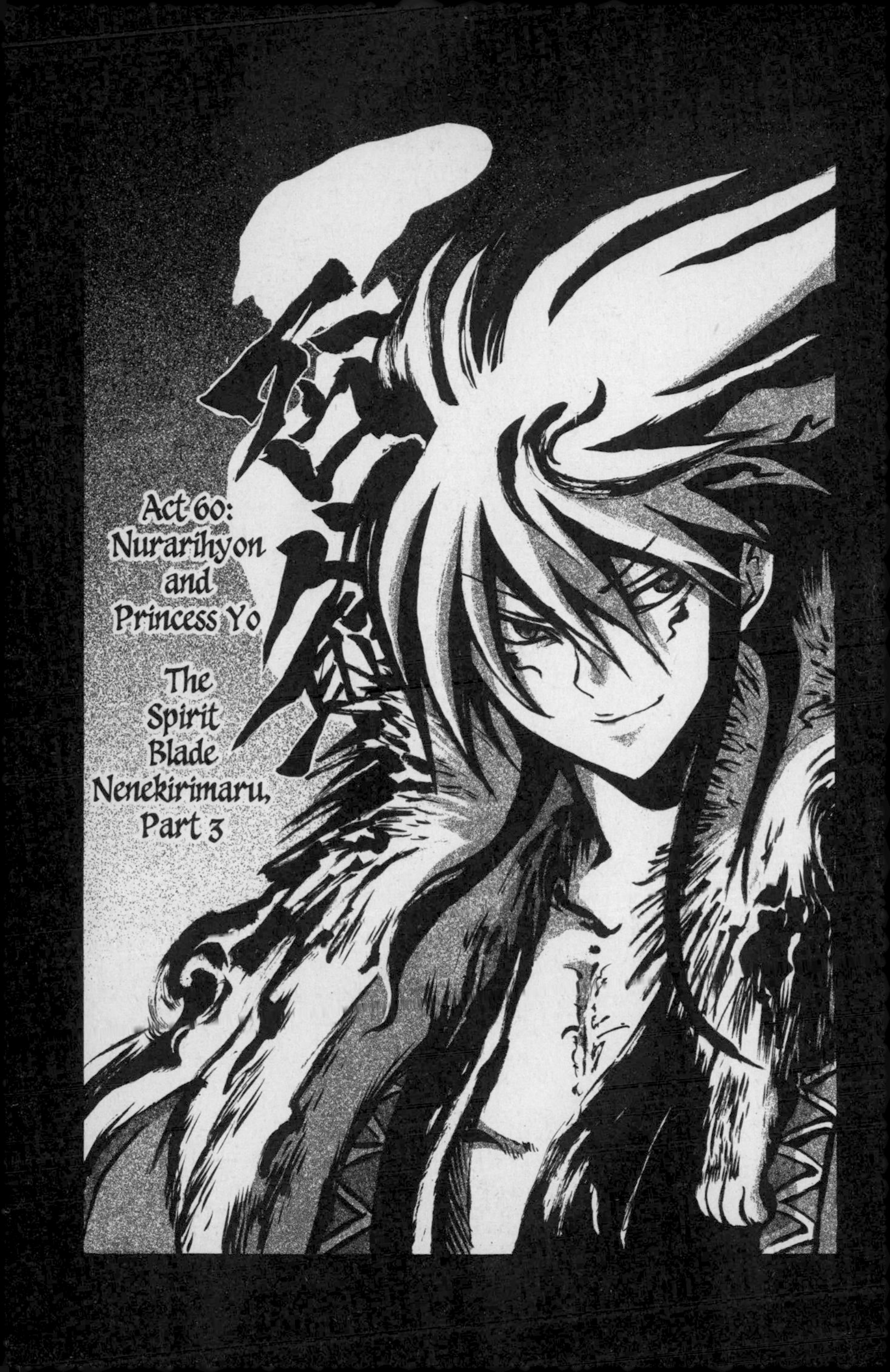
Act 60: Nurarihyon and Princess Yo
The Spirit Blade Nenekirimaru, Part 3

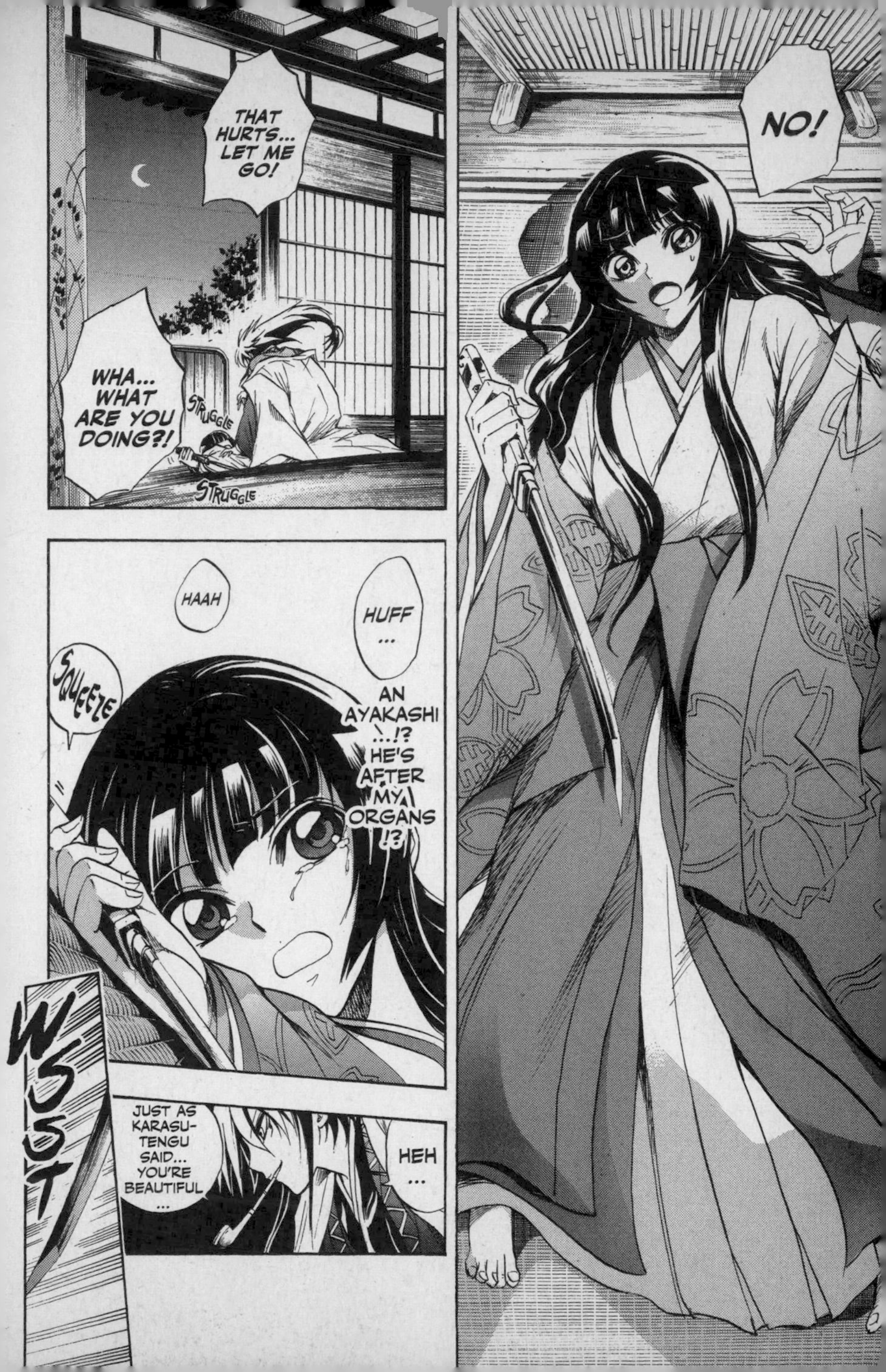
NO!
THAT HURTS... LET ME GO!
WHA... WHAT ARE YOU DOING?!
STRUGGLE
STRUGGLE
HUFF ...
HAAH
AN AYAKASHI ...!? HE'S AFTER MY ORGANS !?
SQUEEZE
HEH ...
JUST AS KARASU-TENGU SAID... YOU'RE BEAUTIFUL ...
WSST

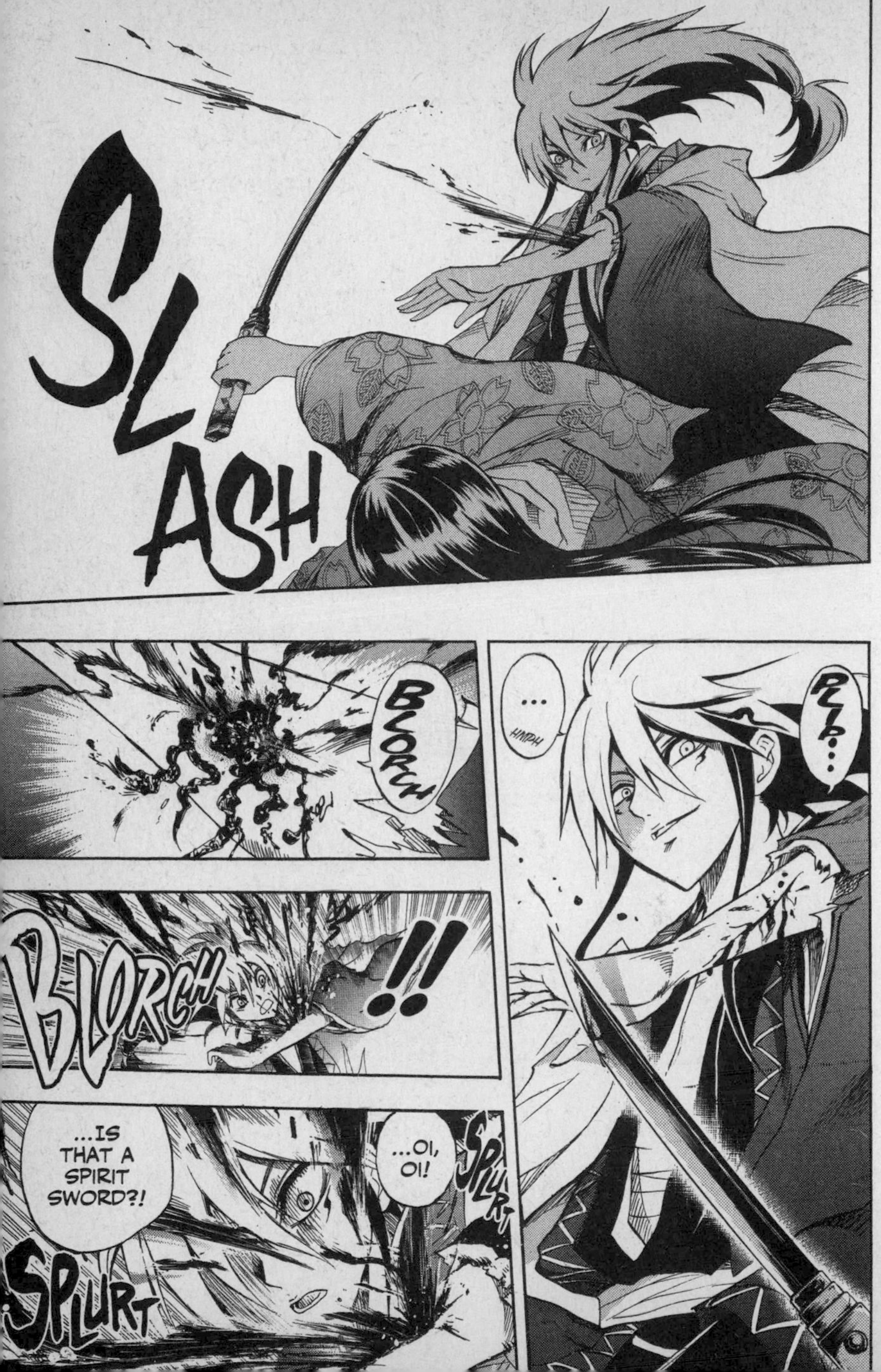
SLASH
...
HMPH
PLIP...
BLORCH
BLORCH
!!
...OI, OI!
...IS THAT A SPIRIT SWORD?!
SPLURT
SPLURT

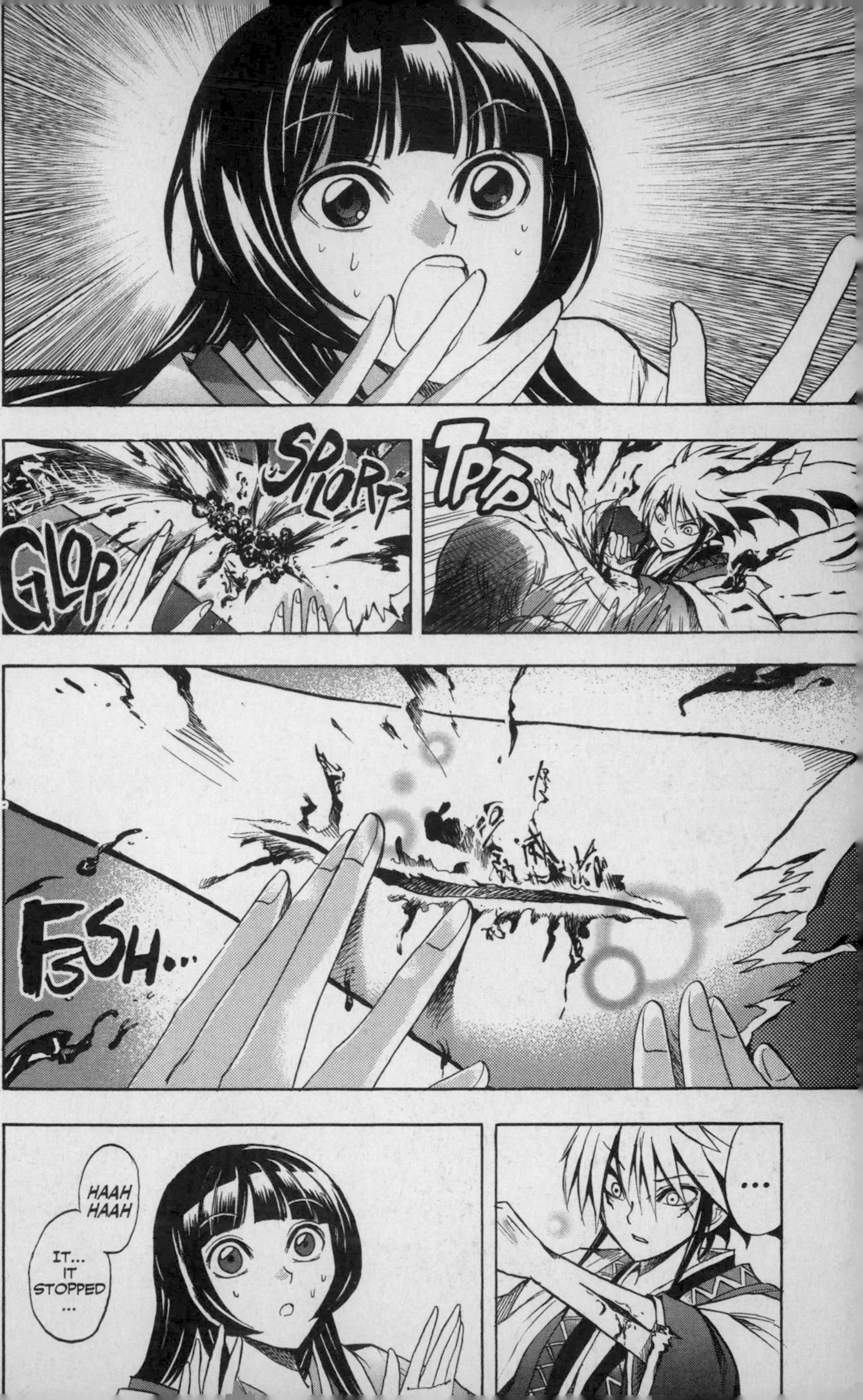
TPTP
SPLORT
GLOP
FSSH...
...
HAAH HAAH
IT... IT STOPPED...

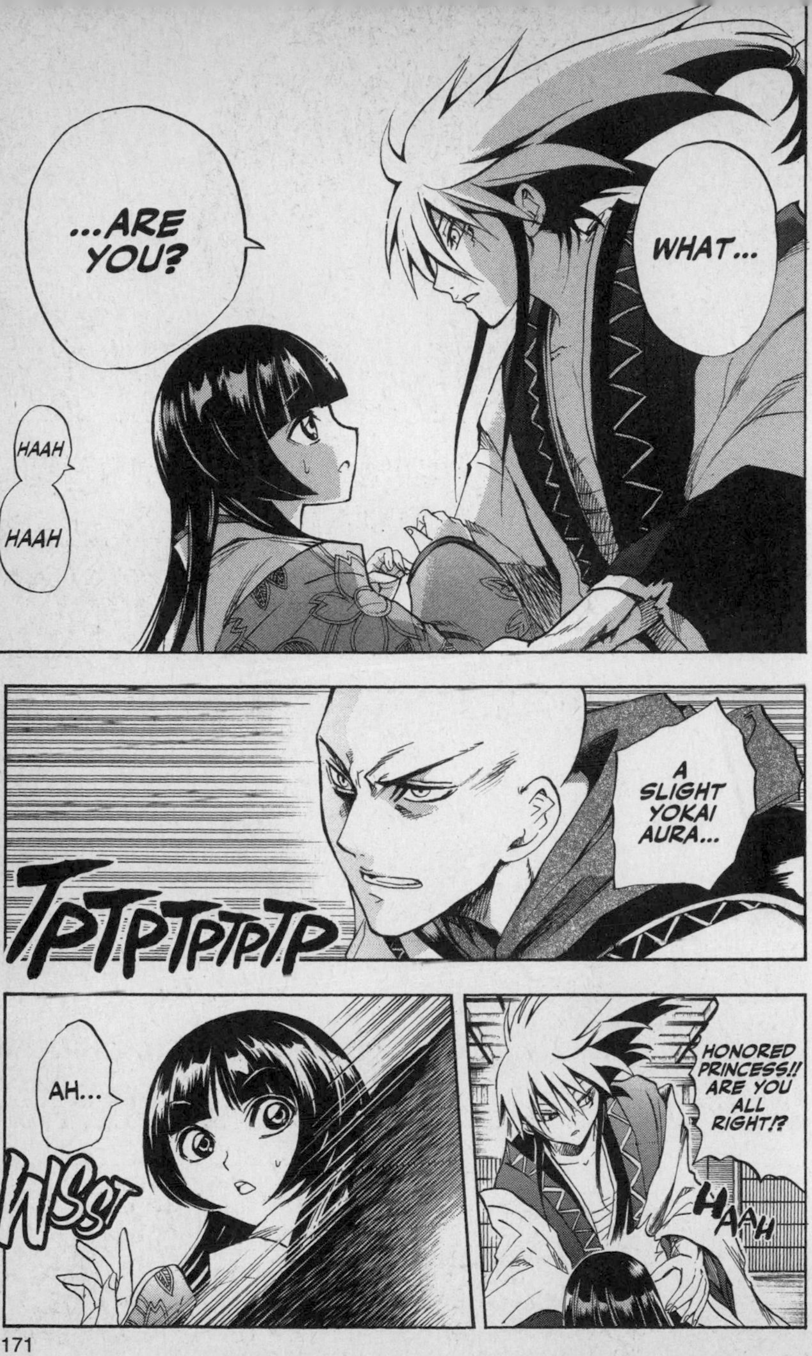
WHAT...
...ARE YOU?
HAAH
HAAH
A SLIGHT YOKAI AURA...
TPTPTPTPTP
HONORED PRINCESS!! ARE YOU ALL RIGHT!?
HAAH
AH...
WSST

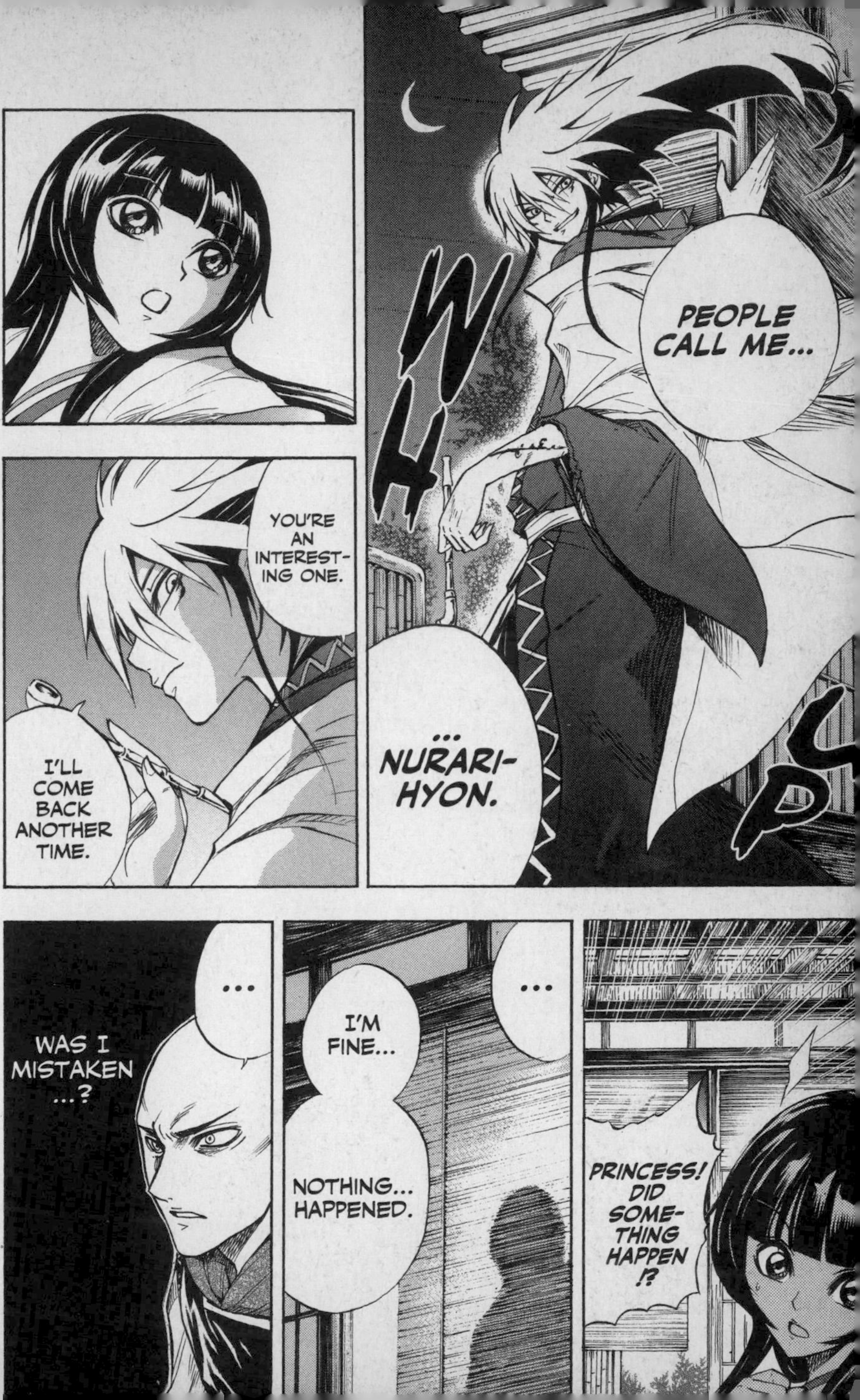
PEOPLE CALL ME...
...NURARI-HYON.
YOU'RE AN INTERESTING ONE.
I'LL COME BACK ANOTHER TIME.
PRINCESS! DID SOMETHING HAPPEN!?
...
I'M FINE...
NOTHING... HAPPENED.
...
WAS I MISTAKEN...?

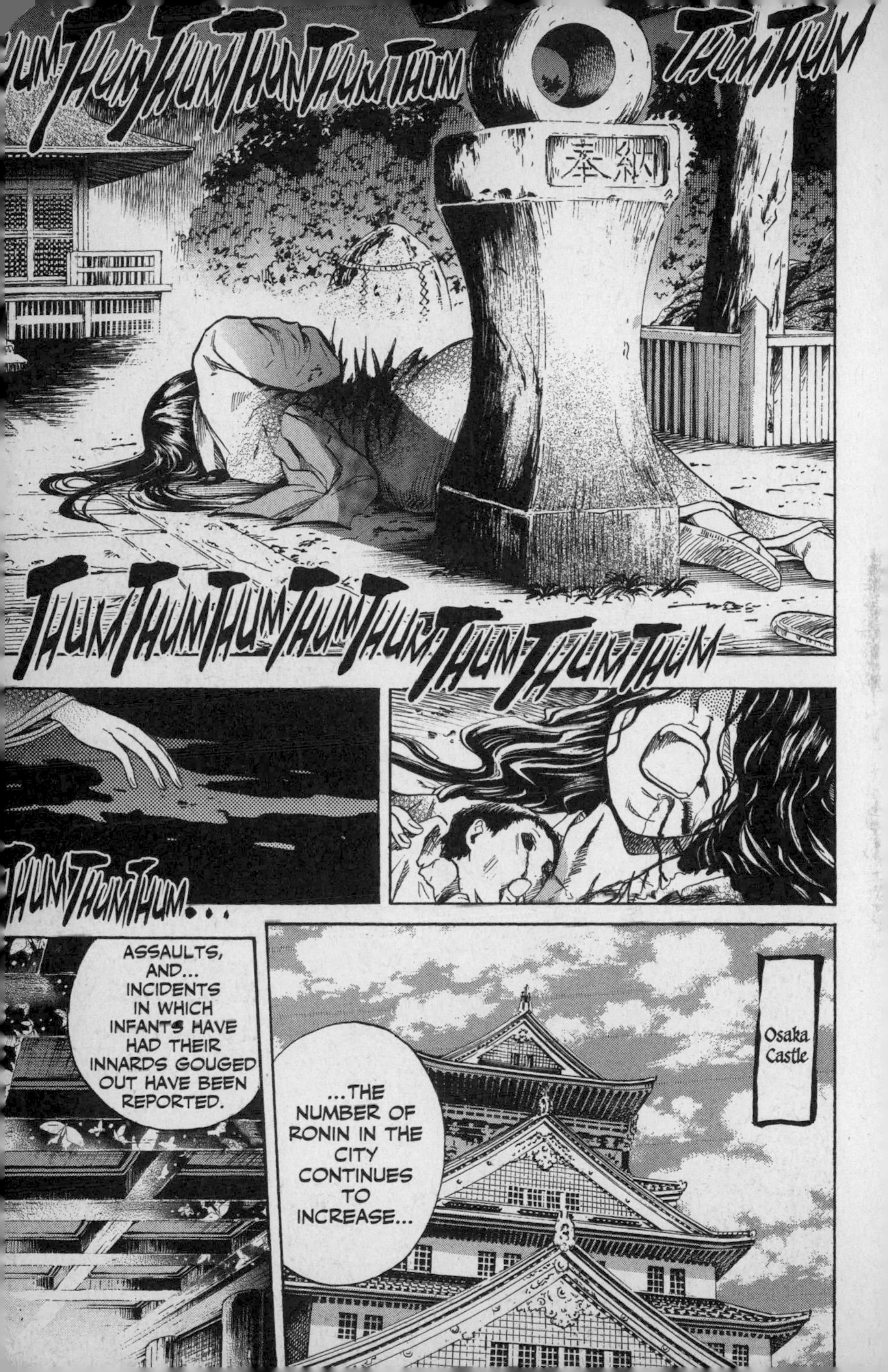
THUM THUM
THUM THUM THUM THUM THUM
奉納
THUM THUM THUM THUM THUM THUM THUM THUM
THUM THUM THUM...
Osaka Castle
...THE NUMBER OF RONIN IN THE CITY CONTINUES TO INCREASE...
ASSAULTS, AND... INCIDENTS IN WHICH INFANTS HAVE HAD THEIR INNARDS GOUGED OUT HAVE BEEN REPORTED.

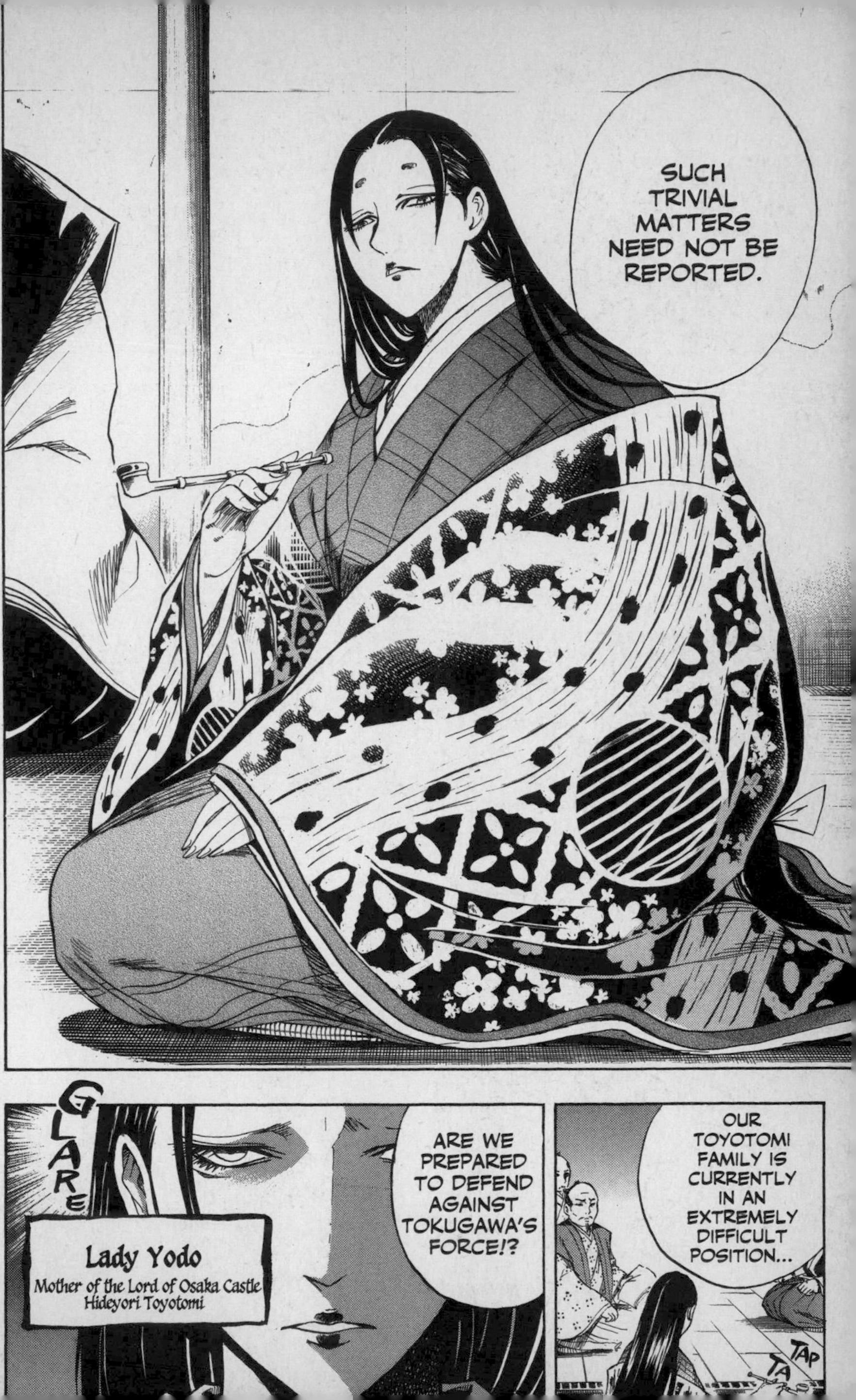
SUCH TRIVIAL MATTERS NEED NOT BE REPORTED.
OUR TOYOTOMI FAMILY IS CURRENTLY IN AN EXTREMELY DIFFICULT POSITION...
TAP
TA
ARE WE PREPARED TO DEFEND AGAINST TOKUGAWA'S FORCE!?
GLARE
Lady Yodo
Mother of the Lord of Osaka Castle Hideyori Toyotomi

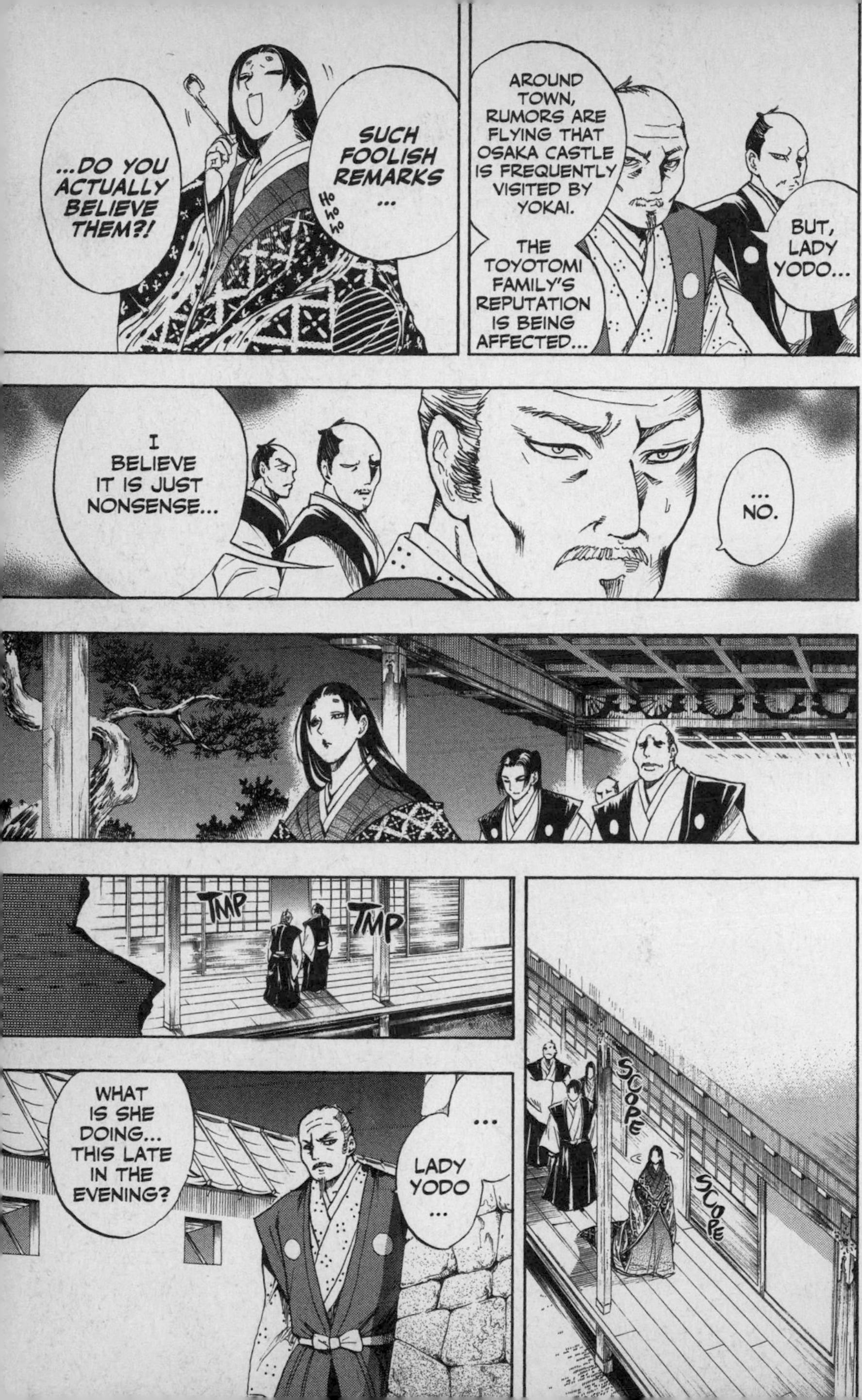
BUT, LADY YODO...
AROUND TOWN, RUMORS ARE FLYING THAT OSAKA CASTLE IS FREQUENTLY VISITED BY YOKAI.
THE TOYOTOMI FAMILY'S REPUTATION IS BEING AFFECTED...
SUCH FOOLISH REMARKS ...
Ho ho ho
...DO YOU ACTUALLY BELIEVE THEM?!
... NO.
I BELIEVE IT IS JUST NONSENSE...
SCOPE
SCOPE
TMP
TMP
... LADY YODO ...
WHAT IS SHE DOING... THIS LATE IN THE EVENING?

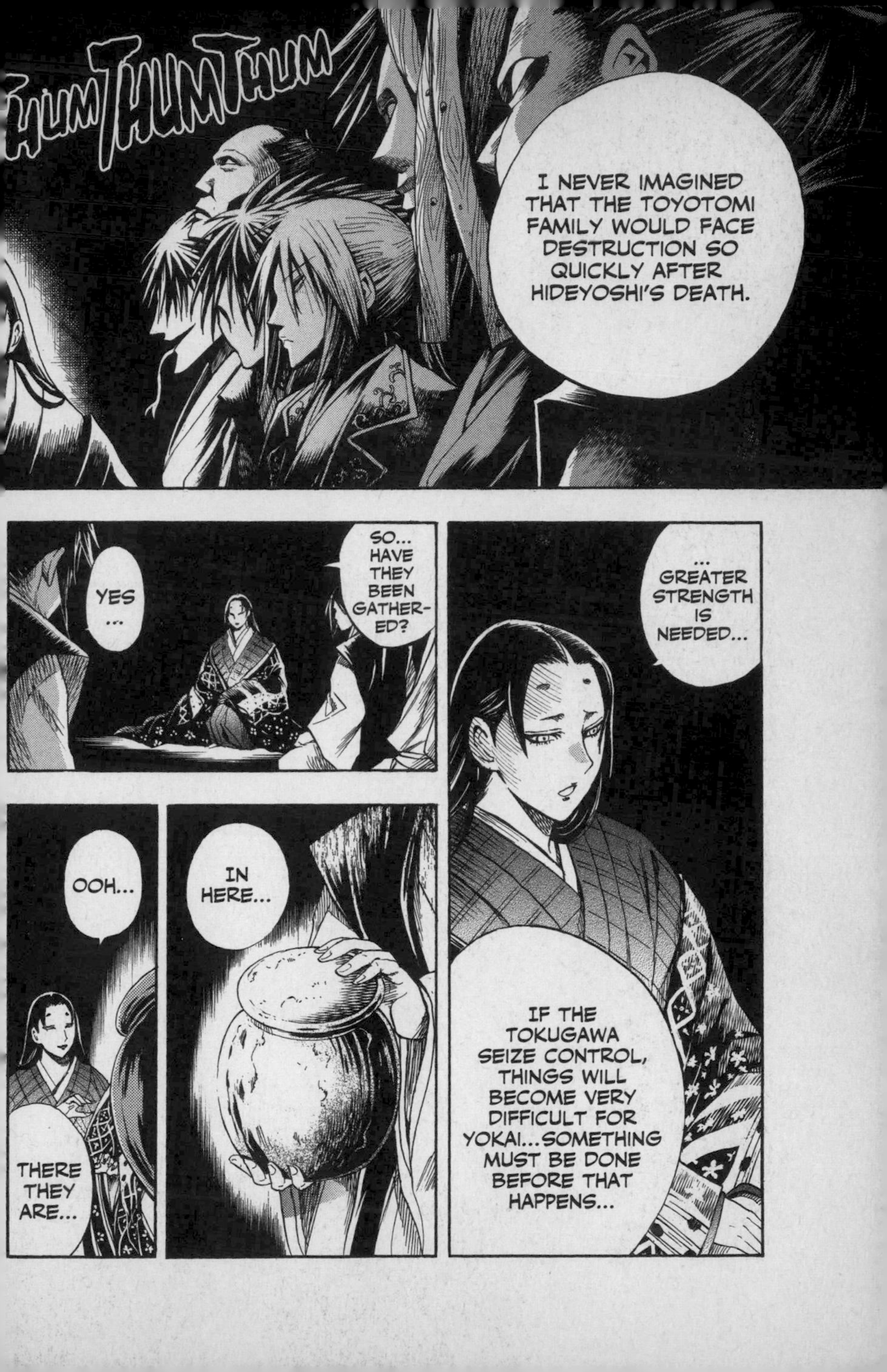
I NEVER IMAGINED THAT THE TOYOTOMI FAMILY WOULD FACE DESTRUCTION SO QUICKLY AFTER HIDEYOSHI'S DEATH.
THUM THUM THUM
... GREATER STRENGTH IS NEEDED...
IF THE TOKUGAWA SEIZE CONTROL, THINGS WILL BECOME VERY DIFFICULT FOR YOKAI...SOMETHING MUST BE DONE BEFORE THAT HAPPENS...
SO... HAVE THEY BEEN GATHERED?
YES ...
IN HERE...
OOH...
THERE THEY ARE...

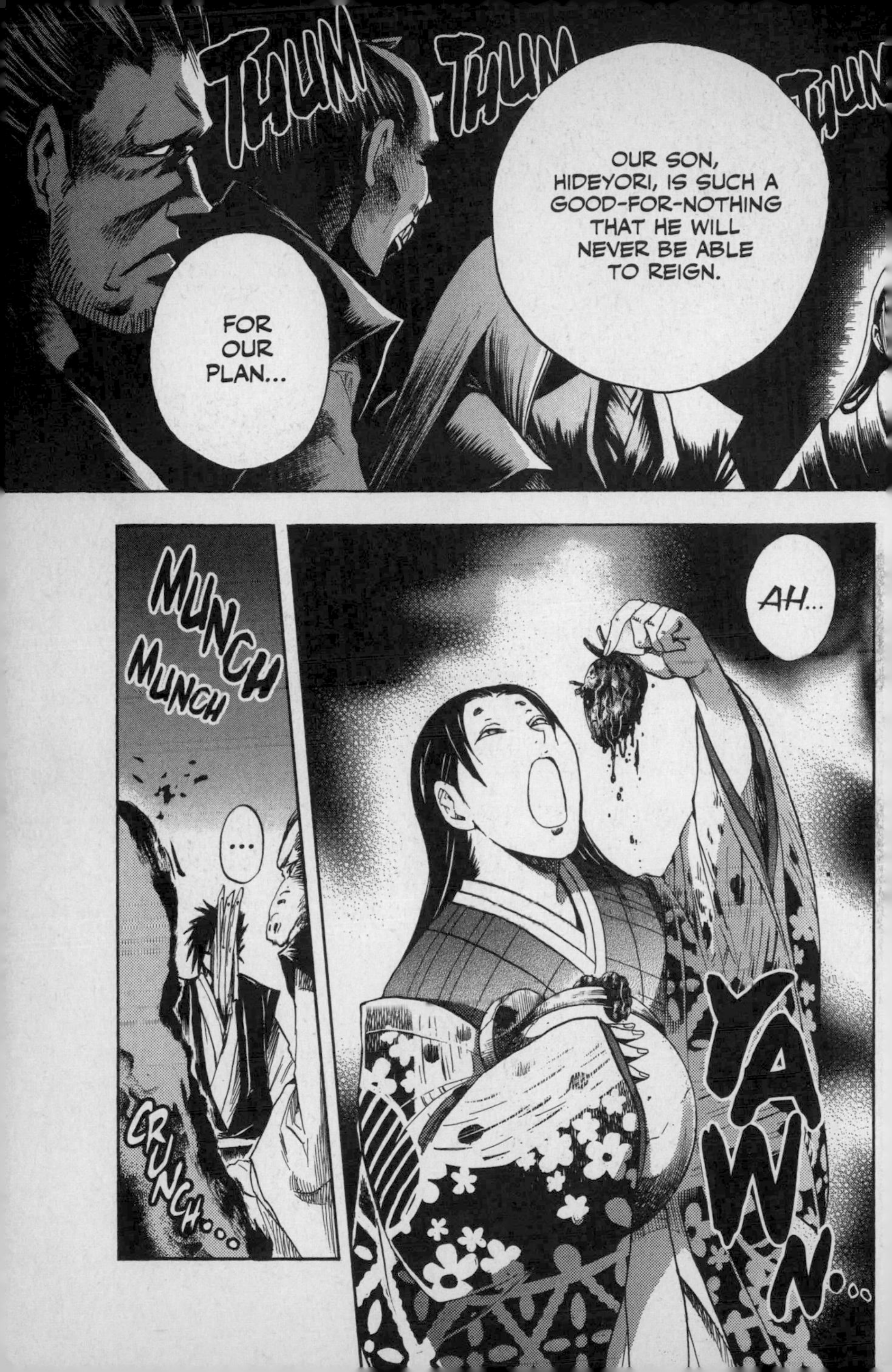
THUM
THUM
THUM
OUR SON, HIDEYORI, IS SUCH A GOOD-FOR-NOTHING THAT HE WILL NEVER BE ABLE TO REIGN.
FOR OUR PLAN...
AH...
YAWN...
MUNCH
MUNCH
...
CRUNCH...

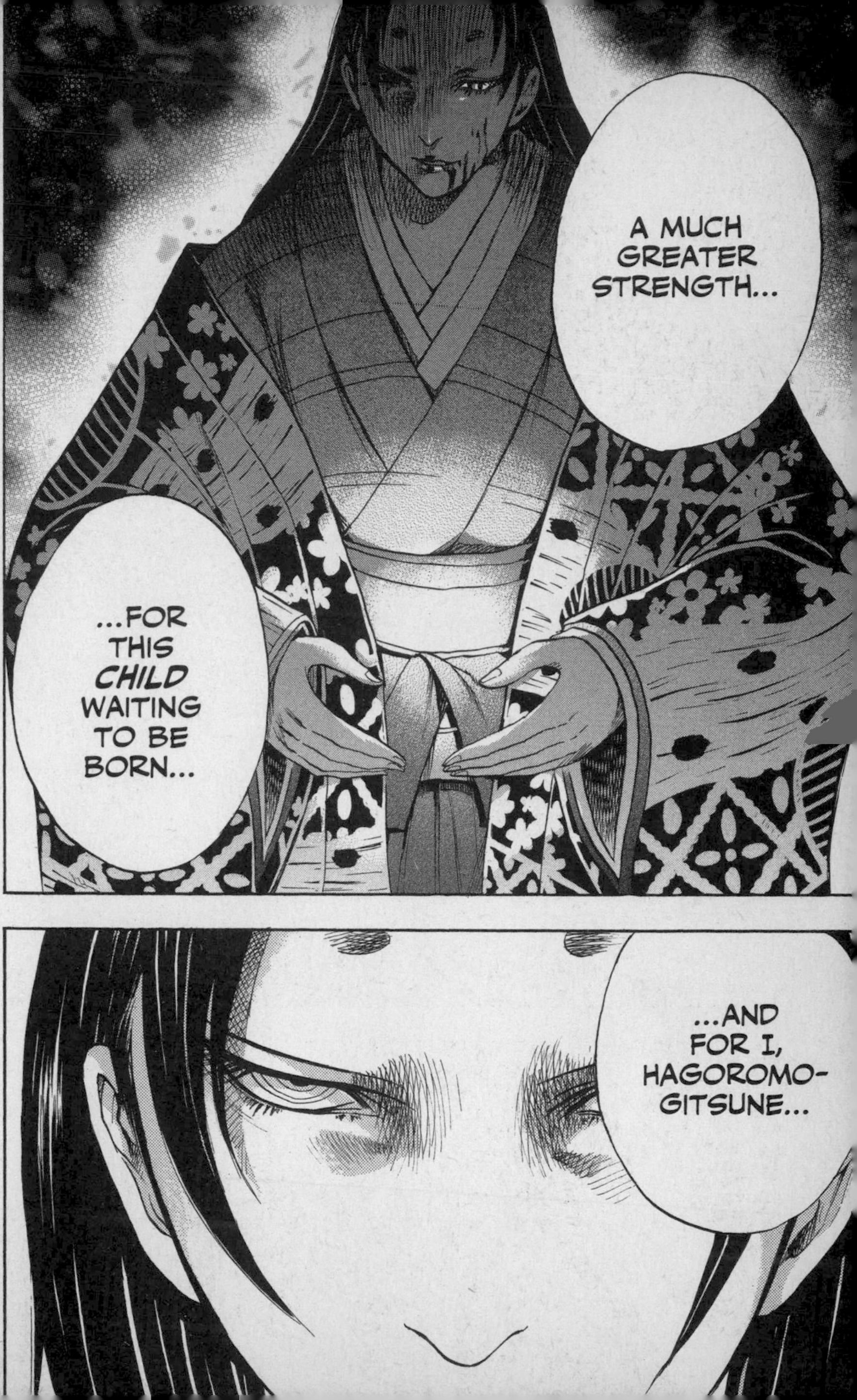
A MUCH GREATER STRENGTH...
...FOR THIS *CHILD* WAITING TO BE BORN...
...AND FOR I, HAGOROMO-GITSUNE...

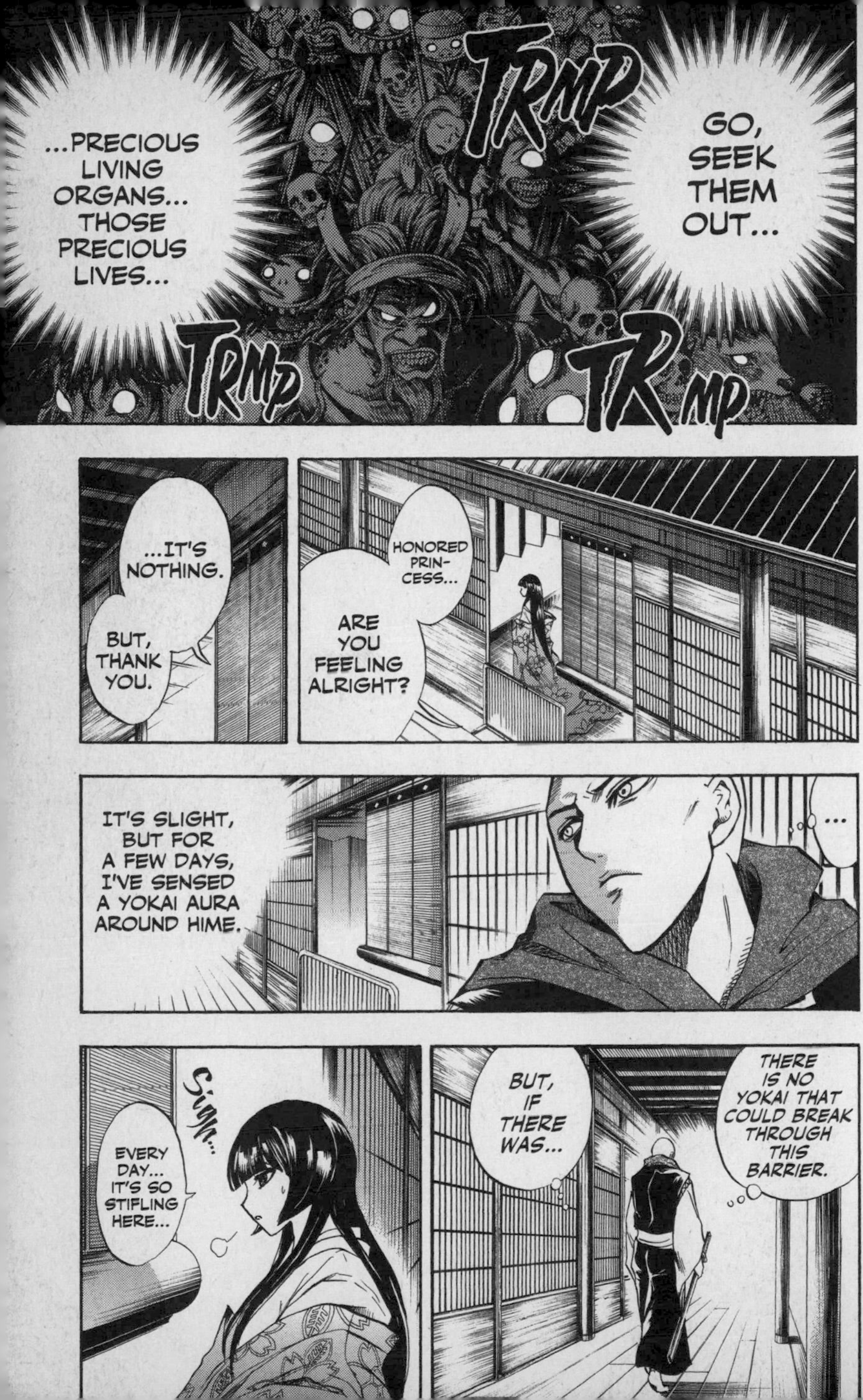
GO, SEEK THEM OUT...
TRMP
...PRECIOUS LIVING ORGANS... THOSE PRECIOUS LIVES...
TRMP
TRMP
HONORED PRIN-CESS...
ARE YOU FEELING ALRIGHT?
...IT'S NOTHING.
BUT, THANK YOU.
...
IT'S SLIGHT, BUT FOR A FEW DAYS, I'VE SENSED A YOKAI AURA AROUND HIME.
THERE IS NO YOKAI THAT COULD BREAK THROUGH THIS BARRIER.
BUT, IF THERE WAS...
SIGH...
EVERY DAY... IT'S SO STIFLING HERE...

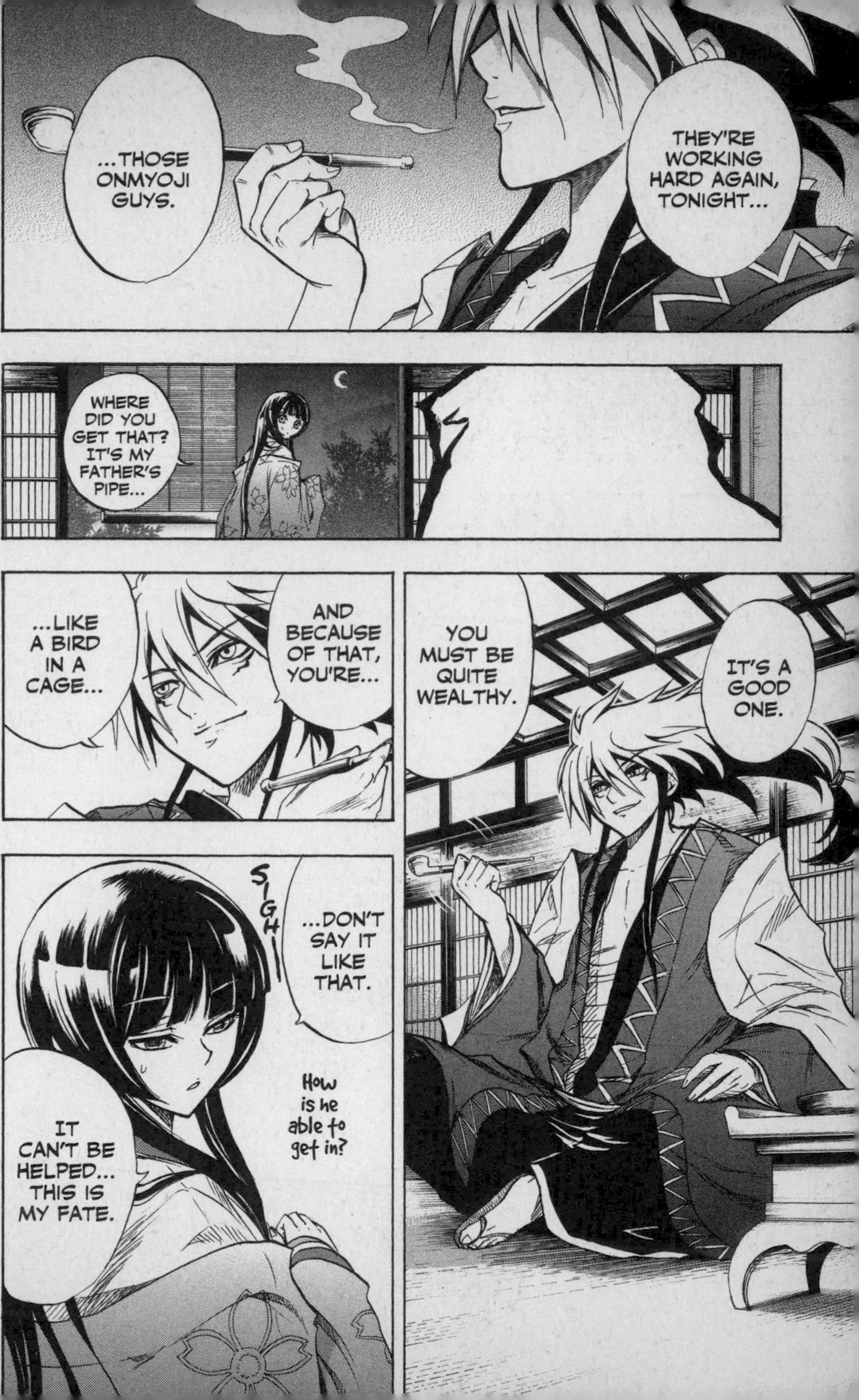
THEY'RE WORKING HARD AGAIN, TONIGHT...
...THOSE ONMYOJI GUYS.
WHERE DID YOU GET THAT? IT'S MY FATHER'S PIPE...
IT'S A GOOD ONE.
YOU MUST BE QUITE WEALTHY.
AND BECAUSE OF THAT, YOU'RE...
...LIKE A BIRD IN A CAGE...
SIGH
...DON'T SAY IT LIKE THAT.
How is he able to get in?
IT CAN'T BE HELPED... THIS IS MY FATE.

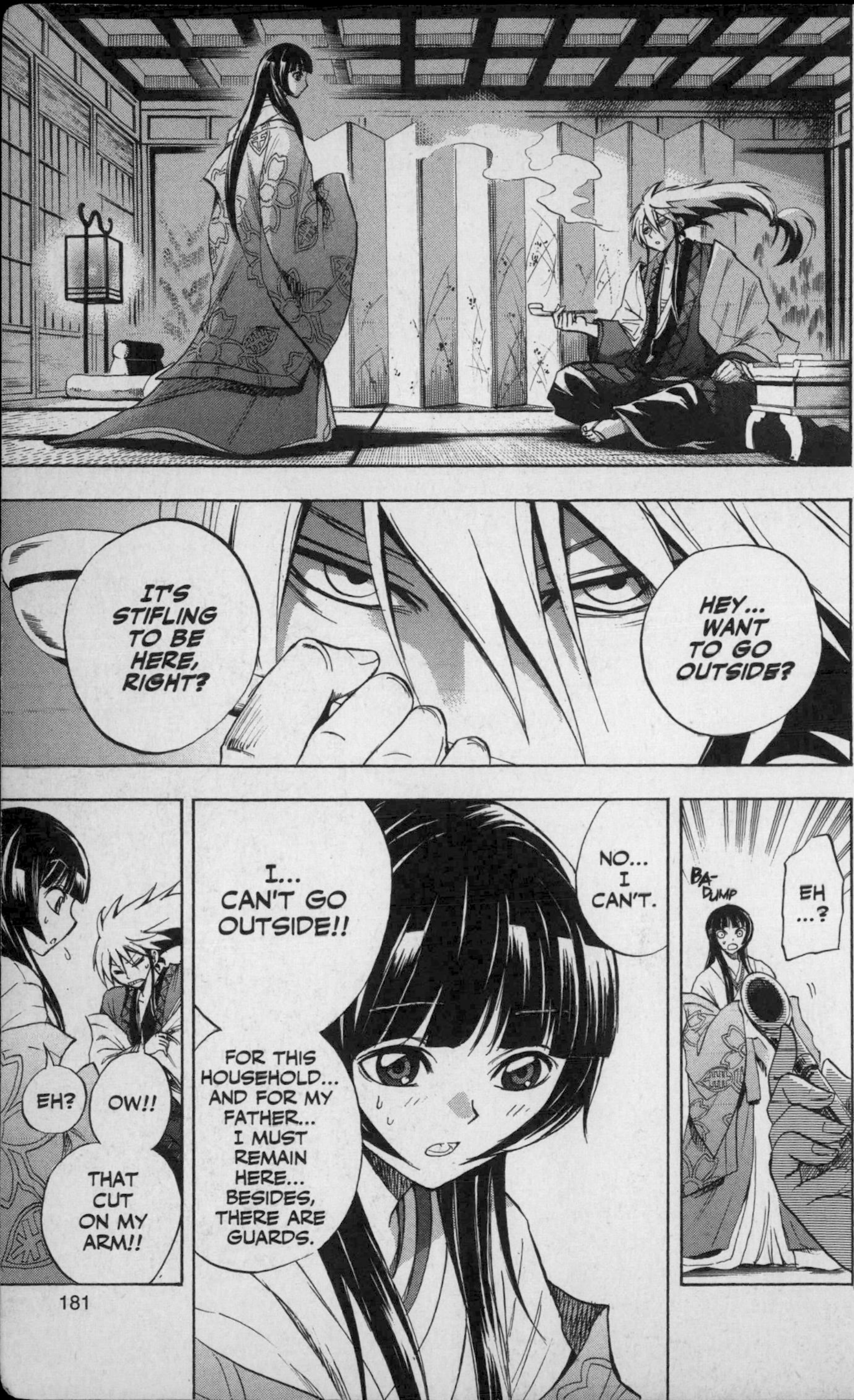
HEY... WANT TO GO OUTSIDE?
IT'S STIFLING TO BE HERE, RIGHT?
EH ...?
BA-DUMP
NO... I CAN'T.
I... CAN'T GO OUTSIDE!!
FOR THIS HOUSEHOLD... AND FOR MY FATHER... I MUST REMAIN HERE... BESIDES, THERE ARE GUARDS.
OW!!
EH?
THAT CUT ON MY ARM!!

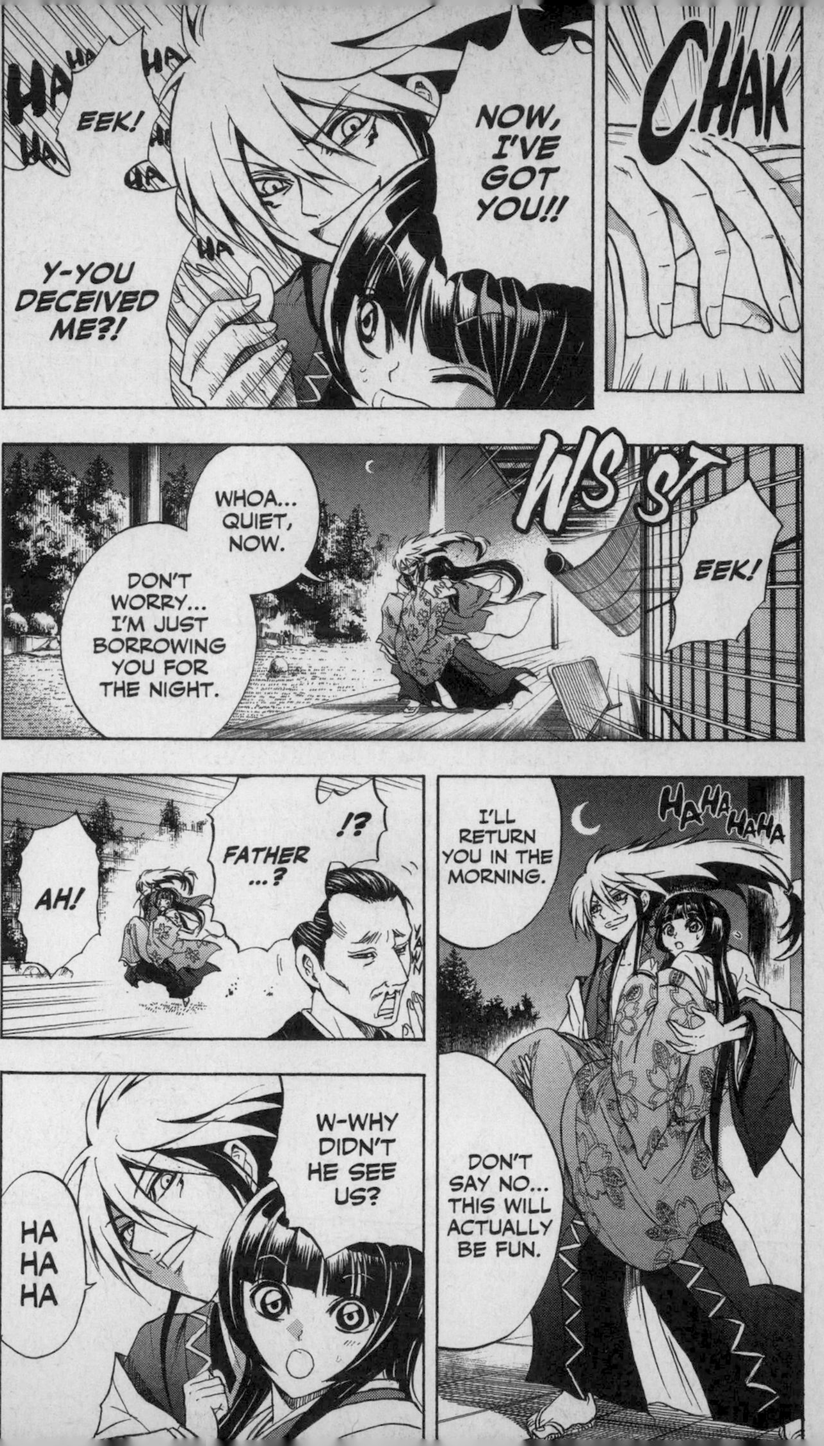
CHAK
NOW, I'VE GOT YOU!!
EEK!
HA HA HA HA HA HA HA HA
Y-YOU DECEIVED ME?!
WISST
EEK!
WHOA... QUIET, NOW.
DON'T WORRY... I'M JUST BORROWING YOU FOR THE NIGHT.
HAHAHAHA
I'LL RETURN YOU IN THE MORNING.
DON'T SAY NO... THIS WILL ACTUALLY BE FUN.
!?
FATHER ...?
AH!
YAWN
W-WHY DIDN'T HE SEE US?
HA HA HA

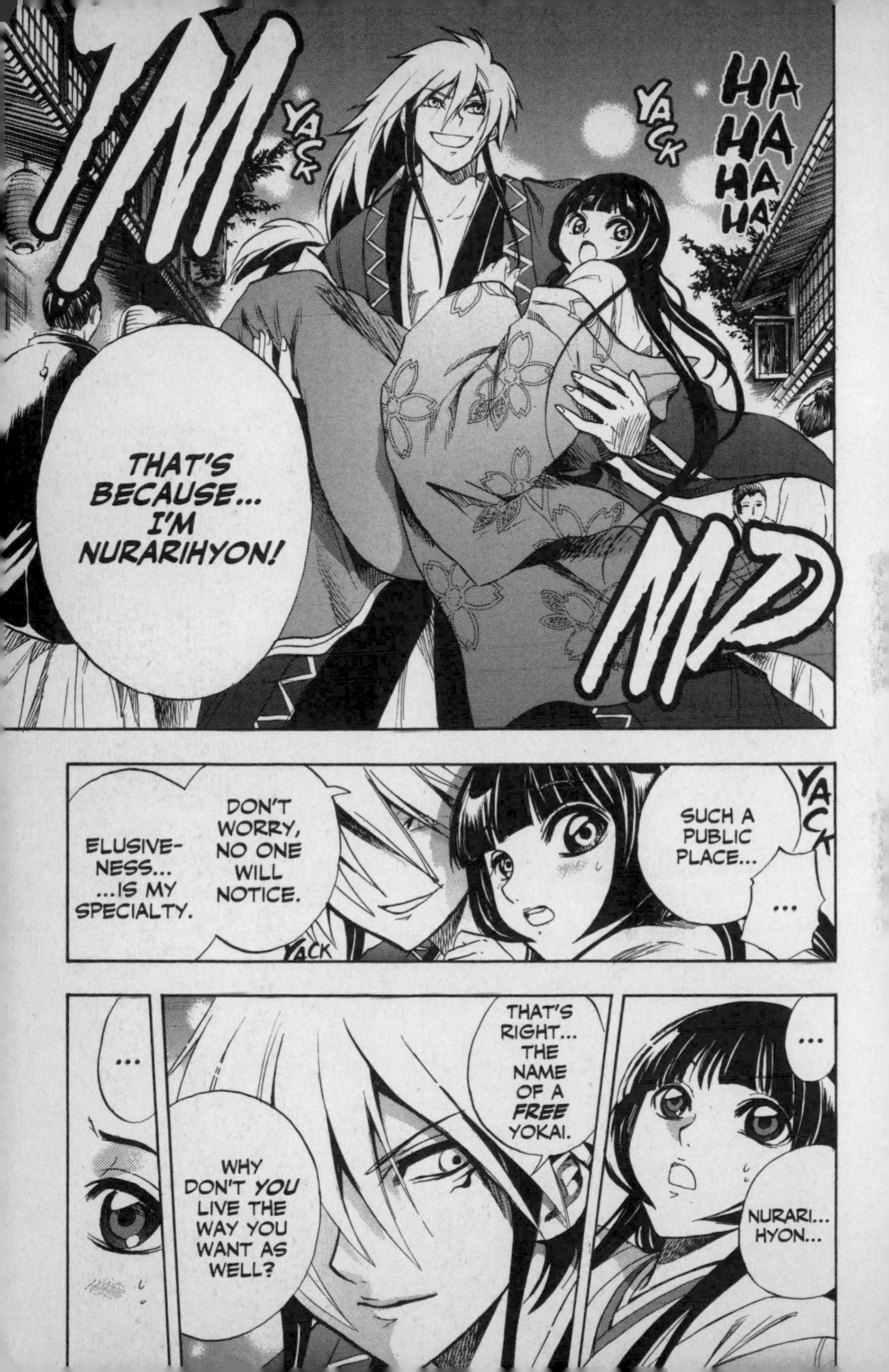
HA HA HA HA
YACK
YACK
THAT'S BECAUSE... I'M NURARIHYON!
YACK
SUCH A PUBLIC PLACE...
...
DON'T WORRY, NO ONE WILL NOTICE.
ELUSIVENESS... ...IS MY SPECIALTY.
YACK
...
NURARI... HYON...
THAT'S RIGHT... THE NAME OF A FREE YOKAI.
WHY DON'T YOU LIVE THE WAY YOU WANT AS WELL?
...

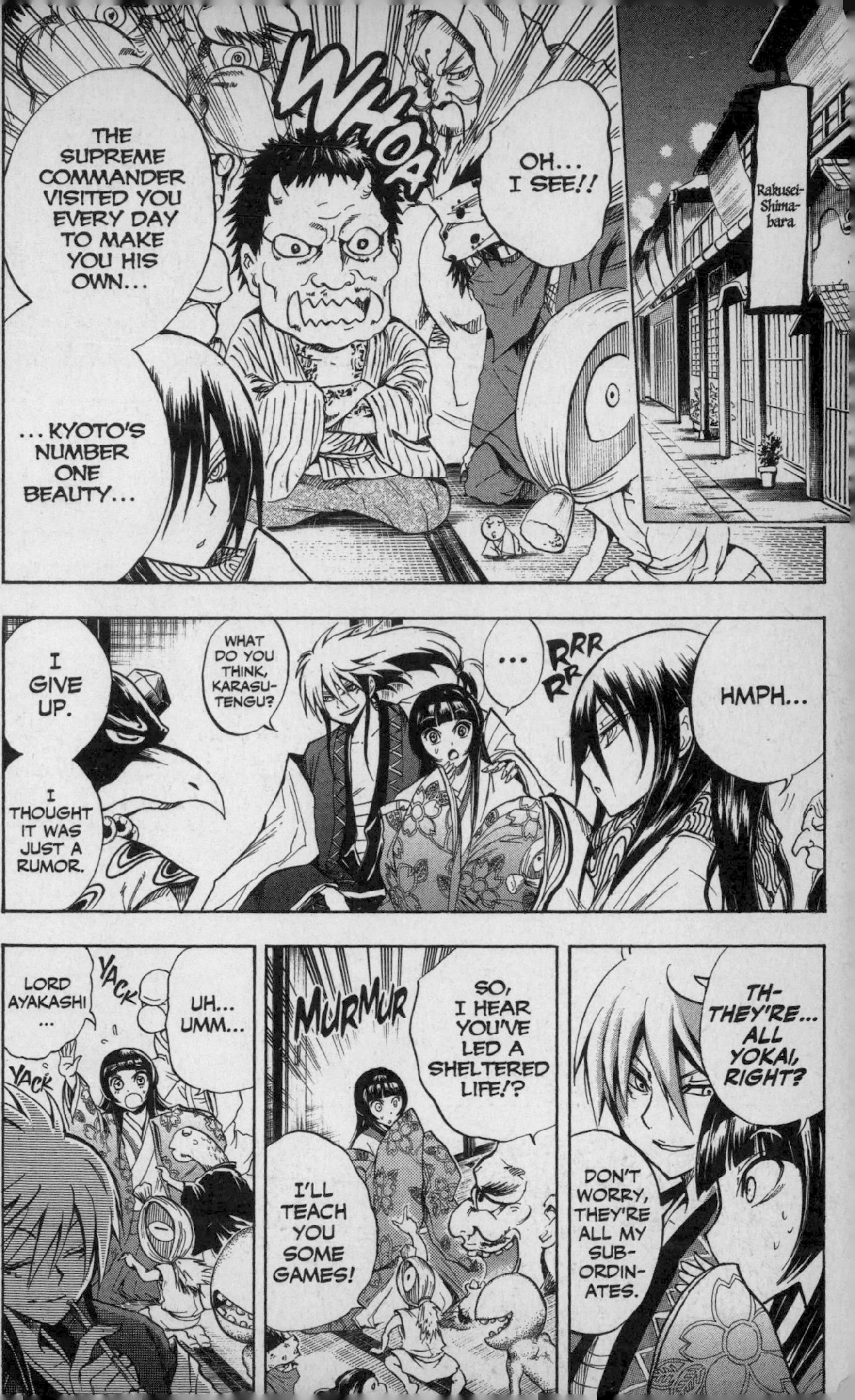
Rakusei-Shimabara
OH... I SEE!!
WHOA
THE SUPREME COMMANDER VISITED YOU EVERY DAY TO MAKE YOU HIS OWN...
...KYOTO'S NUMBER ONE BEAUTY...
HMPH...
RRRRR
...
WHAT DO YOU THINK, KARASU-TENGU?
I GIVE UP.
I THOUGHT IT WAS JUST A RUMOR.
TH-THEY'RE... ALL YOKAI, RIGHT?
DON'T WORRY, THEY'RE ALL MY SUB-ORDIN-ATES.
SO, I HEAR YOU'VE LED A SHELTERED LIFE!?
MURMUR
I'LL TEACH YOU SOME GAMES!
UH... UMM...
YACK
LORD AYAKASHI ...
YACK

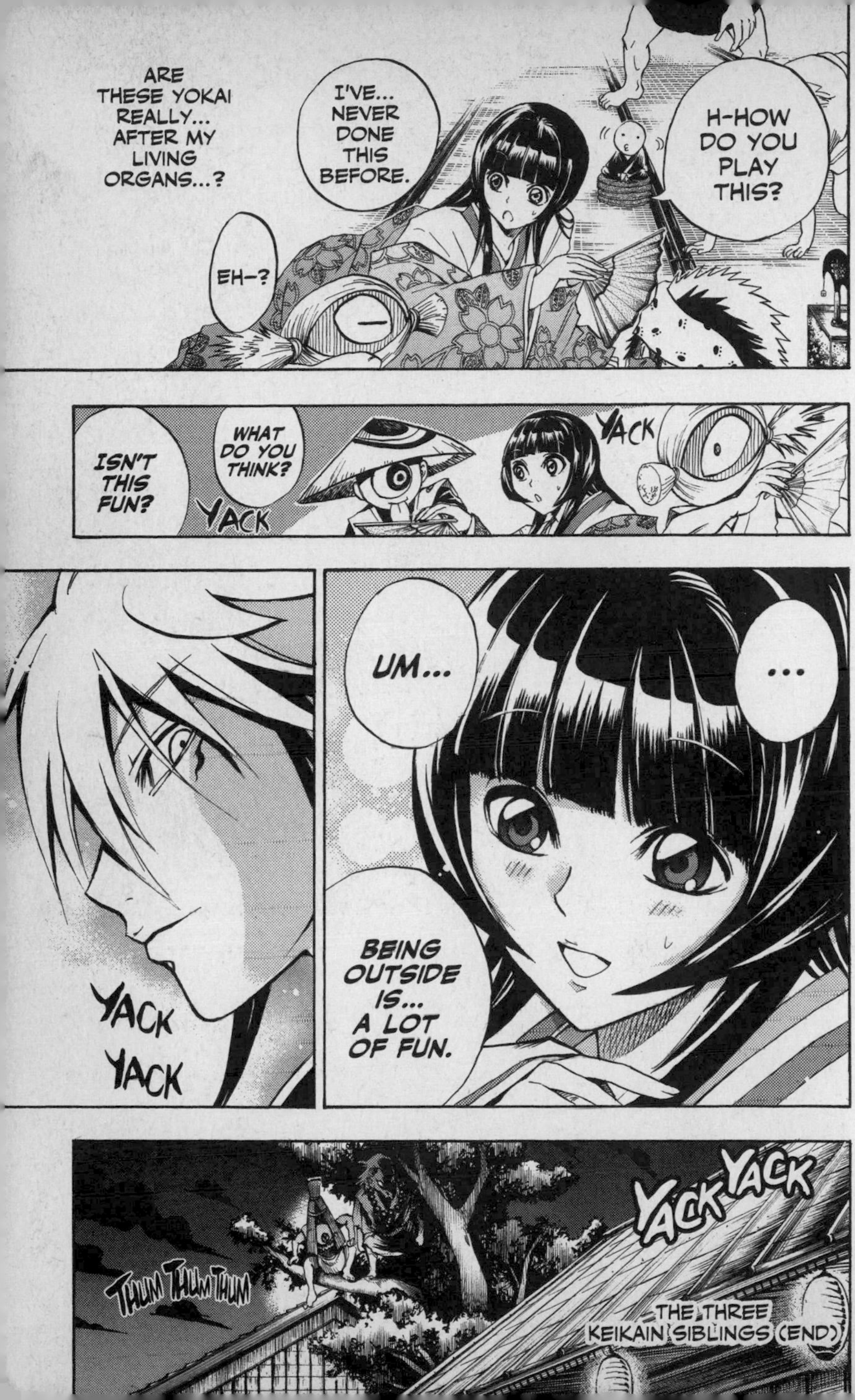
H-HOW DO YOU PLAY THIS?
I'VE... NEVER DONE THIS BEFORE.
ARE THESE YOKAI REALLY... AFTER MY LIVING ORGANS...?
EH-?
YACK
WHAT DO YOU THINK?
ISN'T THIS FUN?
YACK
...
UM...
BEING OUTSIDE IS... A LOT OF FUN.
YACK
YACK
YACK YACK
THUM THUM THUM
THE THREE KEIKAIN SIBLINGS (END)

## YURA KEIKAIN'S

# TRAIN SPLASH

BY: HIROSHI SHIIBASHI

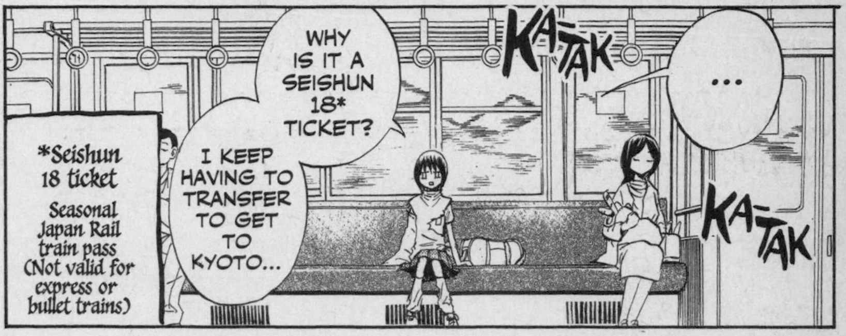
...
KA-TAK
KA-TAK
WHY IS IT A SEISHUN 18* TICKET?
I KEEP HAVING TO TRANSFER TO GET TO KYOTO...
*Seishun 18 ticket
Seasonal Japan Rail train pass (Not valid for express or bullet trains)

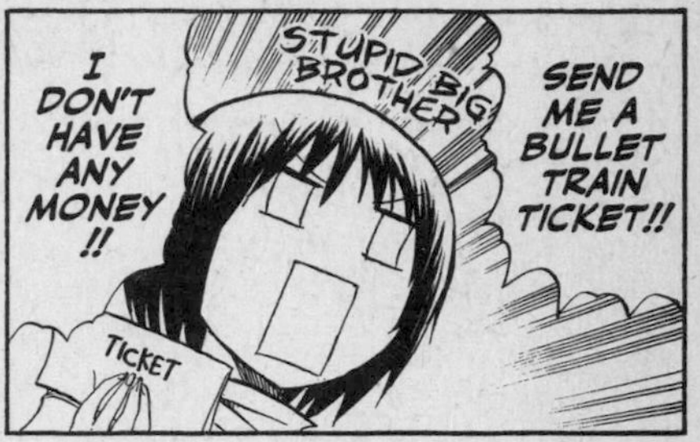
SEND ME A BULLET TRAIN TICKET!!
STUPID BIG BROTHER
I DON'T HAVE ANY MONEY !!
TICKET

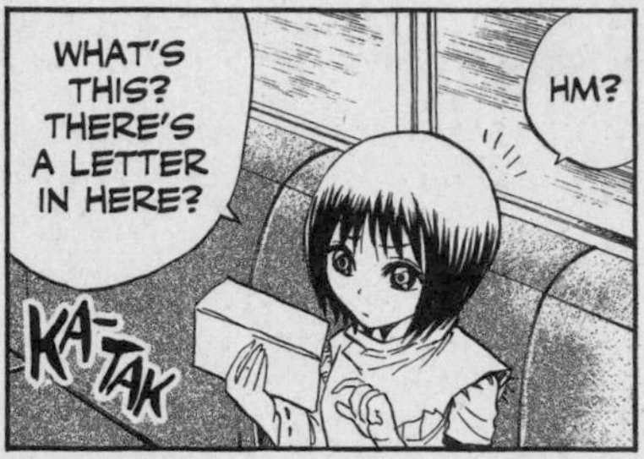
HM?
WHAT'S THIS? THERE'S A LETTER IN HERE?
KA-TAK

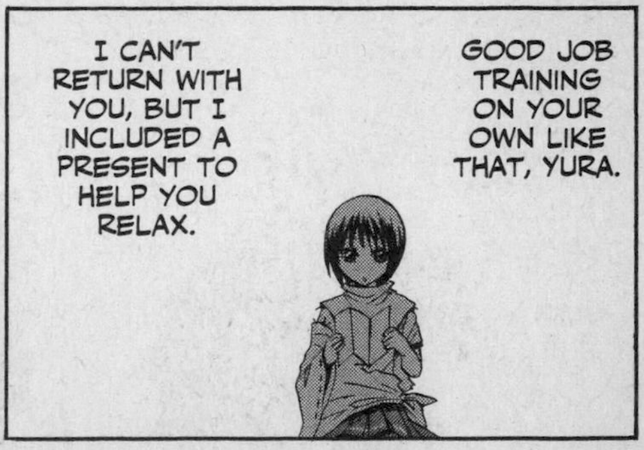
GOOD JOB TRAINING ON YOUR OWN LIKE THAT, YURA.
I CAN'T RETURN WITH YOU, BUT I INCLUDED A PRESENT TO HELP YOU RELAX.

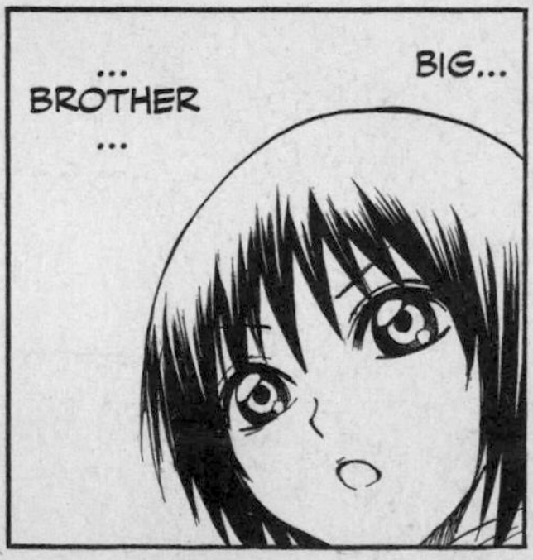
BIG...
... BROTHER ...

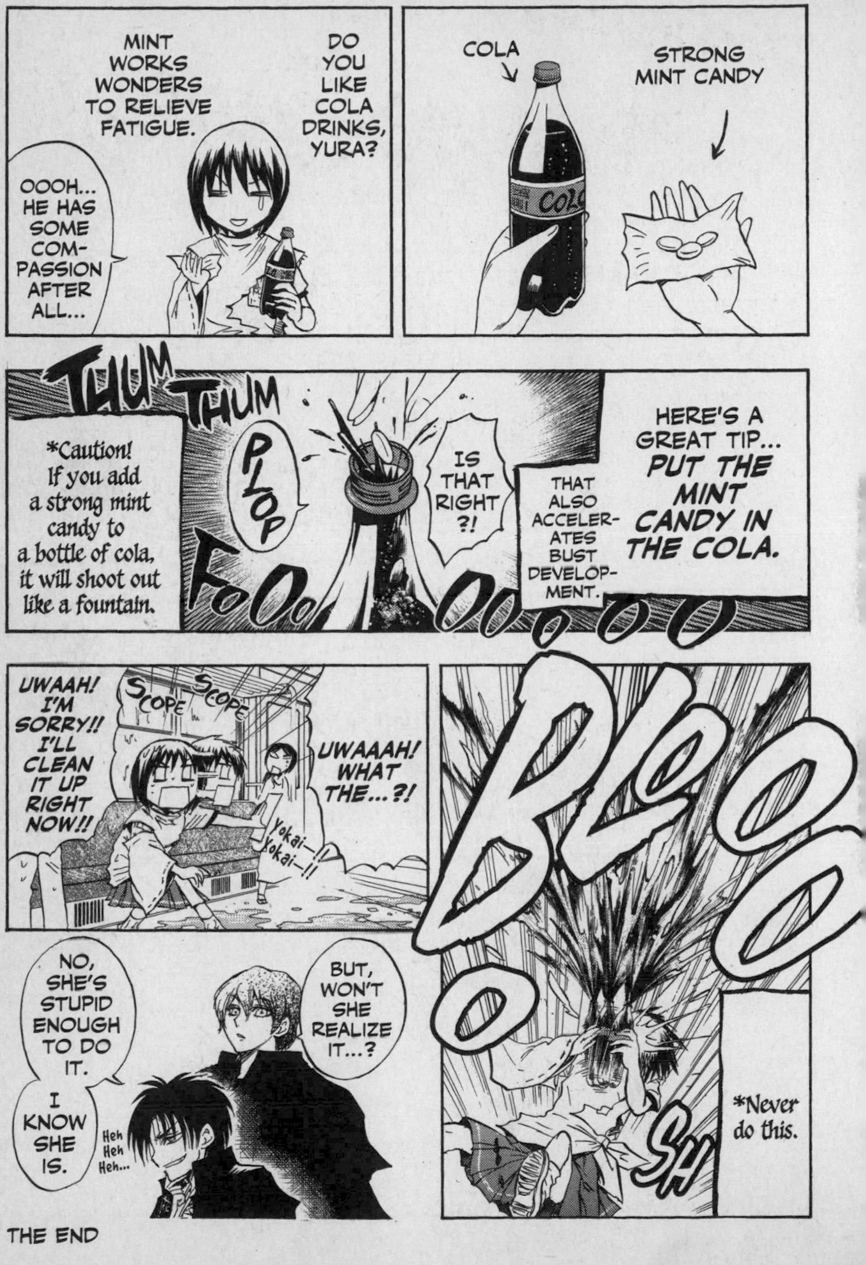
COLA
STRONG MINT CANDY
DO YOU LIKE COLA DRINKS, YURA?
MINT WORKS WONDERS TO RELIEVE FATIGUE.
OOOH... HE HAS SOME COM-PASSION AFTER ALL...
HERE'S A GREAT TIP... *PUT THE MINT CANDY IN THE COLA.*
THAT ALSO ACCELER-ATES BUST DEVELOP-MENT.
IS THAT RIGHT?!
THUM THUM
PLOP
FOOOOOOOOO
*Caution! If you add a strong mint candy to a bottle of cola, it will shoot out like a fountain.
BLOOOOOSH
*Never do this.
UWAAAH! WHAT THE...?!
UWAAH! I'M SORRY!! I'LL CLEAN IT UP RIGHT NOW!!
SCOPE SCOPE
Yokai-- Yokai--!!
BUT, WON'T SHE REALIZE IT...?
NO, SHE'S STUPID ENOUGH TO DO IT.
I KNOW SHE IS.
Heh Heh Heh...

THE END

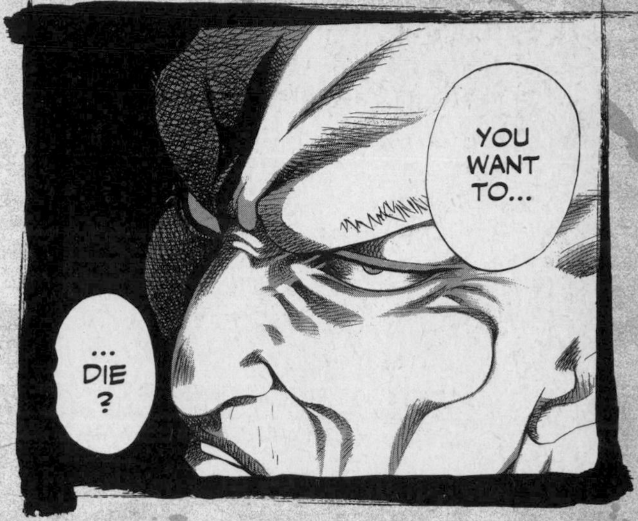
YOU WANT TO...
...DIE?

IN THE NEXT VOLUME...

# ECHOES OF THE PAST

The time is the early 1600s, and the young Nurarihyon has become infatuated with Princess Yo, a girl with mysterious healing powers. He proposes to her. But then Princess Yo is abducted by subordinates of the great yokai Hagoromo-Gitsune. And he wants to cut her apart and steal what makes her special! Find out how Nura's grandfather once had to almost sacrifice it all to save the woman he loved – and how that event still resonates today!

AVAILABLE APRIL 2012!

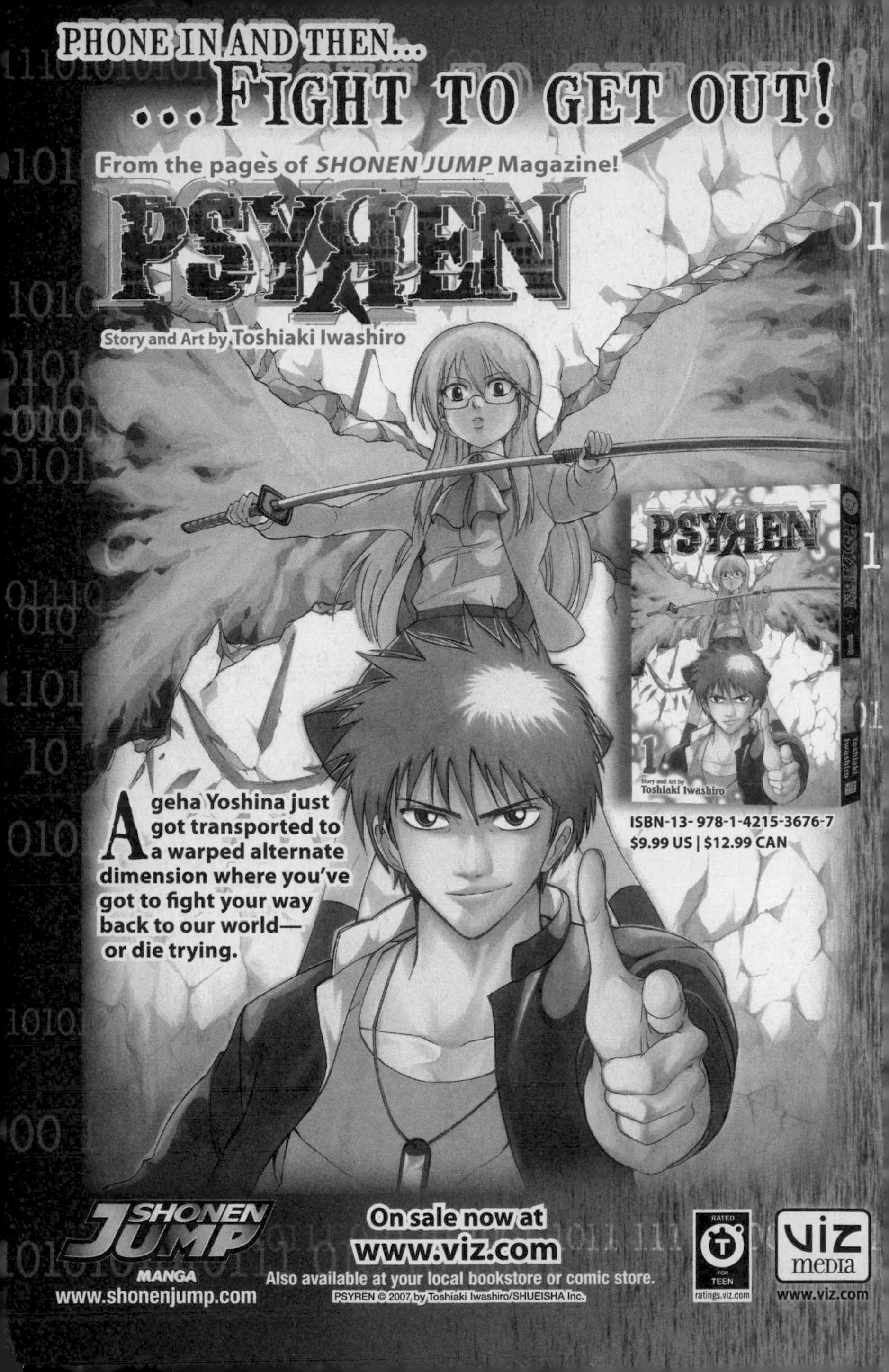
PHONE IN AND THEN...
...FIGHT TO GET OUT!
From the pages of SHONEN JUMP Magazine!
PSYREN
Story and Art by Toshiaki Iwashiro
Ageha Yoshina just got transported to a warped alternate dimension where you've got to fight your way back to our world—or die trying.
PSYREN
1
Story and Art by Toshiaki Iwashiro
ISBN-13- 978-1-4215-3676-7
$9.99 US | $12.99 CAN
SHONEN JUMP MANGA
www.shonenjump.com
On sale now at
www.viz.com
Also available at your local bookstore or comic store.
PSYREN © 2007 by Toshiaki Iwashiro/SHUEISHA Inc.
RATED T FOR TEEN
ratings.viz.com
VIZ media
www.viz.com

# BAKUMAN。

STORY BY TSUGUMI OHBA
ART BY TAKESHI OBATA

From the creators of *Death Note*

## The mystery behind manga making REVEALED!

Average student Moritaka Mashiro enjoys drawing for fun. When his classmate and aspiring writer Akito Takagi discovers his talent, he begs to team up. But what exactly does it take to make it in the manga-publishing world?

Bakuman。, Vol. 1
ISBN: 978-1-4215-3513-5
$9.99 US / $12.99 CAN *

## Manga on sale at store.viz.com

Also available at your local bookstore or comic store

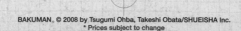

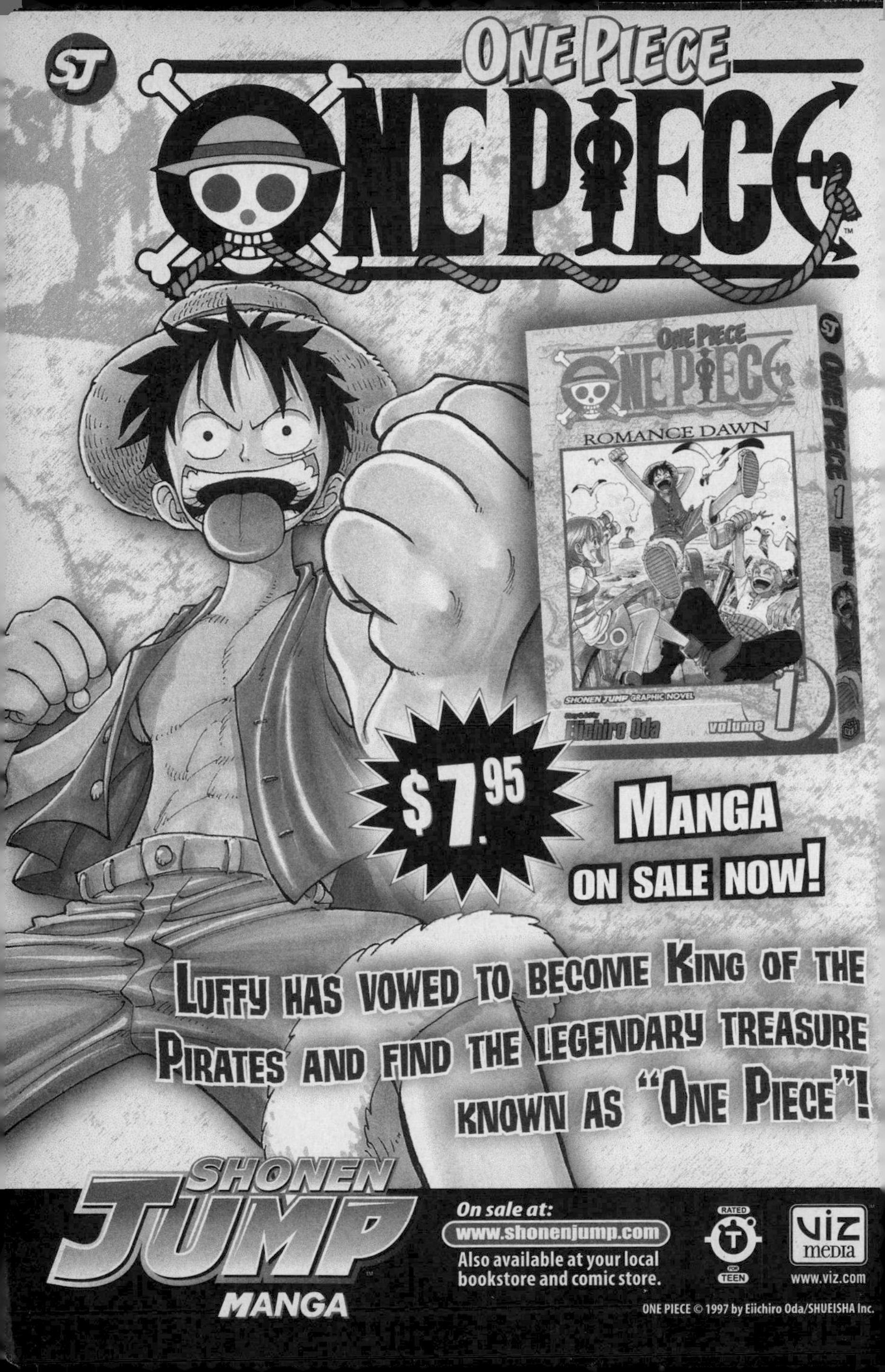